Research and Trends in Data Mining Technologies and Applications

David Taniar, Monash University, Australia

IDEA GROUP PUBLISHING

Hershey • London • Melbourne • Singapore

Acquisition Editor:	Kristin Klinger
Senior Managing Editor:	Jennifer Neidig
Managing Editor:	Sara Reed
Assistant Managing Editor:	Sharon Berger
Development Editor:	Kristin Roth
Copy Editor:	Maria Boyer
Typesetter:	Jamie Snavely
Cover Design:	Lisa Tosheff
Printed at:	Integrated Book Technology

Published in the United States of America by
  Idea Group Publishing (an imprint of Idea Group Inc.)
  701 E. Chocolate Avenue
  Hershey PA 17033
  Tel: 717-533-8845
  Fax: 717-533-8661
  E-mail: cust@idea-group.com
  Web site: http://www.idea-group.com

and in the United Kingdom by
  Idea Group Publishing (an imprint of Idea Group Inc.)
  3 Henrietta Street
  Covent Garden
  London WC2E 8LU
  Tel: 44 20 7240 0856
  Fax: 44 20 7379 0609
  Web site: http://www.eurospanonline.com

Library of Congress Cataloging-in-Publication Data

Research and trends in data mining technologies and applications / David Taniar, editor.
  p. cm. -- (Advanced topics in data warehousing and mining ; vol. 1)
  Includes bibliographical references and index.
  Summary: "This book focuses on the integration between the fields of data warehousing and data mining, with emphasis on applicability to real-world problems; it book provides an international perspective, high-lighting solutions to some of researchers' toughest challenges. Developments in the knowledge discovery process, data models, structures and design offer answers and solutions"--Provided by publisher.
  ISBN 1-59904-271-1 (hardcover) -- ISBN 1-59904-272-X (softcover) -- ISBN 1-59904-273-8 (ebook)
  1. Data mining. 2. Data warehousing. 3. Web databases. I. Taniar, David.
  QA76.9.D343.R49 2006
  005.74--dc22
                          2006032160

British Cataloguing in Publication Data
A Cataloguing in Publication record for this book is available from the British Library.

All work contributed to this book is new, previously-unpublished material. The views expressed in this book are those of the authors, but not necessarily of the publisher.

Research and Trends in Data Mining Technologies and Applications

Table of Contents

Preface.. vi

Section I:
Data Warehousing and Mining

Chapter I
Combining Data Warehousing and Data Mining Techniques for
Web Log Analysis... 1
    Torben Bach Pedersen, Aalborg University, Denmark
    Jesper Thorhauge, Conzentrate, Denmark
    Søren E. Jespersen, Linkage, Denmark

Chapter II
Computing Dense Cubes Embedded in Sparse Data................................ 29
    Lixin Fu, The University of North Carolina at Greensboro, USA

Chapter III
Exploring Similarities Across High-Dimensional Datasets..................... 53
    Karlton Sequeira, Rensselaer Polytechnic Institute, USA
    Mohammed Zaki, Rensselaer Polytechnic Institute, USA

Section II:
Patterns

Chapter IV
Pattern Comparison in Data Mining: A Survey.. 86
    Irene Ntoutsi, University of Piraeus, Greece
    Nikos Pelekis, University of Piraeus, Greece
    Yannis Theodoridis, University of Piraeus, Greece

Chapter V
Mining Frequent Patterns Using Self-Organizing Map........................... 121
    Fedja Hadzic, University of Technology Sydney, Australia
    Tharam Dillon, University of Technology Sydney, Australia
    Henry Tan, University of Technology Sydney, Australia
    Ling Feng, University of Twente, The Netherlands
    Elizabeth Chang, Curtin University of Technology, Australia

Chapter VI
An Efficient Compression Technique for Vertical Mining Methods 143
    Mafruz Zaman Ashrafi, Monash University, Australia
    David Taniar, Monash University, Australia
    Kate Smith, Monash University, Australia

Section III:
Data Mining in Bioinformatics

Chapter VII
A Tutorial on Hierachical Classification with Applications in
Bioinformatics 175
    Alex Freitas, University of Kent, UK
    André C.P.L.F. de Carvalho, University of São Paulo, Brazil

Chapter VIII
Topological Analysis and Sub-Network Mining of
Protein-Protein Interactions 209
    Daniel Wu, Drexel University, USA
    Xiaohua Hu, Drexel University, USA

Section IV:
Data Mining Techiques

Chapter IX
Introduction to Data Mining Techniques via Multiple Criteria
Optimization Approaches and Applications 242
    Yong Shi, University of the Chinese Academy of Sciences, China &
        University of Nebraska at Omaha, USA
    Yi Peng, University of Nebraska at Omaha, USA
    Gang Kou, University of Nebraka at Omaha, USA
    Zhengxin Chen, University of Nebraska at Omaha, USA

Chapter X
Linguistic Rule Extraction from Support Vector Machine
Classifiers 276
    Xiuju Fu, Institute of High Performance Computing, Singapore
    Lipo Wang, Nanyang Technological University, Singapore
    GihGuang Hung, Institute of High Performance Computing, Singapore
    Liping Goh, Institute of High Performance Computing, Singapore

Chapter XI
Graph-Based Data Mining 291
    Wenyuan Li, Nanyang Technological University, Singapore
    Wee-Keong Ng, Nanyang Technological University, Singapore
    Kok-Leong Ong, Deakin University, Australia

Chapter XII
Facilitating and Improving the Use of Web Services
with Data Mining 308
    Richi Nayak, Queensland University, Australia

About the Authors 327

Index 336

Preface

In enterprises, a large volume of data has been collected and stored in data warehouses. Advances in data gathering, storage, and distribution have created a need for integrating data warehousing and data mining techniques. Mining data warehouses raises unique issues and requires special attention. Data warehousing and data mining are inter-related, and require holistic techniques from the two disciplines. The "Advanced Topics in Data Warehousing and Mining" series comes into place to address some issues related to mining data warehouses. To start this series, this volume 1, includes 12 chapters in four sections, contributed by authors and editorial board members from the *International Journal of Data Warehousing and Mining.*

Section I, on Data Warehousing and Mining, consists of three chapters covering data mining techniques applied to data warehouse Web logs, data cubes, and high-dimensional datasets.

Chapter I, "Combining Data Warehousing and Data Mining Techniques for Web Log Analysis" by Torben Bach Pedersen (Aalborg University, Denmark), Jesper Thorhauge (Conzentrate, Demark), and Søren E. Jespersen (Linkage, Denmark), brings together data warehousing and data mining by focusing on data that has been collected in Web server logs. This data will only be useful if high-level knowledge about user navigation patterns can be analyzed and extracted. There are several approaches to analyze Web logs. They propose a hybrid method that combines data warehouse Web log schemas and a data mining technique called Hyper Probabilistic Grammars, resulting in a fast and flexible Web log analysis. Further enhancement to this hybrid method is also outlined.

Chapter II, "Computing Dense Cubes Embedded in Sparse Data" by Lixin Fu (The University of North Carolina at Greensboro, USA) focuses on a sparse input dataset of high-dimensional data whereby both number of dimensions and cardinalities of dimensions are large, but a dense aggregate dataset. The chapter proposes a new dynamic data structure called Restricted Sparse Statistics Trees and a cube evaluation algorithm to efficiently compute dense sub-cubes embedded in high-dimensional sparse input datasets. The proposed algorithm is scalable, as well as incrementally maintainable, which is suitable for data warehousing and the analysis of streaming data.

Chapter III, "Exploring Similarities Across High-Dimensional Datasets" by Karlton Sequeira and Mohammed Zaki (Rensselaer Polytechnic Institute, USA), concentrates on the problem whereby related data collected from a number of different sources may not be able to share the entire dataset. They however may only be willing to share a condensed version of their datasets, due to various reasons, such as privacy issues, dataset size, and so forth. To solve this problem, they propose a framework for constructing condensed models of datasets and algorithms to find similar sub-structure in pairs of such models. Their analysis shows that they could find more interesting results from the combined model than those obtained from independent analysis of the original datasets.

Section II, on Patterns, consists of three chapters covering pattern comparisons, frequent patterns, and vertical mining patterns.

Chapter IV, "Pattern Comparison in Data Mining: A Survey" by Irene Ntoutsi, Nikos Pelekis, and Yannis Theodoridis (University of Piraeus, Greece), provides a thorough survey on pattern comparison. Pattern comparison aims at evaluating how close to each other two patterns are. In this chapter, the authors focus on pattern comparison in frequent itemsets and association rules, clusters and clusterings, and decision trees.

Chapter V, "Mining Frequent Patterns Using Self-Organizing Map" by Fedja Hadzic, Tharam Dillon, and Henry Tan (University of Technology Sydney, Australia), along with Ling Feng (University of Twente, The Netherlands), and Elizabeth Chang (Curtin University of Technology, Australia) investigates a non-traditional approach of extracting frequent patterns using self-organizing map (SOM), which is an unsupervised neural network technique. SOM has normally been used for clustering, but not association rules and frequent itemsets generation. This chapter discusses issues of using a SOM clustering technique for the purpose of generating association rules. It also includes some case studies comparing the SOM approach and the traditional association rule approach.

Chapter VI, "An Efficient Compression Technique for Vertical Mining Methods" by Mafruz Zaman Ashrafi and Kate Smith (Monash University, Australia), highlights the performance problems of many efficient association rule mining algorithms, particularly when the dataset is large or the user-specified support is low, due to a poor treatment of main memory. To solve this problem, this chapter proposes an algorithm for vertical association rule mining that compresses a vertical dataset in an efficient manner by utilizing bit vectors. The performance shows that the proposed compression ratio offers better results than those of the other well-known techniques.

Section III, on Data Mining in Bioinformatics, presents data mining applications in the bioinformatics domain. This part consists of two chapters covering hierarchical classification, and topological analysis and sub-network mining.

Chapter VII, "A Tutorial on Hierarchical Classification with Applications in Bioinformatics" by Alex Freitas (University of Kent, UK) and André C.P.L.F. de Carvalho (University of São Paulo, Brazil), presents a comprehensive tutorial on complex classification problems suitable for bioinformatics applications, particularly the prediction of protein function, whereby the predicted classes are hierarchical in nature.

Chapter VIII, "Topological Analysis and Sub-Network Mining of Protein: Protein Interactions" by Daniel Wu and Xiaohua Hu (Drexel University, USA), reports a comprehensive evaluation of the topological structure of protein-protein interaction networks across different species and confidence levels, by mining and analyzing graphs constructed from public domain bioinformatics datasets. The authors also report some statistical analysis whereby the results obtained are far from a power law, contradicting many published results.

The final section of this volume, Data Mining Techniques, consists of four chapters, covering data mining techniques using multiple criteria optimization, support vector machine classifiers, graph-based mining, and Web services.

Chapter IX, "Introduction to Data Mining Techniques via Multiple Criteria Optimization Approaches and Applications" by Yong Shi (University of the Chinese Academy of Sciences, China and University of Nebraska at Omaha, USA) and Yi Peng, Gang Kou, and Zhengxin Chen (University of Nebraska at Omaha, USA), gives an overview of a series of multiple criteria optimization-based data mining methods that utilize the multiple criteria programming (like multiple criteria linear programming, multiple criteria quadratic programming, and multiple criteria fuzzy linear programming) to solve data mining problems. The chapter includes some case studies, including credit card scoring, HIV-1, and network introduction detection. The authors also highlight some research challenges and opportunities in these areas.

Chapter X, "Linguistic Rule Extraction from Support Vector Machine Classifiers" by Xiuju Fu (Institute of High Performance Computing, Singapore), Lipo Wang (Nanyang Technological University, Singapore), GihGuang Hung (Institute of High Performance Computing, Singapore), and Liping Goh (Institute of High Performance Computing, Singapore), shows how decisions from an SVM classifier can be decoded into linguistic rules based on the information provided by support vectors and decision function. They show that the rule extraction results from the proposed method could follow SVM classifier decisions very well.

Chapter XI, "Graph-Based Data Mining" by Wenyuan Li (Richardson, USA) and Wee-Keong Ng (Nanyang Technological University, Singapore), along with Kok-Leong Ong (Deakin University, Australia), systematically reviews theories and techniques in graph mining. This chapter particularly focuses on approaches that are potentially valuable to graph-based data mining.

Finally, **Chapter XII**, "Facilitating and Improving the Use of Web Services with Data Mining" by Richi Nayak (Queensland University, Australia), presents an overview of an area in which data mining may be useful, especially in the area of Web services. This chapter examines how some of the issues of Web services can be addressed through data mining.

Overall, this volume covers important foundations to research and applications in data mining, covering patterns and techniques, as well as issues of mining data warehouses and an important application domain, namely bioinformatics. The different types of chapters, some of which are surveys and tutorials, while others propose novel techniques and algorithms, show a full spectrum of the coverage of this important topic.

David Taniar

Editor-in-Chief, Journal of International Journal of Data Warehousing and Mining

2006

Section I

Data Warehousing and Mining

Chapter I

Combining Data Warehousing and Data Mining Techniques for Web Log Analysis

Torben Bach Pedersen, Aalborg University, Denmark

Jesper Thorhauge, Conzentrate, Denmark

Søren E. Jespersen, Linkage, Denmark

Abstract

Enormous amounts of information about Web site user behavior are collected in Web server logs. However, this information is only useful if it can be queried and analyzed to provide high-level knowledge about user navigation patterns, a task that requires powerful techniques. This chapter presents a number of approaches that combine data warehousing and data mining techniques in order to analyze Web logs. After introducing the well-known click and session data warehouse (DW) schemas, the chapter presents the subsession schema, which allows fast queries on sequences of page visits. Then, the chapter presents the so-called "hybrid" technique, which combines DW Web log schemas with a data mining technique called Hypertext Probabilistic Grammars, hereby providing fast and flexible constraint-based Web log analysis. Finally, the chapter presents a "post-check enhanced" improvement of the hybrid technique.

Introduction

With the large number of companies using the Internet to distribute and collect information, knowledge discovery on the Web—or *Web mining*—has become an important research area. Web mining can be divided into three areas, namely *Web content mining, Web structure mining,* and *Web usage mining* (also called Web log mining) (Cooley, Srivastava, & Mobasher, 1997). Web content mining focuses on discovery of information stored on the Internet—that is, the various search engines. Web structure mining can be used when improving the structural design of a Web site. Web usage mining, the main topic of this chapter, focuses on knowledge discovery from the usage of individual Web sites.

Web usage mining is mainly based on the activities recorded in the *Web log*, the log file written by the Web server recording individual requests made to the server. An important notion in a Web log is the existence of *user sessions*. A user session is a sequence of requests from a single user within a certain time window. Of particular interest is the discovery of frequently performed *sequences* of actions by the Web user—that is, frequent sequences of visited Web pages.

The work presented in this chapter has to a large extent been motivated by collaboration with the e-learning company Zenaria (*www.zenaria.com*). Zenaria is in the business of creating e-learning, namely interactive stories told through a series of video-sequences. The story is formed by a user first viewing a video-sequence and then choosing between some predefined options, based on the video-sequence. Depending on the user's choice, a new video-sequence is shown and new options are presented. The choices of a user will form a complete story—a *walkthrough*—reflecting the choices made by the individual users. Traditionally, stories have been distributed on CD-ROM, and a *consultant* has evaluated the walkthroughs by observing the users. However, Zenaria now wants to distribute its stories using the Internet (i.e., a walkthrough will correspond to a Web session). Thus, the consultants will now have to use Web usage mining technology to evaluate the walkthroughs.

Data warehousing and database management system (DBMS) technologies excel in handling large amounts of data with good performance and ease-of-use. These technologies support a wide range of complex analysis queries, such as aggregation queries with constraints very well due to techniques such as bitmapped indices, materialized views, and algebraic query optimization. However, certain very specialized analysis queries are not well supported in standard systems. On the other hand, data mining techniques generally handle one type of very specialized analysis query very well, but this often comes at the expense of generality, ease-of-use, and scalability since data must be managed separately in dedicated file structures outside a DBMS. Thus, a lot of advantages can be gained by combining data warehousing/DBMS and data mining technologies (Han, 1997; Hinneburg, Lehner, & Habich, 2000; Sarawagi, Thomas, & Agrawal, 1998).

Much work has been performed on extracting various patterns from Web logs, and the application of the discovered knowledge range from improving the design and structure of a Web site to enabling companies to provide more targeted marketing. One line of work features techniques for working directly on the log file (Cooley et al., 1997; Cooley et al., 1999). Another line of work concentrates on creating aggregated structures of the information in the Web log (Spiliopoulou et al., 1998; Pei et al., 1999). The Hypertext Probabilistic Grammar framework (Borges et al., 1999), utilizing the theory of grammars, is such an aggregated structure. Yet another line of work focuses on using database technology in the clickstream analysis (Andersen et al., 2000; Büchner, Anand, Mulvenna, & Hughes, 2000), building a so-called "data Webhouse" (Kimball & Merz, 2000). Several database schemas have been suggested, for example, the click fact star schema where the individual click is the primary fact (Kimball & Merz, 2000). Several commercial tools for analyzing Web logs exist (Wu, Yu, & Ballman, 1998; Spiliopoulou et al., 1998), but their focus is mostly on statistical measures (e.g., most frequently visited pages), and they provide only limited facilities for clickstream analysis. Finally, a prominent line of work focuses on mining *sequential patterns* in general sequence databases (Agrawal et al., 1995; Agrawal et al., 1996; Pei et al., 1999; Pei, Han, B. Mortazavi-asl, & Zhu, 2000). However, all the mentioned approaches have inherent weaknesses in that they either have huge storage requirements, slow performance due to many scans over the data, or problems when additional information (e.g., user demographics) are introduced into the analysis. Another line of research tries to provide database/data warehouse support for generic data mining techniques, but does not consider Web log mining (Han, 1997; Hinneburg et al., 2000; Sarawagi et al., 1998).

This chapter presents a number of approaches that combine data warehousing and data mining techniques in order to analyze Web logs. After introducing the well-known click and session DW schemas (Kimball & Merz, 2000), the chapter presents the subsession schema which allows fast queries on sequences of page visits (Andersen et al., 2000). Then, the chapter presents the so-called *hybrid technique* (Jespersen, Thorhauge, & Pedersen, 2002), which combines DW Web log schemas (Kimball & Merz, 2000) with a data mining technique called Hypertext Probabilistic Grammars (Borges, 2000), hereby providing fast and flexible constraint-based Web log analysis. Finally, the chapter presents a "post-check enhanced" improvement of the hybrid technique. This chapter is the first to provide an integrated presentation of approaches combining data warehousing and data mining techniques for Web log analysis.

The chapter is organized as follows. The next section presents the well-known click and session fact schemas. Then, the subsession schema is presented, followed by a section on the hybrid approach. Finally, the post-check enhancement of the hybrid approach is presented, followed by a conclusion.

Click and Session Fact Schemas

The Click Fact Schema

The click fact schema uses the individual click on the Web site as the essential fact in the data warehouse (Kimball & Merz, 2000). This will preserve most of the information found in a Web log in the data warehouse. In our case, the click fact schema contains the following dimensions: URL dimension (the Web pages) (note that the fact table has references to both the *requested* page and the *referring* page, also known as the "referrer"), Date dimension, TimeOfDay dimension, Session dimension, and Timespan dimension. We could easily add any desired additional information as extra dimensions, for example, a User dimension capturing user demographics. An example Click Fact schema can be seen in Figure 1.

Figure 1. Click fact schema

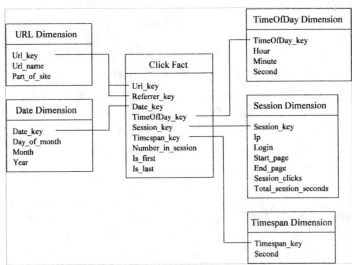

A strong point of this approach is that almost all information from the Web log is retained within the data warehouse. Individual clicks within the individual sessions can be tracked, and very detailed click information is available. This approach can utilize existing OLAP techniques such as pre-aggregation to efficiently extract knowledge on individual pages.

When querying for sequences of clicks, using the click fact schema, several join and self-join operations are needed to extract even relative short sequences (Andersen et al., 2000), severely degrading performance for large fact tables.

The Session Fact Schema

The session fact schema uses the entire session as the primary fact in the data warehouse (Kimball & Merz, 2000), thereby ignoring the individual clicks within a session. Only the requests for the start and end page are stored as a field value on the individual session fact entry. The approach is therefore not suitable for querying for detailed information about sequences of clicks or even individual clicks in a session. Queries on entire sessions are however quite efficient (Andersen et al., 2000). An example session fact schema can be seen in Figure 2. We will not present strong and weak points for this approach, since it is unable to perform analysis of sequences of clicks, which is a key requirement for us.

Figure 2. Session fact schema

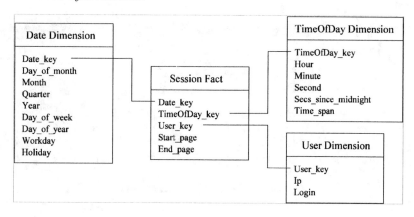

The Subsession Fact Schema

The *subsession fact* schema was first proposed by Andersen et al. (2000) and is aimed specifically at clickstream analysis on sequences of clicks. The approach introduces the concept of using *subsessions* as the fact—that is, explicitly storing all possible *subsequences* of clicks from a session in the data warehouse. This means that for all sessions, subsessions of all lengths are generated and stored explicitly in the data warehouse. In our case, the subsession fact schema has the dimensions Date, Session, TimeOfDay, Timespan, as well as the URL_Sequence dimension capturing the corresponding sequence of Web page requests. An example subsession fact schema can be seen in Figure 3.

Let us compare the SQL queries used to analyze subsessions in the click fact schema and the subsession fact schema. The SQL query used to find the most common subsessions of lengths 2-5 in a click fact table, sorted with the most frequent longest subsessions first, is seen in Figure 4. The || operator denotes concatenation. This query is almost one page of extremely complicated SQL, making it very hard to write correctly for everyone but the most seasoned SQL veterans. Even more importantly, the query has very bad query performance as the (huge) fact table has to be joined to itself up to five times, as well as to five (smaller) dimension tables, requiring a lot of server resources. Because of the complexity of the query, it cannot be efficiently supported by materialized views as found in current DBMSs. Fur-

Figure 3. Subsession fact schema

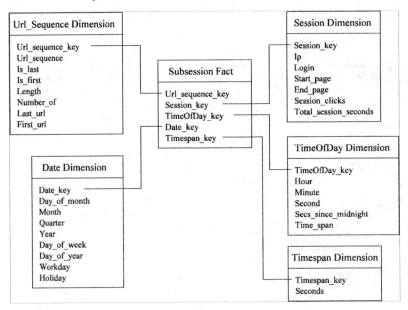

Figure 4. Subsession SQL query for click fact schema (taken from Andersen et al., 2000)

```
SELECT us.url_sequence AS start_url,u2.url_name as end_url, s.length,
        COUNT(*) AS occurences
FROM subsession_fact s,url_sequence us
WHERE us.subsession_key=s.subsession_key AND length<=5

SELECT url_sequence,length,occurences FROM
(
            (SELECT  u1.url_name||u2.url_name as url_sequence,
        2 AS length, COUNT(*) AS occurences
        FROM url_dimension u1,url_dimension u2,click_fact c1,click_fact c2
        WHERE c1.number_in_session=c2.number_in_session-1 AND
        c1.session_key = c2.session_key AND
        c1.url_key=u1.url_key AND c2.url_key=u2.url_key
        GROUP BY url_sequence,length)
UNION ALL
            (SELECT  u1.url_name||u2.url_name|| u3.url_name as url_sequence,
            3 AS length, COUNT(*) AS occurences
            FROM url_dimension u1,url_dimension u2,url_dimension u3,
        click_fact c1,click_fact c2,click_fact c3
        WHERE c1.number_in_session=c2.number_in_session-1 AND
        c2.number_in_session=c3.number_in_session-1 AND
        c1.session_key = c2.session_key AND c2.session_key = c3.session_key AND
        c1.url_key=u1.url_key AND c2.url_key=u2.url_key AND c3.url_key=u3.url_key
            GROUP BY url_sequence,length)
UNION ALL
        (SELECT  u1.url_name||u2.url_name||u3.url_name||u4.url_name AS url_sequence,
            4 AS length, COUNT(*) AS occurences
        FROM url_dimension u1,url_dimension u2,url_dimension u3,url_dimension u4,
        click_fact c1,click_fact c2,click_fact c3,click_fact c4
            WHERE c1.number_in_session=c2.number_in_session-1 AND
        c2.number_in_session=c3.number_in_session-1 AND
        c3.number_in_session=c4.number_in_session-1 AND
        c1.session_key = c2.session_key AND c2.session_key = c3.session_key AND
            c3.session_key = c4.session_key AND
            c1.url_key=u1.url_key AND c2.url_key=u2.url_key AND
            c3.url_key=u3.url_key AND c4.url_key=u4.url_key
            GROUP BY url_sequence,length)
UNION ALL
            (SELECT  u1.url_name|| u2.url_name||u3.url_name||u4.url_name||u5.url_name AS url_sequence,
            5 AS length, COUNT(*) AS occurrences
        FROM url_dimension u1,url_dimension u2,url_dimension u3,url_dimension u4,
            url_dimension u5,click_fact c1,click_fact c2,click_fact c3,click_fact c4,click_fact c5
            WHERE c1.number_in_session=c2.number_in_session-1 AND
        c2.number_in_session=c3.number_in_session-1 AND
        c3.number_in_session=c4.number_in_session-1 AND
        c4.number_in_session=c5.number_in_session-1 AND
        c1.session_key = c2.session_key AND c2.session_key = c3.session_key AND
        c3.session_key = c4.session_key AND c4.session_key = c5.session_key
        c1.url_key=u1.url_key AND c2.url_key=u2.url_key) AND
        c3.url_key=u3.url_key AND c4.url_key=u4.url_key) AND
        c5.url_key=u5.url_key
            GROUP BY url_sequence,length)
)
ORDER BY occurences DESC,length DESC,url_sequence ASC
```

thermore, in the sequence join conditions, for example, "c2.number_in_session=c3. number_in_session-1", the "-1" part of the condition means using indices joining will not be applicable, leading to very long query processing times. If we wanted to find subsessions of length 2-8 instead, the query would be twice as long, with even worse performance.

In contrast, the simple query seen in Figure 4 finds the same answer using a subsession fact table. The query only joins the fact table with one small dimension table, and the query can be efficiently supported by materialized views.

As we have seen, storing subsessions explicitly in the database instead of implicitly (through join-operations) will allow for better performance on queries concerning sequences of clicks. There is a tradeoff between the amount of storage used and query performance, but if a Web site has relatively short sessions, the storage overhead is manageable (Andersen et al., 2000). This technique can answer sequence-related queries much faster than, for example, the click fact schema (Andersen et al., 2000).

However, as hinted above, the longer the sessions, the more storage is needed for storing the information for all subsessions. The number of subsessions generated from a session of length n can be estimated using the formula $0.5^*(n-1)^2$ (Andersen et al., 2000). A study shows that the storage overhead can vary between a factor of 4 and a factor above 20, depending on the characteristics of the sessions on a Web site (Andersen et al., 2000). Some methods for reducing the number of subsessions that are to be stored have been suggested, including ignoring either very short or very long subsessions or ignoring certain subsessions. For example, if only subsessions of length 2-10 are stored, the number of subsession facts will only be nine times the number of click facts, meaning that it is feasible to store them all.

Hypertext Probabilistic Grammars

The nature of Web sites, Web pages, and link navigation has a nice parallel in formal language theory which proves rather intuitive and presents a model for extracting information about user sessions. The model uses a *Hypertext Probabilistic Grammar* (HPG) (Levene et al., 1999) that rests upon the well-established theoretical area of languages and grammars. We will present this parallel using the example Web to the left in Figure 5.

Figure 5. Example Web site and corresponding HPG

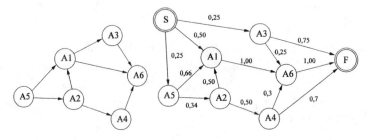

The left side of Figure 5 shows a number of Web pages and the links that connect them. As can be seen, the structure is very similar to a grammar with a number of states and a number of productions leading from one state to another. It is this parallel that the model explores. The model uses all Web pages as states (this is only true if the HPG is created with a so-called "history depth" of 1, to be addressed below) and adds two additional artificial states, the start state S and the end state F, to form all states of the grammar. We will throughout the chapter use the terms state and page interchangeably. From the processing of the sessions in the Web log, each state will be marked with the number of times it has been requested. The probability of a production is assigned based on the information in the Web log so that the probability of a production is proportional to the number of times the given link was traversed relative to the number of times the state on the left side of the production was visited. Note that not all links within a Web site may have been traversed, so some of the links might not be represented in an HPG. The probability of a string in the language of the HPG can be found by multiplying the probabilities of the productions needed to generate the string. Note that Web pages might be linked in a circular fashion and therefore the language of the HPG could be infinite. A HPG therefore specifies a threshold η against which all strings are evaluated. If the probability of the string is below the threshold, the string will not be included in the language of the HPG (with the assigned threshold). This will generate a complete language for a given HPG with a given threshold, L^η. Mining an HPG is essentially the process of extracting high-probability strings from the grammar. These strings are called *rules* (the notion of a rule and a string will be used interchangeably). These rules will describe the most preferred trails on the Web site since they are traversed with a high probability. Mining can be done using both a breath-first and a depth-first search algorithm (Borges, 2000).

A parameter α is used when mining an HPG to allow for mining of rules "inside" the grammar—that is, rules with a leftmost state that has not necessarily been the first request in any session. This is done by assigning probability to productions from the start state to all other states depending on α and whether or not the state is first in a session. An example HPG is shown to the right in Figure 5. Note that, as mentioned above, not all links on the Web pages are necessarily represented in the grammar. The link $A1 \rightarrow A3$ from Figure 5 (left) has not been traversed and is therefore not represented in the grammar. In Figure 5, a Web page maps to a state in the grammar. The HPG can also be generated with a *history-depth N* above 1. With a history-depth of, for example, 2, each state represents two Web pages requested in sequence. The structure of the HPG remains the same, but each state now has a "memory" of the N last states traversed. With $N=3$, a state might then be named $A1A3A5$, for the traversal $A1 \rightarrow A3 \rightarrow A5$. The mining of rules on the HPG using a simple breath-first search algorithm has been shown to be too un-precise for extracting a manageable number of rules. Heuristics have been proposed to allow for a more fine-grained mining of rules from an HPG (Borges et al., 2000). The heuristics are aimed at specifying controls that more accurately and intuitively present relevant rules mined from an HPG and allow for, for example, generation of longer rules and for only returning a subset of the complete ruleset.

Representing Additional Information

An HPG has no memory of detailed click information in the states. Thus, if rules using *additional information*—for example, sessions for users with specific demographic parameters—were to be mined, each production should be split into a number of middle-states, where each middle-state would represent some specific combination of the parameters. Each middle-state should then be labeled with the respective combinations of information. This is illustrated in Figure 6, where A and B are original states and 1 to 7 represent new middle-states. Note that the probability of going from a middle-state to B is 1 for each middle-state.

Note also that Figure 6 only illustrates additional information grouped into seven different categories, which, for example, could be some demographic information about the user. If several different kinds of information were to be represented, the number of middle states would increase exponentially, since all combinations of the different kinds of parameters should potentially be represented for all states in the HPG, thus creating a problem with state explosion. For instance, if the HPG should represent the gender and marital status of users, each production could potentially be split into four middle-states. If the HPG should also represent whether a user had children, each production needs to be split into eight middle states. This factor increases with the cardinality of each additional parameter. This solution scales very poorly. For instance, representing gender, age in years, salary (grouped into ten categories), number of children (five categories), job status (10 categories), and

Figure 6. HPG with additional information

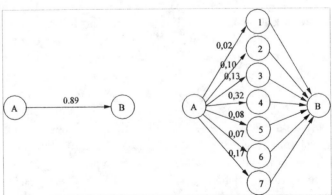

years of working experience could easily require each production to be split into over four million (2∗110∗10∗5∗10∗40) middle states. Doing this for an HPG that includes only ten interconnected states would require over 400 million states (including middle-states) in the full HPG. This is clearly not a scalable solution, since the number of clicks represented might not even be 400 million. Furthermore, the existing algorithms (Borges, 2000) should be expanded to be able to work on this new type of state in the HPG.

Alternatively, a single middle-state could be inserted in each production, containing a structure indicating the distribution of clicks over the parameters. This would effectively reduce the state-explosion but require significant changes to the existing mining algorithms to include parameters in the mining process and to support, for example, mining of rules for a range of parameter-values.

We now discuss pros and cons of the HPG approach.

Pros

The size of an HPG is not proportional to the number of sessions it represents, but to the number of states and productions in the grammar, which makes the model very compact, scalable, and self-contained. Additional sessions can easily be added to an existing HPG and thereby allow for an HPG to grow in the number of sessions represented without growing in size. Performing data mining on an HPG outputs a number of rules describing the most preferred trails on the Web site using probability, which is a relatively intuitive measure of the usage of a Web site. Mining the HPG for a small, high-probability set of rules requires the usage of the described heuristics, which provides the user of the HPG with several parameters in order to tune the ruleset to his or her liking and extract rules for a very specific area.

Cons

The HPG does not preserve the ordering of clicks which is found in the sessions added (using a history depth above 1 will preserve some ordering). Therefore the rules mined could potentially be *false trails* in the sense that none or few sessions include the trail, but a large number of sessions include the different parts of the trail. In order to extract rules for a specific subset of all sessions in the HPG, a *specialized HPG* for exactly these sessions needs to be created. This is because a "complete" HPG does not have a memory of individual clicks and their session, as described above. A collection of sessions can potentially contain a very large number of different subsets, so building and storing specialized HPGs for every subset is not a scalable option, as mentioned above. Therefore, if more specialized HPGs are needed, there would be a need for storing the Web log information so that the desired session could be extracted later on and a specialized HPG could be built and mined.

The Hybrid Approach

Overview

As mentioned in the preceding sections, each approach has some inherent strengths and weaknesses. The click and subsession fact approaches handle additional information easily, but result either in huge I/O or huge storage requirements. On the other hand, an HPG can efficiently mine long rules for a large collection of sessions, but is not able to represent additional information in a scalable way. To remedy this situation, we now present the *hybrid* approach for extracting information about the use of a Web site, utilizing the potential for mining very specific rules present in the HPG approach while still allowing for the representation of additional information using a click fact schema in a data warehouse, utilizing existing DW technology. The main idea is to create HPGs on demand, where each dynamically created HPG represents a specialized part of the information in the Web log. Our proposal for a hybrid approach combines the click fact schema with the HPG model, creating a flexible technique able to answer both general *and* detailed queries regarding Web usage. Using the detailed information from the click fact schema means that almost no data is lost in the conversion from Web log to database.

However, we also need some kind of abstraction or simplification applied to the query results. In short, we want to be able to specify exactly what subset of the information we want to discover knowledge for. An HPG provides us with a simple technique to create an overview from detailed information. The scalability issues and somewhat lack of flexibility in the HPG model must though also be kept in mind as we want to be flexible with regards to querying possibilities. The concept of the hybrid approach is shown in Figure 7.

Figure 7. Overview of the hybrid approach

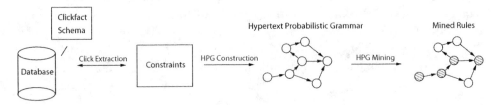

As mentioned above, creating specialized HPGs would require storing the original Web log information and creating each specialized HPG when required. Storing the original Web log file is not very efficient since, for example, a lot of non-optimized string-processing would be required, so some other format needs to be devised. The click fact schema described above provides this detailed level, since it preserves the ordering of the Web log and furthermore offers database functionality such as backup, optimized querying, and the possibility of OLAP techniques such as pre-aggregation to be applied. However, a more subtle feature of the click fact schema actually offers itself directly to the HPG model and proves useful in our solution. The database schema for the click fact table includes unique keys for both the *referrer* and the *destination* for each click. These two keys uniquely identify a specific production within a grammar since each key is a reference to a page and thus a state. Thereby we are able to extract all productions from the click fact table simply by returning all combinations of url_key and referrer_key. Each occurrence of a specific combination of keys will represent a single traversal of the corresponding link on the Web site.

Retrieving all states from an HPG is immediately possible from the click fact schema. The url_dimension table holds information about each individual page on the Web site, therefore a single query could easily retrieve all states in the grammar and a count of how many times the state was visited, both in total and as first or last in a session. The queries can be used to initialize an HPG. This would normally be done using an algorithm iterating over all states in the sessions (Borges, 2000), but using the database representation, the required information can be retrieved in a few simple database queries. Note that some post-processing of the query results are necessary for a nice in-memory representation.

Creating specialized HPGs is indeed possible with this approach. Inserting a *constraint* layer between the database software and the creation process for an HPG will allow for restrictions on the information represented in the HPG. Extending the queries described above to only extract information for clicks with certain characteristics will allow for creation of an HPG only representing this information. Thereby rules mined on this HPG will be solely for clicks with the specific characteristics. Using this concept, specialized HPGs can be created on-demand from the database. For instance, the consultant might be interested in learning about the characteristics of walkthroughs for male, senior salesmen in a company. The consultant will specify this constraint, and the queries above are modified to only extract the productions and the states that apply to the constraint. The queries will therefore only extract the sessions generated by male, senior salesmen in the company, and the HPG built from these sessions will produce rules telling about the characteristic behavior of male, senior salesmen.

This approach utilizes some of the techniques earlier described, but combines them to utilize the strong sides and avoid some of the weak sides.

Pros

The limitations of the "simple" HPG framework of not being able to efficiently represent additional information are avoided with this hybrid approach. The ability to easily generate a specialized HPG overcomes the shortcomings of not being able to store all possible specialized HPGs. Saving the Web log information in the click fact table (and thus in the database) gives us a tool for storing information which arguably is preferable to storing the original log file. A DBMS has many techniques for restoring, querying, and analyzing the information with considerable performance gains over processing on raw textual data such as a log file. Combining the click fact schema, which offers a detailed level of information, and the HPG framework, which offers a more generalized and compact view of the data, will allow for different views on the same data within the same model, without storing information redundantly on non-volatile storage (the extracted HPGs only exist in main memory).

Cons

As the hybrid approach mines results using the HPG, false trails might be presented to the user, which is a characteristic inherited from the general HPG approach. This is obviously a critical issue since this might lead to misinterpretations of the data. Using a history depth greater than 1 might reduce the number of false trails.

Open Issues

The performance of generating specialized HPGs using queries on top of a database is an open issue that will be explored next. The number of rules mined from an HPG should not be too large and the rules should not be too short, so some of the heuristics mentioned above need to be used when mining the HPG to be able to present the information to the user in a manageable way.

Prototype Implementation

The architecture of the hybrid approach prototype is seen in Figure 8. All modules within the system are implemented in Java. The prototype works as follows. First, the Web log file from the Web server is converted into an XML-based format. Then a Quilt query (Chamberlin, Robie, & Florescu, 2000) is executed on the XML file, resulting in a new XML file. An XML parser is then invoked which parses the XML into the click fact schema contained within the database. This part of the system is

Figure 8. Prototype architecture

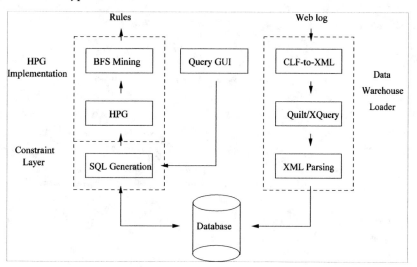

called the *data warehouse loader*. We then use a simple Graphical User Interface (GUI) to control how the SQL query extracting data from the database should be constructed. The SQL generator then constructs four SQL queries which are used to query the database. We call this part the *constraint layer*. The results from these queries are used to construct an HPG structure held in main memory. A BFS mining algorithm then extracts rules from the HPG. This part is named *HPG*.

The system is designing to read information from a Web log. The typical format of a Web log is the Common Log Format (CLF) or the Extended Common Log Format (ECLF). Such Web logs contain the URL requested, the IP address (or a resolved name, if possible) of the computer making the request, and timestamps. An entry in a CLF log file for a single request is seen below:

ask.cs.auc.dk - - [31/Oct/2001:09:48:16 +0100] "GET /education/dat1inf1 HTTP/1.0" 301 314

The identification of users is non-trivial as above. The prototype does not implement any logic to handle user identification, but simply assumes that an IP maps directly to a user. Also, the prototype does not at present include any means to avoid proxy caching of data. Instead of writing a data warehouse loader reading the CLF format directly, we have chosen to convert it into a more high-level format, based on XML. Once in this format, we are able to import and process our log data in a vast variety of programs which provides flexibility. The first step in loading the data into the data warehouse is cleansing the log data. Instead of cleansing directly on the log file using a temporary table in the database, or using other proposed techniques (Cooley et al., 1999), we use the Quilt query language. Quilt is the predecessor of the XQuery language proposed by the W3C and is an SQL-like language for querying an XML structure. We use two Quilt queries to produce an XML file cleansed for irrelevant information and grouped into sessions for each host. When the Web log is transformed into XML, we are ready to load it into the data warehouse. Using a SAX parser, we have implemented separate transformers from XML to the click and subsession warehouse schemas described above. Provided with the XML file, the transformers parse our XML structure into the data warehouse schemas, and the loading is completed. No scheme for handling the uncertainty associated with the decision-time is implemented in the prototype, but it could readily be extended to assume that a predefined timespan was used handling, for example, streaming time for each request. Based on previous work (Cooley et al., 1999), we have chosen to spawn a new session if the dwell time in a session exceeded 25 minutes. The spawning of a new session is handled by the log transformers in the prototype.

The main idea of combining a data warehouse with the HPG technique is the ability to constrain the data on which the HPG is built. We need SQL queries to extract our constrained set of data and then pass it on to a mechanism initializing our HPG. However, the extracted data must first be divided into *session-specific* and *click-specific* information. This distinction is very important, as the constructed HPG could otherwise be incorrect.

Session Specific

Dimensions which are specific to an entire session will, when constrained on one or more of their attributes, *always* return entire sessions as the result. One such dimension is the session dimension. If the click fact schema is constrained to only return clicks referencing a subset of all sessions in the session dimension, it is assured that the clicks returned will form complete sessions. Also, if we assume that all sessions start and finish on the same date, the date dimension will also be session specific. In an HPG context it means that the constructed HPG never has any *disconnected* states—states where no productions are going either to or from.

Click Specific

Dimensions containing information about a single click will, if the click fact table is constrained on a subset of these keys, produce a set of single clicks which are *probably not* forming complete sessions. The probability of this will increase as the cardinality of the attribute grows or the number of selected attributes shrinks. For instance, when constraining on three URLs from a set of 1,000 in the URL

Figure 9. Two-step extraction process

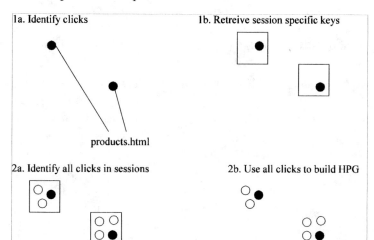

dimension, the clicks returned will properly not constitute complete sessions, and the probability of false trails dramatically increase. Furthermore, the HPG produced will then consist of three states with potentially no productions between them and some productions leading to states not included in this HPG. These three states are disconnected states. To be able to derive any rules from an HPG, we need to have states with productions connecting them.

As we want the approach to provide the overview as well as the detail, these two types of dimensions must be dealt with *before* the HPG is built. The solution proposed here is to constrain the data in two stages. The two stages (see Figure 9) can briefly be described as follows.

First, we retrieve a temporary result using dimensions which are thought to be *click* specific (1a). The temporary result comes from joining the click-specific dimensions with the click fact schema on *all* constrained attributes. The distinct session keys from the temporary result (1b) can be used to get the subset of all clicks having these session keys, which is done in step 2. These distinct keys are session specific and will assure an interconnected HPG. Second, we constrain the result using dimensions which are thought to be *session* specific and the distinct session keys (2a). *All* constraints must be fulfilled on the dimension when joining with the click fact schema. The collection of retrieved clicks is interconnected (2b). Note that both steps in practice will be performed as one query. When executing queries on the database, *java.util.ResultSet* objects are returned. The HPG's initializing method is then provided with the respective *ResultSet* objects and dealt with internally in each method. The method used to initialize the HPG state set will initially run through the *ResultSet* object provided and create a *State* object for each row in the *ResultSet* object. Transparency between the specific SQL query and the result used for HPG initialization is maintained, as the *ResultSet* object is well defined and not affected by a change in the SQL query. The HPG initialization method is at this stage provided with data, and as such, the extraction of data from the data warehouse is completed.

The HPG implementation consists of two parts: the HPG building method and a Breadth First Search (BFS) mining algorithm. The BFS algorithm is chosen instead of the Depth First Search (DFS) algorithm, as the latter has higher memory consumption (Borges, 2000). The only difference between the prototype HPG implementation and work by Borges (2000) is that rules and productions are stored in main memory instead of a database. The HPG implemented in the prototype holds two simple lists in main memory, one for states and one for productions. These lists are initialized from the results from the constraint layer, and the mining process works entirely on these lists.

Experimental Evaluation

We now briefly discuss the results of our experimental evaluation (additional details and figures can be found in Jespersen et al., 2002). In evaluating the hybrid approach, we decided to evaluate the performance of the creation of HPGs on-the-fly both by itself and against a straightforward SQL-query on a subsession schema. The experiments were performed on both a non-optimized and an optimized implementation of the hybrid approach. We decided not to evaluate against a straight forward click fact schema since they perform poorly on sequences of clicks (Andersen et al., 2000) and would perform too poorly to be used for online mining. The *goal* of the experiments is to retrieve information concerning the performance of creating HPGs on-the-fly on top of a database. We have used the Web log from the Computer Science Department at Aalborg University for October 2001, containing 33,000 sessions, with a total of 115,000 valid clicks divided among 27,400 unique pages. The DBMS used in the evaluation is MySQL 4.0.1 running on an Intel 933 Mhz machine. The prototype described above is running on an AMD Athlon 1800 Mhz machine. We adopted the suggested convention (Andersen et al., 2000) of limiting the subsession length to 10 clicks to avoid a massive blowup in number of subsessions generated. Insertion of subsessions yielded a total of 620,000 entries in the subsession fact table divided among 490,000 different subsessions.

In the process of extracting rules from the data warehouse, three main tasks are performed. First, the database is queried for data used to initialize the HPG. Second, the HPG is built in main memory based on the extracted data, and third, the BFS mining algorithm extracts rules from the HPG. To test how the approach performs as the number of states increases, a range query test was performed.

By far the most time-consuming part in the hybrid approach is the database query time. In most cases, more than 90% of the total time is spent on this part. The time used for the BFS mining is very short. The time spent on initializing the HPG only adds little processing time to the overall processing time, usually 5-10%. Thus, it seems that a possible tuning effort should focus on the database query part.

One of the most obvious ways to optimize the database is to create indexes on the key attributes in the click fact schema. Materialized views are another promising opportunity for tuning.

We now compare the hybrid approach to the subsession schema on extraction of information for *all* sessions, *session*-specific constraints, and *click*-specific constraints.

All Sessions

It is found that the non-optimized hybrid approach performs poorer than the subsession schema by a factor of approximately 25. However, the hybrid approach where both the database querying and the BFS mining is optimized takes only 30% longer than the subsession approach. The small performance advantage of the subsession approach comes at a large price: the storage requirements are more than five times higher than for the hybrid approach, due to the need to store subsession of all lengths.

Click-Specific Constraints

The test is performed by extracting information for all sessions containing requests including the string *tbp*, which is a specific personal homepage on the Web site. The hybrid approach proves to be a factor of 10 faster than the subsession schema approach; even in the non-optimized case, the optimized version is 20 times faster.

Session-Specific Constraints

The session-specific constraint is evaluated using a constraint on the *total_session_seconds* field from the *session_dimension* table. The optimized hybrid approach outperforms all the other approaches by an average factor of 3-4. All the other approaches are rather similar in performance. Again, the superior performance of the optimized hybrid approach is accompanied by a storage requirement that is more than five times smaller than the subsession approach.

To conclude, our evaluation of the hybrid approach has shown that the optimized hybrid approach is very competitive when compared to the subsession fact approach.

Even with a storage requirement that is more than five times smaller than for the subsession fact approach, the optimized hybrid approach performs 3-20 times faster. Only for mining all rules, the performance is a little slower, making the hybrid approach the clear winner.

The Post-Check Enhanced Hybrid Approach

Overview

We now describe the concept of false trails in detail, derive the notion of a *true rule,* and present the Post Check Enhanced Hybrid (PEHA) approach for achieving true rules. To understand why a rule extracted from an HPG mining process could be indicating a false trail, it is important to note that the HPG model assumes that the productions expanded from a single state X are entirely dependent upon state X and not on any previous states. This assumption can be overcome somewhat by introducing history depth into the single states in the HPG. Then each state in the HPG models a sequence of, for example, three sequential clicks. The HPG model presented above implicitly used a history depth of 1. Note, that a rule extracted from an HPG is given with a certain probability. This probability can be translated into a number of sessions supporting (under the HPG assumption) the trail of the rule, called the *expected number of sessions,* $E_{sessions}$, by multiplying this probability with the number of sessions that have visited the first state of the rule.

We now want to extend the hybrid approach so that it outputs entirely true rules instead of rules which might be (partly) false—that is, have an incorrect support count.

First, we define an *existing rule*:

- Given a rule R, consisting of a sequence of states $R=s_1 \ldots s_n$, and a support level $S_{sessions}$, indicating the number of sessions which include the sequence of states, R is an *existing rule* if and only if $S_{sessions} \geq 1$.

- We now define a *false rule* to be a rule that is not an existing rule—that is, a rule indicating a sequence of states not traversed by any sessions. We define a *true rule* as:

  - Given an existing rule R, consisting of a sequence of states $R=s_1 \ldots s_n$, with an expected number of users $E_{sessions}$, and a support level $S_{sessions}$, indicating the number of sessions which include the sequence of states, R is a *true rule* if and only if $E_{sessions} = S_{sessions}$.

With the assumption of limited browsing history in the HPG model, the expected number of sessions for a rule might not be the correct support level of the rule.

In extending the hybrid approach, we note that the set of existing rules generated by the HPG model is a superset of the true rules, since a true rule will always be contained in an existing rule. This fact leads us towards an approach where the HPG model is used as a *generator* of *candidate rules,* which can then be validated (modified) to become true rules. In other words, the rules extracted from the HPG are checked against the actual log data to achieve the correct support level. In the following, the set of usage sessions are referred to as the *true traversals.*

To go from candidate rules to true rules, we must develop a way of *post-checking* or *validating* the candidate rules in order to convert them to true rules. This validation does not alter the page sequences, since the HPG ensures that the sequence is valid.

The validation is only an adjustment of the number of sessions having traversed the page sequence, to get the actual support of the page sequence. In essence, we want to adjust $E_{sessions}$ to be equal to $S_{sessions}$. Using the hybrid approach, we already have the framework in place to perform this validation of support level. As described above, we have stored all clickstream information in a click fact schema, so the idea is to use this schema to validate a given rule.

Validating a rule in our click fact schema requires the execution of queries in which we join multiple instances of the click fact table as the click fact schema stores the individual clicks. We want the check of a candidate rule against the click fact schema to result in the number of sessions containing the given rule. By containing, we mean that a session includes the given sequence of Web pages in the rule at least once. If a session contains a sequence more than once, the support is only incremented with one. This definition of support is adopted elsewhere (Agrawal et al., 1995).

Post-Checking Rules

The conditions to be verified for *every* production p $[s_1 \rightarrow s_2]$ in a rule are the following (*number_in_session* captures at what position in the browsing session a given click occurs):

1. s_1 is followed by s_2
2. s_2's *number_in_session* is 1 greater than s_1's *number_in_session*
3. s_1 and s_2 are found within the same session

Furthermore, there are some cases in which additional conditions apply which must be checked as well. The α parameter, used when mining a HPG for (candidate) rules, must also be considered when it is set to 0. Mining with $\alpha=0$ means that all rules mined from the HPG are rules in which the first Web page is also the first page visited in a session. Furthermore, a rule might include the artificial *end*-state, which is not represented in the click fact schema, in its last production, indicating that the previous state was the last in a session. Adding these two special case conditions to the list of checks performed in the query, we get:

1.   if $\alpha=0$, s_1 in $p_1[s_1 \rightarrow s_2]$ *must* have *is_first* = 1
2.   if s_2 in $p_n[s_1 \rightarrow s_2]$ is the artificial *end*-state, s_1 *must* have *is_last* = 1

Note that *is_first* and *is_last* is assumed to be implemented as 1 and 0 in the click fact schema, representing true and false respectively. To clarify how a query would look when checking a given rule, a short example is now presented. Consider the rule $1 \rightarrow 2 \rightarrow 3 \rightarrow E$, where the numbers are the schema identifiers for the specific URLs traversed in the rule—that is, the *url_key* and *referer_key* fields of the click fact table. The parameter α is set to 0, and the state E is the artificial *end*-state. Formally, we must check the productions $p_1[s_1 \rightarrow s_2]$ and $p_2[s_2 \rightarrow s_3]$. The corresponding query used to validate the rule against the click fact schema in the data warehouse is seen below.

```
SELECT COUNT(DISTINCT(cf1.session_key))
FROM Click_fact cf1 INNER JOIN Click_fact cf2 ON
        (cf1.url_key = 1 AND cf1.url_key = cf2.referrer_key AND cf2.url_key = 2
        AND cf1.is_first = 1 AND cf2.number_in_session = cf1.number_in_session+1
        AND cf1.session_key = cf2.session_key)
INNER JOIN Click_fact cf3 ON
        (cf2.url_key = cf3.referrer_key AND cf3.url_key = 3
        AND cf3.is_last = 1 AND cf3.number_in_session = cf2.number_in_session+1
        AND cf2.session_key = cf3.session_key)
```

If $\alpha>0$, the check for *is_first* is omitted, and for rules not ending with the artificial *end*-state, the check for *is_last* is omitted. It is *not* possible to remove a join from the query when the check for *is_first* is not needed. Even though checking for the existence of *referer_key* and *url_key* in the *same* table instance would do the job, condition 2 would be impossible to check. Condition 2 needs to be checked as we could otherwise risk missing pages visited inside session, thus generating wrong results.

The hybrid framework presents a flexible way to add *constraints* on rules extracted from the data warehouse. These constraints should also be applied when post checking a rule, since we should only want to count support for the sessions from which the rule was extracted. The use of constraints in post-checking of rules is quite similar to the use of constraints when creating the HPG in the hybrid approach. For session-specific constraints, a join between the click fact table and the dimension holding the constraint is added to the query. For click-specific constraints, the temporary table used when building the HPG is re-used by adding a join between the temporary table (which holds session-id's fulfilling the click-specific constraints) and the click fact table. An example query using constraints in post-checking a rule is given below. Here, extra joins on the *date_dimension* and the *temp_dimension* is added to illustrate the use of session- and click-specific constraints, respectively.

```
SELECT COUNT(DISTINCT(cf1.session_key))
FROM Click_fact cf1 INNER JOIN Click_fact cf2 ON
        (cf1.url_key = 1 AND cf1.url_key = cf2.referrer_key AND cf2.url_key = 2
        AND cf1.is_first = 1 AND cf2.number_in_session = cf1.number_in_session+1
        AND cf1.session_key = cf2.session_key)
INNER JOIN Click_fact cf3 ON
        (cf2.url_key = cf3.referrer_key AND cf3.url_key = 3
        AND cf3.is_last = 1 AND cf3.number_in_session = cf2.number_in_session+1
        AND cf2.session_key = cf3.session_key)
INNER JOIN date_dimension dd ON
        (cf1.date_key = dd.date_key AND dd.year = 2002)
INNER JOIN Temp_dimension td ON
        (cf1.session_key = td.session_key)
```

Experimental Evaluation

The evaluation of PEHA is aimed at comparing it with an existing Web usage mining approach based on data warehousing technology, namely the subsession schema. Note that we do not compare PEHA to the original hybrid approach since we are only interested in comparing approaches that always provide rules with correct support. The original hybrid approach will always be faster than PEHA since the post-checking phase is not done, but this comes at the cost of sometimes quite incorrect results (Jespersen, Pedersen, & Thorhauge, 2003).

Two datasets are used in the experiments. Experiments are conducted for each dataset, namely the performance using three different ways of constraining the extracted rules (session and click specific, and both). For each constraint type, the threshold used for mining the HPG is varied. By decreasing the support threshold, we experienced an increasing average rule length and rule-set size for both datasets. In order to examine performance using rule-sets with different characteristics, we utilize this property to evaluate the performance for different average lengths of rules. To minimize the effect of distorted results, each experiment is repeated five times and an average is calculated. The sub-tasks of MIMER that are evaluated in this chapter are:

1.   *Query* data warehouse for information used to construct the HPG
2.   *Construction* of the HPG structures in main memory
3.   *Mining* the constructed HPG
4.   *Post-checking* the rules extracted from the HPG

The first Web log (CS) is from the Web site of the Computer Science Department at Aalborg University (*http://www.cs.aau.dk*). The Web site is primarily an information site for students and staff at the institution, but also contains personal homepages with a wide range of content and homepages for individual classes. The second Web log (Bank) is taken from an educational intranet placed at a major Danish financial institution. The Web site contains various courses which can be followed by the employees of the institution. The CS dataset contains 68,745 sessions, with 232,592 clicks, 58,232 unique pages, and an average session length of 3.38. For Bank, the numbers are 21,661, 395,913, 2,368, and 18.23, respectively. Note the differences between the datasets in the average length of a session and the number of unique pages, indicating a more scattered browsing on the CS Web site as opposed to the more continuous browsing on the Bank Web site.

The DBMS used is an industrial system supporting materialized views (for licensing issues, we cannot name the specific DBMS used). The DBMS and MIMER is running on an Athlon XP1800+ with 512 MB of memory and Windows 2000.

For most SQL queries used, matching materialized views are implemented in order to optimize the query performance. Likewise, the queries on the subsession schema are also optimized using materialized views. In the experiments, only rules of length less than 10 are post-checked since the materialized views used are dedicated views for each rule length and not designed to promote the post-checking of longer rules. The space used to hold the materialized views used and the subsession approach are approximately 185 MB and 740 MB, respectively. Each Web log is loaded into the data warehouse using a batch load utility. Because of the very time-consuming task of constructing and loading very long subsessions, only subsessions of length up to 5 is generated, which is ok since we only want to compare the *performance* and not the *correctness* of rule extraction by the two approaches. Additionally, rules longer than 5 will in practice be rare and have low support, and are thus not that interesting from a practical point of view.

The results of extracting and post-checking rules through MIMER using the DB dataset show that MIMER and all of the sub-tasks in MIMER perform in approximately constant time, even as the average rule length is increased. On average, 75% of the total time is used to extract data from the DBMS and construct the HPG structure in main memory. The subtask of querying the data warehouse for information needed to construct the HPG does not at present utilize materialized views to optimize access to the data. Constructing the HPG in main memory takes minimal time partly due to the fact that dedicated structures to hold both productions and states in the HPG have been implemented. Mining the constructed HPG for (candidate) rules takes relatively little time, approximately 50-250 ms. The time used to post-check the candidate rules mined in the previous stage is constant as well. We found that the time used to check a rule scales very well with the average rule length, indicating that no matter the length of a candidate rule in the experiment, post-checking only adds a near constant factor to the total time used. Notice that we would not expect such constant behavior to be achieved *without* the use of materialized views in the DBMS.

Our experiments show that both for click- and session-specific constraints, the post-checks run in almost similar time, indicating that no specific type of single constraint is more time consuming. Performing post-check on a rule for a combined click- and session-specific constraint shows a slight increase in the running time of approximately 200 ms as the average rule length is increased by 2, indicating that adding constraints on several dimensions will increase the running time slightly.

When comparing MIMER to direct queries on the subsession schema, the result is that queries on the subsession schema are several times faster than MIMER, in this case, using click-specific constraints. The subsession schema thereby proves faster at locating true rules compared to MIMER, primarily because all possible rules (of length ≤ 5) are stored explicitly, and finding rules by frequency of occurrence, utilizing materialized views, run relatively fast. In order to run click-specific constraints, the subsession queries use the LIKE statement of the SQL language to extract information "inside" the sequences stored in the schema. Note however that not all click-specific constraints can be implemented on top of the subsession schema, since some information is too finely grained to be stored in the schema, for example, the time spent on a particular page, also referred to as the *dwell-time* of a request.

The tables and materialized views of the subsession approach consume approximately 4.5 times the storage of MIMER for both CS and Bank. The extra space used in the subsession approach comes from the fact that each sub-sequence of clicks found in an entire session of clicks is explicitly stored. One should notice that certain constrained rules are *impossible* to find using the Subsession approach, for example, constraining on how long a certain page has been viewed, also referred to as the *dwelltime*.

In summary, we have found that the average time of post-checking a candidate rule from an HPG runs in approximately constant time, regardless of the length of the rule when utilizing materialized views. The actual running time of the post-check is also dependent on the number of constraints placed on the HPG, but not on the type of constraint as both click- and session-specific constraints run in similar time. Compared to the direct queries on the subsession schema, MIMER performs several times worse, however the flexibility inherent in PEHA and in MIMER allows for more specialized information to be extracted from MIMER. The difference in space usage is clearly in favor of the PEHA approach. Notice that in our experiments, only subsession up to length 5 was generated, and storing longer subsessions would further increase the overhead in space required by the subsession approach.

Conclusion

Motivated by the need to combine data warehousing/DBMS and data mining technologies for Web log analysis, this chapter presented a number of approaches that combine data warehousing and data mining techniques in order to analyze Web logs. After introducing the well-known click and session DW schemas (Kimball & Merz, 2000), the chapter presented the subsession schema which allows fast queries on sequences of page visits (Andersen et al., 2000). Then, the chapter presented the so-called *hybrid technique* (Jespersen et al., 2002), which combines DW Web log schemas (Kimball & Merz, 2000) with a data mining technique called Hypertext Probabilistic Grammars (Borges, 2000), hereby providing fast and flexible constraint-based Web log analysis. Finally, the chapter presented the "post-check enhanced" (PEHA) improvement of the hybrid technique.

The techniques have their own pros and cons, and are suitable for different settings. If the rather high storage use is not a problem, the subsession schema approach is both fast and easy-to-use for sequence-focused queries. If storage use is a problem or more detailed information is needed in queries, the hybrid approach performs well, albeit at the cost of possibly returning imprecise rule support counts. If absolute precision and correctness is mandatory, the PEHA approach offers validation of hybrid result rules at a reasonable cost. This chapter was the first to provide an integrated presentation of these approaches combining data warehousing and data mining techniques for Web log analysis.

References

Agrawal, R., & Srikant, R. (1995). Mining sequential patterns. In *Proceedings of ICDE* (pp. 6-10).

Andersen, J., Giversen, A., Jensen, A.H., Larsen, R.S., Pedersen, T.B., & Skyt, J. (2000). Analyzing clickstreams using subsessions. In *Proceedings of DOLAP* (pp. 25-32). Extended version available as (Tech. Rep. No. 00-5001), Department of Computer Science, Aalborg University, Denmark.

Borges, J. (2000). *A data mining model to capture user Web navigation patterns.* PhD Thesis, Department of Computer Science, University College London, UK.

Borges, J., & Levene, M. (1999). Data mining of user navigation patterns. In *Proceedings of WEBKDD* (pp. 92-111).

Borges, J., & Levene, M. (2000). A fine-grained heuristic to capture Web navigation patterns. *SIGKDD Explorations, 2*(1), 40-50.

Büchner, A.G., Anand, S.S., Mulvenna, M.D., & Hughes, J.G. (1998). Discovering Internet marketing intelligence through Web log mining. *SIGMOD Record, 27*(4), 54-61.

Chamberlin, D.D., Robie, J., & Florescu, D. (2000). Quilt: An {XML} query language for heterogeneous data sources. In *Proceedings of WebDB (Informal Proceedings)* (pp. 53-62).

Cooley, R., Mobasher, B., & Srivastava, J. (1999). Data preparation for mining World Wide Web browsing patterns. *Knowledge and Information Systems, 1*(1), 5-32.

Cooley, R., Srivastava, J., & Mobasher, B. (1997). Web mining: Information and pattern discovery on the World Wide Web. In *Proceedings of ICTAI* (pp. 558-567).

Cooley, R., Tan, P., & Srivastava, J. (1999). Websift: The Web site information filter system. In *Proceedings of the 1999 KDD Workshop on Web Mining.*

Han, J. (1997). OLAP mining: Integration of OLAP with data mining. In *Proceedings of DS-7* (pp. 3-20).

Han, J., & Kamber, M. (2000). *Data mining—concepts and techniques.* San Francisco: Morgan Kaufmann.

Hinneburg, A., Lehner, W., & Habich, D. (2003). COMBI-operator: Database support for data mining applications. In *Proceedings of VLDB* (pp. 429-439).

Jespersen, S., Pedersen, T.B., & Thorhauge, J. (2003). Evaluating the Markov assumption for Web usage mining. In *Proceedings of WIDM* (pp. 82-89).

Jespersen, S., Thorhauge, J., & Pedersen, T.B. (2002). A hybrid approach to Web usage mining. In *Proceedings of DaWaK* (pp. 73-82). Extended version available as (Tech. Rep. No. 02-5002), Department of Computer Science, Aalborg University, Denmark.

Kimball, R., & Merz, R. (2000). *The data Webhouse toolkit.* New York: John Wiley & Sons.

Levene, M., & Loizou, G. (1999). A probabilistic approach to navigation in hypertext. *Information Sciences, 114*(1-4), 165-186.

Pei, J., Han, J., Mortazavi-asl, B., & Zhu, H. (2000). Mining access patterns efficiently from Web logs. In *Proceedings of PAKDD* (pp. 396-407).

Pei, J., Han, J., Mortazavi-Asl, B., Pinto, H., Chen, Q., Dayal, U., & Hsu, M. (2001). PrefixSpan: Mining sequential patterns by prefix-projected growth. In *Proceedings of ICDE* (pp. 215-224).

Sarawagi, S., Thomas, S., & Agrawal, R. (1998). Integrating mining with relational database systems: Alternatives and implications. In *Proceedings of SIGMOD* (pp. 343-353).

Srikant, R., & Agrawal, R. (1996). Mining sequential patterns: Generalizations and performance improvements. In *Proceedings of EDBT* (pp. 3-17).

Spiliopoulou, M., & Faulstich, L.C. (1998). WUM: A Web Utilization Miner. In *Proceedings of WebDB* (pp. 109-115).

Wu, K.-L., Yu, P.S., & Ballman, A. (1998). A Web usage mining and analysis tool. *IBM System Journal, Internet Computing, 37.*

Chapter II

Computing Dense Cubes Embedded in Sparse Data

Lixin Fu, The University of North Carolina at Greensboro, USA

Abstract

In high-dimensional data sets, both the number of dimensions and the cardinalities of the dimensions are large and data is often very sparse, that is, most cubes are empty. For such large data sets, it is a well-known challenging problem to compute the aggregation of a measure over arbitrary combinations of dimensions efficiently. However, in real-world applications, users are usually not interested in all the sparse cubes, most of which are empty or contain only one or few tuples. Instead, they focus more on the "big picture" information—the highly aggregated data, where the "where clauses" of the SQL queries involve only few dimensions. Although the input data set is sparse, this aggregate data is dense. The existing multi-pass, full-cube computation algorithms are prohibitively slow for this type of application involving very large input data sets. We propose a new dynamic data structure called Restricted Sparse Statistics Tree (RSST) and a novel cube evaluation algorithm, which are especially well suited for efficiently computing dense sub-cubes imbedded in high-dimensional sparse data sets. RSST only computes the aggregations of non-empty cube cells where the number of non-star coordinates (i.e., the number of group by attributes) is restricted to be no more than a user-specified threshold. Our innovative algorithms are scalable and I/O efficient. RSST is incrementally maintainable, which makes it suitable for data warehousing and the analysis of streaming data. We have compared our algorithms with top, state-of-the-art cube computation algorithms such as Dwarf and QCT in construction times, query response times, and data compression. Experiments demonstrate the excellent performance and good scalability of our approach.

Introduction

Given n dimensions $D_1, D_2, \ldots, D_n$, where domain values of D_i are in $0..C_i-1$, C_i is the cardinality of D_i, and a measure M, the data cube problem is to compute the aggregation of M over any subset $Q \subseteq D_1 \times D_2 \times \ldots \times D_n$. Domain values other than integers are converted into integers. For example, strings and ordinary domains are mapped into integers starting from 0. Real numbers can be discretized into ranges. SUM, COUNT, and MIN/MAX are typical aggregation operators. In this chapter, we mainly focus on COUNT and SUM operators; others can be implemented similarly.

Data cube facility is essential in data warehousing and OLAP (Gray et al., 1997). Because of the importance of efficient data cube computation and exploration, numerous significant studies have been performed. However, the state-of-the-art algorithms and systems do not scale well in terms of I/O bottleneck. This problem is important because in the data warehousing and analytical data processing environment, the data sets are often very massive. Almost all current technologies build certain structures (e.g., materialized views, indexes, trees, etc.) before answering user queries. The running times of setting up the structures for such large data sets will be dominated by I/O operations. Current top algorithms either entirely ignore the problem of I/O efficiency or do not handle it well. They require multiple passes for large data sets, which makes the data cube computation prohibitively slow or infeasible.

On the other hand, although the input data sets are very large and very sparse (i.e., the vast majority of cubes are empty), the high-level views with few group-bys contain dense data—the typical targets of user navigation. In data cube applications, users (mostly data analyzers and top managers) are usually not interested in the low-level, detailed data, which is the typical focus of daily transactional processing operations. The analytical users are more interested in the highly aggregated, "big picture" information. For example, in a warehouse storing car sales data, a manager may not be so interested in a query like "What is the total sale for golden, Honda Accord

LX sedans that are sold on day *X* and store *Y*?" as in a query for sales grouped by season and manufacturer, for example.

Motivated by the idiom of "make common things fast," we have developed a new method of efficiently evaluating dense, aggregated cubes that are commonly queried so that the number of data passes of original input data sets is minimized. This new I/O efficient strategy will make the analysis for very large data sets feasible. Our major innovations and contributions in this article include the following.

We present a new data structure called RSST (Restricted Sparse Statistics Tree), which binds all the views that have few group-by attributes into *one* compact data structure, thus facilitating the generation, maintenance, and querying of these views. To build RSST, we only need *one* pass of the input data set without any pre-sorting step. BUC algorithm (Beyer & Ramakrishnan, 1999) computes iceberg queries whose aggregates are above certain threshold (we call it *cube aggregation threshold*). Harinarayan, Rajaraman, and Ullman (1996) give an algorithm to select a set of views under the constraint of available space. To our knowledge, RSST is the first structure that binds and computes all the views whose number of group-by attributes is no more than a threshold (we call it *cube dimensionality threshold*). These views occupy the top layers of a view lattice structure.

For large sparse datasets, even restricting the dimensionality of the computed cuboids is not sufficient. The views with group by attributes of large cardinalities are less likely queried. For example, if a table contains 1 million records, and has six dimensions D_1 to D_6 whose cardinalities are 10000, 5000, 1000, 100, 100, and 100 respectively, then on the average the probability that a cuboid of view $D_1 D_2 D_3$ contains one or more tuples is 1/50000. So, we further restrict to the views that the product of the cardinalities of the group-by attributes is no more than the product of a threshold (we call it *cube cardinality threshold*) and the number of records in the data set. Notice that the cube dimensionality threshold and cube cardinality threshold are used for us to focus on the computation of the commonly queried views or cubes. They do not restrict the number of dimensions or the cardinalities of the dimensions of the original input datasets.

We give an efficient cube query algorithm. If the cube queried is dense—that is, its aggregate is above the cube aggregation threshold—it will be answered immediately by in-memory RSST; otherwise, we need only one I/O to compute the aggregate of the cube. Our query algorithm can answer point queries, iceberg queries, range queries, and partial queries.

We have performed comprehensive simulation experiments, paying particular attention to the I/O bottleneck issue. We have implemented three recent top cube computation algorithms such as BUC, Dwarf, and QC Trees, and compared our algorithm with them. The results show that ours is significantly faster.

Related Work

Conceptually, a data cube can be regarded as a d-dimensional array whose cells store the aggregated measures for the sub-cubes defined by their dimensional coordinates (Gray et al., 1997). There are three approaches for data cube implementation: RO-LAP (Relational OLAP), MOLAP (Multidimensional OLAP), and HOLAP (Hybrid OLAP) (Chaudhuri & Dayal, 1997). For example, the algorithm in Agarwal et al. (1996) belongs to the ROLAP camp, while Zhao, Deshpande, and Naughton's (1997) is in MOLAP. In recent years, considerable work has been done on cube computation. The cubing algorithms can be roughly categorized as full cube vs. partial cube computation, or exact cube vs. approximate cube computation. Both of the above example algorithms are full and exact cubing algorithms, computing all the cube cells, including super cubes, exactly. RSST is a partial and exact cube algorithm.

Although stars appear in Gray et al. (1997) to represent super cubes, star pointers are first introduced in a statistics tree structure to actually compute the aggregates of the super cubes (Fu & Hammer, 2000). For dense data sets, packaged arrays are very effective to compute the data cube (Fu, 2004). In Johnson and Shasha (1997), cube trees and cube forests are proposed. Very scant work in the literature addresses the issues of computing the data cube for hierarchical dimensions (e.g., day-month-year for *time* dimension). A family of materialized ST trees (Hammer & Fu, 2001) have been used to improve the performance for queries with constraints on dimension hierarchies. Markl, Ramsak, and Bayer (1999) give a multidimensional hierarchical clustering scheme (MHC) for a fact table with hierarchical dimensions in a data warehouse.

In addition to removing prefix redundancy for dense cubes, recent important work in Sismanis, Deligiannakis, Roussopoulos, and Kotidis (2002) focuses on a new compressed Dwarf structure to remove suffix redundancy for sparse cubes as well. It outperforms Cubetrees in terms of storage space, creation time, query response time, and updates. This algorithm also gives an optimization of clustering data cubes that belong to the same views. However, it requires a pre-sorting of the input records, which needs multiple passes for large data sets. Moreover, each insertion of a record in the sorted file into the structure may incur several additional I/Os in the process of coalescing. This is equivalent to having multiple additional passes for the construction of the dwarf tree. It is not incremental for bulk loading. Another drawback is that updating is complex and somewhat inconvenient.

Rather than computing all the data cubes, Beyer and Ramakrishnan (1999) developed the Bottom-Up Cubing (BUC) algorithm for computing only "iceberg cubes." Similar to some ideas in Apriori (Agrawal & Srikant, 1994) and partitioned-cube (Ross & Srivastava, 1997), BUC is a ROLAP algorithm and may require multiple passes for large data sets. External sorting and accessing large intermediate files slow down BUC-based types of algorithms such as BU-BST, Quotient Cube, and QC-trees that we will discuss in the following paragraph.

In Wang, Feng, Lu, and Yu (2002), the data cube tuples aggregating from the same set of tuples in the input base table are condensed into one physical tuple called base single tuple (BST). BU-BST heuristics is similar to BUC, except that computation quits for BST. Quotient Cube (Lakshmanan, Pei, & Han, 2002) generalizes the idea of BST compression so that all the cubes with the same aggregate value form a class while the drill-down semantics are preserved. More extensive research and complete results over Quotient Cube are given in Lakshmanan, Pei, and Zhao (2003). One of the major contributions of this paper is that it gives a new data structure called QC-trees for storing and searching a quotient cube. However, in the data warehousing environment, both the original table and the temporary class table usually do not fit in memory. The construction of QC-trees requires expensive depth-first searching of the large original tables and sorting temporary class tables. To compute iceberg cubes with complex measures such as AVERAGE, Han, Pei, Dong, and Wang (2001) extend BUC to Top-k BUC and propose the Top-k H-cubing method. Xin, Han, Li, and Wah (2003) compute full or iceberg cubes by integrating the strengths of Top-Down and Bottom-Up approaches.

Due to the complexity and long response times, some algorithms give a quick approximation instead of an exact answer. Sampling is often used in estimations (Acharya, Gibbons, & Poosala, 2000; Gibbons & Matias, 1998). Vitter and Wang (1999) use wavelets to estimate aggregates for sparse data. An interesting idea with a relatively low cost is to refine self-tuning histograms by using feedback from a query execution engine (Aboulnaga & Chaudhuri, 1999).

Materialized views are commonly used to speed up cube queries. A greedy algorithm over the lattice structure to choose views for materialization is given in Harinarayan et al. (1996). Other work related to the selection, indexing, and maintenance of views is addressed by Gupta and Mumick (1999), Labio, Quass, and Adelberg (1997), Lehner, Sidle, Pirahesh, and Cochrane (2000), Mumick, Quass, and Mumick (1997), and Yan and Larson (1995). In an environment with infrequent updates, indexes such as Bitmap, encoded bitmap (Chan & Ioannidis, 1998), and B$^+$-tree can improve the performance of cube queries. Unlike in the OLTP (online transactional processing), the query patterns are usually unpredictable (i.e., ad-hoc) in analytical environment. Therefore, pre-scheduled view materialization and indexing are not sufficient. In summary, although great progress has been made, the evaluation of data cube for very large data sets is still infeasible because current technologies still need multiple passes. In this chapter we propose new I/O-efficient cube algorithms to address this important issue.

Restricted Sparse Statistics Trees

Tree Structure

RSSTs are multi-way trees whose internal nodes are used for branching and whose leaves contain aggregates. A node at level h $(h = 0, 1, ..., n-1)$ contains (index, pointer) pairs. The indexes represent the domain values of the corresponding dimensions, and the pointers direct query paths to nodes at the next level. An additional special index value called *star value*, denoted by $*$, represents the ALL value of dimension h; the corresponding *star pointer* is used to direct the path to the next level for a cube query that has no constraints for dimension h. A root-to-leaf path represents a cuboid (a cube or a cube cell; we use these terms interchangeably). In RSST, the number of non-star pointers along the paths is restricted to be no more than a pre-specified threshold r. We term these data cuboids that have no more than r non-star coordinates *r-dimensional cuboids*. If r is small, we say these cuboids are *low-dimensional*. If r equals n, we are computing the full data cube (i.e., all cuboids). Essentially, we extend the work in Lakshmanan, Ng, Han, and Pang (1999), where constrained frequent set queries with 2-variable constraints are optimized ($r = 2$).

In the example RSST of Figure 1, there are four dimensions, and COUNT operator is implemented. The figure shows the RSST after the first two records (6, 9, 5, 1) and (20, 1, 3, 2) are inserted into an empty tree. We will give details of insertion and loading algorithms in the next subsection. If we set r to be 2, all the root-to-leaf paths have no more than two non-star labels. Along the pointers are the labels of the corresponding domain values. Leaves shown in boxes contain the aggregation values of the cuboids represented by the root-to-leaf paths. Unlike a B-tree, which is an index for only one dimension, RSST deals with multiple dimensions at the same time. The leaves of RSST do not store records or pointers to records. Instead, they store aggregation values only, which saves space since duplicate records or records in the same cuboids are aggregated into the same leaves. In this way, many operations performed on records like sorting/hashing, writing the intermediate data into and reading data from disks, and so forth (Agarwal et al., 1996) are eliminated. In particular, the low-dimensional cuboids tend to contain many duplicates that are aggregated into the same leaves. RSST is a highly condensed data structure.

The reason why we focus on low-dimensional cubes is that in the analytical processing environment, users are mainly interested in the views that have few group-by attributes. In other words, the dense cubes representing the "big picture" are most often queried. For example, among the 22 standard queries in the TPC-H benchmark, 20 of them have no more than three group-by attributes. Another two involve constraints at very fine levels, which are best dealt with by ordinary RD-BMSs. High-dimensional cubes whose coordinates have no or few stars consume most of the storage space, but are rarely queried in real-world applications. Then, why not ignore them and just focus on speeding up the common queries? In the same line, we can also incorporate the concept of density into the tree structure. The cuboids that have non-star dimensions with large cardinalities are more likely sparse. Therefore, we can add another restriction that the product of the cardinalities of the non-star dimensions in the queried cube should be less than certain threshold. The two abovementioned heuristics can be used together. In this way, we focus on the dense, low-dimensional views that are predominantly queried by the users. The tree is unbalanced. All leaves are automatically sorted and naturally indexed by the corresponding root-to-leaf paths. In comparison with complex structures such as Dwarf trees, QC-trees, H-trees, and star-trees, which all have side links and actually become graphs, RSSTs remain simple tree structures, thus rendering simpler implementations and faster runtimes.

As a MOLAP data structure, RSST preserves the advantages of ROLAP in the sense that it only stores non-empty data cubes for sparse data. For example, if the sizes of all four dimensions in the previous example are 1,000, then there are 10^{12} full-dimensional cube cells, most of which are empty. However, in the RSST, we only store *non-empty* cubes. We eliminate the need for special data compression techniques such as (OffsetInChunk, data pairs) that are widely used in MOLAP systems for sparse data.

Figure 1. An example of RSST

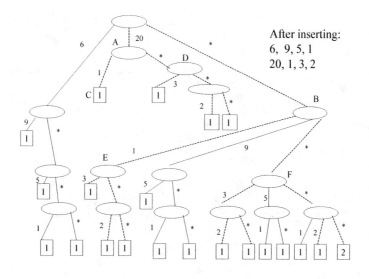

Insertions

The RSST is a dynamic data structure. To generate RSST, we first create a root with an empty list and then repeatedly insert all the input records. Whenever a new record is inserted, starting from the root for the first dimension, we search the entries of the node. If the index is already there, we simply follow its pointer to the next level node. If not, a new node will be created as its child and a new entry of (index, pointer) pair will be added to the node. At the same time we always follow the star pointer to the next level. If the star child is not there, a new child is also created for the star index entry. Figure 2 shows the pseudo-code of a recursive insertion algorithm *insert(cur, level, ns, product, tuple, meas)*.

In Figure 1, we give an example of inserting the second record (20, 1, 3, 2). The whole updated parts of inserting the second record are in dashed lines. Starting from the root, since index 20 is not an entry of the root yet, we create a new node A and add an entry (20, Pa) to the root, where pointer Pa points to the new node A (step 2 of Figure 2). At the same time, we also follow the existing star pointer to node B. For the next value 1, it is not in the lists of node A and node B, so new nodes C and E are created, and corresponding entries (1, Pc), (1, Pe) are added to nodes A, B respectively. Because the star child of A is not there, we need to generate node D and add an entry (*, Pd) to A (step 3). Following the existing star pointer of B to node F, node C is a leaf because the path root-A-C has already two non-star labels. A default COUNT value of 1 is its initial aggregate value (step 1). We can continue similarly for two other domain values 3 and 2. Notice that the COUNT value of

Figure 2. Insertion algorithm

```
Insert a tuple (with a measure "meas") into the current node "cur" on level "level" recursively
ns: #non-stars on the root-to-cur path,
product: product of the cardinalities of the dimensions having non-star labels on the path
insert(cur, level, ns, product, tuple, meas ) {
      if (ns reaches cube dimensionality threshold or product is too large) {
1.        make it be a leaf and aggregate  meas;
          return;} // base case for leaf nodes
      if ( domain value of this level is not an entry of cur) {
2.        create a new node as a child of cur;
          add a new entry;
3.        if (star child is not there)
                  create a star child of cur & add a new entry;
      }
4.    let n1, n2 be the two lower level nodes following the
      Pointers labelled by the domain value & star value
      insert(n1, level+1, ns+1, product*card, tuple, meas);
/        / card is the cardinality of dimension "level"
      insert(n2, level+1, ns,   product,    tuple, meas);
      return;
```

the last leaf increases by one to 2. Continuing the example of Figure 1, two more records (6, 9, 3, 3) and (20, 9, 3, 1) are inserted. The newly created pointers are shown in dashed lines (Figure 3). For other aggregate operators, we simply modify step 1 correspondingly. For example, to implement SUM, we add the measure of the record being inserted to the current aggregate of the leaf. To implement MAX, the max value of these two replaces with the current aggregate of the leaf.

Cutting Sparse Leaves and Generating Runs

Even though the RSST stores only the non-empty data cubes that have a limited number of non-star coordinates, it may still not fit into the available memory for large sparse data sets at some point during the insertion process. Our strategy is to cut off sparse, low-dimensional cubes in the leaves and store them on disks so that they can be retrieved later. In this sense, RSST makes an optimal use of memory space and is used to speed up the most interesting queries. The total number of nodes in the RSST is maintained during the construction and maintenance. Once it reaches a certain threshold (we say, RSST becomes *full*), a cut phase starts. We cut off sparse leaves whose COUNT values are smaller than a threshold *minSup*. So, the size of the RSST always fits in available memory size. The initial *minSup* value can be estimated by the average density of r-dimensional cubes—that is, the total number of records divided by the product of cardinalities of r-non-star dimensions. By default *minSup* is set to 2. It can increase in later cutting phases.

Figure 3. The RSST after inserting the first four records

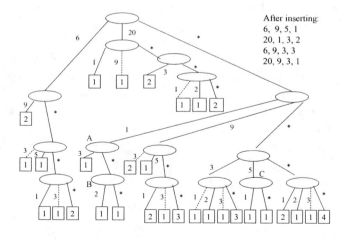

Figure 4. Cutting sparse leaves

```
Cut all sparse leaves and their empty ancestors in the RSST tree
Input: the RSST tree, density threshold minSup
Output: the streamlined RSST, runs of sparse cubes stored on disk;
Method:
1.   Push the root into a stack S;
         while (stack S in not empty) {
         // expand up to the leaf
2.           while (the top node has unprocessed  child & it is not a leaf)
                         push the next unprocessed child on stack
             // process the leaf
3.           if (the aggregate of the leaf < minSup) {
4.                   peek inside the stack upwards to form the leaf's path;
5.                   save this sparse leaf on disk;
6.                   delete this leaf from RSST and pop off stack;
7.                   delete the entry of parent
             } else just pop off stack;
             // process the internal node
8. W         hile ( all the children of the top node are processed) {
9.               if (the top node is an empty internal node)
10.                  delete the node; pop off stack; delete the entry;
                 else just pop off stack}

         }
```

Figure 4 shows the pseudo code for cutting. It is an iterative procedure that uses a stack to store nodes on the path being processed. First, the root is pushed into the stack. We then process each of the root-to-leaf paths in the RSST from left to right one by one. In addition to cutting sparse leaves that form runs on disks (lines 4 and 5), the empty internal nodes are also deleted (lines 9 and 10). Once a child is deleted, the corresponding entry should also be deleted (lines 6 and 7).

Suppose that the aggregation threshold *minSup* is set to be 2. Continuing on Figure 3, we expand the first path 6-9 to the first leaf by pushing nodes on the stack. It is dense, therefore, we check the next two paths 6-*-3 and 6-*-5. Since their leaves are sparse, they are cut off from the tree. Other paths can be processed similarly. Empty internal nodes (e.g., nodes A, B, and C in Figure 3) must also be cut and the corresponding entries in their parent nodes should be deleted. All memory space resulting from cutting is reclaimed for later insertions. The sparse leaves being cut in one cutting phase form a run and are stored on disks. For example, the first run formed by the cutting of the sparse leaves in Figure 3 contains 20 cubes: (6, *, 3, *), (6, *, 5, *), (6, *, *, 1) ..., (*, *, *, 3). The RSST after cutting off the sparse leaves and empty internal nodes is shown in Figure 5.

Figure 5. The RSST after cutting

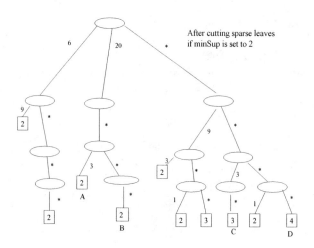

Construction of RSSTs: Loading

Once the cutting phase is finished, the insertion of records resumes until RSST is full again, at which time a new cutting phase starts. Repeated iterations of inserting and cutting continue until all input data are processed. If the available memory can hold all the cubes, no cutting phase is necessary. The RSST then contains all non-empty, low-dimensional cuboids. If cutting does happen, after all input records are inserted, we need make a final cut so that the RSST only retains low-dimensional dense cubes in memory. In this case, the loading process generates multiple runs (see lines 1-3 of Figure 6).

Since the same data cuboids may be scattered across multiple runs due to the different ordering of input records, aggregating them together may qualify them as dense, low-dimensional cubes. In addition, there may be a case where a cube is sparse and cut, but later it becomes dense and is retained in memory. The query result of matching RSST alone will give a wrong answer. To resolve these issues, we merge all the runs into one output run (lines 4-5). We use a modified version of a loser tree (Horowiz, Sahni, & Mehta, 1995) to accomplish this. A loser tree is a complete binary tree used to merge a set of ordered runs into one merged run. The fields of a node in the loser tree are cube coordinates, aggregate value of the cube, and run index, which is used to track which run the output cuboid is from. A couple of issues need special care here. First, if the coordinates of a cube are equal to those of a node in the loser tree during upward travel, the aggregate values of the two cubes are just simply aggregated. Second, when a run is depleted during

Figure 6. Construction of RSST

```
Input: base table
Output: RSST tree and a merged run file storing sparse cubes

Load () {
1.  Open and scan the input file record by record;
2.  Insert each record into the RSST tree;
3.  if ( available memory cannot hold the tree ) {
            cut all the sparse leaves and all the empty internal nodes;
            store the sparse leaves in separate runs (on disk files);
    }

4.  setup a loser tree by reading cubes into the buffers from the run files;
5.  merge the runs into the final run through an output buffer;
6.  Re-insert the elements in output buffer into the tree;
7.  if ( aggr of a cube > minSup or the coordinates matches a path in tree)
            re-insert into the tree or update the aggregates of the leaves;
        else write it into the merged run file for later retrieval;
}
```

Figure 7. The final RSST after inserting and cutting

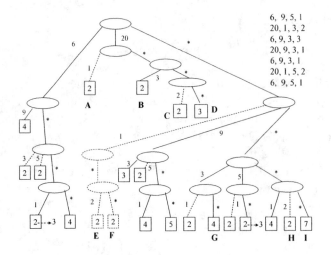

merging, a sentinel cube with infinity coordinates is filled. Notice that the "infinity" value is a large number plus the run index so that the different "infinities" are not erroneously merged.

Continuing on Figure 5, suppose three more records (6, 9, 3, 1), (20, 1, 5, 2), (6, 9, 5, 1) are inserted. After cut, the second run contains 13 cubes: (6, *, 3, *), (6, *, 5, *), (20, 1, *, *), ..., (*, *, *, 2). The RSST after cut is shown in Figure 7, with dotted parts excluded. Now, we merge the first two runs. The first three cubes in the output buffer are (6, *, 3, *), (6, *, 5, *), (6, *, *, 1), whose aggregates of the first two are 2.

For each cuboid from output buffer, we first check if its coordinates match a path of RSST. If yes, the aggregate value of the matched leaf is updated. For example, (6, *, *, 1) matches a path of RSST, so its COUNT increases from 2 to 3. If its aggregate value is above the threshold *minSup*, it becomes a dense cube and should be inserted into the RSST. However, this insertion is just the insertion of a new path. It is different from the insertion in the early insertion algorithm, which also requires it to visit or create the star paths. For example, new path (6, *, 3, *) with COUNT value of 2 must be inserted. If the cube (e.g., (6, *, *, 3)) is neither dense nor in the RSST, it is sparse and stored in the final merged run for later retrieval (lines 6-7). Figure 7 is the final tree. The parts with broken lines are newly inserted. The final merged run contains 11 cubes: (6, *, *, 3), (20, 9, *, *), (20, *, 5, *), (20, *, *, 1), (*, 1, 3, *), (*, 1, 5, *), (*, 9,*, 3), (*, *, 3, 2), (*, *, 3, 3), (*, *, 5, 2), and (*, *, *, 3). The loading process is shown in Figure 8.

Notice that we only need one pass of the original input data to insert all the records. The runs to be merged contain only the sparse, low-dimensional cubes which could be of significantly smaller sizes than the input dataset. Furthermore, the merging process can be run as a daemon process. When all the input records are inserted into RSST, queries can be immediately evaluated for quick approximations. The estimated aggregate is between the quick answer from RSST and the quick answer plus the minSup*num_runs.

Figure 8. Prototype subsystem of loading

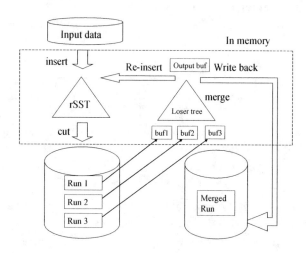

Space Complexity of RSST and the Threshold Values

The size of RSST in terms of total number of nodes is polynomial $O(n^r)$ instead of exponential $O(2^n)$. The maximal number of nodes N_i at level i are given as follows:

$$for\ r = 2,\quad N_i = 2i - 2,\quad i > 2$$
$$for\ r = 3,\quad N_i = 2N_{i-1} - (i - 2)(i - 3), i > 4, N_4 = 8$$

The actual size of the RSST depends on a number of factors such as the number of dimensions, cardinality and data distribution of each dimension, the number of records that have been inserted, and input data ordering. Although we do not have a mathematical formula to compute the RSST size from these factors, we can control it by applying the thresholds formerly introduced. Through the cube dimensionality threshold r, users can specify the number of group-by attributes in the materialized views. It is typically no more than 4. The cardinality threshold can be initially set according to average density estimated as total-number-of-records/product of non-star cardinalities. These two thresholds influence how fast the tree grows. The cube aggregation threshold *minSup* determines how extensive the cutting goes. It has an influence on the sizes of the runs and indirectly the total number of runs. By default, it is set to 2. We allow two modes of setting this threshold: fixed mode and automatic mode. In fixed mode, user-given minSup stays the same across all cuts. In automatic mode, when the RSST is close to full after a cut and the runs are small, *minSup* will increase in some fashion (e.g., doubled each time).

The thresholds provide users the flexibility of controlling the behavior of the algorithm according to their needs and *a priori* knowledge of input data and queries. If we set *minSup* to 1, r to n, and cardinality threshold to infinity, then the full cube is computed. Notice that regardless of these threshold values, the tree never grows out of available memory because when it nears full, a cutting phase is triggered.

Incremental Maintenance of RSSTs

We have described the insertion and cutting procedures on the RSST. In the analytical applications and data warehousing, the main refreshing operations are insertions and bulk loading. Although deletions and updates (can be regarded as a combination of insertions and deletions) are common in transactional data processing of traditional DBMSs, they are rare in data warehousing and OLAP.

To delete a record, we can traverse the RSST by following the pointer corresponding to the domain value and the star pointer at each level as insertions do. When a leaf is reached, the measure value of the record is subtracted from the aggregate value of the leaf. If there is no entry for the domain value of the record being deleted at the level of the node, the common prefix composed by the path from the root to that node should be expanded into r-dimensional cubes and save them to match sparse cubes in the merged run. For example, suppose the second record (20, 1, 3, 2) is to be deleted. After traversal, we find that the leaves A-I in Figure 7 are matched and their aggregates decrease by one. The unmatched common prefixes are (*, 1, 3, *) and (*, *, 3, 2), which are then matched with the merged run. If matching, the measure value (the default is one here for COUNT operation) is subtracted from the aggregate values of the matched cubes. So, RSST is incrementally maintainable. In particular, our bulk load and insertion operations share the same process of the RSST construction.

Answering Queries

Point Queries and Iceberg Queries

A point query can be represented by a tuple q $(q_0, q_1,...,q_{n-1})$, where q_i is in $0..C_i-1$ or a special value *. Since we only compute the low-dimensional cuboids, the number of non-star coordinates in the query is restricted to be no more than a given threshold r. It is straightforward to evaluate such a query. Starting from the root of the RSST, we follow the pointers indexed by $q_0, q_1,...,$ and so on to the next level nodes until a leaf is reached. The aggregate value of that leaf is returned as the query answer. At any node along the path, if no entry can be matched with the query value at the level of the node, query q is then matched with sparse cubes in the merged run. While merging the runs, we have also set up a page table whose entries are the coordinates of the first cubes of the pages. The target page of query q is first found in the page table. The target page is swapped into the memory. The cube is then found in the loaded page using binary search, and its aggregate is returned as the final answer if the cuboid queried is non-empty. If the memory can hold the page table, we only need at most *one* I/O operation to retrieve a point query. Otherwise, one or more levels of indirection may be necessary. For example, $q = (20, *, 3, *)$ will eventually reach leaf B and the answer is 2. Query (6, *, *, 3) is not in the RSST, but matches a cube in the merged run and the answer is 1. Query (20, *, 7, *) matches neither, so the final answer is 0.

For an iceberg query, if its threshold in the HAVING clause of SQL is larger than the cube aggregation threshold *minSup*, the query can be computed simply from the RSST. Otherwise, checking the sparse cubes in the merged run is necessary. If RSST can hold all the r-dimensional cuboids, both point queries and iceberg queries can be evaluated by the tree in memory without any I/O operations.

Range Queries and Partial Queries

If a query specifies a range constraint or an arbitrary subset constraint on a dimension, it is a range query or a partial query. Given such a query, we extract the constrained domain values and store them using n vectors $v_0, v_1, \ldots, v_{n-1}$, each containing the chosen values for a dimension. If dimension i is absent, v_i contains one single star * value. These vectors are called *selected values sets* (SVSs) of the query. We provide our evaluation algorithm for SVSs. Starting from the root of the SST, our algorithm follows the paths directed by the SVS until it will encounter related leaves. The access paths are determined by $v_0 \times v_1 \times \ldots \times v_{n-1}$, the cross product of the selected values. If the domain value is not in the index list of a node P, the path stops at node P because there is no dense cube for this path. If the tree holds all cubes, then the other query paths starting from here can be pruned. Otherwise, the aggregation of the visited leaves is returned to users as a quick approximation. The accuracy of estimation depends on the *minSup* value. If users require an exact answer, the unmatched cubes are checked with the merged run and aggregated. The pseudo code is shown in Figure 9.

Suppose a cube query COUNT (*; {1, 9}; {3, 5}; *) is submitted and the RSST shown in Figure 7 and the merged run are used to evaluate the query. We first compute its SVS: $v_0 = \{*\}$, $v_1 = \{1, 9\}$, $v_2 = \{3, 5\}$, and $v_3 = \{*\}$. Starting from the root, follow the star pointer to the next level node. Then follow the pointer labeled 1 and the traversal stops there. The query result is still 0. The common prefix (*, 1) is expanded to (*, 1, 3, *), (*, 1, 5, *) stored in a vector Q. Check the second value 9 of v_2 and follow the pointer labeled 9. Further tracking along the pointers for 3 and 5 leads to fall-off leaves. After adding them up, the result becomes 5. A quick

Figure 9. Answering cube queries with RSST

```
1  double query(n, level, SVS) {
     // aggregate all the related fall-off leaves in the subtree rooted at
     // node n on level "level" as the returned quick approximation;
     // SVS is the input selected vectors extracted from the input query;
2      sum = 0;
3      if n is a leaf then  // base case
4         for each selected value e in v level do
5             if e is in the list of node n then
6                 sum =sum+ aggregate of the leaf corresponding to e;
7         return sum;
8      level = level +1;
9      for each selected value e in v level-1 do
10     if e is in the list of node n then
11         sum =sum+query(child of n following e, level, SVS);
12     return sum;
13 }
```

approximate query result of 5 is returned. Next, we can refine the result by matching the paths stored in Q with the runs generated previously. The result is updated from 5 to 7 (after aggregating (*, 1, 3, *), (*, 1, 5, *) in the run).

For large range and partial queries, vector Q may contain a large number of tree-unmatched sparse cubes. Instead of matching each of them individually against the merged run file, we have designed a more efficient new "zigzag" method to accomplish. We use a simple example shown in Figure 10 to illustrate. The columns under column heads Q and pageTable are the vectors storing the paths. We use integers here for explanation purpose only. The values are strictly increasing. Buddies (i.e., the cubes in Q that are in the same page) and their target page numbers are also listed in the right columns in the figure. Starting from the first cube, find its target page index is 0. The right-pointing arrow corresponds to the "zig" step which computes the target page index of this cube (the page before the pointed one). At the "zag" step (left-pointing arrow) are the buddies if any are found. Since 40 is larger than 7, it is in a different page. So, there cube 5 alone is in page 0. The target page of 40 is one before the pointed 54 (i.e., page 2). The next cube in column Q that is greater than or equal to 54 indicates the buddies of 40 (from 40 to the one before the pointed). So cubes 40 and 44 are buddies on page 2. Other steps are similar.

Figure 10. "Zigzag" matching method

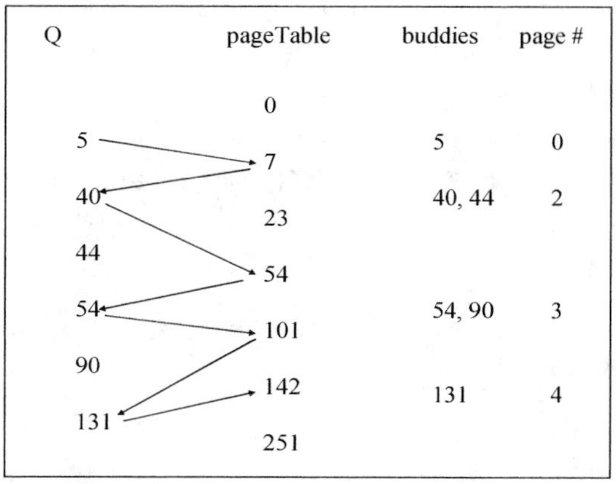

Q	pageTable	buddies	page #
	0		
5	7	5	0
40	23	40, 44	2
44	54		
54	101	54, 90	3
90	142	131	4
131	251		

Simulation Results

Setup for Simulation

We have implemented our RSST algorithm, BUC, Dwarf, and QC-tree in C++ language. We compare with them because they represent recent top data cube algorithms. We have conducted comprehensive experiments on the construction times and query response times by varying the number of records, the number of dimensions, the cardinalities of the dimensions, and data distributions. Our BUC implementation is based on the paper of Beyer and Ramakrishnan (1999). However, that paper only implements the internal BUC. To investigate its overall behavior including I/O operations, we implement both internal BUC and external BUC, and some other features in the paper such as switching from counting sort to quick sort, and duplicate elimination as well. We have also adapted BUC algorithm to RBUC, the dimensionality-restricted BUC, where only low-dimensional cubes are computed using modified BUC.

In Dwarf implementation, we first use the sorting algorithm in Standard Template Library (STL) to sort the original table if it fits in memory. Otherwise, an external merging sorting is used. We use a stack to store the nodes in the current path. All the nodes are written to a disk in the order of closing. During coalescing, we bring back the nodes in the previous subtrees into the memory by referring to their disk addresses. For QCT (QC-tree) implementation, first the temporary classes are computed by applying a recursive DFS (depth-first search) procedure described in Lakshmanan et al. (2003). In our implementation, we regard the star value as the largest, thus deferring the construction of the star subtree to the end. If we first create the nodes in the star subtree, we have to bring into memory the nodes that have drill-down links, which significantly increases the number of I/Os. It is difficult to modify Dwarf and QCT algorithms so as to restrict the dimensionality of queried data cubes. All experiments are conducted on a Dell Precision 330 with 1.7GHZ CPU, 256MB memory, and the Windows 2000 operating system.

Varying Number of Records

In this set of experiments, we fixed the number of dimensions to five, each of size 20. We use data in Zipf distribution of factor 2 for each dimension. The number of records increases from 10,000 to 1,000,000. The cube aggregation threshold *minSup* and cube dimensionality threshold in RSST are set to 2 and 3 respectively.

The runtimes of Figure 11 are the times for constructing the data structures. In QCT, the times of computing the temporary classes (i.e., the QC table) are recorded. The Dwarf construction times already include the pre-sorting times. Our RSST is about two times faster than the closest competitor Dwarf in this case. The query evaluation times are much faster than construction times. We measure the query times using total response times of 1,000 random queries. The queries are generated by first randomly choosing three dimensions where random numbers within the domains are selected as queried values. All other coordinates in the queries are star values. RSST is much faster than other algorithms (Figure 12).

Figure 11. Construction times for varying number of records

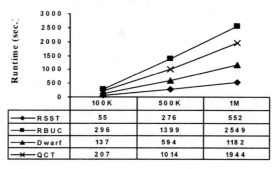

Figure 12. Query response times for varying number of records

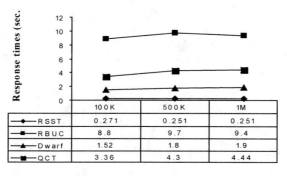

Figure 13. Varying number of dimensions

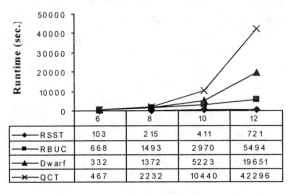

	6	8	10	12
RSST	103	215	411	721
RBUC	668	1493	2970	5494
Dwarf	332	1372	5223	19651
QCT	467	2232	10440	42296

Number of dimensions

Varying Number of Dimensions

In this subsection we investigate the behavior of the algorithms while increasing the number of dimensions. We use data of Zipf distribution (factor is 2), the number of records is 100,000, and the cardinality of each dimension is fixed to 1,000. The number of dimensions increases from 6 to 12. Figure 13 shows the construction times. Clearly, RSST and RBUC are scalable with respect to the number of dimensions, while Dwarf and QCT have steep increases of construction times with respect to the increase of dimensions. For high-dimensionality data, RSST is faster than Dwarf and QCT.

Varying Cardinalities

We use uniform data and set the number of records to be 100,000. The cardinalities of three dimensions are the same, which increase from 20 to 500. The construction times are recorded in Figure 14. RSST is scalable in terms of cardinalities. The construction time of RSST is not sensitive to the changes of dimension orders (Table 1).

Figure 14. Varying cardinalities using uniform distributed data

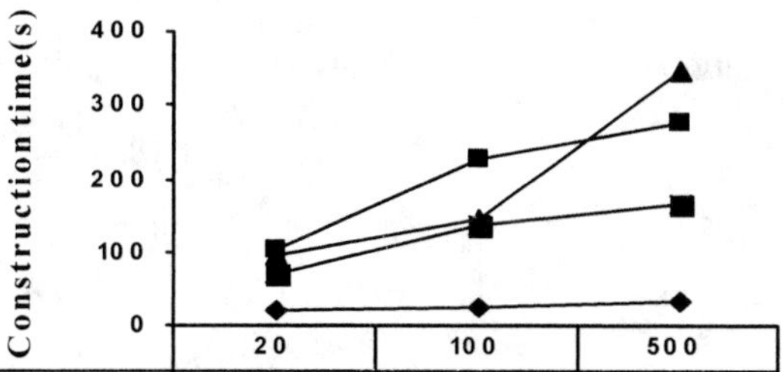

	20	100	500
RSST	21.4	26.2	32.8
BUC	103	227.8	278
Dwarf	93.2	142.6	348
QCT	70	135	167

Cardinalities

Table 1. Construction times of varying dimension orders

Cons. times(s)	RSST	RBUC	Dwarf	QCT
500, 100, 50, 10	44.4	679	299	453
10, 50, 100, 500	52.2	602	441	825

Conclusion

In this chapter, we present a new data structure called RSST, which stores the cuboids whose number of group by attributes is no more than a certain threshold. In practice, these cuboids, especially the dense ones, are most often queried. Based on RSST, a cubing algorithm has been given. RSST retains the dense cubes, but dynamically cuts off sparse cubes that are rarely or never queried, and stores them on disks for later retrieval if necessary. RSST can also automatically choose the dimension combinations according to cube cardinality threshold. These methods combined can efficiently compute the dense cuboids embedded in large high-dimensional data sets. RSST is incrementally maintainable.

Our comprehensive sets of experiments have shown that RSST is I/O efficient and scalable in terms of number of records, number of dimensions, and dimension cardinalities. RSST is insensitive to dimension orders and is especially suitable for skewed data sets.

References

Aboulnaga, A., & Chaudhuri, S. (1999). Self-tuning histograms: Building histograms without looking at data. In *Proceedings of the 1999 ACM SIGMOD International Conference on Management of Data (SIGMOD '99)*, Philadelphia (pp. 181-192).

Acharya, S., Gibbons, P.B., & Poosala, V. (2000). Congressional samples for approximate answering of group-by queries. In *Proceedings of the 2000 ACM SIGMOD International Conference on Management of Data (SIGMOD '00)*, Dallas, TX (pp. 487-498).

Agarwal, S., Agrawal, R., Deshpande, P., Naughton, J., Sarawagi, S., & Ramakrishnan, R. (1996). On the computation of multidimensional aggregates. In *Proceedings of the International Conference on Very Large Databases*, Mumbai (Bomabi), India (pp. 506-521).

Agrawal, R., & Srikant, R. (1994, September 12-15). Fast algorithms for mining association rules in large databases. In C. Zaniolo (Ed.), In *Proceedings of 20th International Conference on Very Large Data Bases*, Santiago de Chile, Chile (pp. 487-499). San Francisco: Morgan Kaufmann.

Beyer, K., & Ramakrishnan, R. (1999). Bottom-up computation of sparse and iceberg CUBEs. In S.B. Davidson & C. Faloutsos (Eds.), *In Proceedings of the 1999 ACM SIGMOD International Conference on Management of Data (SIGMOD '99)*, Philadelphia (pp. 359-370).

Beyer, K., & Ramakrishnan, R. (1999). Bottom-up computation of sparse and iceberg CUBEs. In C. Faloutsos (Ed.), In *Proceedings of the 1999 ACM SIGMOD International Conference on Management of Data (SIGMOD '99)*, Philadelphia (pp. 359-370).

Chan, C.Y., & Ioannidis, Y.E. (1998). Bitmap index design and evaluation. In *Proceedings of the 1998 ACM SIGMOD International Conference on Management of Data (SIGMOD '98)*, Seattle, WA (pp. 355-366).

Chaudhuri, S., & Dayal, U. (1997). An overview of data warehousing and OLAP technology. *SIGMOD Record, 26*(1), 65-74.

Fu, L. (2004). Computation of dense data cubes using packaged arrays. In *Proceedings of the International Conference on Internet Computing 2004 (IC'04)*, Las Vegas, NV (pp. 116-120).

Fu, L., & Hammer, J. (2000, November). CUBIST: A new algorithm for improving the performance of ad-hoc OLAP queries. In *Proceedings of the ACM 3rd International Workshop on Data Warehousing and OLAP*, Washington, DC (pp. 72-79).

Gibbons, P.B., & Matias, Y. (1998). New sampling-based summary statistics for improving approximate query answers. In *Proceedings of the 1998 ACM SIGMOD International Conference on Management of Data (SIGMOD '98)*, Seattle, WA (pp. 331-342).

Gray, J., Chaudhuri, S., Bosworth, A., Layman, A., Reichart, D., Venkatrao, M. et al. (1997). Data cube: A relational aggregation operator generalizing group-by, cross-tab, and sub-totals. *Data Mining and Knowledge Discovery, 1*(1), 29-53.

Gupta, H., & Mumick, I. (1999). Selection of views to materialize under a maintenance cost constraint. In *Proceedings of the International Conference on Management of Data*, Jerusalem, Israel (pp. 453-470).

Hammer, J., & Fu, L. (2001, September). Improving the performance of OLAP queries using families of statistics trees. In *Proceedings of the 3rd International Conference on Data Warehousing and Knowledge Discovery (DaWaK '01)*, Munich, Germany (pp. 274-283).

Han, J., Pei, J., Dong, G., & Wang, K. (2001). Efficient computation of Iceberg cubes with complex measures. *ACM SIGMOD Record,* In *Proceedings of the 2001 ACM SIGMOD International Conference on Management of Data* (Vol. 30, pp. 1-12).

Harinarayan, V., Rajaraman, A., & Ullman, J.D. (1996). Implementing data cubes efficiently. *SIGMOD Record, 25*(2), 205-216.

Horowiz, E., Sahni, S., & Mehta, D. (1995). *Fundamentals of data structures in C++*. W.H. Freeman & Company.

Johnson, T., & Shasha, D. (1997). Some approaches to index design for cube forests. *Bulletin of the Technical Committee on Data Engineering, IEEE Computer Society, 20*(1), 27-35.

Labio, W., Quass, D., & Adelberg, B. (1997). Physical database design for data warehouses. In *Proceedings of the International Conference on Database Engineering*, Birmingham, UK (pp. 277-288).

Lakshmanan, L.V.S., Ng, R., Han, J., & Pang, A. (1999). Optimization of constrained frequent set queries with 2-variable constraints. In *Proceedings of the 1999 ACM SIGMOD International Conference on Management of Data*, Philadelphia (pp. 157-168).

Lakshmanan, L.V.S., Pei, J., & Han, J. (2002). Quotient cube: How to summarize the semantics of a data cube. In *Proceedings of 28th International Conference on Very Large Databases (VLDB '02)*, Hong Kong, China (pp. 778-789).

Lakshmanan, L.V.S., Pei, J., & Zhao, Y. (2003, June 9-12). QC-trees: An efficient summary structure for semantic OLAP. In A. Doan (Ed.), In *Proceedings of the 2003 ACM SIGMOD International Conference on Management of Data*, San Diego, CA (pp. 64-75). ACM Press.

Lehner, W., Sidle, R., Pirahesh, H., & Cochrane, R.W. (2000). Maintenance of cube automatic summary tables. In *Proceedings of the 2000 ACM SIGMOD International Conference on Management of Data (SIGMOD '00)*, Dallas, TX (pp. 512-513).

Markl, V., Ramsak, F., & Bayer, R. (1999, August 2-4). Improving OLAP performance by multidimensional hierarchical clustering. In *Proceedings of the 1999 International Database Engineering and Applications Symposium (IDEAS '99)*, Montreal, Canada.

Mumick, I.S., Quass, D., & Mumick, B.S. (1997). Maintenance of data cubes and summary tables in a warehouse. In *Proceedings of the 1997 ACM SIGMOD International Conference on Management of Data (SIGMOD '97)*, Tucson, AZ (pp. 100-111).

Ross, K.A., & Srivastava, D. (1997). Fast computation of sparse datacubes. In *Proceedings of the 23rd VLDB Conference (VLDB '97)*, Athens, Greece (pp. 116-125).

Sismanis, Y., Deligiannakis, A., Roussopoulos, N., & Kotidis, Y. (2002). Dwarf: Shrinking the PetaCube. In *Proceedings of the 2002 ACM SIGMOD International Conference on Management of Data (SIGMOD '02)*, Madison, WI (pp. 464-475).

Vitter, J.S., & Wang, M. (1999). Approximate computation of multidimensional aggregates of sparse data using wavelets. In *Proceedings of the 1999 ACM SIGMOD International Conference on Management of Data (SIGMOD '99)*, Philadelphia (pp. 193-204).

Wang, W., Feng, J., Lu, H., & Yu, J.X. (2002). Condensed cube: An effective approach to reducing data cube size. In *Proceedings of 18th IEEE International Conference on Data Engineering (ICDE '02)*, San Jose, CA (pp. 155-165).

Xin, D., Han, J., Li, X., & Wah, B.W. (2003, September 9-12). Star-cubing: Computing iceberg cubes by top-down and bottom-up integration. In J.C. Freytag, P.C. Lockemann, S. Abiteboul, M.J. Carey, P.G. Selinger, & A. Heuer (Eds.), In *Proceedings of 29th International Conference on Very Large Data Bases*, Berlin, Germany (pp. 476-487). San Francisco: Morgan Kaufmann.

Yan, W.P., & Larson, P. (1995). Eager aggregation and lazy aggregation. In *Proceedings of the 8th International Conference on Very Large Databases*, Zurich, Switzerland (pp. 345-357).

Zhao, Y., Deshpande, P.M., & Naughton, J.F. (1997). An array-based algorithm for simultaneous multidimensional aggregates. *SIGMOD Record, 26*(2), 159-170.

Chapter III

Exploring Similarities Across High-Dimensional Datasets

Karlton Sequeira, Rensselaer Polytechnic Institute, USA

Mohammed Zaki, Rensselaer Polytechnic Institute, USA

Abstract

Very often, related data may be collected by a number of sources, which may be unable to share their entire datasets for reasons like confidentiality agreements, dataset size, and so forth. However, these sources may be willing to share a condensed model of their datasets. If some substructures of the condensed models of such datasets, from different sources, are found to be unusually similar, policies successfully applied to one may be successfully applied to the others. In this chapter, we propose a framework for constructing condensed models of datasets and algorithms to find similar substructure in pairs of such models. The algorithms are based on the tensor product. We test our framework on pairs of synthetic datasets and compare our algorithms with an existing one. Finally, we apply it to basketball player statistics for two National Basketball Association (NBA) seasons, and to breast cancer datasets. The results are statistically more interesting than results obtained from independent analysis of the datasets.

Introduction

Often, data may be collected by a number of sources. These sources may be geographically far apart. There are a number of disadvantages in transferring the datasets from their source to a central location for processing. These include less reliability, security, higher computational and storage requirements, and so forth. It may be preferable to share condensed models of the datasets. Similarly, for reasons like confidentiality agreements, it may be required to use condensed models of datasets, which obfuscate individual details while conveying structural information about the datasets. Lastly, the datasets may have slightly different dimensionality or transformations like rotations, with respect to each other. This may preclude simply appending the datasets to each other and processing them.

If *unusually similar* substructure can be detected from the condensed models of some of the datasets, then policies successfully applied to one may be successfully applied to the others. For example, two consumer markets (*A* and *B*) differing in geography, economy, political orientation, or some other way may have some unusually similar consumer profiles. This may prompt sales managers in B to use successful sales strategies employed by sales managers in A for consumer profiles in which they are unusually similar. Also, profiles which are *unusually dissimilar* to any of those in the other graph are particularly interesting. The latter is analogous to the problem of finding contrast sets (Bay & Pazzani, 2001). Additionally, determining similarities and dissimilarities between snapshots of a dataset taken over multiple time intervals can help in identifying how the dataset characteristics evolve over time (Ganti, Gehrke, Ramakrishnan, & Loh , 1999).

A dataset may be a set of points drawn in possibly different proportions, from a mixture of unknown, multivariate, and perhaps non-parametric distributions. A significant number of the points may be noisy. There may be missing values as well. We currently assume that the dataset may belong to non-identical attribute spaces, which are mixtures of nominal and continuous variables. The datasets may be subject to translational, rotational, and scaling transformations as well. High-dimensional datasets are inherently sparse. It has been shown that under certain reasonable assumptions on the data distribution, the ratio of the distances of the nearest and farthest neighbors to a given target is almost 1 for a variety of distance functions and data distributions (Beyer, Goldstein, Ramakrishnan, & Shaft, 1999). Hence, traditional distance metrics which treat every dimension with equal importance have little meaning. Algorithms using such dissimilarity measures as a building block for application to high-dimensional datasets may produce meaningless results due to this lack of contrast.

In this chapter, we explore similarities across datasets using a two-step solution:

1. *Constructing a **condensed model** of the dataset.* This involves finding the components of the model, and relationships between these components. In our case, the components are subspaces. The condensed model is a weighted graph where the vertices correspond to subspaces and the weighted edges to relationships between the subspaces. A condensed model allows: (a) sharing of dataset summaries, (b) noise and outlier removal, and (c) normalization and dataset scaling.

2. *Identifying similarities between the condensed models.* In our solution, this reduces to finding structurally similar **subgraphs** in the two models and matching vertices between the structurally similar subgraphs.

In previous work (Sequeira & Zaki, 2004), we have shown algorithms to find components of the model. In this chapter, we make the following contributions:

1. We propose two kinds of **similarity measures** for subspaces (components). The first kind is projection based—that is, it uses the similarity of the projections of the subspaces. The other is support based—it uses the number of points shared by the subspaces.

2. We provide algorithms for identifying *unusually similar* substructure from the condensed models corresponding to pairs of datasets with possibly differing dimensionality.

3. We test our framework with synthetic datasets and apply it to finding similar substructure in models constructed from basketball player statistics and breast cancer datasets. Inferences from the similar substructure are found to be logically meaningful. Further, they reveal information, which remains unknown under independent dataset analysis.

Preliminaries

Consider dataset D_A having d_A dimensions. If $S_{A,i}$ is the domain of the ith dimension, then $S_A = S_{A,1} \times S_{A,2} \times ... \times S_{A,d_A}$ is the high-dimensional space for D_A, where $D_A = \{x_i | i \in [1,m,] x_i \in S_A\}$. Similarly, $D_B = \{y_i | i \in [1,n,] y_i \in S_B\}$. If the range $S_{A,i}$ of each dimension is divided into ξ equi-width intervals, then S_A has a grid superimposed over it. Accordingly, we have the following definition: a **subspace** is a grid-aligned hyper-rectangle $[l_1, h_1] \times [l_2, h_2] \times ... \times [l_d, h_d]$, $\forall i \in [1, d,]$ $[l_i, h_i] \subseteq S_{A,i}$. Here for a given interval $[l_i, h_i]$, we have $l_i = (aS_{A,i})/\xi$ and hi $= (bs_{A,i})/\xi$, where a,b are non-negative integers, and a<b≤ξ.

If $[l_i, h_i] \subset S_{A,i}$, the **subspace** is said to be *constrained* in dimension *i*—that is, the subspace does not span the entire domain of the dimension *i*, A subspace that is constrained in all the dimensions to a single interval—that is, b−a=1 is referred to as a *grid cell*.

If our algorithm to find components in a dataset finds $|V_A|$ components/subspaces internal to *DA*, the relationships between these subspaces are expressed by a $|V_A| \times |V_A|$ matrix $w_A : S_A \times S_A \rightarrow \Re$.

We also use the following notations for the rest of this chapter: let $A = (a_{i,j})_{1 \leq i, j \leq m,n}$ and $B = (b_{kl})_{1 \leq k, l \leq p,q}$ be two matrices. If $m = n$, $Tr[A] = \Sigma_{i \in [1,m]} a_{i,i}$ is the trace of *A*. A^T refers to the transpose of *A*.

$\| A \|_F = (\sum_{i=1}^{m} \sum_{j=1}^{n} | a_{i,j} |^2)^{1/2}$, is the Frobenius norm of *A*. *ones(m,n)* returns a m×n matrix containing all ones. The tensor product of A and B is a *mp×nq* matrix, and is defined as:

$$A \otimes B = \begin{pmatrix} a_{1,1}B & a_{1,2}B & \dots & a_{2,n}B \\ a_{2,1}B & a_{2,2}B & \dots & a_{2,n}B \\ a_{m,1}B & a_{m,2}B & \dots & a_{m,n}B \end{pmatrix}$$

An *n×n* matrix *X* is called *normal*, if it can be written as $X = U_X D_X U^T_X$, where U_X is a unitary matrix containing the eigenvectors of *X*, and D_X is a diagonal matrix containing the eigenvalues of $X .\lambda_{X,i}$ denotes the *i*th eigenvalue, where $\forall i \in [1, n-1]$, $\lambda_{X,i} \geq \lambda_{X,i+1}$, and $U_{X,i}$ denotes the eigenvector corresponding to $\lambda_{X,i}$. If $\lambda_{X,1} > \lambda_{X,2}$, $\lambda_{X,1}$ and $U_{X,1}$ are called the dominant eigenvalue and dominant eigenvector respectively.

If $S = [s_1, s_2 \dots]$ where $s_1, s_2 \dots$ are column vectors, then *vec(S)* creates a column vector by stacking its column vectors one below the other, so that $vec(S) = [s_1^T \ s_2^T \ \dots]^T$.

Let V_A and V_B be the components (subspaces) of datasets D_A and D_B, respectively. Let *P* be the function, which takes as argument a mapping $f:V_A \rightarrow V_B$, and returns a permutation matrix (typically, a permutation matrix is a square matrix)—that is, a $|V_A| \times |V_B|$ matrix, such that:

$$P_f(u,v) = \begin{cases} 1 \ if & f(u) = v \\ 0 & otherwise \end{cases} \quad (1)$$

If f is a one-to-one mapping, then if $|V_A| \leq |V_B|$ ($|V_A| > |V_B|$), the rows (columns) of P are orthogonal to each other and $PP^T = I$ ($P^T P = I$). As in Van Wyk and Van Wyk (2003), we want f which minimizes the associated error function err, which we define as:

$$err(f \mid w_A, w_B) = \parallel w_A - P_f w_B P_f^T \parallel_F \tag{2}$$

A mapping f from a subset of subspaces corresponding to w_A to a subset corresponding to w_B is *unusually similar*, if the probability of finding another mapping f' between these subsets, by MonteCarlo sampling as later in this chapter, such that $err(f \mid w_A, w_B) > err(f' \mid w_A, w_B)$ is very low.

Example

Let D_A and D_B be two datasets as shown in Table 1, with domains $[0,1000)$ for each dimension. $D_A(p_1, d_1)$ refers to row p_1, column d_1 of dataset D_A. If we discretize the domain of each dimension into 10 intervals (i.e., $\xi = 10$), then the grid cells surrounding the points in D_A, D_B yield the datasets D'_A, D'_B in Table 2. For example, $D_A(p_1, d_1) = 915$. Therefore, $D'_A(g_1, d_1) = \lfloor \frac{915}{1000} \times \xi \rfloor = 9$. Thus, p_1 is constrained to the last interval in dimension d_1—that is, $[900, 1000)$. We then run a subspace mining algorithm (e.g., SCHISM (Bay & Pazzani, 2001), CLIQUE (Ganti et al., 1999)) on each of the discretized datasets independently and find two sets of subspaces S and S' corresponding to D_A and D_B respectively, as shown in Table 3. Here -1 implies that the dimension is unconstrained. $S(c_1, d_2) = 5$ means that the subspace c_1 in the set S of subspaces is constrained to interval 5 in dimension d_2 —that is, $[500, 600)$. Subspaces may be constrained to more than one interval in a dimension.

Typically, **subspace** mining algorithms also partition the dataset based on the subspaces it finds. Let us assume that the subspace mining algorithm assigns p_1, p_2 to $c_1, p_3, p_4,$ p_5 to c_2, p_6, p_7, p_8 to c_3 and labels p_9 as noise. Similarly, it assigns p'_1, p'_2, p'_3, p'_4 to c'_1; p'_5, p'_6, p'_7 to c'_2 vand labels p'_8 as noise.

Given such subspaces and the points assigned to them, we wish to construct **condensed models** of the datasets, which can be used to discover structurally similar subspaces across the two datasets without having access to the datasets or their schema. For example, in Table 3, if d_2 corresponds to d'_4 and d_4 corresponds to d'_2, then c_1 and c'_1 are both constrained in the same dimension and to the same interval—that is, $[500, 600)$. Also, c_2 and c'_2 are constrained in the same dimensions to similar intervals. Hence, $c_1 \approx c'_1$ and $c_2 \approx c'_2$. Thus, we wish to recover the mapping between c_1 and c'_1, and c_2 and c'_2.

Table 1. Original data

D_A	d_1	d_2	d_3	d_4	d_5	D_B	d_1'	d_2'	d_3'	d_4'	d_5'
p_1	915	561	866	657	661	p_1'	889	710	591	564	679
p_2	965	575	534	860	365	p_2'	854	189	641	564	666
p_3	217	506	121	452	303	p_3'	553	869	449	612	199
p_4	758	512	357	423	289	p_4'	779	690	203	598	872
p_5	276	531	327	418	335	p_5'	88	453	965	541	324
p_6	268	520	351	348	454	p_6'	391	436	193	578	301
p_7	239	514	369	301	451	p_7'	574	450	220	588	270
p_8	237	510	377	650	472	p_8'	805	60	803	525	152
p_9	33	118	144	388	280						

Table 2. Discretized data

D_A'	d_1	d_2	d_3	d_4	d_5	D_B'	d_1'	d_2'	d_3'	d_4'	d_5'
g_1	9	5	8	6	6	g_1'	8	7	5	5	6
g_2	9	5	5	8	3	g_2'	8	1	6	5	6
g_3	2	5	1	4	3	g_3'	5	8	4	6	1
g_4	7	5	3	4	2	g_4'	7	6	2	5	8
g_5	2	5	3	4	3	g_5'	8	4	9	5	3
g_6	2	5	3	3	4	g_6'	3	4	1	5	3
g_7	2	5	3	3	4	g_7'	5	4	2	5	2
g_8	2	5	3	6	4	g_8'	8	6	8	5	1
g_9	3	1	1	3	2						

Table 3. Two sets of subspaces

S	d_1	d_2	d_3	d_4	d_5
c_1	-1	5	-1	-1	-1
c_2	-1	5	-1	4	3
c_3	2	5	3	-1	4

S'	d_1'	d_2'	d_3'	d_4'	d_5'
c_1'	-1	-1	-1	5	-1
c_2'	-1	4	-1	5	2

Related Work

Our two-step solution to finding *unusually similar* substructure across datasets involves:

1. Constructing a condensed model of the dataset; this involves two sub-steps:
    a. finding components in the dataset
    b. constructing a condensed model from the components
2.   Identifying similarities between the condensed model

Finding Components in the Dataset

We find components in the dataset using a subspace mining algorithm called SCHISM (Bay & Pazzani, 2001), which finds sets of possibly overlapping subspaces, for example, set S from dataset D_A in the example above. It partitions the points in the datasets using these subspaces. *Note that any other hyper-rectangular subspace mining algorithm—for example, MAFIA (Beyer et al., 1999), CLIQUE (Sequeira & Zaki, 2004), and so forth—may be used to find the subspaces and partition the dataset.* Hence, we do not delve into the details of the SCHISM algorithm.

Constructing Condensed Models from the Components

We condense the dataset using a weighted graph, where the vertices correspond to subspaces and the weights on the edges to similarities between the subspaces. While we are unaware of much related work on similarities between subspaces, it is noteworthy that subspaces are also clusters. Accordingly, we review some of the existing similarity measures used for comparing clusterings.

Clusterings may be compared based on the number of point pairs, in which the two clusterings C, C' agree or disagree. Each pair of dataset points is assigned to one of four categories N_{00}, N_{01}, N_{10}, and N_{11}. Pairs of points in N_{00} are assigned to distinct clusters in both C and C', those in N_{01} are assigned to the same cluster in both C and C', those in N_{01} are assigned to the same cluster in C but to distinct clusters in C', and so on. If the dataset has n points, $N_{00}+N_{01}+N_{10}+N_{11}=n(n-1)/2$.

Accordingly there exists the **Rand index**:

$$Rand(C,C') = \frac{N_{11} + N_{00}}{N_{11} + N_{10} + N_{01} + N_{00}}$$

and the **Jaccard index**

$$Jaccard(C,C') = \frac{N_{11}}{N_{11} + N_{10} + N_{01}}$$

to compare the clusterings. Further Meila (2003) proposes the VI (variance of information) metric to compare clusterings: $VI(C,C') = H(C) + H(C') - 2I(C,C')$, where $H(C) = \sum_{i=1}^{|C|} - p_i log(p_i)$, $p_i = \frac{n_i}{n}$ and where $I(C,C') = \sum_{i=1}^{|C|}\sum_{j=1}^{|C'|} p_{i,j} log(\frac{p_{i,j}}{p_i p_j})$, $p_{i,j} = \frac{|C_i \cap C_j'|}{n}$, with n_i being the number of points in C_i, the ith cluster in C. This implies that p_i and $p_{i,j}$ are simply the *support* of clusters C_i and $C_i \cap C_j$ respectively, according to the traditional definition of support in the data mining literature (Bay & Pazzani, 2001).

Thus, these clustering (dis)similarity measures use (dis)similarity in support overlap to express cluster similarity.

Identifying Similarities Between Condensed Models of Different Datasets

Ganti et al. (1999) compare datasets by comparing their respective models. The datasets share a common schema. A dataset may be typically modeled by a decision tree, a set of clusters, or a set of frequent itemsets. The model consists of a set of pairs. Each pair consists of an "interesting region" in the dataset (called the *structural component*) and the fraction of the dataset (called the *measure component*) it accounts for. They then partition the attribute space using hyperplanes, which (as per the type of model chosen) define the leaves, clusters or frequent itemsets, induced by the models of the two datasets. Using a single scan of each dataset, they can compute the fraction of each dataset in each distinct hyperspace, resulting from the superposition of the two models of the datasets. They then compare these fractions, corresponding to different datasets but the same hyperspace, using a "difference" function and combine the resulting "deviation" using an "aggregation" function which returns a measure of the similarity of the datasets. This method does not leverage the structure present in the data and hence is susceptible to translational transformations.

Much of the existing work in the database community (Bay & Pazzani, 2001) assumes the datasets have identical schema and that access to both datasets simultaneously is possible. By utilizing the underlying structure in the datasets, we avoid making such assumptions.

Li, Ogihara, and Zhu (2002) use a variant of the mutual information between datasets D_A and D_B, modeled by sets of maximal frequent itemsets (MFIs) F_A and F_B, which is defined as: $I(F_A, F_B) = \sum_{i \in F_A, j \in F_B} \frac{|i \cap j|}{|i \cup j|} log(1 + \frac{|i \cap j|}{|i \cup j|}) * min(|i|, |j|)$. They assume an identical schema for two datasets and define the similarity between the datasets as: $\frac{I(F_A, F_B) * 2}{I(F_A, F_A) + I(F_B, F_B)}$. To test for significance of similarity, they propose bootstrapping-based approaches in which disjoint pairs of subsets of the attributes are drawn at random from samples of the given datasets. The similarity between the pairs of samples is used to estimate the distribution of similarity between the two datasets. They then generalize their approach to heterogeneous datasets, of which matchings between some of the attributes of the two datasets are known. These matchings are used to identify matchings of at least ξ attributes of one dataset with those of the other.

There have been a number of graph matching algorithms, stemming from work in the field of computer vision, regarding applications like image registration, object recognition, and so forth. Many of the past approaches involve matching between labeled or discrete-attributed graphs (Bunke, 1999; Carcassoni, 2002; Kalviainen & Oja, 1990; Van Wyk & Van Wyk, 2003). Like the solutions to many other NP-hard problems, graph matching algorithms may be *enumerative* (Bunke, 1999; Shapiro & Haralick, 1985) or *optimization based* (Carcassoni, 2002; Van Wyk & Van Wyk, 2003). Most of these algorithms assume the graphs lie in the same space, which is usually low dimensional (i.e., two or three dimensions).

The concept "two vertices are similar, if vertices they are related to are similar" allows recursive definition of inter-vertex similarity. This idea is used explicitly or implicitly by a number of propagation-based algorithms (Melnik, Garcia-Molina, & Rahm, 2002) for a range of applications. The recursive definition causes similarity to flow from one vertex to the other.

Blondel, Gajardo, Heymans, Senellart, and Van Dooren (2004) show that given w_A and w_B (the similarity among the subspaces with the two datasets), $|V_A| \times |V_B|$ similarity matrix S, whose real entry $s_{i,j}$ represents the similarity between vertex i of G_A and j of G_B, can be obtained as the limit of the normalized even iterates of $S_{k+1} = w_B S_k w_A^T + w_B^T S_k w_A$. Note that this model does not assume that w_A and w_B are symmetric. This algorithm has time complexity of matrix multiplication, which is currently $O(=n^{2.376})$. We compare our algorithms with Blondel's algorithm.

Gionis, Mannila, and Tsaparas (2005) examine the problem of finding a clustering that agrees as much as possible with a set of given clusterings on a given dataset of objects. They provide an array of algorithms seeking to find either: (i) the clustering that minimizes the aggregate number of disagreements with the given set of clusterings (clustering aggregations), or (ii) a partition of the objects into two groups, such that the sum of aggregate dissimilarities between objects in the same group and aggregate similarities between objects in different groups is minimized (correlation clustering). Here the (dis)similarities between objects are defined using the given clusterings. This differs from our work, in that the same dataset is used to produce each clustering.

Constructing a Condensed Model of the Dataset

We represent each dataset D_A by a weighted graph $G_A(V_A, E_A, w_A)$, where V_A is the set of subspaces found by the subspace mining algorithm, $E_A \subseteq V_A \times V_A$ is the set of edges between the subspaces in the dataset, and $w_A : S_A \times S_A \to \Re$ is the adjacency matrix/set of weights on the edges of the graph G_A, indicating similarity between components/subspaces in the condensed model/graph of G_A. Depending on whether we use support or similarity of projections as the basis for comparing subspaces, we prescribe the following subspace similarity measures.

Support-Based Subspace Similarity

Each subspace $u \in V_A$ partitions the space S_A into a clustering containing two clusters—that is, u and $S_A \backslash u$. Accordingly, if $C_u, C_{u'}$ are the clusterings yielded by subspaces $u, u' \in V_A$, we can define $w_A v(u, u')$ using $Jaccard(C_u, C_{u'})$ and $Rand(C_u, C_{u'})$. Additionally, we experiment with using the VI measure of Meila (2003): $w_A(u, u') = exp(-VI(C_u, C_{u'}))$.

Projection-Based Subspace Similarity

Consider the case where the datasets being modeled are sets of points sampled in different proportions with respect to each other from the same mixture of multivariate distributions. Then, correctly matching these distributions using support-based subspace similarity measures is unlikely. Accordingly, we seek similarity measures which use similarity of the projections of the subspaces.

We define the similarity between subspace $R \in V_A$ and a grid cell Q surrounding a point $r \in D_A$ using the Jaccard-coefficient as:

$$\rho(r \in Q, R \in V_A) = \frac{1}{d_A} \sum_{i=1}^{d_A} \frac{|Q_i \cap R_i|}{|Q_i \cup R_i|} \tag{3}$$

Here, Q_i, R_i refer to the set of intervals spanned by subspaces Q, R respectively, in dimension i. If dimension i of R is unconstrained, then $|R_i| = \xi$.

For example, using our running example,

$$\rho(p_1 \in g_1, c_1) = \frac{1}{d_A}\left(\frac{1}{\xi} + \frac{1}{1} + \frac{1}{\xi} + \frac{1}{\xi} + \frac{1}{\xi}\right) = 0.28.$$

Based on the subspaces found by the subspace mining algorithm, it is possible, for example using nearest neighbors, to assign points in the dataset to subspaces. Using the assignment of points to subspaces, we have devised two similarity measures: AVGSIM and HIST.

AVGSIM

Each subspace may be thought to be more accurately approximated by the points assigned to it. As we know the similarity between the grid cell around each point and every subspace found by the subspace mining algorithm using $\rho()$ from Equation 3, the similarity between two subspaces $u \in V_A, u' \in V_A$ can be defined as:

$$w_A(u,u') = \frac{\sum_{r \in u} \rho(r,u')}{|u|} + \frac{\sum_{r \in u'} \rho(r,u)}{|u'|} \qquad (4)$$

From our running example:

$$\rho(p_1 \in g_1, c_2) = 0.24, \rho(p_2 \in g_2, c_2) = 0.44, \rho(p_3 \in g_3, c_1)$$
$$= \rho(p_4 \in g_4, c_1) = \rho(p_5 \in g_5, c_1) = 0.28$$

Then, $w_A(c_1,c_2) = \dfrac{0.24+0.44}{2} + \dfrac{0.28+0.28+0.28}{3} = 0.62.$

To ensure that $\forall u \in V_A, w_A(u,u) = 1$, we normalize by setting:

$$w_A(u,u') = \frac{w_A(u,u')}{\sqrt{w_A(u,u) \times w_A(u',u')}}.$$

HIST

Based on the coordinates of points assigned to each subspace in V_A, we estimate discrete p.d.f.s. for each dimension for each subspace. If each dimension of the d_A-dimensional dataset is discretized into ξ equi-width intervals, then $u(i,j)$ corresponds to the fraction of points assigned to vertex/subspace u, which are discretized to the jth interval in the ith dimension. Using our running example, there are two points p_1, p_2 assigned to subspace c_1. Both of them are discretized to the interval 5 in the dimension d_2—that is, $[500,600)$. Therefore, $c_1(2,5) = \dfrac{2}{2} = 1$. Accordingly,

$$w_A(u,u') = \frac{1}{d_A\xi}\sum_{i=1}^{d_A}\sum_{j=1}^{\xi}sim(u(i,j),u'(i,j)) \tag{5}$$

where $sim : [0,1]\times[0,1] \to [0,1]$ is a similarity function.

Note that this $w_A()$ requires no normalization if we use the Gaussian or increasing weighted $sim()$ function shown below. Otherwise, normalization is required. We have tested a number of symmetric similarity functions:

- **Dot product:** $sim(a,b) = a \times b$

- **Gaussian weighted:** $sim(a,b) = exp(\dfrac{-(a-b)^2}{2s^2})$

- **Increasing weighted:** $sim(a,b) = \dfrac{1}{1+\dfrac{|a-b|}{s}}$

where s is a user-defined parameter controlling the spread of sim. Note that our similarity measures are both symmetric and independent of the number of points assigned to each subspace.

Identifying Similarities Between Condensed Models

Once we have the internal similarity among the subspaces within each dataset in the form of weighted graphs, to find similarities between the dataset graphs, we test three algorithms. One (**OLGA**) uses the tensor product, the next (**EigenMatch**) uses ideas from the first and Blondel's algorithm, and the last uses MonteCarlo sampling.

OLGA

We combine the graphs G_A and G_B into a single bipartite graph:

$G = (V_A \cup V_B, E \subseteq V_A \times V_B, \Pi)$. Π is a $|V_A|\times|V_B|$ matrix of pairwise vertex similarities.

To find Π, we construct the product graph (see function **ProductGraph** in Figure 1 $G' = (V_A \times V_B, E' \subseteq (V_A \times V_B)\times(V_A \times V_B), w_{A,B})$, where $w_{A,B} : E' \to \Re$ is the adjacency matrix, indicating similarity between vertices corresponding to pairs of subspaces from underlying graphs of G'. Let $\beta(A,B) = sim(w_A(u,u'), w_B(v,v'))$, then:

$$w_{A,B}((u,v),(u',v')) = \begin{cases} \beta(A,B) & if \quad \beta(A,B) > \tau \\ 0 & otherwise \end{cases} \tag{6}$$

where τ is a user-specified threshold, used to minimize noise and limit space complexity of the algorithm. As $w_A(u,u')$, $w_B(v,v')$ depend on G_A, G_B respectively, the weight of an edge in product graph G' is high, if the weights on the corresponding edges in the underlying graphs are similar. Thus, we do not explicitly compare dimensions of vertices in the two graphs, thereby making no assumptions on identical schema. Let $S = vec(\Pi)$ (as defined above) and $l = |V_A \| V_B|$ length column vector. Using the concept, "two vertices are similar, if vertices they are related to, are similar," then similarity between $u \in V_A$ and $v \in V_B$ is a function of all the vertices in V_A and V_B, and the relationships that u and v have with them, respectively. If S_i denotes S at iteration i, we can write this as (with $u' \in V_A, v' \in V_B$):

$$
\begin{aligned}
S_i((u,v)) &= \sum w_{A,B}((u,v),(u',v')) S_{i-1}((u',v')) \\
&= w_{A,B}((u,v),:) \cdot S_{i-1} \\
\textit{Then, } S_i &= w_{A,B} \cdot S_{i-1}
\end{aligned}
$$

where $w_{A,B}((u,v),:)$ returns the $(u,v)^{th}$ row of $w_{A,B}$. As shown in Figure 1, we set the initial similarities—that is, all entries in S_0—to 1.0 (line 6). We then iterate using Equation 7 (line 8). We determine convergence by checking to see if the Frobenius norm of the residual at the end of each iteration is less than a user-specified threshold ε (line 9).

As we are looking for a matching between vertices from G_A to G_B, we may unstack the vector S and use the resulting $|V_A| \times |V_B|$ matrix as the adjacency matrix of the bipartite graph G (i.e.,Π).

Ideally, Π is a permutation matrix which minimizes $err(f|w_A, w_B)$ (Equation 2). Typically however, Π is a real matrix. Hence, we need to *round* Π to a permutation matrix. We use the **Match** function to do the same. **Match** returns $f: V_A \rightarrow V_B$. There are a number of matching algorithms, for example, stable matching, the Kuhn-Munkres algorithm (Kuhn, 1955), perfectionist egalitarian polygamy (Melnik et al., 2002), and so forth. We can formulate the *rounding* as finding a matching which maximizes the sum of the weights on the edges of the matching. Finding such a **matching** (also called an *alignment*) is called *bipartite weighted matching,* which has earlier been optimally solved by the Hungarian algorithm (Kuhn, 1955). This algorithm has complexity $O(\max\{|V_A|,|V_B|\})^3)$. This is equivalent to partitioning G into a number of clusters such that no cluster contains two vertices from the same graph, and the total of the similarity among the vertices within each cluster is maximized. **Match,** unless otherwise mentioned, refers to the Hungarian algorithm. There are other approximate matching algorithms of lower complexity. We do not take into account the complexity of **Match** while stating complexity of the algorithms, as it is a parameter. This idea is similar to similarity propagation in Melnik et al. (2002). However, they use directed, labeled graphs.

If $w_{A,B}$ is normal, it is diagonalizable. If it has a dominant eigenvalue,

$$S_i = \frac{w_{A,B} \cdot S_{i-1}}{\| w_{A,B} \cdot S_{i-1} \|_F} \; Then, \; S' = \lim_{i \to \infty} S_i = \frac{w_{A,B} \cdot S'}{\| w_{A,B} \cdot S' \|_F} \tag{7}$$

Rearranging, $(w_{A,B} - \| w_{A,B} \cdot S' \|_F \cdot I)S' = 0$, where I is the $l \times l$ identity matrix. Note, this is the characteristic equation for $w_{A,B}$. Then, $w_{A,B}$ has a dominant eigenvalue $\lambda_1 = \| w_{A,B} \cdot S' \|_F$ and dominating eigenvector S'. The rate of convergence is determined by the ratio $\frac{\lambda_2}{\lambda_1}$ (Golub & Van Loan, 1996).

If *sim* returns the scalar product of its inputs and $\tau = 0$, then $w_{A,B}((u,v),(u',v')) = w(u,u')w(v,v')$ and $w_{A,B} = w_A \otimes w_B$, as defined above. If $w_{A,B}$ corresponds to the tensor product, further improvements in the time and space complexity of the algorithm are possible. Accordingly, we have **FastOLGA** algorithm in Figure 1.

It is known (West, 1996) that the set of eigenvalues of the tensor product of two matrices is the set of values in the tensor product of the eigenvalues of these matrices, that is:

Figure 1. Matching two graphs

```
ProductGraph( G, G_A, G_B ):
1.  ∀(u,v) ∈ (V_A × V_B) create vertex (u,v)
2.  ∀(u,u') ∈ (V_A × V_A)
3.      ∀(v,v') ∈ (V_B × V_B)
4.          add edge ((u,v),(u',v')) using Eq. 6

OLGA( G_A, G_B, τ, k ):
5.  ProductGraph( G, G_A, G_B )
6.  S_0 = ones(|V_A|, |V_B|)
7.  for i=1:k
8.      S_i = (w_{A,B} · S_{i-1}) / ‖ w_{A,B} · S_{i-1} ‖_F
9.      if ‖ S_i − S_{i-1} ‖_F < ε  break
10. return Match( S_k )

FastOLGA( G_A, G_B ):
11. Find U_{A,1}, λ_{A,1}, λ_{A,2}
12. Find U_{B,1}, λ_{B,1}, λ_{B,2}
13. if λ_{A,1} ≠ λ_{A,2} and λ_{B,1} ≠ λ_{B,2}
14.     S = U_{A,1} ⊗ U_{B,1}
15.     return Match( S )
```

$$w_{A,B} = w_A \otimes w_B \Rightarrow 1 \leq i, j \leq |V_A|, |V_B|, \lambda_{w_A,i} \lambda_{w_B,j}$$

is an eigenvalue of $w_{A,B}$. Hence, the dominant eigenvalue of the tensor product of $w_{A,B}$ (if it exists) is the product of the dominant eigenvalues of the w_A and w_B. This implies that convergence is achieved if both w_A and w_B have dominant eigenvalues (line 13). Similarly, the set of eigenvectors of the tensor product of two matrices is the set of values in the tensor product of the eigenvectors of these matrices. This implies that $S' = U_{A,1} \otimes U_{B,1}$, using notation from above for dominant eigenvectors. Finding a **maximal matching** in the tensor product of the dominant eigenvectors corresponds to projecting the longer eigenvector onto the space of the smaller eigenvector and permuting the dimensions of the former, such that their cosine similarity is maximized (i.e., aligning them).

The dominant eigenvector of an $n \times n$ matrix can be determined in $O(n^2)$ time (lines 11,12) using QR factorization (Golub & Van Loan, 1996), and the tensor product of $|V_A|$ and $|V_B|$ length vectors is computed in $|V_A| \cdot |V_B|$ steps (line 14). This allows computation of S' in $O(max(|V_A|^2, |V_B|^2))$ time (i.e., faster than the Blondel algorithm).

EigenMatch

The main result of the **OLGA** algorithm is that it approximately reduces graph matching to the problem of aligning the dominant eigenvectors of the two graphs to be matched. This raises the question: why not try to align more than just the dominant eigenvectors? Accordingly, we analyze the optimization function *err* in 2. As $Tr[ww^T] = \| w \|_F^2$,

$$\min_P \| w_A - Pw_B P^T \|_F^2$$
$$= \min_P Tr[(w_A - Pw_B P^T)(w_A - Pw_B P^T)^T]$$
$$= \min_P Tr[w_A w_A^T + Pw_B P^T Pw_B^T P^T$$
$$- w_A Pw_B P^T - Pw_B P^T w_A]$$
$$= \| w_A \|_F^2 + \min_P \| Pw_B P^T \|_F^2$$
$$- Tr[w_A Pw_B P^T + Pw_B P^T w_A]$$

As the trace of the product of two square matrices is independent of the order of multiplication, $Tr[w_A(Pw_B P^T)] = Tr[(Pw_B P^T)w_A]$. Also, $\| w_A \|_F^2, \| Pw_B P^T \|_F^2$ are terms related to the magnitude of the matched subgraphs, while the latter two terms pertain to the structure of the matching. Hence the problem reduces to $\max_P Tr[w_A P w_B P^T]$. If w_A, w_B are normal matrices, then using eigen decomposition,

$$\max_P Tr[w_A P w_B P^T]$$
$$= \max_P Tr[U_A D_A U_A^T P U_B D_B U_B^T P^T]$$
$$= \max_P Tr[(D_A U_A^T P U_B D_B U_B^T P^T) U_A]$$
$$= \max_P Tr[D_A (U_A^T P U_B) D_B (U_B^T P^T U_A)]$$
$$= \max_W Tr[D_A W D_B W^T] \text{ where } W = U_A^T P U_B$$

Blondel et al. (2004) use normalized even iterates of $S_{k+1} = w_A S_k w_B$ to find similarities between normal matrices w_A, w_B. We adopt this idea, so that $W_{k+1} = D_A W_k D_B$. We drop the normalization as it is a constant for a single iteration. However, instead of an iterative algorithm, we choose a good seed and utilize just one iteratio'—$W_1 = D_A W_0 D_B$. For the seed, we use the **FastOLGA** algorithm (line 2), which aligns the dominant eigenvectors. Substituting in W, we get $D_A W_0 D_B = U_A^T P U_B$. Rearranging, we get:

$$P = U_A D_A W_0 D_B U_B^T, \text{ where } W_0 = FastOLGA(w_A, w_B) \tag{8}$$

$U_X D_X = [U_{X,1} \lambda_{X,1} \ U_{X,2} \lambda_{X,2} \ldots]$. Thus, each eigenvector of w_A and w_B will then be weighted by its eigenvalue. Then during rounding of P, the matching algorithm will be fully cognizant of the smaller eigenvalues as well.

Accordingly, we have the algorithm **EigenMatch** as shown in Figure 2. This algorithm has the same time complexity as eigen decomposition—that is, $O(n^3)$ (Golub & Van Loan, 1996).

Figure 2. Matching all eigenvectors

EigenMatch (G_A, G_B):
1. $w_A = U_A D_A U_A^T, w_B = U_B D_B U_B^T$
2. $W_0 =$ **FastOLGA**(w_A, w_B)
3. $P = U_A D_A W_0 D_B U_B^T$
4. return **Match**(P)

Matching Using MonteCarlo Sampling

One way of estimating the unusualness of matchings produced by our algorithms involves generating random **matchings** and comparing the *err* value of the best of these, with that produced by our algorithms. Accordingly, if $|V_A|>=|V_B|$, we generate a random permutation of the numbers $[1,|V_A|]$ and map the first $|V_A|$ numbers of this permutation to the vertices numbered $[1,|V_B|]$ of G_B. Otherwise, we swap the graphs and get the mapping in the same way. We call this *MonteCarlo sampling.*

We repeat this sampling a number of times, evaluate them using the *Zscore* described further on, and keep the one with the best *Zscore*. The number of such samples generated is controlled by the time taken to run **OLGA**. This ensures that **OLGA** and **MonteCarlo sampling** have the same amount of time to find the matching.

Experiments

In evaluating the performance of the algorithms, we pay attention to the following measures:

- **Execution time**
- **Number of matches (#(matches)):** It is the number of D_B's matchable components that are correctly matched. A component in D_B is *matchable* if there exists a known, unusually similar component in D_A.
- *Zscore*: We estimate the distribution of $err(f|w_A, w_B)$ (Equation 2) by generating a number of **matchings** using **MonteCarlo sampling** and computing the *err*. Using this distribution, the mean and standard deviation can be determined, and the scores corresponding to the mapping found by an algorithm are normalized to get the *Zscore*. Thus, the *Zscore* is the number of standard deviations from the mean. Very negative *Zscore* implies that the corresponding matching is very unlikely to have happened by MonteCarlo sampling, and such a matching is said to have found *unusually similar* substructure.

Experiments on **OLGA**, Blondel's algorithm, and MonteCarlo sampling were carried out on a SUN Sparc 650 MHz machine running on Solaris O/S with 256 MB RAM in C++. Blondel's algorithm, **EigenMatch, FastOLGA,** and MonteCarlo sampling were also implemented on a Pentium 2 GHz machine running on Windows XP with 256MB RAM in Matlab.

Synthetic Datasets

We use synthetic datasets to test the performance of our algorithms and similarity measures, as dataset and algorithm parameters are varied. By generating the datasets ourselves, we can verify the correctness. Our program for generating synthetic datasets is based on that previously described in Sequeira and Zaki (2004). It has the following set of parameters:

1.   Average number of dimensions (d)
2.   Average number of points in a dataset (n)
3.   Average number of embedded subspaces (k)
4.   Average probability that a subspace is constrained in a dimension (c)
5.   Average probability that a subspace is constrained in the same dimension as the previous subspace (o)
6.   Amount of perturbation (p)
7.   Type of transformation

First, $1.5k$ subspaces are generated one after the other. They are by default multivariate normal, with means in each dimension $\mu(j \in [1, d])$, chosen from U[0,1000), where U[l,h] implies a uniform distribution over the interval [l,h]. The standard deviation in each dimension $\sigma(j \in [1, d])$ is by default set to 20. A dimension is constrained with probability c. Two serially generated subspaces are constrained in the same dimension with probability o. Their means are constrained to be within 2 standard deviations of each other, to allow overlapping of subspaces. Unconstrained dimensions have means chosen from U[0,1000).

For $i \in \{1,2\}$, for dataset D_i, n_i, k_i are chosen uniformly from U($5n$, $1.5n$) and U($5k$, $1.5k$) respectively. The first k_i subspaces are embedded in D_i after perturbing their parameters using a transformation. There are three types of transformations:

-   **Noisy:** $\forall j \in [1, d], \mu(j) = \mu(j) + U(-p, p) * 1000$
    $\sigma(j) = \sigma(j) * (1 + U(-p, p))$

-   **Translation:** $\mu(j) = \mu(j) + i * p * 1000$

-   **Scaling:** $\sigma(j) = \sigma(j) * (1 + ip/5)$

where p is the perturbation parameter. Each embedded subspace accounts for at least 1% of the total number of points. The actual number of points corresponding to a subspace is a function of the imbalance factor:

$$a, a = \frac{\max_l \alpha_l}{\min_l \alpha_l}$$

where α_l is the fraction of D_i generated using parameters of the lth subspace embedded in D_i. Noisy points, which account for 5% of the points in D_i, are multivariate uniform—that is, each coordinate is chosen from U[0,1000].

In experiments shown below, we assume that the subspace mining algorithm finds the embedded subspaces correctly, so as to isolate the contributions of this chapter. Thus, we test only the graph creation and matching algorithms described in this chapter. We tested the algorithms by matching synthetic datasets having embedded subspaces. As we serially insert subspaces, for every pair of datasets, we ensure that the dataset with the larger number of embedded subspaces includes all subspaces embedded in the other dataset. The datasets have, on average, n=1000 points and d=50 dimensions and k=25 embedded subspaces, except those with k>40 subspaces, which have n=10000 points. Unless otherwise stated, c=o=0.5, p=0.03, a=4.0, we use the noisy transformation and Gaussian weighted $sim()$function. By default, we try to map a 27-vertex graph to a 34-vertex one using **OLGA** and the HIST similarity measure. For **OLGA,** we set τ=.925, k=30. We evaluate the algorithms based on the #(matches) and its $Zscore$, as some parameter in the dataset is varied or the subspace similarity function is varied.

Comparison of Similarity Functions

We first tested the similarity functions by attempting to match each graph to itself. As expected, we found that while the linear algebra-based algorithms succeed in doing so, the MonteCarlo sampling often does not. We have not shown these results, due to space constraints.

In Figures 3, 5, and 7 we compare **OLGA**'s performance in terms of #(matches) as some parameter, namely, p,o and c, used in generating the embedded subspaces is varied. Note that #(matches) is virtually the same for both measures, except parameter p, where HIST performs better at p>0.05. It also outperforms AVGSIM in terms of $Zscore$ as seen in Figures 4, 6, and 8. This suggests that HIST favors a more global solution as compared to AVGSIM. This occurs because it develops a profile for the entire subspace, including dimensions for which the subspace is not constrained, whereas AVGSIM takes more of a discretized approach. Also, there exist some values of these parameters, for which HIST's $Zscore$ drops below that of the optimal matching, in spite of having a significantly lower #(matches). This happens for extreme settings of the parameters. It suggests that $Zscore$ and hence err quality measures are best suited to matching datasets having a low amount of perturbation.

Figure 3. #(matches) v/s p

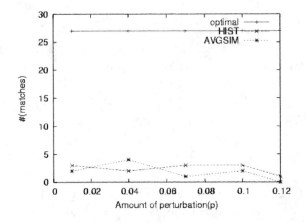

In Figures 9 and 10, we compare the effect that different transformations on the dataset have on similarity measures. We notice that AVGSIM is consistently outperformed by HIST in the *Zscore* category, emphasizing the robustness of the latter. In terms of #(matches), HIST is outperformed for the noisy transformation because again it tries to optimize globally. Thus, in general HIST outperforms AVGSIM.

Comparison of Support-Based Similarity Functions

Early in this chapter, we discussed three functions used to compare clusterings. We then showed how to use them to find support-based subspace similarity. From Figure 11, Jaccard Index outperforms Rand Index and VI Metric.

Comparison of Mapping Algorithms

Firstly, we found experimentally that **FastOLGA** and Blondel's algorithm always arrive at the identical matching, suggesting that the similarity transformation found by Blondel's algorithm is basically the tensor product of the dominant eigenvectors. Note however that our algorithm is theoretically faster than Blondel's. In view of this result, we show their results combined except for the timing results.

In Figures 12, 13, and 14, we compare the performance of **OLGA** and **EigenMatch** with that of Blondel's algorithm (Blondel et al., 2004) and the best matching produced in terms of *Zscore* by MonteCarlo sampling. Note that for Figure 12, the log scale is used for the y-axis. Although **OLGA** is the most consistent performer, the best matching produced by MonteCarlo sampling (denoted in the figures as ``best Mon-

MonteCarlo") performs well for matching small graphs, as it has a smaller state space to search. In Figure 13, **EigenMatch** outperforms the others in minimizing the *Zscore* more often than not. However, **EigenMatch** is unreliable in terms of #(matches) it produces. It sometimes produces no matches, while for $k = 75$, it perfectly matches 13 vertices. This is because it attempts global optimization in trying to align all the eigenvectors. **OLGA,** by virtue of using the *sim* function, prunes the graph and hence tries to find unusually similar matches. Hence, it typically outperforms Blondel's algorithm. Also note that while Blondel's algorithm converges faster than the other algorithms, it is provably slower than **FastOLGA** and produces the same results. We have verified this using our Matlab simulation, but have not shown it in the graph, as efficient simulation of **OLGA** in Matlab is non-trivial.

All the algorithms have running time independent of n and d. Hence, results for these are not shown.

Applications

As stated earlier in the chapter, our framework may be applied to monitoring evolution of datasets over time. Rather than use dataset snapshots, we use the statistics of players from the NBA, averaged annually from two consecutive basketball seasons, namely, 2003-04 (dataset A) and 2004-05 (dataset B). They are accessible at *http://sports.yahoo.com/nba/stats/*.

Another possible application of our framework is the mining of related but schematically differing datasets. We use two datasets pertaining to breast cancer (Beyer et al., 1999) donated to the UCI ML repository at *ftp://ftp.ics.uci.edu/pub/machine-learning-databases/breast-cancer-wisconsin*, obtained from the University of Wisconsin Hospitals, Madison from Dr. William H. Wolberg.

Finally, we apply our methodology on time series microarray datasets from the cell cycle of *S. Cerevisiae*.

NBA Data Analysis

Datasets A and B contain statistics for 443 and 464 players respectively. Each dataset has 16 columns: number of games played, average minutes played per game, average field goals, 3-pointers and free throws made and attempted, offensive and defensive rebounds, assists, turnovers, steals, blocks, personal fouls, and points per game. In this application, we seek to find groups of players having similar performance across the two seasons. If models of performance for the two seasons yield structurally similar clusters which overlap in their members, then these overlapping members are likely to have very similar performance. Consider the following scenario in which such knowledge may be employed: let players, say E, F, and G, currently belonging to distinct teams P, Q, and R respectively, all wish to leave their current team. If by

Figure 4. Zscore v/s p

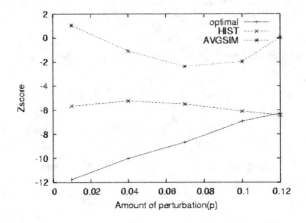

Figure 5. #(matches) v/s o

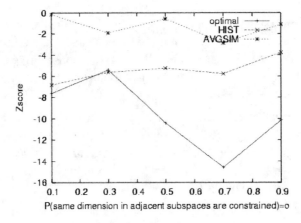

Figure 6. Zscore v/s o

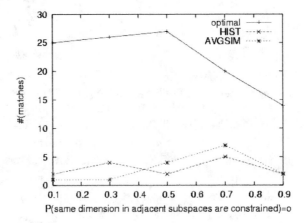

Figure 7. #(matches) v/s c

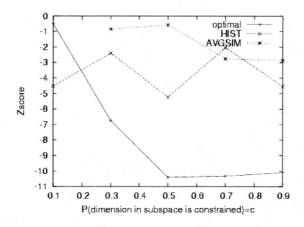

Figure 8. Zscore v/s c

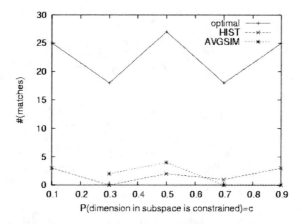

Figure 9. #(matches) v/s transformation

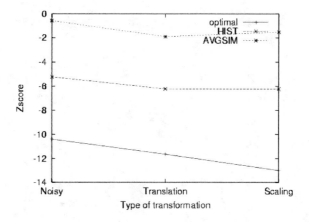

Figure 10. Zscore v/s transformation

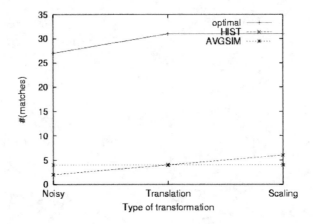

Figure 11. Clustering Comparison Functions

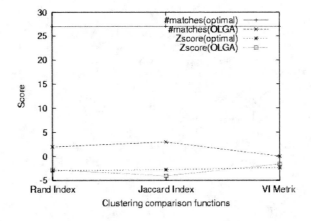

Figure 12. #(matches) v/s k

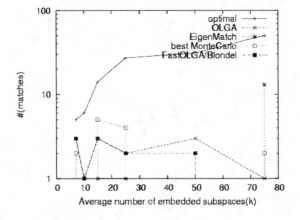

Figure 13. Zscore v/s k

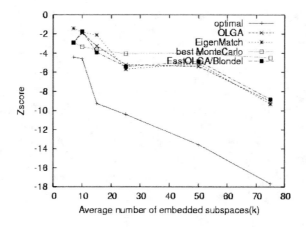

Figure 14. Time v/s k

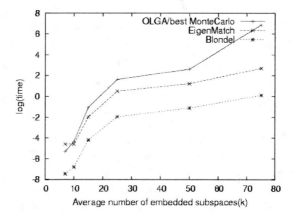

our clustering models for the two seasons, it is known that players E and F belong to structurally similar clusters, then they show similar performance across the two seasons, prompting management at *P* and *Q* to consider "exchanging" them.

The statistics of each year yield a set of clusters/subspaces, 22 for dataset A and 15 for dataset B, for which we construct a graph using methods described above. We then structurally matched the two graphs using **OLGA.** For each pair of matched clusters, we report the intersection set of players. We found clusters as shown in Figure 4, preserved structurally, with respect to the rest of the dataset, across the two years. In basketball, there are primarily three positions at which the players play: 'center', 'forward', and 'guard'. Within these three positions there are further variants, like 'power forward', 'point guard', and so on. The position at which the NBA players played (i.e., *player position*) is not a column in our datasets. Examination of the cluster members revealed that the clusters primarily had members having the same player position.

For example, in the first cluster, out of six members, four—Curtis Borchardt, Ervin Johnson, Kendrick Perkins, and Stanislav Medvedenko—all play as 'centers'. Across both datasets, the probabilities of a randomly chosen player being either 'center', 'forward', or 'guard' are approximately the same and are given as p('center')=0.25, p('forward')=0.42, p('guard')=0.33. If the six players were drawn independently with replacement from this distribution, the probability that k of them are 'centers' is binomially distributed with parameters n=6 and p=0.25. Accordingly, the p-value of this cluster is bounded by the area of the tail of this distribution, to the right of k=4. Thus, p-value= $\sum_{k=4}^{n} \binom{n}{k} p^k (1-p)^{n-k} = \sum_{k=4}^{5} \binom{5}{k}(0.25)^k (0.75)^{5-k} = 0.0562$, which may be considered to be statistically significant. As player position was not a part of the dataset, this analysis has provided us with a new insight. Also, it was found that all the players in the clusters do not start the game and come off the bench. As the players in the same cluster, as found by our algorithm, are typically in the same position, exchanging them seems very reasonable.

The cluster from dataset A corresponding to the first cluster in Table 4 has 50 players, of which 11, 25, and 14 are 'centers', 'forwards', and 'guards', respectively. These players are alike in that they belong in the lower third in terms of attempts at field goals, 3-pointers, and free throws; middle third for field goals made; and upper third for number of games played. Such a cluster has high entropy with respect to the player position. None of these categories singly yield statistically significant p-values. The same is true for the corresponding cluster from dataset B as well. The corresponding cluster in B has players belonging to the lower third in terms of attempts at field goals, 3-pointers, and free throws; number of field goals and free throws made; number of blocks and personal fouls; and average minutes per game. The six players reported in the table. Thus, structural alignment of the models for the datasets produces higher-entropy clusters with respect to those of the original models, with respect to the hidden variable (i.e., player position).

Breast Cancer Data Analysis

The first dataset (X) has nine dimensions/columns having integral values between 1 and 10 for clump thickness, uniformity of cell shape and size, marginal adhesion, bare nuclei, and so forth, and 699 samples/rows. There are a few missing values as well. Thirty-five percent of the samples are malignant (M) and the rest are benign.

Table 4. Structurally similar clusters from two NBA seasons

Common Cluster Members	Characteristic	p-value
Curtis Borchardt, Ervin Johnson, KendrickPerkins, Stanislav Medvedenko, Walter McCarty, Lonny Baxter	4/6 are 'centers'	0.0562
Calbert Cheaney, Howard Eisley, Kendall Gill, Anfernee Hardaway, Jumaine Jones, Mickael Pietrus, James Posey, Kareem Rush, Theron Smith	7/9 are 'forwards'	0.062
Jeff Foster, Mark Madsen, Jamal Sampson	3/3 are 'centers'	0.0156
Brevin Knight, Tyronn Lee, Jeff McInnis, Latrell Sprewell, Maurice Williams	4/5 are 'guards'	0.0436

The second dataset (Y) has 30 dimensions/columns corresponding to three statistics (mean, standard error, max) for each of 10 real-valued features (radius, symmetry, area, texture, etc.) of the cell nuclei drawn from 569 samples/rows. Thus, the schema for X and Y is different. In Y, 37.25% are malignant and the rest are benign.

Each sample in both X and Y is labeled as either malignant or benign. Our goal is to discover these labels using unsupervised, rather than supervised learning techniques. Using SCHISM (Sequeira & Zaki, 2004), we find 36 clusters in X and 21 in Y. After creating the graphs and matching the clusters structurally, we examine the labels of the samples in matched clusters. Let $p(M, u \in V_X)$, $p(M, v \in V_Y)$ denote the probability that a sample drawn uniformly at random from clusters u,v respectively, from graphs corresponding to datasets X,Y respectively, is labeled malignant. Then if our framework finds that $P_j(u,v)=1$, from Equation 1—that is, the cluster u of X is matched to cluster j of Y—we found that $p(M,u) \approx p(M,v)$ (i.e., we found a strong correlation between labels of elements of matched clusters). In Table 5, we report the probabilities of $p(M, u \in V_X)$ and $p(M, v \in V_Y)$ $\forall P_j(u,v)=1$ and $p(M,u) \neq p(M,v)$. The first column, interpreted as cluster 0 of the second dataset (Y), has all its elements labeled as malignant, while cluster 31 of the first dataset (X) has three of its five elements (i.e., 3/5=0.6) labeled as malignant. Such findings allow us to search for correlations between the two spaces corresponding to X and Y. Although, the clusters found in both datasets are predominantly malignant, our algorithm correctly matches the benign ones—that is, cluster 2 of Y with cluster 23 of X, and the higher entropy clusters 16 of Y with 25 of X. A few of the clusters matched do not have a high correlation, as we forcibly attempt to match every cluster in Y to some cluster in X. Blondel's algorithm produces a worse mapping, in that it matches a cluster of

Table 5. Structurally similar clusters from schematically different breast cancer datasets and $p(M,u) \neq p(M,v)$. Here $v \in V_Y, u \in V_X$, and $\delta^2 = ((p(M,v) - p(M,u))^2$.

(v,u)	(0,31)	(2,23)	(4,13)	(8,3)	(11,24)	(14,34)	(16,25)	(17,28)	(19,35)	(20,2)
$p(M,v)$	1.0	0.021	0.933	0.5	0.97	1.0	0.833	0.833	1.0	0.8
$p(M,u)$	0.6	0.027	1.0	1.0	1.0	0.56	0.77	1.0	0.28	1.0
δ^2	0.16	0.0000036	0.0044	0.25	0.0009	0.193	0.0044	0.027	0.50	0.04

malignant samples with a cluster of predominantly benign samples. We compare the results from the algorithms by measuring the correlation between the matched clusters using:

$$corr(f) = \frac{\sum_{v \in V_Y} exp(-(p(M,v) - p(M,f(v)))^2)}{\sum_{v \in V_Y} exp(-1)}$$

Accordingly, we find $corr(f_{OLGA}) = 2.586$ and $corr(f_{BLONDEL}) = 2.0636$, where f_{OLGA} and $f_{BLONDEL}$ are the mappings produced by **OLGA** and Blondel's algorithm, respectively. Thus, **OLGA** outperforms Blondel's algorithm for the breast cancer dataset.

Microarray Data

With a large number of noisy, high-dimensional gene expression datasets becoming available, there is a growing need to integrate information from heterogeneous sources. For example, different clustering algorithms, designed to serve the same purpose, may be run on a dataset, and we may wish to integrate output from the two algorithms. Alternatively, the same algorithm may be run on two datasets differing only slightly in experimental conditions. In the first example, the algorithm provides heterogeneity, while in the latter, it is the experimental conditions.

In our specific application, we look at three microarray datasets, called GDS38, GDS39, and GDS124, pertaining to the *Saccharomyces cerevisiae* (yeast) cell cycle (to access the datasets, visit *http://www.ncbi.nlm.nih.gov/projects/geo/gds/gds_browse. cgi*). The datasets contain expression values of the different genes of yeast sampled over its cell cycle. The cultures are synchronized by different mechanisms, namely, alpha factor block-release(*A*), centrifugal elutriation (*E*), and cdc15 block release

(*C*). GDS38 (i.e., *A*) has 16 samples/columns taken at seven-minute intervals, while GDS39 (i.e., *E*) has 14 samples/columns taken at 30-minute intervals, and GDS124 (i.e., *C*) has 25 samples/columns taken from almost three full cell cycles. Datasets A and E have 7,680 genes/rows, while C has 8,832 rows. The entry in the ith row and j^{th} column of the dataset corresponds to the gene expression value for the jth time sample of gene i during the cell cycle of yeast. Microarray datasets are known to be very noisy. Also, these datasets have a large number of missing values as well.

It is hypothesized that genes which exhibit similar expression patterns may be co-regulated—that is, having similar regulation mechanisms. Hence, we are looking for subspaces having similar expression patterns. We use SCHISM (Sequeira & Zaki, 2004) to find these subspaces. We use $\xi=3$. This discretizes gene expression values into three categories: under-expressed (first interval), normal (second interval), and over-expressed (third interval). Thus, the subspaces correspond to a subset of the genes/rows which are simultaneously either under-expressed or normal or over-expressed for some subset of the time samples/columns. SCHISM returns 13 and 25 subspaces for datasets GDS38 and GDS39 respectively. We then construct the graphs for each dataset and match the underlying subspaces/vertices using **OLGA**. We examined the genes in the intersection of the matched subspaces to verify the efficacy of our algorithms. We submitted the list of genes in the intersection of the matched subspaces to the SGD Gene Ontology (GO) Term Finder (for details, see *http://db.yeastgenome.org/cgi-bin/GO/goTermFinder*) tool. This tool searches for significant shared GO terms, or parents of the GO terms, used to describe the genes in the submitted list of genes to help discover what the genes may have in common. A small sample of their results is shown in Table 6.

The first row of Table 6 is interpreted as follows: Genes SUM1 and BRE1 are associated with the process of chromatin silencing at telomere. These genes actually belong to a cluster of seven genes, but out of 7,274 genes in yeast, there are 42 involved in this process. Using the right tail of the binomial distribution, GO TermFinder reports the p-value (measure of statistical significance) as 0.00068. Further, they are also associated with gene silencing, and the p-value is 0.00215. SUM1 and BRE1 belong to a subspace of 193 genes when SCHISM is applied to dataset GDS38. This results in a much lower p-value and is hence not reported as statistically significant. This is true for other clusters reported too. Thus, the condensed model technique yields smaller, more statistically interesting clusters, by leveraging information from multiple sources.

Table 6. GO-based interpretation of similar substructure

Gene Ontology(GO) Term	p-value	Genes
chromatin silencing at telomere	0.00068	SUM1, BRE1
telomeric heterochromatin formation	0.00068	
gene, chromatin silencing	0.00215	
regulation of metabolism	0.00561	BRE1, ADR1, SUM1
organelle organization and biogenesis	0.00918	BRE1, ADR1, SUM1, SPC110
ribosome biogenesis	4.13e-05	MAK16, SPB4, CGR1 ...
ribosome biogenesis and assembly	0.0001	... TSR2, RLP7, NOP4
dicarboxylic acid transporter activity	0.00059	SFC1, DIC1
recombinase activity	0.00059	KEM1, RAD52
cytoskeletal protein binding	0.00251	NUM1, BNR1, ASE1, MLC2
transcription cofactor activity	0.00885	SPT8, SWI6, ARG81
signal transduction	0.01704	COS111, BEM2
DNA replication	0.00194	ECO1, DPB2
DNA repair	0.00402	
response to DNA damage stimulus	0.00551	
response to endogenous stimulus	0.00551	
growth	0.0078	TEC1, BEM2

Conclusion

From the *Zscore* values obtained by the algorithms, it is obvious that the algorithms find *unusually similar* matchings with respect to MonteCarlo sampling. The p-values of the inferences from the application to the NBA datasets confirm this. It is evident that **OLGA** and **EigenMatch** succeed in finding similar subspaces based on the structure of the dataset alone, without sharing the datasets. The experiments on the breast cancer data suggest that correlations between clusters in related datasets of differing schema may also be inferred, using our framework.

As part of future work, we hope to extend our algorithms to finding common substructure across multiple datasets. Also, currently our similarity measures are best suited to finding similarities between hyperrectangular subspaces. Patterns in datasets may require less restrictive descriptions, for example, coherent patterns in NBA datasets, curves, and so forth. We hope to develop similarity measures for such patterns as well.

Acknowledgments

This work was supported in part by NSF CAREER Award IIS-0092978, DOE Career Award DE-FG02-02ER25538, and NSF grants EIA-0103708 and EMT-0432098. Karlton Sequeira is now at Amazon.com, but the work was done while he was at RPI.

References

Agrawal, R., Gehrke, J., Gunopulos, D., & Raghavan, P. (1998). Automatic subspace clustering of high dimensional data for data mining applications. In *Proceedings of the ACM SIGMOD Conference on Management of Data.*

Bay, S., & Pazzani, M. (2001). Detecting group differences: Mining contrast sets. *Data Mining and Knowledge Discovery, 5*(3), 213-246.

Bennett, K.P., & Mangasarian, O.L. (1992). Robust linear programming discrimination of two linearly inseparable sets. *Optimization Methods and Software, 1,* 23-34.

Beyer, K., Goldstein, J., Ramakrishnan, R., & Shaft, U. (1999). When is nearest neighbors meaningful? In *Proceedings of the International Conference on Database Theory.*

Blondel, V., Gajardo, A., Heymans, M., Senellart, P., & Van Dooren, P. (2004). A measure of similarity between graph vertices: Applications to synonym extraction and Web searching. *SIAM Review, 46*(4), 647-666.

Bunke, H. (1999). Error correcting graph matching: On the influence of the underlying cost function. *IEEE Transactions on Pattern Analysis and Machine Intelligence, 21*(9), 917-922.

Carcassoni, M., & Hancock, E. (2002). Alignment using spectral clusters. In *Proceedings of the British Machine Vision Conference.*

Ganti, V., Gehrke, J., Ramakrishnan, R., & Loh, W. (1999). A framework for measuring changes in data characteristics. In *Proceedings of the ACM Symposium on Principles of Database Systems.*

Gionis, A., Mannila, H., & Tsaparas, P. (2005). Clustering aggregation. In *Proceedings of the IEEE International Conference on Data Engineering.*

Nagesh, H., Goil, S., & Choudhary, A. (2001). Adaptive grids for clustering massive data sets. In *Proceedings of the SIAM Data Mining Conference.*

Golub, G., & Van Loan, C. (1996). *Matrix computations* (3rd ed.). Baltimore: Johns Hopkins University Press.

Han, J., & Kamber, M. (2001). *Data mining: Concepts and techniques.* San Francisco: Morgan Kaufmann.

Kalviainen, H., & Oja, E. (1990). Comparisons of attributed graph matching algorithms for computer vision. In *Proceedings of the Finnish Artificial Intelligence Symposium.*

Kuhn, H. (1955). The Hungarian method for the assignment problem. *Naval Research Logistics Quarterly, 2,* 83-97.

Li, T., Ogihara, M., & Zhu, S. (2002). *Similarity testing between heterogeneous datasets.* Technical Report UR-CS-TR781, Computer Science Department, University of Rochester, USA.

Meila, M. (2003). Comparing clusterings by the variation of information. In *Proceedings of the International Conference on Learning Theory.*

Melnik, S., Garcia-Molina, H., & Rahm, E. (2002). Similarity flooding: A versatile graph-matching algorithm. In *Proceedings of the IEEE International Conference on Data Engineering.*

Neuwald, A., Liu, J., & Lawrence, C. (1995). Gibbs motif sampling: Detection of bacterial outer membrane repeats. *Protein Science, 4,* 1618-1632.

Sequeira, K., & Zaki, M. (2004). SCHISM: A new approach to interesting subspace mining. In *Proceedings of the IEEE International Conference on Data Mining.*

Shapiro, L., & Haralick, M. (1985). A metric for comparing relational descriptions. *IEEE Transactions on Pattern Analysis and Machine Intelligence, 7*(1), 90-94.

Van Wyk, B., & Van Wyk, M. (2003). Orthonormal Kronecker product graph matching. *Lecture Notes in Computer Science, 2726,* 107-117. Berlin: Springer-Verlag.

West, D. (1996). *Introduction to graph theory.* Englewood Cliffs, NJ: Prentice-Hall.

Wolberg, W.H., Street, W.N., Heisey, D.M., & Mangasarian, O.L. (1995). Computer-derived nuclear features distinguish malignant from benign breast cytology. *Human Pathology, 26,* 792-796.

Section II

Patterns

Chapter IV

Pattern Comparison in Data Mining:
A Survey

Irene Ntoutsi, University of Piraeus, Greece

Nikos Pelekis, University of Piraeus, Greece

Yannis Theodoridis, University of Piraeus, Greece

Abstract

Many patterns are available nowadays due to the widespread use of knowledge discovery in databases (KDD), as a result of the overwhelming amount of data. This "flood" of patterns imposes new challenges regarding their management. Pattern comparison, which aims at evaluating how close to each other two patterns are, is one of these challenges resulting in a variety of applications. In this chapter we investigate issues regarding the pattern comparison problem and present an overview of the work performed so far in this domain. Due to heterogeneity of data mining patterns, we focus on the most popular pattern types, namely frequent itemsets and association rules, clusters and clusterings, and decision trees.

Introduction

Nowadays a large quantity of raw data is collected from different application domains (business, science, telecommunication, health care systems, etc.). According to Lyman and Varian (2003), "The world produces between 1 and 2 exabytes of unique information per year, which is roughly 250 megabytes for every man, woman, and child on earth". Due to their quantity and complexity, it is impossible for humans to thoroughly investigate these data collections directly. Knowledge discovery in databases (KDD) and data mining (DM) provide a solution to this problem by generating compact and rich semantics representations of raw data, called *patterns* (Rizzi et al, 2003). With roots in machine learning, statistics, and pattern recognition, KKD aims at extracting valid, novel, potentially useful, and ultimately understandable patterns from data (Fayyad, Piatetsky-Shapiro, & Smyth, 1996). Several pattern types exist in the literature mainly due to the wide heterogeneity of data and the different techniques for pattern extraction as a result of the different goals that a mining process tries to achieve (i.e., what data characteristics the mining process highlights). Frequent itemsets (and their extension, association rules), clusters (and their grouping, clusterings), and decision trees are among the most well-known pattern types in data mining.

Due to the current spreading of DM technology, even the amount of patterns extracted from heterogeneous data sources is large and hard to be managed by humans. Of course, patterns do not raise from the DM field only; signal processing, information retrieval, and mathematics are among the fields that also "yield" patterns. The new reality imposes new challenges and requirements regarding the management of patterns in correspondence to the management of traditional raw data. These requirements have been recognized by both the academic and the industrial parts that try to deal with the problem of efficient and effective pattern management (Catania & Maddalena, 2006), including, among others, modeling, querying, indexing, and visualization issues.

Among the several interesting operations on patterns, one of the most important is that of *comparison*—that is, evaluating how similar two patterns are. As an application example, consider a supermarket that is interested in discovering changes in its customers' behavior over the last two months. For the supermarket owner, it is probably more important to discover what has changed over time in its customers' behavior rather than to preview some more association rules on this topic. This is the case in general: the more familiar an expert becomes with data mining, the more interesting it becomes for her to discover changes rather than already-known patterns. A similar example also stands in the case of a distributed data mining environment, where one might be interested in discovering what differentiates the distributed branches with respect to each other or, in grouping together branches of similar patterns. From the latter, another application of similarity arises, that of exploiting similarity between patterns for meta-pattern management—that is, applying data mining techniques over patterns instead of raw data (e.g., Xin, Han, Yan, & Cheng, 2005).

So far, the importance of defining similarity operators between patterns has been justified. However, this definition is not so straightforward. At first, there are a lot of different pattern types like association rules, frequent itemsets, decision trees, clusters, and so forth; so similarity operators should be defined for each pattern type. Secondly, except for patterns of the same pattern type, an interesting extension would be the comparison between patterns of different pattern types, for example, a cluster with a decision tree (extracted from the same raw data set). Furthermore, an important aspect is that of examining whether similarity between patterns reflects in some degree the similarity between the original raw data. From an efficiency point of view, this is desirable, since the pattern space is usually of lower size and complexity.

In the next sections we overview the work performed so far in the area of data mining patterns comparison. Due to the widespread use of the data mining pattern types, we mainly focus on three basic pattern types that have been used extensively in KDD literature, namely frequent itemsets and association rules, clusters and clusterings, and decision trees.

The chapter is organized as follows. First, we present the above mentioned basic pattern types in detail. We then overview the work regarding the comparison of frequent itemsets and association rules, and focus on decision trees' comparison. We present the related work regarding the comparison of clusters and clusterings, along with the general frameworks for the comparison/monitoring of data mining patterns that have appeared in the literature. Finally, we conclude the chapter.

Data Mining Patterns

According to Rizzi et al. (2003), patterns can be defined as compact and rich in semantics representations of raw data—*compact* by means that they summarize in some degree the amount of information contained in the original raw data, and *rich in semantics* by means that they reveal new knowledge hidden in the huge amount of raw data.

A variety of pattern types exists in the literature due to the heterogeneity of the raw data from which patterns are extracted and the different goals that each mining task tries to accomplish. Different pattern types highlight different characteristics of the raw data; for example, *frequent itemsets* capture the correlations between attribute values, *clusters* reveal natural groups in the data, whereas *decision trees* detect characteristics that predict (with respect to a given class attribute) the behavior of future records (Ganti & Ramakrishnan, 2002).

Ganti, Gehrke, and Ramakrishnan (1999) introduced the *2-component property* of patterns. The central idea of their work is that a broad class of pattern types (called 'models') can be described in terms of a *structural component* and of a *measure component*. The structural component identifies "interesting regions," whereas the measure component summarizes the subset of the data that is mapped to each region. In other words, the structural component describes the pattern space, whereas the measure component quantifies, in some way, how well the pattern space describes the underlying raw data space.

The *2-component property* of patterns has been extended in Rizzi et al. (2003), where the authors introduced a general model for patterns, including also a *source component* that describes the data set from which patterns have been extracted and an *expression component* that describes the relationship between the source data space and the pattern space. We refer to the 2-component property of patterns since, as will be shown from the related work, most of the similarity measures exploit these components.

In the following subsections we present three popular data mining pattern types that are relevant to this work, namely frequent itemsets (and their extensions, association rules), clusters (their groupings, clusterings), and decision trees.

Frequent Itemsets and Association Rules

Frequent itemsets and association rules mining are strongly related to each other by means that frequent itemsets mining is the first step towards association rules mining. In this section we present more detail on both of them.

The Frequent Itemset Mining (FIM) problem is a core problem in many data mining tasks, although it was first introduced in the context of market basket analysis. To define the FIM problem, we will follow the work by Agrawal, Imielinski, and Swami (1993): Let I be a set of distinct items and D be a database of transactions where each transaction T contains a set of items $T \subseteq I$. A set $X \subseteq I$ with $|X| = k$ is called k-itemset or simply itemset. The frequency of X in D equals to the number of transactions in D that contain X, that is, $fr_D(X) = |\{T \in D: X \subseteq T\}|$. The percentage of transactions in D that contain X is called *support* of X in D, that is, $supp_D(X) = fr_o(x)/|D|$. An itemset X is called *frequent* if its support is greater than or equal to a user-specified minimum support threshold σ called *minSupport*, $supp_D(X) \geq \sigma$. The FIM problem is defined as finding all itemsets X in D that are frequent with respect to a given *minSupport* threshold σ. Let $F_\sigma(D)$ be the set of frequent itemsets extracted from D under *minSupport* threshold σ.

The set of frequent itemsets forms the itemset lattice L in which the lattice property holds: an itemset is frequent iff all of its subsets are frequent. The lattice property allows as enumerating all frequent itemsets using more compact representations like closed frequent and maximal frequent itemsets.

A frequent itemset X is called *closed* if there exists no frequent superset $Y \supseteq X$ with $supp_D(X) = supp_D(Y)$. Let $C_\sigma(D)$ be the set of closed frequent itemsets extracted from D under *minSupport* threshold σ. By definition, $C_\sigma(D)$ is a lossless representation of $F_\sigma(D)$ since both the lattice structure (i.e., frequent itemsets) and lattice measure (i.e., their supports) can be derived from *CFIs*. On the other hand, a frequent itemset is called *maximal* if it is not a subset of any other frequent itemset. Let $M_\sigma(D)$ be the set of maximal frequent itemsets extracted from D under *minSupport* threshold σ. Unlike $C_\sigma(D)$, $M_\sigma(D)$ is a lossy representation of $F_\sigma(D)$, since it is only the lattice structure (i.e., frequent itemsets) that can be determined from *MFIs*, whereas frequent itemsets supports are lost (Zaki & Hsiao, 2005). Practically, *CFIs* can be orders of magnitude less than *FIs*, and *MFIs* can be orders of magnitude less than *CFIs* (Zaki & Hsiao, 2005).

Recalling the *2-component property* of patterns, we can say that in case of frequent itemsets, the *structure component* consists of the itemset itself, that is the items that form it, whereas the *measure component* consists of itemset support.

The association rules mining (ARM) problem was first introduced by Agrawal et al. (1993), motivated mainly by the market basket analysis domain, and could be defined as follows: Let D be a database of transactions, where each transaction consists of a set of distinct items I, called itemsets. An association rule is a implication of the form $X \rightarrow Y$, where $X \subseteq I$, $Y \subseteq I$ and $X \cap Y = \emptyset$ (X and Y are itemsets). The rule is associated with a *support s* and a *confidence c*. The rule $X \rightarrow Y$ is said to have support s, if $s\%$ of the transactions in D contain $X \cap Y$, whereas it is said to have confidence c, if $c\%$ of the transactions in D that contain X also contain Y.

The association rules mining problem consists of two steps. In the first step the set of frequent itemsets is calculated, which is then used as input to the second step where the association rules are finally extracted. So, association rules provide some additional information than frequent itemsets.

Recalling the *2-component property* of patterns, we can say that in case of association rules, the *structure component* consists of the left-hand side (also called head) and the right-hand side (also called body), whereas the *measure component* consists of rule confidence and support.

Decision Trees

Decision trees (DTs), first introduced by Hunt, Marin, and Stone (1966), are commonly used for classification due to their intuitive representation that makes them easy understandable by humans.

In this section, we provide some basic concepts on decision trees following the work by Mitchell (1997). DTs are used to classify instances by sorting them down to the tree from the root to some *leaf node*, which provides the classification of the instance. Each *internal node* of the tree specifies a test on some attribute of the instance with regard to some of its values, and each branch descending from that node corresponds to one of the possible values for this attribute.

A *leaf node* corresponds to problem classes with some weight factor, which depends specific on the amount of instances that follow the specific path down to the tree and fall into each class. In the worst case, for each leaf node there is a weight associated with all classes. In the simple case, however, each leaf corresponds to only one class (actually this is the case of practical use).

More formally, let D be a set of problem instances to be classified. Let $A_1, A_2,..., A_m$ be the attributes on which classification will be based (*predictor attributes*), where attribute A_i has domain $D(A_i)$. Let C be the *class attribute*, *that is*, the attribute to be predicted, with domain $D(C) = \{C_1, C_2,..., C_k\}$, where k is the number of classes. A decision tree T over D provides a classification of D instances into classes based on tests over the predictor attributes.

Predictor attributes might be either numerical, categorical, or ordinal. Recall that in a *numerical attribute,* the domain is ordered (e.g., age, income), and in a *categorical or nominal attribute,* the domain is a finite set without any natural ordering (e.g., colors, gender), whereas in a *ordinal attribute* the domain is ordered, but absolute differences between values is unknown (e.g., preference scale). Usually, numerical attributes are discretized and treated as categorical attributes.

According to FOCUS (Ganti et al., 1999), a DT partitions the raw data space into a set of regions. Each leaf node of the tree corresponds to one region, and furthermore each region is associated with a set of measures, each measure corresponding to the fraction of problem instances that result in this region for some of the problem classes.

Recalling the *2-component property* of patterns, we can say that in case of a decision tree, the *structure component* consists of a set of regions (one per leaf node of the tree), whereas the *measure component* consists of a set of measures associated with these regions (in the worst case a leaf node contains k measures, i.e., one for each class).

Clusters and Clusterings

Clustering is the unsupervised classification of data into natural groups (called clusters) so that data points within a cluster are more similar to each other than to data points in other clusters (Jain, Murty, & Flynn, 1999). The term *unsupervised* stands for the fact that there is no *a priori* knowledge about the partition of the data. In a more formal definition, we can state that a clustering C_i is the partition of a data set D into sets $C_1, C_2, ..., C_K$ called clusters such that $C_i \cap C_j = \varnothing$ and $\bigcup_{j=1}^{K} C_j = D$. This definition stands for *hard clustering*, where a data set instance is associated with only one cluster. A more "relaxed" definition is that of *soft clustering*, where an instance is associated with every cluster to a certain extent (or probability) indicated by a weight.

Clustering algorithms are based on some *distance function* that evaluates in which cluster an object should be assigned. There is also an *evaluation function* that evaluates how good the achieved clustering is. For example, minimizing the distance of each data point from the mean of the cluster to which it is assigned could be thought of as such a criterion.

Due to its broad application areas, the clustering problem has been studied extensively in many contexts and disciplines including data mining. As a result, a large number of clustering algorithms exists in the literature (see Jain et al., 1999, for a survey). In fact, there is not only one correct answer in a clustering problem, rather many answers can be found.

Different clustering algorithms proposed in the literature use a variety of cluster definitions. Han and Kamber (2000) propose the following categorization for the major clustering methods:

- *Partitioning methods* that create K partitions of the data (K is defined by the user) where each partition corresponds to a cluster. K-means and K-medoids algorithms belong to this category.

- *Hierarchical methods* that create a hierarchical decomposition of the data set. Depending on how the hierarchical decomposition is formed, that is, in a bottom-up or top-down fashion, they are classified into agglomerative and divisive methods correspondingly. In both cases, a distance function between clusters is required and as such, minimum, maximum, mean, or average distance can be used.

- *Density-based methods* that continue to grow a cluster as long as the density (i.e., number of data points) in its "neighbor" exceeds some threshold. DBScan algorithm belongs to this category.

- *Grid-based methods* that quantize the object space into a finite number of cells that form a grid structure. STING and CLIQUE algorithms belong to this category.

- *Model-based methods* that hypothesize a model for each of the clusters and finds the best fit of the data to the given model. Statistical approaches like COBWEB algorithm and neural network approaches are the two major approaches in this category.

Recalling the *2-component property* of patterns, we can state that in case of clusters, this property depends on the definition of the cluster itself. For example, in case of a "partitioning cluster," its structure could be defined by its center and radius, as in *K*-means, or by its centroid and radius as in *K*-medoids algorithm. In case of a "hierarchical cluster," its structure could be defined as the set of data points that fall into it. In case of a "density-based cluster," its structure could be defined by the cluster distribution function (i.e., the mean and the standard deviation of the distribution). Regarding the measure component, a possible measure is cluster support (i.e., the percentage of data set records that fall into this cluster). Other measures, like the intra-cluster distance within the cluster or the average distance of cluster records from the center or the centroid of the cluster could be used as well.

Comparing FIM or ARM Results

In this section we present the work performed so far regarding the comparison of FIM results (i.e., sets of frequent itemsets) and ARM results (i.e., association rules). In case of FIM results, related work demonstrates methods that utilize the comparison between sets of frequent itemsets in order to compare the underlying raw data sets. In case of association rules, related work gives emphasis on the temporal aspects of rules, namely the necessary operations to maintain and monitor rules evolution over time. However, these are ad hoc approaches to measure the distance between association rules, as well as incremental techniques to update previously discovered rules.

Comparing Sets of Frequent Itemsets

In order to define the similarity between frequent itemsets, let us consider two sets of itemsets (or itemsets lattices) A and B, like the ones illustrated in Figure 1. Each itemset is described through the 2-component property as a pair *<structure, measure>*. Suppose also that both A and B were generated under the same *minSupport* threshold from the data sets D and E respectively which are defined over the same set of items I. The problem we try to deal with is how similar to each other A and B are.

Parthasarathy and Ogihara (2000) propose the following metric for the comparison of sets of frequent itemsetswhere θ is a scaling parameter that is specified by the user and reflects how significant the variations in support are for the user. For $\theta = 0$, the measure component (i.e., support) carries no significance. For $\theta = 1$, the measure component is of equal importance with the structure component.

$$dis(A,B) = 1 - \frac{\sum\limits_{X \in A \cap B} max\ \{0, 1 - \theta * |\text{supp}_D\ (X)| - \text{supp}_E\ (X)|\}}{|A \cup B|} \qquad (1)$$

Recalling the example of Figure 1, the intersection of the two sets is: $A \cap B = \{a\}$. Assuming $\theta = 1$, $dis(A,B) = 1max\{0, 1\theta^*|0.40.6|\}/5 = 0.84$, according to Equation 1.

In fact, the measure of Parthasarathy and Ogihara (2000) utilizes frequent itemsets comparison for data set comparison. The authors consider that $dis(D, E) = dis(A, B)$ based on the intuition that itemsets indicate the correlations within the data sets to be compared.

Ganti et al. (1999) propose the FOCUS framework for quantifying the deviation between two data sets D and E in terms of the pattern sets A and B, respectively, they induce. In order to compare the pattern sets, the authors introduce the notion of *Greatest Common Refinement (GCR)*. GCR is a kind of refinement of the structure components (recall the *2-component property* of patterns) of the models to be compared (see General Frameworks section for more detail on FOCUS).

In case of frequent itemsets, the GCR of the two sets to be compared is their union. Using absolute difference as the difference function and sum as the aggregation function, an instantiation of the FOCUS framework is as follows:

$$dis_{abs}(A, B) = \sum\limits_{X \in A \cup B} |\text{supp}_D(X) - \text{supp}_E(X)| \qquad (2)$$

Since maximum distance occurs when A and B are totally different, the normalized (in $[0...1]$) distance can be defined as:

$$dis(A, B) = \frac{\sum\limits_{X \in A \cup B} |\text{supp}_D(X) - \text{supp}_E(X)|}{\sum\limits_{X \in A \cup B} |\text{supp}_D(X) + \text{supp}_E(X)|} \qquad (3)$$

Figure 1. Two lattices of frequent itemsets (A on the left, B on the right)

Especially for the frequent itemsets case, authors provide an upper bound regarding the distance between the two pattern sets which does not only require re-querying the original raw data space. In this case, if an itemset X only appears in one of the pattern sets (e.g., in A), FOCUS considers that it also appears in B with support equal to 0 without re-querying the original data set E from which B has been extracted.

Recalling the example of Figure 1, $GCR(A, B)$ is given below in the form: $<X$, $supp_D(X), supp_E(X)>$ for each itemset X belonging to $A \cup B$: $GCR(A,B) = \{<a: 0.4, 0.6>, <b: 0.2, 0>, <c: 0, 0.4>, <ab: 0.2, 0>, <ac: 0, 0.4>\}$. Hence, $dis(A, B) = (|0.4 \tilde{0}.6| + |0.\tilde{2}0| + |\tilde{0}0.4| + |0.\tilde{2}0| + |\tilde{0}0.4|) / (|0.\tilde{4}0| + |0.\tilde{2}0| + |0.\tilde{2}0| + |0.\tilde{6}0| + |0.\tilde{4}0| + |0.\tilde{4}0|)$ = 1.4 / 2.2 = 0.64, according to Equation 3.

As with the measure of Parthasarathy and Ogihara (2000) presented above, FOCUS also utilizes frequent itemsets comparison for data comparison. The authors justify that using pattern comparison for data comparison is meaningful since the interesting characteristics of the data sets are captured by the induced pattern models.

Li, Ogihara, and Zhu (2003) exploit the dissimilarity between two sets of MFIs in order to compare the data sets from which MFIs have been extracted. If $A = \{X_i, supp_D(X_i)\}$ and $B = \{X_i, supp_E(Y_j)\}$, X_i, Y_j are the MFIs in D, E respectively, then their metric is defined as follows:

$$dis(A, B) = 1 - \frac{2I_3}{|I_1 + I_2|} \qquad (4)$$

where

$$I_3 = \sum_{i,j} \frac{|X_i \cap Y_j|}{|X_i \cup Y_j|} * \log(1 + \frac{|X_i \cap Y_j|}{|X_i \cup Y_j|}) \min(supp_D(X_i), supp_E(Y_j))$$

$$I_1 = \sum_{i,j} \frac{|X_i \cap X_j|}{|X_i \cup X_j|} * \log(1 + \frac{|X_i \cap X_j|}{|X_i \cup X_j|}) \min(supp_D(X_i), supp_D(X_j))$$

$$I_2 = \sum_{i,j} \frac{|Y_i \cap Y_j|}{|Y_i \cup Y_j|} * \log(1 + \frac{|Y_i \cap Y_j|}{|Y_i \cup Y_j|}) \min(supp_E(Y_i), supp_E(Y_j))$$

I_3 can be considered as a measure of "mutual information" between A and B; the term $|X_i \cup Y_j|/|X_i \cap Y_j|$ represents the fraction of itemsets in common, whereas the fraction $2/|I_1 + I_2|$ serves as a normalization factor.

Recalling the example of Figure 1 and applying Equation 4, it arises that $I_1 = 1.04$, $I_2 = 1.88$, $I_3 = 0.61$; hence $dis(A, B) = 0.58$.

Once more, the pattern space, MFIs in this case, has been exploited towards evaluating similarity in raw data space. The authors support that using MFIs is meaningful since MFIs encapsulate the information regarding the associations among the data sets.

Concluding, we can state that the similarity measures between sets of itemsets have been introduced in order to evaluate the similarity between the underlying raw data sets and not per se. All of these measures make use of the structure (i.e., items that form an itemset) and of the measure components (i.e., the support of an itemset) of frequent itemsets. The measures of Parthasarathy-Ogihara and FOCUS are based on some kind of 1-1 matching between itemsets (i.e., an itemset of the first set is matched to only one itemset of the second set, and an "optimal" score, according to some criteria, is calculated), whereas the measure of Li et al. utilizes N-M matching (all itemsets of the first set are matched to all itemsets of the second set, and an "average" score is calculated). Comparing the Parthasarathy-Ogihara and FOCUS measures, we can state that the first is based on the intersection of the two sets to be compared ($A \cap B$), whereas the second also makes use of the itemsets that appear in the difference sets (A-B, B-A).

All of these measures could be expressed as instantiations of the PANDA framework (Bartolini, Ciaccia, Ntoutsi, Patella, & Theodoridis, 2004) (see General Frameworks section for more details on PANDA). Following the PANDA terminology, a frequent itemsets could be considered as a simple pattern, whereas a set of frequent itemsets could be considered as a complex pattern. Several similarity measure configurations might arise within the PANDA framework for the FI comparison case, by just arranging the following issues: (a) how the similarity between two frequent itemsets (simple patterns) is evaluated (b) how the simple patterns of the two sets (complex patterns) are matched (c) how the scores of the matched patterns are aggregated into an overall similarity score.

Comparing Association Rules

Comparison of association rules can be defined on rules features such as support, confidence, or their bit-vector representations. These direct features are very limited in capturing the interaction of rules on the data and characterize only a single rule.

Toivonen, Klemettinen, Ronkainen, Hatonen, and Mannila (1995) proposed a first approach of defining distance between rules based on the overlap of their market baskets. More specifically, the authors define the distance between two rules $X \Rightarrow Z$ and $Y \Rightarrow Z$ as the amount of rows where the rules differ:

$$dis(X \Rightarrow Z, Y \Rightarrow Z) = \left| \frac{m(XZ) \cup m(YZ)}{m(XYZ)} \right| = |m(XZ)| + |m(YZ)| - 2|m(XYZ)| \qquad (5)$$

where $m(X)$ is the number of matching rows for attribute set X. The problem with this metric is that it grows as the number of market baskets in the database increases.

Gupta, Strehl, and Ghosh (1999) argue that this can be corrected by normalization (i.e., dividing the measure by the size of the database). However, the measure is still strongly correlated with support, as high support rules will on average tend to have higher distances to everybody else. For example, two pairs of rules, both pairs consisting of non-overlapping rules, may have different distances. This is an undesired property. Furthermore, high support pairs have a higher distance than low support pairs.

As an improvement to this metric, Gupta et al. (1999) proposed a new distance measure based on a conditional probability estimate:

$$d_{i,j} = P\left(\overline{BS_i} \vee \overline{BS_j} \mid BS_i \vee BS_j\right) = 1 - \frac{\left|m\left(BS_i, BS_j\right)\right|}{\left|m\left(BS_i\right)\right| + \left|m\left(BS_j\right)\right| - \left|m\left(BS_i, BS_j\right)\right|}$$

(6)

where the set BS_i is the union of items in the left- and right-hand sides of rule i, and $m(X)$ is the set of all transactions containing itemset X. This distance function, called the *Conditional Market-Basket Probability (CMBP)*, results in a distance of 1 for rules having no common market baskets, while rules valid for an identical set of baskets are at a distance of 0.

A specialized approach regarding similarity between association rules was proposed by Lent, Swami, and Widom (1997), who consider the problem of clustering association rules of the form $A \cup B \Rightarrow C$ where the left-hand side attributes (A and B) are quantitative, while the right-hand side attribute (C) is categorical. A segmentation is defined as the collection of all clustered association rules for a specific value C. Having as input a set of two-attribute association rules over binned data, the methodology forms a two-dimensional grid where each axis corresponds to one of the left-hand side attributes. All the corresponding association rules for a specific value of the right-hand side attribute are plotted on this grid. The goal is to find the minimum number of clusters that cover the association rules within this grid. Lent et al. (1997) introduce a series of algorithms to form clusters of adjacent association rules in the grid.

A similar line of research concentrates on the statistical properties of rules by considering their lifetime, meaning the time in which they are sufficiently supported by the data. When data is continuously collected over a long period, the concepts reflected in the data change over time. This requires the user to monitor the discovered rules continuously. Except the well-known but application-dependent solution of an appropriate partitioning scheme, formal methods have been proposed for application-independent partitioning of data. In Chen and Petrounias (1999), the authors focus on the identification of valid time intervals for previously discovered association rules. They propose a methodology that finds all adjacent time intervals during which a specific association holds, and furthermore all interesting periodicities that a specific association has.

Such temporal aspects of rules are also taken into account in the rule monitor of Agrawal, Psaila, Wimmers, and Zaki (1995), and Liu et al. (2001). In Agrawal et al. (1995), upward and downward trends in the statistics of rules are identified using an SQL-like query mechanism. Liu et al. (2001) count the significant rule changes across the temporal axis. They pay particular attention on rules that are "stable" over the whole time period—that is, that do not exhibit significant changes—and contradict them with rules that show trends of noteworthy increase or decrease. Liu et al. (2001) further study the discovery of "fundamental rule changes." More analytically, they detect changes on support or confidence between two successive timepoints by applying a X^2-test.

Baron and Spiliopoulou (2001, 2002, 2003), and Baron, Spiliopoulou, and Günther (2003) introduced Pattern Monitor (PAM), a framework for efficiently maintaining data mining results. PAM builds on a temporal rule model. More specifically, the temporal representation of the patterns follows the Generic Rule Model (GRM) presented in Baron and Spiliopoulou (2001, 2002), where a rule R is a temporal object with signature:

$$R = ((ID, query, body, head), \{(timestamp, statistics)\}) \tag{7}$$

ID is an identifier, ensuring that rules with the same body (antecedent) and head (consequent) have the same ID. The query is the data mining query, while the statistics depend on the rule type. Support, confidence, and certainty factor of association rules are statistics considered in this work. Based on this representation schema, the authors introduce a *change detector mechanism,* a mechanism for identifying changes to a rule statistics which exhibit a particular strength. Statistical significance is used to assess the strength of pattern changes.

Recently, a series of methods having intrinsic the notion of similarity have emerged and focus on maintaining and updating previously discovered knowledge, thus being able to deal with dynamic data sets. Such a popular approach is that of incremental mining in which the knowledge about already extracted association rules is reused. Updating association rules was first introduced in Cheung, Han, Ng, and Wong (1996), and in Cheung, Ng, and Tam (1996). These approaches, as well as subsequent ones, are based on the abstract framework of that the problem of updating association rules can be solved by maintaining the large itemsets. In this initial approach the authors proposed the Fast Update (FUP) algorithm (the framework of which is similar to that of Apriori and DHP) for computing the large itemsets in the updated database. Furthermore, optimization techniques for reducing the size of the database as well as the pool of candidate itemsets during the update process are discussed.

In Cheung, Lee, and Kao (1997), the FUP algorithm was generalized for handling insertions to and deletions from an existing set of transactions.

Subsequently, Ayan, Tansel, and Arkun (1999) proposed the Update with Early Prunning (UWEP), which employs a dynamic look-ahead pruning strategy in updating the existing large itemsets by detecting and removing those that will no longer remain large after the contribution of the new set of transactions. In Thomas, Bodagala, and Ranka (1997), and Sarda and Srinivas (1998), the concept of negative border (Toivonen, 1996) is used to compute the new set of large itemsets when new transactions are added to or deleted from the database.

As inferred from the previous discussion, there are three main lines of research regarding the similarity issue between association rules: (a) ad hoc solutions which can be only applied to special forms of association rules (b) time-oriented rule monitoring (c) incremental approaches which focus on keeping the rules up to date with respect to the underlying raw data.

Naturally, an approach combining the above characteristics is an emerging research issue in the domain.

Comparing Decision Trees

Ganti et al. (1999) argue that the difference between different decision tree models is quantified as the amount of work required to transform one model into the other, which is small if the two models are "similar" to each other, and high if they are "different". According to FOCUS (Ganti et al., 1999), the decision tree induced by a data set identifies a set of regions. Each region is described through a set of attributes (structure component) and corresponds to a set of raw data (measure component). If the structures extracted from the data sets to be compared are identical, then the deviation between the data sets equals their measures deviation.

More specifically, the authors define the 2-component property of a decision tree model M as $\langle \Gamma_M, \Sigma(\Gamma_M, D) \rangle$ where $\Gamma_M = \{1 \leq i \leq l\}$ is the set of regions defined as a subset of the attribute space, $\Sigma(\Gamma_M, D) = \{\sigma(\gamma_M^i, D): \gamma_M^i \in \Gamma_M\}$, and $\sigma(\gamma_M^i, D)$ is the selectivity of the region γ_M^i (the fraction of tuples in data set D that correspond to this region). So, when the structural components of the two models M_1 and M_2 are identical ($\Gamma_{M1} = \Gamma_{M2}$) then, the amount of work for transforming $\Sigma(\Gamma_{M1}, D_1)$ into $\Sigma(\Gamma_{M2}, D_2)$ is the aggregate of the differences between $\sigma(\gamma_{M1}^i, D_1)$ and $\sigma(\gamma_{M2}^i, D_2)$, $i = 1, ..., |\Gamma_{M1}|$. The difference, at a region, between the measures of the first and the second models is given by a *difference function* (not necessarily the usual difference operator "-"), and the aggregate of the differences is given by an aggregate function. If f is a difference function and g is an aggregate function, the formal definition of the deviation when the structural components of the two models are identical is:

$$\delta_{f,g}^{1}(M_1, M_2) \overset{def}{=} g\left(\left\{ f\left(\kappa_{D_1}^{1}, \kappa_{D2}^{1}, |D_1|, |D_2|\right), ..., f\left(\kappa_{D_1}^{l}, \kappa_{D2}^{l}, |D_1|, |D_2|\right)\right\}\right) \tag{8}$$

where l denotes the number of regions and $j \in \{1,2\}, \kappa_{D_j}^{i} = \sigma\left(\gamma_i, D_j\right) \cdot |D_j|$ denotes the absolute number of tuples in D_j that are mapped into $\gamma_{M_j}^{i} \in \Gamma_{M_j}$.

In the general case, however, structures differ and thus a first step is required to make them identical by "extending" them to their GCR. This extension involves splitting regions until they became identical. Then the measures components for each region are computed either directly or by querying back the raw data space. In this case the deviation of the two models is defined as:

$$\delta_{f,g}(M_1, M_2) \overset{def}{=} \delta_{f,g}^{1}\left(\left\langle \Gamma_{GCR(M_1,M_2)}, \Sigma\left(\Gamma_{GCR(M_1,M_2)}, D_1\right)\right\rangle, \left\langle \Gamma_{GCR(M_1,M_2)}, \Sigma\left(\Gamma_{GCR(M_1,M_2)}, D_2\right)\right\rangle\right) \tag{9}$$

Another approach to quantify the deviation between two data sets D_1 and D_2 is to find how well a decision tree model M induced by the first data set represents the second data set. To estimate this deviation, Breiman, Friedman, Olshen, and Stone (1984), Loh and Vanichsetakul (1988), and Loh and Shih (1997) utilize the notion of *misclassification error,* which in the case of decision trees corresponds to the fraction of tuples in a data set that a decision tree misclassifies. In this particular case, let C be the class label predicted by M for tuple $t \in D_2$. If the true class of t is different from C, then t is said to be misclassified by M.

Thus the overall misclassification error $ME^M(D_2)$ of M with respect to D_2 is given by the following equation:

$$ME^M(D_2) \overset{def}{=} \frac{\left|\left\{t \in D_2 \wedge M \; missclassifies \; t\right\}\right|}{|D_2|} \tag{10}$$

An additional methodology that can be employed to measure differences between two data sets is that of the *chi-squared metric.* A prerequisite for the utilization of this metric is the ability to partition the attribute space into a grid consisting of disjoint regions. This requirement, which is the base of the FOCUS framework (Ganti et al., 1999), is met by decision trees and has been utilized by D'Agostino and Stephens (1986) as a means to indicate how the chi-squared metric describes whether two data sets have the same characteristics. More specifically, the chi-squared metric for D_1 and D_2 is given by the subsequent equation:

$$X^2(D_1, D_2) = \sum_{i=1}^{n} |D_2| \cdot \frac{\left(m_{r_i}(D_1) - m_{r_i}(D_2)\right)^2}{m_{r_i}(D_1)} \tag{11}$$

where $r_1, ..., r_n$ is the grid of disjoint regions and $m_r(D_i)$ is the measure of a region r with respect to D_i.

Similarly with the incremental approaches for maintaining and updating association rules, techniques that adjust decision trees inducted by dynamic data sets have been also proposed. Such an approach introducing a series of tree-restructuring methods was firstly presented in Utgoff (1989) and Utgoff, Berkman, and Clouse (1997). The disadvantage of these techniques is that it is assumed that the entire database fits in main memory, and as such the subject of scalability with respect to data size is not addressed.

This issue is handled in Gehrke, Ganti, Ramakrishnan, and Loh (1999), where BOAT, an incremental algorithm for the maintenance decision trees, is introduced. In case of an ad hoc change, BOAT adjusts a tree in a two-step process. Initially, it classifies the amount of change at a node as *drastic* or *moderate,* and depending on this categorization it adjusts the corresponding splitting criterion following different tactics on numerical and categorical criterions. The adjustment of a tree node is based on additional information deliberately kept in the node. Such annotated information concerns a confidence interval of around the point where the splitting occurs, the set of tuples that fall within this interval, a histogram where each bin contains the class distribution of the previously tuples in the range implied by the splitting criterion, and a list of the best splitting criterions at that node for the remaining attributes.

The above description shows that the issue of similarity between decision trees is an open research topic, as some of the special features of decision trees, basically emanating of their complicated structure (e.g., order of the splitting attributes), are not handled in current efforts.

Comparing Clusters and Clusterings

The notion of similarity between two clusters is fundamental in clustering algorithms. In fact the division of a data set into clusters is based on the similarity between clusters, since the goal of clustering is grouping together the most similar data points and assigning dissimilar data points into different clusters.

Several distance measures have been proposed in the literature in order to compare two clusters as a step of cluster generation algorithms. The definition of these measures assumes that we are able to quantify how similar two data points are. In case of numerical data, this distance is usually expressed by some *p-norm*-based distance measure like the well-known Manhattan distance (1-norm distance), Euclidean distance (2-norm distance), and so forth. In case of categorical data, alternative approaches have been exploited, like the Jaccard coefficient used by the ROCK algorithm (Dunham, 2003). In this case the similarity between two data points (e.g., two customers' transactions) equals to the number of common items of the two transactions divided by all items appearing in both transactions.

Regarding the distance between two clusters, several measures based on set theory are utilized by cluster generation algorithms (Dunham, 2003). The *single linkage* distance calculates the smallest distance between an element in one cluster and an element in the other. The *complete linkage* distance calculates the largest distance between an element in one cluster and an element in the other. The *average* distance calculates the average distance between the elements of the two clusters. The *centroid* distance calculates the distance between the centroids of the two clusters (recall here that the centroid of a cluster is the mean of its elements and it is not required to be an actual point in the cluster). The *medoid* distance calculates the distance between the medoids of the two clusters (recall here that the medoid of a cluster is a centrally located element in the cluster).

There are also many paradigms in the literature that exploit the notion of similarity between two clusters in order to perform cluster monitoring or spatial clustering. Among others, we mention the work by Neill, Moore, Sabhnani, and Daniel (2005) on a new class of space-time clusters for the rapid detection of emerging clusters demonstrated for indicating emerging disease outbreaks. Their method consists of two parts: time series analysis for computing the expected number of cases for each spatial region on each day, and space-time scan statistics for determining whether the actual numbers of cases in some region are significantly higher than expected on the last W days (W is the window size). Towards the same direction is the work by Aggarwal (2005) for modeling and detecting spatiotemporal changes in clusters. Clusters are modeled through a kernel function, and at each spatial location X, the kernel density is computed. For each time point t, two estimates of density change are computed, the backward $\tilde{th}_t$ and the forward estimate $t+h_t$ upon a sliding time window. Their difference is the velocity density (or evolution density) of the location X. This model also identifies the data properties that mostly contribute to change.

Furthermore, some of the measures regarding clustering comparison (to be discussed in the sequel) could also be utilized in this case by considering that a cluster is a clustering of size one, that is, it contains only one cluster.

Concluding, we can state that several measures for cluster comparison have been proposed in the literature either in the context of clustering algorithms or in the context of cluster monitoring across the time axis. These measures exploit both the data points that belong in the clusters and the features regarding cluster structure like centroids, medoids, or density functions. The different measures, however, depend on the clustering algorithm used for the generation of clusters, and thus they cannot be applied for the comparison of patterns of arbitrary type.

In the following section we discuss in more detail the comparison of clustering results, a problem that appears quite often in the literature due to its broad range of applications.

Comparing Sets of Clusters

Defining similarity between sets of clusters (i.e., clusterings) results in a variety of applications. Some approaches compare clusterings extracted from the same data set but under different algorithms, thus evaluating the quality of the different clustering algorithms. Other approaches compare clusterings extracted from the same data set under the same algorithm, but with different parameters (e.g., different K values in case of K-means algorithm), thus evaluating the impact of the parameters on the resulting clusterings.

There are also more generic approaches that compare clusterings extracted from different but homogeneous data sets (i.e., data sets defined over the same attribute space). In this case, the applications are broader. Consider, for example, the distributed data mining domain, where it is often required to group together similar clusterings (e.g., group together branches of a supermarket with similar customers profiles so as to apply common marketing strategies to each group). In this case, grouping requires using some similarity function to compare clusterings. Alternatively, consider monitoring of clusterings results over time; in this case the notion of similarity between two clusterings is crucial by means that monitoring is based on being able to quantify how similar two snapshots of the pattern base are (e.g., detect changes in customers profiles of a branch over time).

Generally speaking, we can think of clustering similarity as a way of accessing the "agreement" between two clustering results (Meila, 2003).

Comparing Clustering Results from the Same Data Set

In order to define the similarity between two clusterings, let us consider a data set D of n data points and two clusterings over D, namely Cl_1, Cl_2, of K_1, K_2 clusters respectively.

Meila (2003) provides an overview of the related work on comparing different clustering results produced from the same data set D under different mining parameters (different algorithms or different parameters over the same algorithm).

According to this work, the comparison between two clusterings Cl_1, Cl_2 can be virtually represented through a contingency matrix M of size $K_1 \ X \ K_2$, where the $[Cl_{1i}, Cl_{2j}]$ cell contains the number of data points that belong to both clusters C_i (of clustering Cl_1) and C_j (of clustering Cl_2). The different clustering comparison criteria are categorized into three types:

1.   Criteria based on counting pairs
2.   Criteria based on cluster matching
3.   Criteria based on variation of information (VI)

In the next paragraphs we present more detail on each of these types (see a thorough presentation and analysis in Meila, 2003).

The first category of criteria, criteria based on counting pairs, is based on counting the pair of points on which the two clusterings agree/disagree. Let us define the following quantities:

- N_{11}: The number of data point pairs (x_i, $x_j \in D$) that are clustered in the same cluster under both Cl_1 and Cl_2 clusterings.

- N_{00}: The number of data point pairs (x_i, $x_j \in D$) that are clustered in different clusters under Cl_1 and Cl_2 clusterings.

- N_{10}: The number of data point pairs (x_i, $x_j \in D$) that are clustered in the same cluster under Cl_1 clustering but not under Cl_2 clustering.

- N_{01}: The number of data point pairs (x_i, $x_j \in D$) that are clustered in the same cluster under Cl_2 clustering but not under Cl_1 clustering.

It holds that $N_{11}+N_{00}+N_{10}+N_{01}=n$. Let also n_{k1}, n_{k2} be the number of data points belonging to clusters C_{k1}, C_{k2} respectively, and let n_{k1k2} be the number of data points belonging to both C_{k1} and C_{k2} clusters.

The different measures proposed in the literature for this category make use of the above mentioned parameters. We present some characteristic examples (see Meila, 2003, for a detailed representation).

Wallace (1983) proposed the two following asymmetric criteria:

$$W_I(Cl_1, Cl_2) = \frac{N_{11}}{\sum C_{k_1} \in Cl_1 (n_{k1} * (n_{k1} - 1)/2)},$$

$$W_{II}(Cl_1, Cl_2) = \frac{N_{11}}{\sum C_{k_{12}} \in Cl_2 (n_{k2} * (n_{k2} - 1)/2)} \quad (12)$$

where W_I (respectively W_{II}) represents the probability that a pair of data points which are in the same cluster under Cl_1 (respectively Cl_2) are also in the same cluster under Cl_2 (respectively Cl_1).

Fowlkes and Mallows (1983) introduced the following symmetric criterion which is based on the number of pair of data points clustered together:

$$F(Cl_1, Cl_2) = \sqrt{W_I(Cl_1, Cl_2) * W_{II}(Cl_1, Cl_2)} \tag{13}$$

In Rand (1971), the Rand index criterion has been proposed which is defined as the fraction of pair of data points for which there is an agreement in both clusterings:

$$R(Cl_1, Cl_2) = \frac{N_{11} + N_{00}}{n * (n-1)/2} \tag{14}$$

By just ignoring the "negative" agreements, the well-known Jaccard coefficient arises:

$$J(Cl_1, Cl_2) = \frac{N_{11}}{n * (n-1)/2} \tag{15}$$

Another criterion is the Mirkin distance metric (Mirkin, 1996) defined as:

$$M(Cl_1, Cl_2) = \sum_{C_{k_1} \in Cl_1} \left(n_{k1}^2\right) + \sum_{C_{k_2} \in Cl_2} \left(n_{k2}^2\right) - 2 * \sum_{C_{k_1} \in Cl_1} \sum_{C_{k_2} \in Cl_2} \left(n_{k1k2}^2\right) \tag{16}$$

The second category of criteria, criteria based on set matching (Meila, 2003), is based on finding for each cluster $C_1 \in Cl_1$ a cluster $C_2 \in Cl_1$ that consist "best match" of C_1. The notion of "best matching" is implemented as follows: the contingency matrix M is scanned in decreasing order, and the cluster C_2 with which C_1 shares the larger number of data points (with respect to the other clusters of Cl_2) is considered to be its match. Ignoring the row and the column of the contingency matrix for which the "best matching" has been achieved and repeating the above procedure, the "second matching" is found and so on until $min(K_1, K_2)$ matches are found.

Based on this logic, several measures have been proposed. For example, Larsen and Aone (1999) proposed the following measure:

$$L(Cl_1, Cl_2) = \frac{1}{K_1} * \sum_{k_1} \left(\max_{k_2} \left(\frac{2 * n_{k1k2}}{n_{k1} + n_{k2}} \right) \right), k_1 \in Cl_1, k_2 \in Cl_2 \tag{17}$$

whereas Meila and Heckerman (2001) proposed the following measure:

$$H(Cl_1, Cl_2) = \frac{1}{K_1} * \sum_{k_2 = match(k_1)} n_{k1k2}, k_1 \in Cl_1, k_2 \in Cl_2 \tag{18}$$

Van Dongen (2000) proposed this measure:

$$D(Cl_1, Cl_2) = 2n - \sum_{k1} \max_{k2} n_{k1k2} - \sum_{k2} \max_{k1} n_{k1k2}, k_1 \in Cl_1, k_2 \in Cl_2 \tag{19}$$

In this category also belongs the "classification error" (CE) clustering distance discussed in Meila (2005) which expresses the minimum error of classifying Cl_2 results according to Cl_1 results. CE distance measure is given by:

$$d_{CE}(Cl_1, Cl_2) = 1 - \frac{1}{n} \max_{\sigma} \sum_{k_1=1}^{K_1} n_{k_1, \sigma(k_1)} \tag{20}$$

In the above formula it is assumed that $K_1 \leq K_2$ and σ is an injective mapping of clusters $\{1...K_1\}$ of Cl_1 to clusters $\{1...K_2\}$ f Cl_2. For each σ, a partial correspondence between clusters of Cl_1 and those of Cl_2 is created, and then the classification error of Cl_2 with regard to Cl_1 is computed (think of clustering as a classification task). Among all the possible correspondences, the one with the minimum classification error is d_{CE}. To find the "best correspondence," a naive solution is to examine all possible correspondences and then choose the one with the minimum CE, however this is a solution of high complexity. A polynomial time complexity solution is also available by reducing the problem to the maximum bipartite graph matching problem of the graph theory domain and use either the exact solution provided by the Hungarian algorithm (Kuhn, 1955) or some approximate solution like in Gabow and Tarjan (1989).

Meila (2003) introduced the variation of information method which belongs to the third category of clustering comparison criteria, criteria based on variation of information. This measure is based on the notion of the entropy associated with a clustering which is defined as:

$$H(Cl) = -\sum_{k=1}^{K} P(k) * \log P(k) \tag{21}$$

and $P(k)$ is the probability of occurrence of cluster k, defined as $P(k)=n_k/n$.

The variation of information (VI) metric computes the amount of information that is lost or gained in changing from one clustering to the other and is expressed as:

$$VI(Cl_1, Cl_2) = H(Cl_1) + H(Cl_2) - 2 * I(Cl_1, Cl_2) \tag{22}$$

where $I(Cl_1, Cl_2)$ is the mutual information between the two clusterings defined as:

$$I(Cl_1, Cl_2) = \sum_{C_{k_1} \in K_1} \sum_{C_{k_2} \in K_2} P(k1, k2) * \log \frac{P(k1, k2)}{P(k1) * P(k2)} \tag{23}$$

and $P(k_1, k_2)$ is the joint probability that a point belongs to C_{k1} in Cl_1 and to C_{k2} in Cl_2 and is defined as: $P(k_1, k_2) = |C_{k1} \cap C_{k2}|/n$.

Alternatively, the VI measure can be expressed as:

$$VI(Cl_1, Cl_2) = H(Cl_1 | Cl_2) + H(Cl_2 | Cl_1) \tag{24}$$

where the first term expresses the loss in information about Cl_1, whereas the second term expresses the gain in information about Cl_2 when going from Cl_1 to Cl_2. Although, as presented above, this measure stands for hard clustering, it can be extended to apply to soft clustering as well (in this case, however, it is not a metric).

Summarizing, we can say that the first category of criteria—criteria based on counting pairs—evaluates two clusterings by examining how likely it is for them to group a pair of data points in the same cluster or separate it in different clusters. This category is mainly based on the relationships between data points and is restricted to hard clustering only (Zhou, Li, & Zha, 2005).

The second category of criteria—criteria based on set matching—is based on the notion of "matching" between a cluster of the first clustering and one among the clusters of the second clustering. This "matching" is evaluated in terms of the data points that are grouped together (i.e., in the same cluster) under both clusterings. The proposed measures in this category are based on some greedy technique so as to find the cluster matches. At each step the matching with the greatest score is selected, and finally the scores of the matched clusters are aggregated to produce a total score. However this technique does not lead to the global optimal matching score, but it can fall into some local optima. An exception is the CE error measure, which finds the global optimal solution. Furthermore, this category does not work well in cases of clusterings that contain different number of clusters, since in this case some clusters might be ignored during the comparison process (Zhou et al., 2005).

The third category of criteria—criteria based on the variation of information—is based on the amount of information loss/gain as going from one clustering to the other. The VI metric can be applied to soft clustering as well, but in this case it is not a metric.

All three categories are based on the membership of data points to clusters. However, clusters are usually described not only by their members (i.e., data points), but also by other properties like cluster centroid/medoid or some cluster density function. The description of a cluster depends of course on the algorithm used for its generation as mentioned earlier in this chapter.

Towards this direction, Zhou et al. (2005) proposed a new measure which takes also into account the distance between cluster representatives. The proposed measure is a metric and stands for both hard and soft clustering. In fact, Zhou et al. (2005) proposed two measures. The first one is based on the membership of data points to clusters and comes from the Mallows distance–a metric between probability distributions in statistics. The formula that stands for soft clustering (the hard clustering is a special case of this formula) is as follows:

$$D(Cl_1, Cl_2) = \min_{w_{k,j}} \sum_{k=1}^{K} \sum_{j=1}^{J} w_{k,j} \sum_{i=1}^{N} |p_{i,k} - q_{i,j}| \qquad (25)$$

where $p_{i,k}$ ($q_{i,j}$ respectively) is the probability that the point i belongs to cluster k (j respectively) of Cl_1 (Cl_2 respectively) and $w_{k,j}$ is the "weight" of matching cluster k with cluster j. This weight depends on the importance of a cluster within a clustering (a possible solution is to consider all clusters of equal importance or to define a weight based on the percentage of data points assigned to the cluster with respect to the total number of data points). The Mallows distance can be interpreted as a global optimal cluster matching schema between the two clusterings.

The second measure proposed by Zhou et al. (2005) takes also into account the distance between cluster centroids yielding thus more intuitive results. This measure is given by the following formula:

$$D(Cl_1, Cl_2) = \min_{w_{k,j}} \sum_{k=1}^{K} \sum_{j=1}^{J} \left(1 - \frac{2}{a_k + b_j} * w_{k,j} \right) * \sum_{i=1}^{N} p_{i,k} * q_{i,j} * L(k,j) \qquad (26)$$

where $L(k,j)$ is the distance between the centroids of cluster k (belonging to Cl_1) and of cluster j (belonging to Cl_2).

If we would like to place the measures of Zhou et al. (2005) into the categorization of Meila (2003), we could say that they belong to the second category of clustering comparison criteria, those based on set matching. In contrast to the majority of measures in this category, and together with the CE error measure, the Zhou et al. (2005) measures provide a global optimal solution. Furthermore, their second measure exploits also information regarding cluster structures, like the distance between the centroids of the clusters, whereas previous measures exploit only the data points participating in each cluster.

To conclude with measures for comparing clusterings results over the same data set, we can say that a variety of such measures have been proposed in the literature with applications in evaluating different clustering algorithms, different clustering criteria, and so forth. The majority of these measures are based on the membership of data points to clusters, whereas there are also approaches that also take into account parameters concerning cluster structure, like the distance between cluster centroids.

Comparing Clustering Results from Different Data Sets

The measures presented in the previous section have been introduced towards comparison of clustering results over the same data set. In the general case however, what is required is the comparison between clusterings resulted from different homogeneous data sets—that is, data sets defined over the same attribute space. Consider, for example, comparing clusterings of customer behavior produced by two different branches of a supermarket. Several measures have been proposed towards this aim, and we will present them in more detail. It is obvious that these measures could also be applied towards comparison of clustering results over the same data set presented in the previous subsection.

The FOCUS framework (Ganti et al., 1999) proposes a way for clustering comparison based on the GCR. A cluster model is a special case of the decision tree model mentioned above, however we will give some details on this correspondence for better understanding. Each cluster corresponds to a region which is described through a set of constraints over the attributes (structure component) and is associated with the fraction of tuples in the raw data set that is assigned to this cluster (measure component). The GCR of two clusterings resulted from data set D, and E is formed up by splitting clusters regions of the two clusterings until they become identical. Then the deviation between the data sets equals the deviation between them over the set of all regions in the GCR.

The PANDA framework (Bartolini et al., 2004) could be exploited towards clustering comparison. According to PANDA terminology, a cluster could be considered as a simple pattern, whereas a clustering could be considered as a complex pattern. Defining how two clusters should be compared, how simple clusters of the two clusterings should be matched, and how the scores of the matched clusters should be aggregated, a total score could be calculated that expresses the similarity between the two clusterings to be compared. Different instantiations of the PANDA framework result in several different similarity configurations.

Moreover, some of the measures presented in the previous subsection could also be utilized towards comparing clustering results over different data sets.

To conclude with measures for comparing clustering results over a different data set, we can say that only a few attempts exist in the literature–most of the work is towards comparing clusterings over the same data set. However, performing comparison over different data sets' clustering results in a variety of useful applications and could also be exploited towards clustering monitoring or towards second-generation clustering (i.e., clustering over clusterings).

General Frameworks

Despite the individual approaches towards comparing specific pattern types, more general approaches (frameworks) have been also proposed in the literature (in fact, there exist only a few attempts towards this direction). In this section, we will present these approaches in more detail.

Ganti et al. (1999) presented the **FOCUS** framework for measuring the deviation between two data sets D and E. Although designed for data set comparison, the FOCUS framework actually utilizes the comparison between the corresponding pattern sets. The intuition behind this hypothesis is that interesting data characteristics in a data set are captured by a model induced from the data set. In that work, authors introduced the *2-component property of patterns,* already discussed in this chapter.

If the induced models have different structure components, a first step is required to make them identical by extending them to their *Greatest Common Refinement.* For better understanding, we can think of GCR as a way of refining the structure of the models to be compared, which is achieved by splitting down the models to be compared until identical regions are formed. Then, the deviation between the data sets equals the deviation between them over the set of all regions in the GCR. A difference function that calculates the deviation of two regions and an aggregate function that aggregates all these differences are required; depending on the choice of these functions, several instantiations of the FOCUS framework might arise. Deviation computation requires the measures of all regions in GCR to be computed with respect to both data sets D and E, so the comparison in pattern space (*patterns*) also involves the data space (*raw data*).

The FOCUS framework works for three well-known data mining pattern types, namely frequent itemsets, clusters, and decision trees. The further details on each case have already been presented in the corresponding sections of this work.

Bartolini et al. (2004) proposed the **PANDA** framework for the comparison of both simple and complex patterns. *Simple* patterns are those defined over raw data (e.g., a cluster of data points), whereas *complex* patterns are those defined over other patterns (e.g., a set of clusters, i.e., clustering). Authors adopt the 2-component property of patterns introduced by FOCUS, thus patterns are expressed through a structure and a measure component, and their similarity is evaluated in terms of both of these components (Figure 2).

The similarity between two simple patterns p_1, p_2 is evaluated by combining, by means of an aggregation function, f_{aggr}, the similarities between both the structure ($p_1.s, p_2.s$ respectively) and the measure components ($p_1.m, p_2.m$ respectively):

$$\text{sim}(p_1, p_2) = f_{aggr}(\text{sim}_{struct}(p_1.s, p_2.s), \text{sim}_{meas}(p_1.m, p_2.m)) \tag{27}$$

Regarding the structural similarity, if the two patterns have the same structure, then their measure similarity is only considered. In the general case, however, the patterns to be compared have different structural components, thus a preliminary step is needed to "reconcile" the two structures so as to make them comparable (by calculating, for example, the amount of work required to turn one structure to the other). Regarding the measure components' similarity, several measures could be used like absolute difference or relative difference. Regarding the aggregation function, either sum or weighted sum could be exploited.

Evaluation of similarity between complex patterns follows the same logic depicted in Figure 2. However, the structure of complex patterns now consists of several other patterns. Within the PANDA framework, the similarity between structures of complex patterns depends in turn on the similarity between component patterns. Similarity is conceptually evaluated in a bottom-up fashion and can be adapted to specific needs/ constraints by acting on two fundamental abstractions:

1. The *coupling type,* which is used to establish how component patterns can be matched

2. The *aggregation logic*, which is used to combine the similarity scores obtained for coupled component patterns into a single overall score representing the similarity between the complex patterns.

Depending on the instantiations of the different blocks of the framework (coupling type, aggregation logic, structure similarity, and measure similarity), various similarity function configurations can be defined within the PANDA framework.

Comparing the above frameworks, we can state that both FOCUS and PANDA frameworks try to give a general solution to the problem of pattern comparison

Figure 2. Assessment of similarity between two patterns

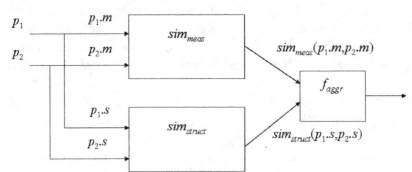

between patterns of the same pattern type. PANDA framework could be thought of as an extension of the FOCUS framework by means that it provides a wide variety of matching criteria (coupling type) in contrast to the specific type of GCR matching provided by FOCUS. Furthermore, it is more generic since it can be applied to arbitrarily complex patterns, like Web site structures, and not only to patterns for which their GCR can be defined (like frequent itemsets, decision trees, and clusters). Also, it works exclusively in the pattern space and does not involve the raw data space as well, thus it is more efficient.

Except for frameworks for pattern comparison, frameworks for pattern monitoring over time and efficient pattern updating have been also proposed in the literature. Their goal is monitoring and understanding pattern changes over time (recall the dynamic nature of data); in some cases, however, monitoring concerns raw data (instead of patterns) and utilizes corresponding patterns towards this aim.

Ganti, Gehrke, and Ramakrishnan (2000) proposed the DEMON framework for mining systematically evolving data across the temporal dimension, where "systematically" means that data changes through additions or deletions of blocks of records (a block is a set of records added simultaneously to the database). DEMON mainly focuses on efficient updating of models (i.e., pattern base) by detecting changes in raw data. To find data changes, authors build on their prior work, the FOCUS framework. After detecting (across the time dimension) the data blocks that have been changed, these blocks are processed in order to maintain the corresponding models. Also, authors describe efficient model maintenance algorithms for frequent itemsets and clusters.

Baron and Spiliopoulou (2001, 2002) introduced Pattern Monitor (**PAM**), a framework for efficiently maintaining data mining results. In contrast to other approaches which consider only part of a pattern, either its content–that is, the relationship in the data the pattern reflects—or the statistical properties of the pattern, authors model rules as integrated temporal objects, which may exhibit changes in either of these two aspects.

PAM builds on the temporal rule model already presented in this chapter. The core of PAM implements the change detector and a series of heuristics to identify not only significant, but also interesting rule changes which take different aspects of pattern reliability into account.The *Occurrence-Based Grouping Heuristic* reveals not patterns observed within a specific time interval, but patterns that are present in each period and, as such, reflect (part of) the invariant properties of the underlying data set. The *Corridor-Based Heuristic* defines a corridor (around the time series of a pattern) as an interval of values, which is dynamically adjusted at each time point to reflect the range of values encountered so far. In *Interval-Based Heuristic,* the range of values of the time series is partitioned into intervals of equal width, so an alert for a pattern R is raised for each time point t_i at which the value of the time series is in a different interval than for t_{i1}.

Furthermore, due to the fact that the change detector returns at each time point t_i the set of all patterns, whose observed statistic measure has changed with respect to the previous period, and the fact that this set is usually large as patterns overlap in content, the authors introduce the term *atomic change* to identify a minimal set of patterns whose characteristic is that there are no components (i.e., the body and the head) that have themselves experienced a change.

Baron et al. (2003) distinguish rules into *permanent rules* that are always present (though they may undergo significant changes) and *temporarily rules* that appear only temporarily and indicate periodic trends.In Baron and Spiliopoulou (2003), PAM was applied in a different case study following an evaluation procedure intending to use the monitor not only to identify rule changes of a particular strength, but also to check whether old rules still hold.

Concluding the presentation of frameworks for pattern monitoring, we can state that they are very important by means that they give insights on how raw data and corresponding patterns evolve over time (recall that most of the data collected nowadays are dynamic). These frameworks utilize methods for pattern comparison in order to detect significant changes across the time axis. Furthermore they can also be applied towards efficient maintenance of pattern bases (i.e., data mining results). However, the DEMON framework gives more emphasis on frequent itemsets and clusters, while the PAM framework focuses mainly on association rules, thus there is no some generic approach supporting monitoring and maintenance for all data mining pattern types.

In this section we have presented the work performed so far towards developing generic frameworks for pattern comparison. The importance of such frameworks is straightforward since there are several different pattern types in the literature, so being able to deal with issues like comparison under a common framework forms an elegant solution. We also presented the work regarding frameworks for pattern monitoring and maintenance which are based on comparing consecutive snapshots of the database or pattern base.

Although some steps have already been done towards a generic, universal way of comparison, the current methods concern specific pattern types, thereas their extension to other pattern types is not so straightforward.

Conclusion

In this work, we presented an overview of the research performed so far in the area of data mining patterns comparison focusing on popular data mining pattern types, namely frequent itemsets and association rules, clusters and clusterings, and decision trees. Despite individual approaches towards comparing specific types of patterns, more general approaches (frameworks) have been also presented.

As demonstrated by the related work, several ad-hoc approaches for similarity assessment of particular pattern types have been proposed in the literature. All of these measures utilize information regarding the pattern space that a pattern describes (i.e., structure component) as well as information about how well the pattern represents the underlying raw data space (measure component).

All of these measures are pattern-type specific, and if we follow this rationale, new similarity measures should be defined each time a new pattern type emerges. It is obvious that this solution is not so efficient, especially nowadays where new types of data or patterns arise continuously from various domains, for example, bio-informatics, telecommunications, audio/visual entertainment, and so forth. A nice solution to this problem would be some pattern-type-independent similarity measure(s).

Furthermore, related work is currently limited to similarity assessment between patterns of the same pattern type. In the general case, however, even patterns from different pattern types should be able to be compared. As a motivating example, consider the problem of comparing a decision tree and a clustering both extracted from different branches of the same supermarket.

As demonstrated by the related work, similarity in pattern space has been utilized towards similarity assessment in underlying raw data space, based on the intuition that patterns encompass most of the information lying in the corresponding raw data. However, the effect of mining parameters on this correspondence usually is ignored. In case of FIM problem, for example, *minSupport* threshold used for the generation of patterns and the adopted lattice representation—i.e. frequent, closed frequent, or maximal frequent itemsets—could be considered as such parameters.

Thus, a future direction would be associating distance in pattern space with distance in the original raw data space from which patterns have been extracted through some data mining process. This direction would result in a wide variety of applications, since pattern space is usually of lower complexity than raw data space.

Acknowledgment

This research is partially supported by the Greek Ministry of Education and the European Union under a grant of the "Heracletos" EPEAEK II Program (2003-2006).

References

Aggarwal, C.C. (2005). On change diagnosis in evolving data streams. *IEEE Transactions on Knowledge and Data Engineering, 17,* 587-600.

Agrawal, R., Imielinski, T., & Swami, A. (1993). Mining association rules between sets of items in large databases. In *Proceedings of the 1993 ACM SIGMOD International Conference on Management of Data (pp.* 207-216*)*. Washington, DC: ACM.

Agrawal, R., Psaila, G., Wimmers, E.L., & Zaki, M. (1995). Querying shapes of histories. In U. Dayal, P.M.D. Gray, & S. Nishio (Eds.), *Proceedings of the 21st International Conference on Very Large Data Bases (pp. 502-514)*. Zurich, Switzerland: Morgan Kaufmann.

Ayan, N.F., Tansel, A.U., & Arkun, E. (1999). An efficient algorithm to update large itemsets with early pruning. In *Proceedings of the 5th ACM SIGKDD International Conference on Knowledge Discovery and Data Mining* (pp. 287-291). San Diego, CA: ACM.

Baron, S., & Spiliopoulou, M. (2001). Monitoring change in mining results. In Y. Kambayashi, W. Winiwarter, & M. Arikawa (Eds.), In *Proceedings of the 3rd International Conference on Data Warehousing and Knowledge Discovery* (pp. 51-60). Munich, Germany: Springer.

Baron, S., & Spiliopoulou, M. (2002). *Monitoring the results of the KDD process: An overview of pattern evolution*, In J. Meij (Ed.), *Dealing with the data flood: mining data, text and multimedia* (pp. 845-863). The Hague, The Netherlands: STT.

Baron, S., & Spiliopoulou, M. (2003). Monitoring the evolution of Web usage patterns. In B. Berendt, A. Hotho, D. Mladenic, M. Someren, M. Spiliopoulou, & G. Stumme (Eds.), *Proceedings of Web Mining: From Web to Semantic Web, 1st European Web Mining Forum* (pp. 181-200). Cavtat-Dubrovnik, Croatia: Springer.

Baron, S., Spiliopoulou, M., & Günther, O. (2003). Efficient monitoring of patterns in data mining environments. In L.A. Kalinichenko, R. Manthey, B. Thalheim, & U. Wloka (Eds.), In *Proceedings of the 7th East European Conference on Advances in Databases and Information Systems* (pp. 253-265). Dresden, Germany: Springer.

Bartolini, I., Ciaccia, P., Ntoutsi, I., Patella, M., & Theodoridis, Y. (2004). A unified and flexible framework for comparing simple and complex patterns. In J.-F. Boulicaut, F. Esposito, F. Giannotti, & D. Pedreschi (Eds.), In *Proceedings of the 8th European Conference on Principles and Practice of Knowledge Discovery in Databases* (pp. 96-499). Pisa, Italy: Springer.

Breiman, L., Friedman, J., Olshen, R., & Stone, C. (1984). *Classification and regression trees.* Belmont, CA: Wadsworth International Group.

Catania, B., & Maddalena, A. (2006). *Pattern management: Practice and challenges.* In J. Darmont & O. Boussaïd (Eds.), *Processing and managing complex data for decision support* (pp. 280-317). Hershey, PA: Idea Group Publishing.

Chen, X., & Petrounias, I. (1999). Mining temporal features in association rules. In *J.M. Zytkow & J. Rauch (Eds.),* In *Proceedings of the 3rd European Conference on Principles and Practice of Knowledge Discovery in Databases* (pp. 295-300). Prague, Czech Republic: Springer.

Cheung, D.W.-L., Han, J., Ng, V., & Wong, C.Y. (1996). Maintenance of discovered association rules in large databases: An incremental updating technique. In S.Y.W. Su (Ed.), In *Proceedings of the 12th International Conference on Data Engineering* (pp. 106-114). New Orleans, LA: IEEE Computer Society.

Cheung, D.W.-L., Lee, S.D., & Kao, B. (1997). A general incremental technique for maintaining discovered association rules. In R.W. Topor & K. Tanaka (Eds.), In *Proceedings of the 5th International Conference on Database Systems for Advanced Applications* (pp. 185-194). Melbourne, Australia: World Scientific.

Cheung, D.W.-L., Ng, V.T.Y., & Tam, B.W. (1996). Maintenance of discovered knowledge: A case in multi-level association rules. In *Proceedings of the 2nd International Conference on Knowledge Discovery and Data Mining* (pp. 307-310). Portland, OR: AAAI Press.

D'Agostino, R.B., & Stephens, M.A. (Eds.). (1986). *Goodness-of-fit techniques.* New York: Marcel Dekker.

Dongen, S.V. (2000). Performance criteria for graph clustering and Markov cluster experiments. Technical Report. Amsterdam: Center for Mathematics and Computer Science.

Dunham, M.H. (2003). *Data mining: Introductory and advanced topics.* Upper Saddle River, NJ: Prentice-Hall.

Hunt, E.B., Marin, J., & Stone, P.T. (1966). *Experiments in induction.* New York: Academic Press.

Fayyad, U.M., Piatetsky-Shapiro, G., & Smyth, P. (1996). From data mining to knowledge discovery: An overview. In U.M. Fayyad, G. Piatetsky-Shapiro, P. Smyth, & R. Uthurusamy (Eds.), *Advances in knowledge discovery and data mining* (pp. 1-34). Newport Beach, CA: AAAI/MIT Press.

Fowlkes, E.B., & Mallows, C.L. (1983). A method for comparing two hierarchical clusterings. *Journal of the American Statistical Association, 78,* 553-569.

Gabow, H.N., & Tarjan, R.E. (1989). Faster scaling algorithms for network problems. *SIAM Journal of Computation, 18,* 1013-1036.

Ganti, V., Gehrke, J., & Ramakrishnan, R. (1999). A framework for measuring changes in data characteristics. In *Proceedings of the 18th ACM SIGACT-SIG-MOD-SIGART Symposium on Principles of Database Systems* (pp. 126-137). Philadelphia: ACM Press.

Ganti, V., Gehrke, J., & Ramakrishnan, R. (2000). Demon: Mining and monitoring evolving data. In *Proceedings of the 16th International Conference on Data Engineering* (pp. 439-448). San Diego, CA: *IEEE Computer Society.*

Ganti, V., & Ramakrishnan, R. (2002). *Mining and monitoring evolving data.* In J. Abello, P.M. Pardalos, & M.G.C. Resende (Eds.), *Handbook of massive data sets* (pp. 593-642.). Norwell, MA: Kluwer Academic.

Gehrke, J., Ganti, V., Ramakrishnan, R., & Loh, W.-Y. (1999). Boat—optimistic decision tree construction. In A. Delis, C. Faloutsos, & S. Ghandeharizadeh (Eds.), In *Proceedings of the ACM SIGMOD International Conference on Management of Data* (pp. 169-180). Philadelphia: ACM Press.

Gupta, G.K., Strehl, A., & Ghosh, J. (1999). Distance-based clustering of association rules. In *Proceedings of ANNIE 1999, Intelligent Engineering Systems Through Artificial Neural Networks 9* (pp. 759-764).

Han, J., & Kamber, M. (2000). *Data mining: Concepts and techniques.* San Francisco: Morgan Kaufmann.

Jain, K., Murty, M.N., & Flynn, P.J. (1999). Data clustering: A review. *ACM Computer Surveys, 31*(3), 264-323.

Kuhn, H. (1955). Hungarian method for the assignment problem. *Naval Research Quarterly, 2,* 83-97.

Larsen, B., & Aone, C. (1999). Fast and effective text mining using linear-time document clustering. In *Proceedings of the 5th ACM SIGKDD International Conference on Knowledge Discovery and Data Mining* (pp. 16-22). San Diego, CA: ACM.

Lent, B., Swami, A.N., & Widom, J. (1997). Clustering association rules. In W.A. Gray & P. Larson (Eds.), In *Proceedings of the 13th International Conference on Data Engineering.* Birmingham, UK: IEEE Computer Society.

Li, T., Ogihara, M., & Zhu, S. (2003). Association-based similarity testing and its applications. *Intelligent Data Analysis, 7,* 209-232.

Liu, B., Hsu, W., & Ma, Y. (2001). Discovering the set of fundamental rule changes. In *Proceedings of the 7th ACM SIGKDD International Conference on Knowledge Discovery and Data Mining* (pp. 335-340). *San Francisco: ACM.*

Liu, B., Ma, Y., & Lee, R. (2001). Analyzing the interestingness of association rules from the temporal dimension. In N. Cercone, T.Y. Lin, & X. Wu (Eds.), In *Proceedings of the 2001 IEEE International Conference on Data Mining (pp. 377-384).* San Jose, CA: IEEE Computer Society.

Loh, W.-Y., & Shih, Y.-S. (1997). Split selection methods for classification trees. *Statistica Sinica, 7,* 815-840.

Loh, W.-Y., & Vanichsetakul, N. (1988). Tree-structured classification via generalized discriminant analysis (with discussion). *Journal of the American Statistical Association, 83,* 715-728.

Lyman, P., & Varian, H.R. (2003). *How much information.* Retrieved January 30, 2006, from *http://www.sims.berkeley.edu/research/projects/how-much-info*

Meila, M. (2003). Comparing clusterings by the variation of information. In B. Schlkopf & M.K. Warmuth (Eds.), In *Proceedings of the 16th Annual Conference on Computational Learning Theory (pp. 173-187).* Washington, DC: Springer.

Meila, M. (2005). Comparing clusterings: An axiomatic view. In L. De Raedt & S. Wrobe (Eds.), In *Proceedings of the 22nd International Conference on Machine Learning* (pp. 577-584). Bonn, Germany: ACM.

Meila, M., & Heckerman, D. (2001). An experimental comparison of model-based clustering methods. *Machine Learning, 42,* 9-29.

Mirkin, B. (1996). *Mathematical classification and clustering.* London: Kluwer Academic Press.

Mitchell, T. (1997). *Machine learning.* New York: McGraw-Hill.

Neill, D.B., Moore, A.W. Sabhnani, M., & Daniel, K. (2005). Detection of emerging space-time clusters. In R. Grossman, R. Bayardo, & K.P. Bennett (Eds.), In *Proceedings of the 11th ACM SIGKDD International Conference on Knowledge Discovery and Data Mining* (pp. 218-227). Chicago: ACM.

Parthasarathy, S., & Ogihara, M. (2000). Clustering distributed homogeneous datasets. In D.A. Zighed, H.J. Komorowski, & J.M. Zytkow (Eds.), In *Proceedings of the 4th European Conference on Principles of Data Mining* (pp. 566-574). Lyon, France: Springer.

Rand W.M. (1971). Objective criteria for the evaluation of clustering methods. *Journal of the American Statistical Association, 66,* 846-850.

Rizzi, S., Bertino, E., Catania, B., Golfarelli, M., Halkidi, M., Terrovitis, M., Vassiliadis, P., Vazirgiannis, M., & Vrachnos, E. (2003). Towards a logical model for patterns. In I.-Y. Song, S.W. Liddle, T.W. Ling, & P. Scheuermann (Eds.), In *Proceedings of 22nd International Conference on Conceptual Modeling* (pp. 77-90). Chicago: Springer.

Thomas, K.A.S. Bodagala, S., & Ranka, S. (1997). An efficient algorithm for the incremental updation of association rules in large databases. In D. Heckerman, H. Mannila, & D. Pregibon (Eds.), In *Proceedings of the 3rd International Conference on Knowledge Discovery and Data Mining* (pp. 187-190). Newport Beach, CA: AAAI Press.

Sarda, N.L., & Srinivas, N.V. (1998). An adaptive algorithm for incremental mining of association rules. In E.B. Fernandez & K.R. Nair (Eds.), In *Proceedings of the 9th International Workshop on Database and Expert Systems Applications* (pp. 310-315). Vienna, Austria: IEEE Computer Society.

Toivonen, H. (1996). Sampling large databases for association rules. In T.M. Vijayaraman, A.P. Buchmann, C. Mohan, & N.L. Sarda (Eds.), In *Proceedings of 1996 International Conference on Very Large Data Bases* (pp. 134-145). Bombay, India: Morgan Kaufmann.

Toivonen, H., Klemettinen, M., Ronkainen, P., Hatonen, K., & Mannila, H. (1995). Pruning and grouping of discovered association rules. *Workshop Notes of the ECML-95 Workshop on Statistics, Machine Learning, and Knowledge Discovery* (pp. 47-52). Heraklion, Greece: Mlnet.

Utgoff, P.E. (1989). Incremental induction of decision trees. *Machine Learning, 4,* 161-186.

Utgoff, P.E., Berkman, N.C., & Clouse, J.A. (1997). Decision tree induction based on efficient tree restructuring. *Machine Learning, 29,* 5-44.

Wallace, D.L. (1983). Comment. *Journal of the American Statistical Association, 78,* 569-576.

Xin, D., Han, J., Yan, X., & Cheng, H. (2005). Mining compressed frequent-pattern sets. In K. Bohm, C.S. Jensen, L.M. Haas, M.L. Kersten, P. Larson, & B.C. Ooi (Eds.), In *Proceedings of the 31st International Conference on Very Large Data Bases* (pp. 709-720). Trondheim, Norway: ACM.

Zaki, M., & Hsiao, C.-J. (2005). Efficient algorithms for mining closed itemsets and their lattice structure. *IEEE Transactions on Knowledge and Data Engineering, 17,* 462-478.

Zhou, D., Li, J., & Zha, H. (2005). A new Mallows distance-based metric for comparing clusterings. In L. De Raedt & S. Wrobe (Eds.), In *Proceedings of the 22nd International Conference on Machine Learning* (pp. 1028-1035). Bonn, Germany: ACM.

Chapter V

Mining Frequent Patterns Using Self-Organizing Map

Fedja Hadzic, University of Technology Sydney, Australia

Tharam Dillon, University of Technology Sydney, Australia

Henry Tan, University of Technology Sydney, Australia

Ling Feng, University of Twente, The Netherlands

Elizabeth Chang, Curtin University of Technology, Australia

Abstract

Association rule mining is one of the most popular pattern discovery methods used in data mining. Frequent pattern extraction is an essential step in association rule mining. Most of the proposed algorithms for extracting frequent patterns are based on the downward closure lemma concept utilizing the support and confidence framework. In this chapter we investigate an alternative method for mining frequent patterns in a transactional database. Self-Organizing Map (SOM) is an unsupervised neural network that effectively creates spatially organized internal representations of the features and abstractions detected in the input space. It is one of the most popular clustering techniques, and it reveals existing similarities in the input space by per-

forming a topology-preserving mapping. These promising properties indicate that such a clustering technique can be used to detect frequent patterns in a top-down manner as opposed to the traditional approach that employs a bottom-up lattice search. Issues that are frequently raised when using clustering technique for the purpose of finding association rules are: (i) the completeness of association rule set, (ii) the support level for the rules generated, and (iii) the confidence level for the rules generated. We present some case studies analyzing the relationships between the SOM approach and the traditional association rule framework, and propose a way to constrain the clustering technique so that the traditional support constraint can be approximated. Throughout our experiments, we have demonstrated how a clustering approach can be used for discovering frequent patterns.

Introduction

With large amounts of data continuously collected and stored, organizations are interested in discovering associations within their databases for different industrial, commercial, or scientific purposes. The discovery of interesting associations can aid the decision-making process and provide the domain with new and invaluable knowledge. Association rule mining is one of the most popular data mining techniques used to discover interesting relationships among data objects present in a database. A large amount of research has gone toward the development of efficient algorithms for association rule mining (Agrawal, Imielinski, & Swami, 1993; Agrawal, Mannila, Srikant, Toivonen, & Verkamo, 1996; Feng, Dillon, Weigana, & Chang, 2003; Park, Chen, & Yu, 1997; Tan, Dillon, Feng, Chang, & Hadzic, 2005; Zaki, 2001; Zaki, Pathasarthy, Ogihara, & Li, 1997). The algorithms developed have different advantages and disadvantages when applied to different domains with varying complexity and data characteristics. Frequent pattern discovery is an essential step in association rule mining. Most of the developed algorithms are a variant of Apriori (Agrawal et al., 1996) and are based on the downward closure lemma concept with the support framework. Besides the fact that the problem is approached differently, commonality that remains in most of the current algorithms is that all possible candidate combinations are first enumerated, and then their frequency is determined by scanning of the transactional database. These two steps, candidate enumeration and testing, are known to be the major bottlenecks in the Apriori-like approaches, which inspired some work towards methods that avoid this performance bottleneck (Han, Pei, & Yin, 2000; Park, Chen, & Yu, 1995). Depending on the aim of the application, rules may be generated from the frequent patterns discovered, and the support and confidence of each rule can be indicated. Rules with high confidence often cover only small fractions of the total number of rules generated, which makes their isolation more challenging and costly. In general, the task of frequent patterns discovery can have problems with complex real-world data, as for a transaction that contains n-items, the space complexity is usually of the order 2^n. To reduce the complexity of the task in such difficult situations, interest arose in the development of algorithms for mining maximal patterns (Bayardo, 1998; Burdick, Calimlim, & Gehrke, 2001; Lin & Kedem, 1998; Zaki & Gouda, 2003) and closed patterns (Pasquier, Bastide, Taouli, & Lakhal, 1999; Pei, Han, & Mao, 2000; Wang, Han, & Pei, 2003; Zaki & Hsiao, 1999). A maximal pattern is a frequent pattern in which no proper superset is frequent, and a closed pattern is a pattern that has no superset with the same support. The main implication behind mining maximal or closed patterns is that the computational cost is greatly reduced without resulting in loss of information. The set of all frequent patterns can be derived from the maximal or closed pattern set obtained. In this study we aim at investigating an alternative method for mining frequent/maximal patterns from a transactional database.

Self-Organizing Map (SOM) (Kohonen, 1990) is a type of neural network that uses the principles of competitive or unsupervised learning. In unsupervised learning there is no information about a desired output, as is the case in supervised learning. This unsupervised learning approach forms abstractions by a topology-preserving mapping of high-dimensional input patterns into a lower-dimensional set of output clusters (Sestito & Dillon. 1994). These clusters correspond to frequently occurring patterns of features among the input data. Due to its simple structure and learning mechanism, SOM has been successfully used in various applications and has proven to be one of the effective clustering techniques (Kohonen, 1990; Deboeck & Kohonen, 1998; Sestito & Dillon, 1994; Visa, Toivonen, Vanharanta, & Back, 2001).

The useful properties of SOM mentioned above have motivated us to investigate whether the method can be applied to the problem of frequent pattern discovery in the association rule framework sense. More specifically, it needs to be determined whether the notion of finding frequent patterns can be interchangeably substituted with the notion of finding clusters of frequently occurring patterns in the data. There is a relationship between the task of separating frequent from infrequent patterns from data and the task of finding clusters in data, as a cluster could represent a particular frequently occurring pattern in the data. A cluster would in this case correspond to a pattern, and hence it would be interesting to see whether a cluster set obtained from a clustering technique can correspond to a set of frequent patterns obtained through the Apriori approach. We want to investigate whether the clustering approach can automatically filter out the infrequent patterns and detect only the frequent ones. In other words the clustering technique can be used to detect frequent patterns in a top-down manner, as opposed to the traditional approach that employs a bottom-up lattice search. Furthermore we would like to find the necessary restrictions or limitations on the clustering technique so that the extracted patterns satisfy the specified support constraints.

Problem Statement

Mining frequent itemsets is a fundamental and essential step in the discovery of association rules. Let $T(n)$ denote a transactional database consisting of n transactions. Each transactional record R from $T(n)$ is made up of a subset of items from the allowed vocabulary of items $V = \{1,2,3...m\}$. An itemset or a pattern refers to any subset of the items contained in vocabulary V. The support of a pattern X is the number of transactional records from $T(n)$ which contain X. A pattern is considered frequent if its support is higher or equal to the pre-specified minimum support (σ). Given a large transactional database and a minimum support threshold (σ), the task of frequent pattern discovery is to discover patterns that occur in at least σ transactions of the database.

Mining Frequent Itemsets using SOM

SOM (Kohonen, 1990) is an unsupervised neural network that effectively creates spatially organized "internal representations" of the features and abstractions detected in the input space. It consists of an input layer and an output layer in the form of a map (see Figure 1). SOM is based on the competition among the cells in the map for the best match against a presented input pattern. Each node in the map has a weight vector associated with it, which are the weights on the links emanating from the input layer to that particular node. When an input pattern is imposed on the network, a node is selected from among all the output nodes as having the best response according to some criterion. This output node is declared the 'winner' and is usually the cell having the smallest Euclidean distance between its weight vector and the presented input vector. The 'winner' and its neighboring cells are then updated to match the presented input pattern more closely. Neighborhood size and the magnitude of update shrink as the training proceeds. After the learning phase, cells that respond in similar manner to the presented input patterns are located close

*Figure 1. SOM consisting of two input nodes and 3 * 3 map*

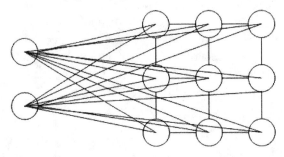

to each other, and so clusters can be formed in the map. Existing similarities in the input space are revealed through the ordered or topology-preserving mapping of high-dimensional input patterns into a lower-dimensional set of output cluster. When used for classification purposes, SOM is commonly integrated with a type of supervised learning in order to assign appropriate class labels to the clusters. After the learning phase has come to completion, the weights on the links could be analyzed in order to represent the learned knowledge in a symbolic form. One such method is used in 'Unsupervised BRAINNE' (Sestito & Dillon, 1994), which extracts a set of symbolic knowledge structures in the form of concepts and concept hierarchies from a trained neural network. A similar method is used in the current work. After the supervised learning is complete, each cluster will have a rule or pattern associated with it, which determines which data objects are covered by that clusters.

It was mentioned that SOM is good at mapping high-dimensional input patterns into a lower-dimensional set of output clusters. As we map higher-dimensional space into a lower-dimensional space, there are only two possibilities. Either the data in lower-dimensional space represents the data from higher-dimensional space in compressed form, or the data in the lower-dimensional space is corrupted because there is not enough resolution (map size) to store the data. Putting mining frequent patterns into the context, we will investigate a relationship between isolating frequent patterns from infrequent patterns and mapping higher-dimensional space into lower-dimensional space. The relationship becomes important when there is a correspondence between the two frameworks. The key to realize such correspondence lies in understanding the way SOM learns without supervision.

The notion of competitive learning hints that the way knowledge is learned by SOM is competitive based on certain criteria. Therefore, with a smaller output space, the level of competition increases. Patterns exposed more frequently to SOM in the training phase are more likely to be learned, while the ones exposed less frequently are more likely to be disregarded. The number of nodes in the output space, width x height, in SOM is normally set less than or equal to 2^n, where n denotes the number of features in the input space—that is, the dimension of input space. The frequently occurring patterns (or rules) will influence the organization of the map to the highest degree, and hence after training the resulting clusters correspond to the most frequently occurring patterns. The patterns that are not covered by any clusters have not occurred often enough to have an impact on the self-organization of the map and are often masked out by frequent patterns.

Input Transformation

A transactional record, R can be represented as a tuple of items from 1 to n number of items, $\{I_1, I_2, ..., I_n\}$. A transactional database T, of size s, consists of many records $\{R_1, ..., R_s\}$. For a record R_i, if an item I_j is a part of the record, then it will have a corresponding value 1, and 0 when the opposite condition occurs. Representing transactional records in this way is suitable for the SOMs input layer.

Training the SOM

SOM needs to be trained with a large set of training data until it reaches a terminating condition. The terminating condition is reached when either the number of training iterations (epochs) has reached its maximum or the mean square error (mse) value has reached its minimum or a pre-specified limit. The mse value should be chosen small enough so that the necessary correlations can be learned. On the other hand it should be large enough to avoid the problem of over-fitting, which results in a decrease of the generalization capability (Sestito & Dillon, 1994).

Cluster Labeling

Once the SOM has been sufficiently trained, the pattern(s) that each output node in the map represents need to be determined. This is achieved by analyzing the weight vectors of each node and determining which input is contributory for that node. We have used the threshold technique adopted from Sestito and Dillon (1994) where an input i is considered contributory 1 to an output node o if the difference between the weight on the link from i to o and the maximum weight component in the weight vector of o is below a pre-specified threshold. Note also that a threshold is chosen, so that if all the weight components in the weight vector of an output node are below this threshold, then none of the inputs are considered contributory. An input is considered inhibitory 0 if the weight is below a pre-specified threshold T_{inh}, which is commonly chosen to be close to zero. The inputs that are not selected, as either of the above are considered as a "don't care" (-1) in the related rule. The output nodes that represent the same patterns are grouped together into a cluster, and those clusters now represent the frequent patterns or rules from the database. In Figure 2, {0,1,0,0,1}, {0,1,1,0,1}, and {0,1,0,1,0} are examples of rules with no "don't cares." {1,1,-1,-1,-1}, {1,0,-1,1,-1}, and {-1,-1,-1,1,-1} are rules with

Figure 2. Extracted rules with and with no "don't cares"

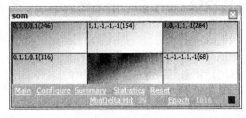

"don't cares." Whenever a rule contains a "don't care" for a particular attribute, it indicates that the input patterns captured by the rule had this particular attribute present as well as absent in many cases. Due to this property rules with "don't cares" produce multiple rules, by considering "don't care" attributes as both contributory and inhibitory. As an example, a rule with two "don't cares" {1,0,-1,1,-1} would produce four rules, {1,0,0,1,0}, {1,0,1,1,0}, {1,0,1,1,1}, and {1,0,0,1,1}.

In some cases the nodes from the map could represent a mixture of instances of topographically adjacent clusters and as such would not have a separate conceptual existence. The rules extracted from nodes of this type should not be taken into account. To determine which nodes' rules we should take or discard, we formulated a means of separating them using a threshold technique. We apply the same principle as a threshold technique for extracting rules described in Sestito and Dillon (1994) and introduce a hit count measure. In Figure 2, the hit count is the value in the bracket, to the right of the extracted rules. The hit count value of each cell in SOM is normalized against the total epoch. The maximum normalized value H_{max} is determined as the fraction of the highest hit count over the number epoch. We take the rules that satisfy:

$$| H_{max} - H_i | < T \tag{1}$$

T is a chosen threshold value with typical value equal to 0.1. Rules that do not satisfy the above equation will be discarded. We continue with candidate counting in the next step. For now all frequent patterns are stored in the frequent patterns set L.

Candidate Counting

In the previous step most frequent patterns were discovered. The next step would be to count each occurrence of the pattern in L and all patterns that form a subset of L or partial subset of L. One of the fastest ways to count the occurrences of a candidate in a database is to use the hash-based approach (Park, et al., 1995, 1997). We can use this technique to do candidate counting by taking the vector elements as the hash-key. For example, the vector {0,1,0,1,0} can uniquely map to integer 10, {0,1,1,0,0} to integer 12, and so on. A rule X {0,1,1,0,0} is a subset of rule Y {1,1,1,0,0}. We will refer to a particular rule r as a partial subset of another rule $r2$, if they have some items in common but r is not a subset of $r2$. For example, rule Z {0,0,1,0,1} is a partial subset of rule Y {1,1,1,0,0}, as $Z \cap Y \neq \{\}$ and $Z \not\subset Y$. Patterns that only form partial subsets will be separately stored in L_{part}. This is to differentiate such rules from the frequent rules set L, since rules that form partial subsets with L might not be frequent. Detecting a pattern as a sub-pattern of any particular pattern can be done by using Boolean AND operation. To check if a pattern S forms a subset of pattern P, the following condition must be satisfied: if $S\ AND\ P = S'$ and $S = S'$ then S is sub-pattern of P. The partial subset is the minimum condition to determine whether a pattern is to be considered or not. We only count the patterns in L, their subsets, and their partial subsets, while ignoring the rest of the patterns.

Frequent Pattern Generation

Frequent pattern generation is an important step in association rule mining. In fact, most of the computation cost is concentrated at this step (Park, et al., 1997). Generation of association rules can be done in a more straightforward manner once all frequent patterns are detected. In this chapter we concentrate on the problem of frequent pattern generation. The downward closure lemma states that if a pattern is frequent, then its sub-pattern must also be frequent. The previous step discovered all the frequent patterns. Furthermore, any subset of the discovered frequent patterns must then be frequent. A frequent itemset is called a maximal frequent itemset if there is no other frequent itemset that is its proper superset. The frequent patterns set L corresponds to the maximal pattern set with some additional frequently occurring patterns. Once the maximal frequent patterns are discovered, all other frequent patterns can be derived. The next step in the pipeline derives the maximal frequent pattern set from all the frequent patterns. The maximal frequent patterns set L_{max} will be generated from L as in Figure 3.

Next, all possible candidates will be enumerated from the set L_{max}. So, rather than enumerating all possible patterns, the proposed approach also generated a smaller number of candidates from the maximal patterns. For example, if {0,1,1,1,0} is one of the maximal patterns, the enumeration in Table 1 is obtained.

Once the complete set of candidates C is generated from each of the maximal patterns previously constructed, the counting can be done by performing the dot product

Figure 3. Generating L_{max}

```
Lmax = L
k = LongestPattern(L)  // start with the
                       // longest pattern
while(k > 0){
foreach(p in Lmax){
  if(Length(p) == k){
      foreach pp in Lmax{
        if(pp != p){ // pp is subset of p
          if(DotProduct(p, pp) == pp)
             remove(pp, Lmax) // pp is removed from L
        }
      }
    }
  }
  k--;
}
```

Table 1. Candidates enumerated from {0,1,1,1,0}

Candidates
{0,0,0,1,0}
{0,0,1,0,0}
{0,0,1,1,0}
{0,1,0,0,0}
{0,1,0,1,0}
{0,1,1,0,0}

Figure 4. Counting candidates

```
foreach(q in C){
  foreach(p in L){
    if(DotProduct(q, p) == q)  // if q 5 p
        q.count = q.count + p.count;
  }
  foreach(pp in L_part){
    if(DotProduct(q, pp) == q) // if q 5 pp
q       .count = q.count + p.count;
  }
}
```

operation between patterns in C and L, and C and L_{part}. In the previous step we have counted the support of each pattern in L as well as patterns in L_{part}. Figure 4 shows how the support count is determined from the enumerated candidates.

The final step is to generate the frequent pattern set (FREQ-PATTERN) from the complete set of candidates C with respect to the minimum support threshold σ. Patterns that have a support ratio lower than σ are pruned from the frequent pattern set. Once this set is generated, association rule generation can be done in a more straightforward manner as in Apriori-based algorithms.

Approximating Support Threshold by Restricting the Map Size

From the above described process, it may occur to the reader that the approach does not avoid the candidate testing bottleneck, as at the end the database is scanned to determine the frequent pattern set. At this stage this is done to make the approach compatible to the results obtained using the traditional approach. The frequent pattern discovery using the traditional approach is parameterized by the support and confidence framework. However, if we are to use a clustering approach like SOM for detecting frequent patterns, support threshold would not be an appropriate measure to use. Rather the method using SOM would be parameterized by the chosen map dimension, which will play a role in the frequency of the discovered patterns. As already mentioned reduction of map size increases the competition between patterns to be projected onto the output space, and hence patterns with low frequency will disappear from the map. On the other hand, the larger the map, the more patterns will be discovered. As a property of SOM is to compress the input space and present the abstraction in a topology-preserving manner, a heuristic to determine the map size will be based on the number of input attributes, the size of the data set, and the frequency that the user is after.

We mentioned previously that the size of output space width x height in SOM is set less than or equal to 2^n, where n denotes the dimension of input space. With n inputs there will be a total of $(2^n - 1)$ possible patterns, and to set the map size equal to 2^n would defeat the purpose of using SOM, as there would be enough resolution to isolate each input pattern into a separate cluster, rather than collecting frequently occurring patterns into clusters. At this early stage we have not as yet obtained the exact formula, but during our investigation it appeared that a good approximation to the support threshold σ would be to set the map size equal to $(\text{size}(Tdb) / \sigma)$, where $\text{size}(Tdb)$ is the number of transactions in Tdb. The reasoning behind this comes from the observation that there should be a relationship between the allowed space for patterns to occur in the input space and the allowed space for them to be projected in the output space. If a set of patterns is to occur n times in a database, then one could assume that there exist a part of the database of size $(\text{size}(Tdb) / (\sigma))$ where all these patterns occur at least once. In the output space the patterns have a chance to either be projected or not, and choosing the map size of $(\text{size}(Tdb)) / (\sigma))$ should only allow enough resolution for those patterns which have occurred σ times in the database. This is only an estimate as the frequency distribution comes into play. However, at this early stage it appeared to be a good indicator for the required map dimension. If some kind of frequency distribution is known beforehand, it definitely should play a role in determining the map size. It should also be noted that other factors come into play for complex databases. This is due to the fact that at a higher support threshold, many more unwanted patterns exist which compete for the allowed space. They are unwanted in the sense that their support is insufficient, but because they still occur frequently, they may have an effect on the self-organization of the map. Through their repeated occurrence the characteristics of these unwanted patterns may be reflected on the part of the map, thereby disallowing space for other wanted patterns. In this case the SOM's learning parameters need to be adjusted so that the competition for the restricted output space is even higher. In other words the self-organization of the map should only be affected by the wanted patterns, and they should win over the output space even if their increase in support over other patterns is only minimal. Note that if we had a very large database, where $(size(Tdb)/ \sigma) > (2^n - 1)$, there would be enough input space to contain all the patterns; and hence to ensure the completeness of results, the output space should be set to $(2^n - 1)$ (divided by a certain threshold, as many patterns are sub-patterns of others).

Results and Discussion

In this section, we present some of our preliminary experimental results that validate the correctness of the proposed technique and indicate some appropriate ways of using SOM for frequent pattern extraction. The section is split into three parts which are exclusive from each other with respect to the set of experiments performed. The aim of the first part is to show how a complete set of frequent patterns can be extracted using SOM. As the first part indicates that the initial patterns detected by

Table 2. Transaction of items, T_1

Transaction	Count
{A,B}	2
{A,C}	2
{A,D}	10
{B,D}	80
{B,E}	40
{C,D}	2
{D,E}	1
{A,C,D}	40
{A,D,E}	25
{B,C,E}	80
{B,C,D,E}	2
{A,B,C,D,E}	5

Table 3. SOM learning parameters

MSE: 1E-04	Mean square error threshold
E: 0.2	Threshold for zero vector
T: 0.1	Threshold
Tinh: 0.05	Threshold for inhibitor input
α: 0.1	Learning rate
Neighbor: (width + height) / 2	Neighbor spread

Table 4. Extracting frequent patterns with SOM

SOM	Frequent Rules (L)
	{A,0,C,D,0} {0,B,C,0,E} {0,B,0,D,0}
	{0,B,0,0,E} {A,0,C,D,0} {A,0,0,D,E} {A,0,0,D,0} {0,B,0,D,0} {0,B,C,0,E}
	{0,B,0,0,E} {0,B,C,0,E} {0,B,0,D,0} {A,B,0,0,0} {A,0,0,D,E} {A,0,0,D,0} {A,0,C,D,0}
	{0,B,0,D,0} {A,B,0,0,0} {0,B,0,D,0} {0,0,0,D,E} {A,0,0,D,E} {A,B,C,D,E} {A,0,0,D,0} {0,B,0,0,E} {0,B,C,0,E} {A,0,C,D,0}

SOM consist of maximal patterns and possibly other patterns with high frequency, in part two we use a simple illustrative example to show how restricting the map size can produce the same maximal patterns as by using the minimum support framework. Finally in part three we use a more complex syntactic data set to compare the maximal patterns obtained using SOM and GenMax algorithm (Zaki & Gouda, 2003). Varying support thresholds were used and the size of the map was adjusted accordingly.

Mining Frequent Patterns

At this stage, we are interested in examining the possibility of using a clustering technique for mining frequent patterns, and as such we do not use complex data sets. Instead, an artificial transactional data set was generated that can be seen in Table 2.

Table 5. L & L_{part} generated from T_1

L	Count
{B,D}	80
{A,C,D}	40
{B,C,E}	80
{B,E}	40
{A,D}	10
{A,C}	2
{C,D}	2

L_{part}	Count
{A,B}	2
{D,E}	1
{A,D,E}	25
{B,C,D,E}	2
{A,B,C,D,E}	5

Table 6. L_{max} generated from L

L_{max}
{B,D}
{A,C,D}
{B,C,E}

The transactions in T_1 are randomly distributed in the database. The frequencies of items are chosen specifically to simulate real-world transactional data. Patterns appear at different frequencies and at different length. The longest pattern has size 5, and so if complete candidates ought to be generated, there will be, 2^5-1, 31 possible combinations.

The SOM was initialized with parameters as suggested in Sestito and Dillon (1994) (see Table 3).

Applying the technique described earlier, frequent rules (patterns) set L was generated as shown on the right side of Table 4. We can see that additional patterns are extracted when the output dimension is increased. The next step is candidate counting, and we describe the counting process for the first example of Table 4. The following rules are obtained with the indicated occurrence count as shown in Table 5.

Next, L_{max} is obtained from L using the technique described in Figure 3 (see Table 6).

Figure 5. Comparison result of FREQ-PATTERN set generated from T_1 using SOM and Apriori

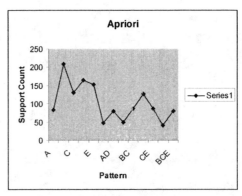

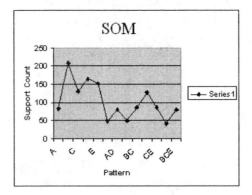

Table 7. Comparison result of FREQ-PATTERN set generated from T_1 using SOM and Apriori

SOM		Apriori	
Rule	**Count**	**Rule**	**Count**
A	84	A	84
B	209	B	209
C	131	C	131
D	165	D	165
E	153	E	153
AC	47	AC	47
AD	80	AD	80
CD	49	CD	49
BC	87	BC	87
BE	127	BE	127
CE	87	CE	87
ACD	40	ACD	40
BCE	80	BCE	80

Finally, by enumerating and counting the patterns from L_{max}, the following FREQ-PATTERN set is obtained. Figure 5 and Table 7 show that the obtained results are equivalent with the Apriori approach.

It is quite interesting to see that the results obtained using SOM and Apriori algorithm are the same. The results show that for this scenario, the notion of discovering clusters of frequent patterns (rules) can be interchangeably substituted with frequent patterns (rules) generation. From the experiments we can see that the ability of SOM to map high-dimensional input patterns into a lower-dimensional set of output clusters forms a desirable property in the context of association rule mining. Such ability traps frequent patterns quite elegantly by limiting the output space. The benefits of this property would be even more noticeable in situations where input dimensions are large, as the costly generation of all the candidate patterns would be avoided.

The result also suggests that there is some kind of relation between the fractions of number of output space over the input space with the support parameter in Apriori algorithm. By tracing back the process of generating frequent patterns set using Apriori algorithm and consulting results in Table 7, it can be seen that such result is obtained by specifying the minimum support σ of about ~0.114-0.16. Working out the Apriori approach, it can be found that *DE* in particular has a support count of 33 in T_1, and it is the next pattern after the pattern with the lowest count in Figure 5, *AC* for 2-itemset. Note that there are in total 289 numbers of records in T_1 that validate the figure above, $\sigma_{DE} = 33/289 = 0.114$ and $\sigma_{AC} = 47/289 = 0.16$. Following that point, we could agree that σ must therefore lie in between σ_{DE} and σ_{AC}. This is very close to the fraction of the dimension of the SOM chosen, 2×2, over the input space, 2^5: 4/32 = 0.125.

Mining Maximal Patterns

For the purpose of this experiment, we have created an example transactional database shown in Table 8. The transactional database ($T(n=7)$) consists of six items (*A B C D E F*). The transactions are displayed on the left of Table 8, and the set of all frequent and maximal patterns for the support thresholds of two and three are shown on the right.

When using the SOM for extracting maximal patterns, the only adjustment is that once the rules are extracted using the threshold technique previously described, we count the occurrences of the extracted rules (patterns) and delete any subsets of an already determined frequent pattern. This needs to be done in order to make the results compatible to maximal patterns obtained using the minimum support framework. When wanting to demonstrate the SOM's capability of extracting the maximal patterns for the simple example above, the map size has to be set very small in order to demonstrate the capability of projecting a larger input space onto a smaller output space. If we choose the map size too large (e.g., 6 * 6), it would defeat the

Table 8. Set of frequent and maximal patterns for example transactional database

Transaction	MinSup = 2		Itemset size	MinSup = 3	
	Frequent Itemsets	Maximal Itemsets		Frequent Itemsets	Maximal Itemsets
ABCF	A, B, C, D, F		1	A, B, C, D, F	
BCDF	AB, AC, AF, BF, BC, BD, BF, CD, CF, DF		2	AB, AC, AF, BC, BD, BF, CD, CF, DF	DF
ACF	ABC, ABF, BCD, BCF, CDF, ACF, BDF		3	ABC, ABF, BCD, BCF	BCD
ABCDF	ABCF, BCDF	ABCF, BCDF	4	ABCF	ABCF
DF					
BCD					
ABCEF					

Figure 6. SOM after training on Tdb from Table 8 (mimicking support = 2)

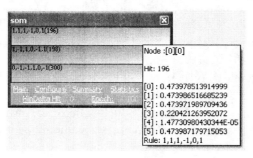

Figure 7. SOM after training on Tdb from Table 8 (mimicking support = 3)

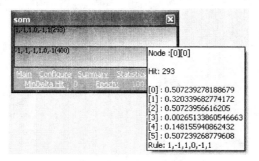

purpose of demonstration. There would be enough resolution to isolate each input pattern into a separate cluster, as there are 31 (i.e., 2^n-1) possible combinations of attributes in this example. The example database in Table 8 is very simple and hence we have chosen to use the exact heuristic previously described (size(Tdb)/ σ). The state of the map after training on Tdb from Table 8 when the map size was restricted to mimic support 2 and 3 is shown in Figures 6 and 7 respectively. On the right of the figures, the weight vector of the first node is displayed. After the extraction of rules and deletion of subsets from frequent patterns, maximal patterns identical to the ones displayed in Table 8 were obtained. This simple example demonstrated the generalization capability of SOM as the information from the input space is compressed onto lower dimensional output space. It is a desirable property for the frequent pattern extraction problem as the infrequent patterns were automatically filtered out without going through the process of candidate generation.

Results Comparison with GenMax

For this experiment we have created a dataset consisting of 10 items and 100 transactions where the frequency is randomly distributed. The aim is to compare the similarity of the maximal pattern sets obtained using GenMax algorithm (Zaki & Gouda, 2003) and using the proposed technique for varying support thresholds. We have chosen support of 2, 3, 5, 7, and 10 for GenMax and SOM's map size of (8*8), (8*7), (7*6), (6*6), and (6*5) respectively. The chosen map size is an approximation using the heuristic described earlier. Note that extra resolution was added to (size(Tdb) / σ) heuristic, because in reality a cluster could cover multiple nodes from the map, and extra resolution is needed to allow for self-organization to occur in the map. The frequency distribution will influence which patterns are easily projected while others could be missed. Furthermore, for increasing support the learning parameters had to be adjusted in a way so that it becomes highly competitive in that confined space. The reason for the necessary increase in competition was discussed earlier in the chapter. Table 9 displays the learning parameters used for varying support thresholds. Once the rules are extracted using the threshold technique previously described, we count the occurrences of the extracted rules (patterns) and delete

Table 9. Learning parameters used for varying support thresholds

	$\sigma = 2$	$\sigma = 3$	$\sigma = 5$	$\sigma = 7$	$\sigma = 10$
Map size	8 * 8	7* 7	7 * 6	6 * 6	6 * 5
α	0.1	0.4	0.6	0.7	0.9
T	0.2	0.2	0.2	0.2	0.2
T_{inh}	0.05	0.03	0.02	0.01	0.01
Neighborhood	4	3	2	2	2
Epochs	1000	1000	600	600	150
E	0.2	0.2	0.2	0.2	0.2
MSE	0.0001	0.0001	0.0001	0.0001	0.0001

Figure 8. The difference in the number of maximal patterns detected by the two techniques

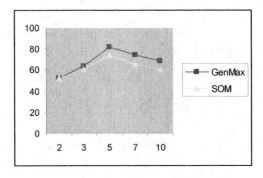

any subsets of an already determined frequent pattern. This results in the set of maximal patterns.

Figure 8 shows the difference in the number of maximal patterns obtained using the two techniques for varying support thresholds. When support was set to 2, the maximal patterns obtained were identical, whereas once support was increased, a small number of patterns were missed by SOM. Note that we performed other experiments where the map size was slightly increased for higher support thresholds, and as expected the whole set of maximal patterns was detected. However, in this section we aim at indicating some main issues and problems that occur when trying to mimic the support threshold by restricting the map size. Our initial heuristic appears promising, but as the support is increased, some patterns are missed. For higher support thresholds one would intend to shrink the map size so that only highly occurring patterns are projected, but for the reasons described earlier, this will not suffice. Other learning parameters also need adjustment so that it becomes highly competitive in that confined space. Generally speaking we want to adjust all the SOM parameters in such way so that the self-organization and projection that occurs in the map is mainly (or only) affected by the frequent patterns. Only if a certain pattern in the database occurs often enough (at wanted support) should the map be affected. Throughout our experimentation we have experienced that certain parameters may cause the map to converge in less time, and similar results could be obtained through the change in different learning parameters. For example at $\sigma = 10$, similar results were obtained by training the map for longer time using a smaller learning rate. As sufficient results were obtained only after 150 epochs, this indicates that there exist different combinations of learning parameter values that will produce the same results, and hence for highly complex data, close estimates could be obtained after short training. Due to the learning parameters of SOM being dependent on each other, the exact guidelines for mimicking support cannot be provided at this early stage of research into frequent pattern discovery using SOM. Here we have provided some initial guidelines for using SOM for frequent pattern extraction, and the experiments demonstrated that SOM is in fact able to extract frequent/maximal patterns. There will be more investigation needed into finding the exact parameters so that the total set of maximal patterns would be guaranteed. However, the authors believe that if SOM is to be used efficiently for frequent pattern discovery, the support threshold would be replaced by a threshold where major decisive factors are the output space size and the intensity of competition that occurs within that limited space. In other words the traditional and SOM technique for frequent pattern discovery are parameterized differently, and whereas support and confidence framework parameterize the traditional approach, output space dimension and intensity of competition parameterize the SOM approach.

Conclusion and Future Work

This study has investigated an alternative method for frequent pattern extraction by using the Self-Organizing Map. Throughout the experiments we have demonstrated how a clustering technique can be used to automatically filter out the infrequent patterns. Frequent patterns are detected in a top-down manner, as opposed to a traditional approach that employs a bottom-up lattice search. Furthermore the SOM approach is parameterized by the size of the output dimension as opposed to the support threshold in the traditional approach. Some immediate challenges that occur when mimicking the support threshold by restricting the output size were indicated. Many factors come into play when the support threshold is increased, and a more thorough investigation on the adjustment of SOM's learning parameters with respect to support threshold is left as future work. At this stage, we are quite satisfied with the validity and correctness of the proposed approach when applied to simple data sets. It shows that SOM has some desirable and promising properties for the problem of frequent pattern mining. It would be interesting to explore more on the efficiency of the technique in comparison to existing Apriori algorithms when applied to real-world data with higher complexity. Adjusting the learning parameters of SOM in a certain way can provide a sufficient solution in much less training time. In very complex data sets where the traditional approach using the support framework fails due to enormous amount of candidates that need to be generated and tested, a clustering approach to frequent pattern extraction may need to be adapted where the support threshold will be replaced by the output space and intensity of competition thresholds. Besides the fact that few patterns could be missed, the method would provide a good approximation in cases where the traditional bottom-up approaches fail due to inherent complexity.

References

Agrawal, R., Imielinski, T., & Swami, A. (1993). Mining association rules between sets of items in large databases. In *Proceedings of ACM SIGMOD*, Washington, DC (pp. 207-216).

Agrawal, R., Mannila, H., Srikant, H., Toivonen, R., & Verkamo, A.I. (1996). Fast discovery of association rules. *Advances in knowledge discovery and data mining* (pp. 307-328). AAAI Press.

Bayardo, R.J. (1998, June). Efficiently mining long patterns from databases. In *Proceedings of the ACM SIGMOD Conference on Management of Data*.

Burdick, D., Calimlim, M., & Gehrke, J. (2001, April). MAFIA: A maximal frequent itemset algorithm for transactional databases. In *Proceedings of the International Conference on Data Engineering*.

Deboeck, G., & Kohonen, T. (1998). *Visual explorations in finance using self-organizing maps*. London: Springer-Verlag.

Feng, L., Dillon, T.S., Weigana, H., & Chang, E. (2003). An XML-enabled association rule framework. In *Proceedings of DEXA'03* (pp. 88-97). Prague.

Han, J., Pei, J., & Yin, Y. (2000, May). Mining frequent patterns without candidate generation. In *Proceedings of the ACM SIGMOD Conference on Management of Data*, Dallas, TX.

Kohonen, T. (1990). The self-organizing map. In *Proceedings of the IEEE*, 78(9), 1464-1480.

Lin, D., & Kedem, Z.M. (1998, March). Pincer-search: A new algorithm for discovering the maximum frequent set. In *Proceedings of the 6th International Conference on Extending Database Technology* (pp. 105-119).

Park, J.S., Chen, M.S., & Yu, P.S. (1995). An effective hash-based algorithm for mining association rules. In *Proceedings of the 1995 ACM-SIGMOD International Conference on Management of Data (SIGMOD'95)*, San Jose, CA (pp. 175-186).

Park, J.S., Chen, M.S., & Yu, P.S. (1997). Using a hash-based method with transaction trimming for mining association rules. *IEEE Transactions on Knowledge and Data Engineering, 9*(5), 813-826.

Pasquier, N., Bastide, Y., Taouil, R., & Lakhal, L. (1999, January) Discovering frequent closed itemsets for association rules. In *Proceedings of the 7th International Conference On Database Theory (ICDT'99)*, Jerusalem, Israel (pp. 398-416).

Pei, J., Han, J., & Mao, R. (2000, May). Closet: An efficient algorithm for mining frequent closed itemsets. In *Proceedings of the SIGMOD International Workshop on Data Mining and Knowledge Discovery*.

Sestito, S., & Dillon, T.S. (1994). *Automated knowledge acquisition*. Sydney: Prentice-Hall of Australia.

Tan, H., Dillon, T.S., Feng, L., Chang, E., & Hadzic, F. (2005). X3-Miner: Mining patterns from XML database. In *Proceedings of Data Mining 2005*, Skiathos, Greece.

Visa, A., Toivonen, J., Vanharanta, H., & Back, B. (2001, January 3-6). Prototype matching—finding meaning in the books of the bible. In J. Ralph & H. Sprague (Eds.), *Proceedings of the 34th Annual Hawaii International Conference on System Sciences (HICSS-34)*, HI.

Wang, J., Han, J., & Pei, J. (2003, August). CLOSET+: Searching for the best strategies for mining frequent closed itemsets. In *Proceedings of the 2003 ACM SIGKDD International Conference on Knowledge Discovery and Data Mining (KDD'03)*, Washington, DC.

Zaki, M.J. (2002). Efficiently mining frequent trees in a forest. In *Proceedings of SIGKDD '02*, Edmonton, Alberta, Canada.

Zaki, M.J., & Gouda, K. (2003). Fast vertical mining using diffsets. In *Proceedings of the 9th ACM SIGKDD International Conference on Knowledge Discovery and Data Mining (KDD-2003)* (pp. 326-335).

Zaki, M.J., & Hsiao, C.-J. (1999, October). *CHARM: An efficient algorithm for closed association rule mining* (Tech. Rep. No. 99-10). Computer Science Department, Rensselaer Polytechnic Institute, USA.

Zaki, M.J., Parthasarathy, S., Ogihara, M., & Li, W. (1997, August). New algorithms for fast discovery of association rules. In *Proceedings of the 3rd International Conference on Knowledge Discovery in Databases* (pp. 283-286).

Chapter VI

An Efficient Compression Technique for Vertical Mining Methods

Mafruz Zaman Ashrafi, Monash University, Australia

David Taniar, Monash University, Australia

Kate Smith, Deakin University, Australia

Abstract

Association rule mining is one of the most widely used data mining techniques. To achieve a better performance, many efficient algorithms have been proposed. Despite these efforts, many of these algorithms require a large amount of main memory to enumerate all frequent itemsets, especially when the dataset is large or the user-specified support is low. Thus, it becomes apparent that we need to have an efficient main memory handling technique, which allows association rule mining algorithms to handle larger datasets in the main memory. To achieve this goal, in this chapter we propose an algorithm for vertical association rule mining that compresses a vertical dataset in an efficient manner, using bit vectors. Our performance evaluations show that the compression ratio attained by our proposed technique is better than those of the other well-known techniques.

Introduction

One of the most widely used data mining techniques is association rule mining. Association rule mining algorithms iterate a dataset many times to enumerate frequent itemsets that exist in the transactions of a given dataset. However, a dataset scan is considered as an I/O exhaustive process (Zaki, 1999). A single scan can take a significant amount of time when it is large. Therefore, the performance degrades if the mining algorithm requires multiple dataset scans.

Many algorithms have been proposed to reduce the cost of dataset scan (Zaki, 1999; Zaki, 2003; El-Hajj & Zaiane, 2003; Han, Pei, & Yin, 2000; Doug, Manuel, & Johannes, 2001; Shenoy et al., 2000). These algorithms use various techniques, such as compression (Han et al., 2000), intersection (Zaki, 1999, 2003; Doug et al., 2000; Shenoy et al., 2000), and indexing (El-Hajj & Zaiane, 2003), to name a few. In spite of these efficient techniques, they still incur a common problem: all of these algorithms are inherently dependent on the amount of main memory (Geothals, 2003). Since the size of the main memory is limited, when the dataset is large and/or the support is low, the main memory size required by these algorithms never seems to be enough. Consequently, it is not surprising that these algorithms are unable to finish the mining task, or have to downgrade the performance significantly (Geothals, 2003).

Since main memory plays a significant role in association rule mining performance, in recent years several novel techniques have been proposed (Zaki, 2003; El-Hajj & Zaiane, 2003; Han et al., 2000; Doug et al., 2000; Shenoy et al., 2000) in order to efficiently use main memory. These techniques generally cut down the dataset size, so that the mining algorithms will be able to finish the mining task on bigger datasets, or with a low support.

We are motivated by the abovementioned fact that main memory is an important resource and, to improve performance, we need to use it in an efficient way without exceeding its capacity. To enhance main memory capacity, in this chapter we propose an algorithm that uses a bit-oriented approach to compress vertical tid dataset. The proposed technique keeps track of the differences between two tids and converts the differences into a bit format; finally, it stores these bits into a bit vector in an efficient way, so the resultant bit vector has only a few unused bits.

The important outcome of this method is that the proposed technique is not biased, which means that it does not depend on a particular dataset characteristic (i.e., dense or sparse) or the user-specified support. Rather, it has the ability to compress the original dataset regardless of dataset size, type, or user-specified support. Our performance evaluation also shows that it achieves a good compression ratio in all scenarios. Therefore, it is able to keep large datasets and allows the mining algorithms to perform mining tasks on such datasets.

The rest of this chapter is organized as follows. At first, we discuss the background of association mining. The reason that we need efficient main memory is then described. Then we present our proposed efficient main memory compression algorithm. The proposed method uses a bit-oriented approach to compress vertical tid dataset. It keeps track of differences between two tids and converts the differences into a bit format, and finally, stores these bits into a bit vector in an efficient way, so the resultant bit vector has only a few unused bits. The important outcome of this method is that the proposed technique is not biased, which means that it does not depend on particular dataset characteristics (i.e., dense or sparse) or the user-specified support. Rather, it has the ability to compress the original dataset regardless of dataset size, type, or user-specified support. Then, we present the performance evaluation and comparison, followed by a discussion of the proposed algorithm. And finally, we present the summary.

Background

Association rule mining can be stated as follows: Let $I=\{I1, I2, \dots, Im\}$ be a set of distinct attributes, also called literals. Let D be the database of transactions, where each transaction T has a set of items such that $T \subseteq I$, and unique identifier (tid). The set of items also known as itemset, and the number of items in an itemset is called the length of an itemset. The support of an itemset X is the number of transactions occurring as a subset. An itemset is frequent if the itemset has user-specific support. An association rule is an implication of the form $X \Rightarrow Y$, where $X \subseteq I, Y \subseteq I$ are itemsets, and $X \cap Y = \varphi$. Here, X is called antecedent, and Y consequent. The rule $X \Rightarrow Y$ has *support s* in transaction set D, if and only if $s\%$ of transactions in D contains $X \cup Y$ and holds with *confidence c* in transaction set D, if and only if $c\%$ of transactions in D that contains X also contains Y.

An association rule mining algorithm discover rules in two different phases. In the first phase, it generates all frequent itemsets. An itemset is considered to be frequent if all items of that set collectively occur in the dataset for a specific number of times defined by the user. This user-specified threshold value is known as support. In the second and final phases, it discovers rules from the frequent itemsets generated by the first phase. Since an association rule can be expressed in $A \rightarrow B$ where A is antecedent itemset and B is the consequence itemset and $A \cup B$ is the frequent itemset, hence to generate the rules, association rule mining algorithms place the subset of each frequent itemset in the antecedent and consequence in an appropriate manner so that the union of the antecedent and consequence itemset becomes the frequent itemset. To measure the strength of a rule, it uses another user-specified value known as confidence, which is the percentage of the antecedent itemsets that collectively occur with the consequence itemset.

The frequent itemset generated by the first phase is used in the second phase to generate association rules. Therefore, all association rule mining algorithms focus on how to improve the performance of the first phase (Zaki, 1999; Zaki, 2003; El-Hajj & Zaiane, 2003; Han et al., 2000; Doug et al., 2001; Shenoy et al., 2000); that is, how to enumerate frequent itemsets. However, generating all frequent itemsets not only requires massive computation, but also accumulates a huge main memory. For example, if a given dataset has n number of items, then theoretically there are 2n numbers of potential frequent itemsets and, to enumerate these itemsets, efficient methods are required to traverse all search spaces (Zaki, 1999). In addition, holding all intermediate itemsets also consumes a huge amount of main memory.

Search Technique

Association rules are generated from frequent itemsets. However, enumerating all frequent itemsets is computationally expensive. For example, if a transaction of a database contains 30 different items, one can generate up to 230 itemsets. To mitigate the enumeration problem, we found two basic searching approaches in the data mining literature. The first approach uses breadth-first searching techniques that search through the dataset iteratively by generating the candidate itemsets. It works efficiently when the user-specified support threshold is high. On the other hand, the performance downgrades drastically when the support is low.

The second approach uses depth-first searching techniques to enumerate frequent itemsets. This search technique performs better, especially when the user-specified support threshold is low, or if the dataset is dense (i.e., items frequently occur in transactions). For example, Éclat (Zaki, 1999) determines the support of k-itemsets by intersecting the tidlists (i.e., Transaction ID) of the lexicographically first two (k-1) length subsets that share a common prefix. However, this approach may run out of main memory when there are large numbers of transactions.

Dataset Layout

Transactional datasets used in the association rule mining can be divided into two different layouts, such as horizontal and vertical. Let us now discuss the details of those layouts.

Horizontal Layout

In the horizontal layout, each row has a transaction ID (tid) followed by the items that appeared in that transaction as depicted in Figure 1. Most association rule mining algorithms (Agrawal, Imielinski, & Swami, 1993; Agrawal & Srikant, 1994; Klemettinen, 1994; Han et al., 2000; El-Hajj & Zaïane, 2003; Brin, 1997; Savasere 1995) use this layout to generate frequent itemsets. The main advantage of this layout is that the mining algorithms can take advantage of skipping the rows that do not have any frequent itemsets in the previous iterations. For example, we are interested to find all frequent itemsets from the dataset shown at Figure 1. Suppose at a given user-specified support constraint, items such as 'rice', 'soap', and 'toy' turn out to be infrequent after the first iteration. Then, after the first iteration, all mining algorithms use this dataset layout able to skip transaction #11 because that contains only those three items. Furthermore, one can also find many identical rows when the dataset is loaded in the main memory, and subsequently it reduces the dataset size as well as the frequent itemset generating cost. For example, transactions #5 and #10 shown in the dataset plotted in Figure 1 are identical; thus, we can reduce the frequent itemset enumeration cost if these transactions are processed at once during the support enumeration.

Although the horizontal layout has the above benefits, this approach suffers major problems because one cannot perform an intersection between different items of the dataset. In fact, algorithms that use this layout often read many items that are considered as infrequent after the first iteration (El-Hajj & Zaiane, 2003). For example, at a given user-specified support constraint, ≥ 3 items such as 'toothpaste' and 'pasta' turn out to be infrequent. Despite these items being infrequent at first iteration, the mining algorithms that use this dataset layout are unable to ignore those transactions where these items appeared because the other items of those transactions are frequent. Subsequently, a significant amount of time could be spent reading these useless infrequent items.

Figure 1. Horizontal dataset layout

Transaction #	Item Purchased
1	bread, milk, toothpaste
2	bread, cheese, milk,
3	cereal, coffee, cheese, milk
4	beef, coffee, milk
5	bread, sugar, tea
6	milk, potatoes, sugar
7	cheese, tea
8	bread, coffee, cheese, milk, pasta, sugar
9	beef, coffee, pasta
10	bread, sugar, tea
11	rice, soap, toy
12	battery, beef, potatoes, rice

Vertical Layout

The vertical dataset (Zaki, 1999, 2003; Shenoy et al., 2000; Doug et al., 2001) layout can further be divided into two different types such as: vertical tid and vertical bit vector as shown in Figures 2(a) and 2(b). In the former approach, each row has an item followed by all transactions # where that item appeared. The main benefit of vertical tid is that it allows intersect, thereby enabling us to ignore all infrequent items/itemsets. For example, suppose at a given user-specified support constraint, ≥ 3 items such as 'toothpaste' and 'pasta' turn out as infrequent after the first iteration. Since all mining algorithms use this layout and employ intersect to enumerate the support of an itemset, there is never a need to read any useless infrequent items in a subsequent iteration. The latter approach uses a bit that is 0 or 1 to represent the whole dataset as shown in the Figure 2(a). In other words, it holds the whole dataset

Figure 2. Vertical dataset layout: (a) vertical tidset and (b) vertical bit vector

Item	Transaction #
bread	1, 2, 5, 8, 10
battery	12
beef	4, 9, 12
cheese	2, 3, 7, 8
cereal	3
coffee	3, 4, 8, 9
milk	1, 2, 3, 4, 6, 8
pasta	8, 9
potatoes	6, 12
rice	11, 12
soap	11
sugar	5, 6, 8, 10
tea	5, 7, 10
toothpaste	1
toy	11

(a)

Item	Transaction #
bread	1 1 0 0 1 0 0 1 0 1 0 0
battery	0 0 0 0 0 0 0 0 0 0 0 1
beef	0 0 0 1 0 0 0 0 1 0 0 1
cheese	0 1 1 0 0 0 1 1 0 0 0 0
cereal	0 0 1 0 0 0 0 0 0 0 0 0
coffee	0 0 1 1 0 0 0 1 1 0 0 0
milk	1 1 1 1 0 1 0 1 0 0 0 0
pasta	0 0 0 0 0 0 0 1 1 0 0 0
potatoes	0 0 0 0 0 1 0 0 0 0 0 1
rice	0 0 0 0 0 0 0 0 0 0 1 1
soap	0 0 0 0 0 0 0 0 0 0 1 0
sugar	0 0 0 0 1 1 0 1 0 1 0 0
tea	0 0 0 0 1 0 1 0 0 1 0 0
toothpaste	1 0 0 0 0 0 0 0 0 0 0 0
toy	0 0 0 0 0 0 0 0 0 0 1 0

(b)

in a bit vector. Each distinct item of a dataset has n number of index, and each of the index positions is set at either '0' or '1'. If an item appears in the transaction, then the corresponding index position of that item is set '1' or otherwise '0'. Since in the dense dataset every distinct item appears very frequently, the vertical bit vector is able to compress the whole dataset significantly. However, it is unable to compress the sparse dataset because in a sparse dataset, items appear in the transaction only after a long interval.

Why Main Memory is an Issue

Performance improvement of the frequent itemset mining method can normally be attained in two ways, including the use of efficient mining techniques (Han et al., 2000; Zaki, 1999; Zaki & Gouda, 2003; El-Hajj & Zaïane, 2002) and efficient main memory utilization (Geothals, 2003). However, if during the mining task, the algorithm exceeds the main memory limit, the mining process will take a long time regardless of how efficient the mining technique is. In other words, efficient mining techniques will be efficient if, and only if, there is an abundant space in the main memory, so that the mining process will not exceed the main memory limit. For example, Apriori uses an efficient data structure such as hash tree or tier to store all intermediate candidate itemsets in the main memory and to extract exact support of the frequent itemset of the next iteration. However, when the length of frequent itemsets is large, then despite these efficient dataset structures, Apriori is unable to accommodate intermediate frequent itemsets in the main memory. For example, if the length of a current candidate itemset is 30, this implies that there are more than 536.8 million subset frequent itemsets; the storage of these frequent itemsets and their corresponding support in the main memory by employing a hash tree requires more than 4 GB main memory space.1 Since finding frequent itemsets of this length (30) from telecommunication and census dataset is not uncommon (Zaki & Gouda, 2003), Apriori is therefore often unable to enumerate all frequent itemsets from such a dataset.

In recognition of this drawback of Apriori, in recent years several innovative techniques have been proposed (Shenoy et al., 2000; Han et al., 2000; Zaki, 1999, 2003) in order to efficiently use main memory. These techniques compress and cut down the dataset size, so that the mining algorithms will be able to finish the mining task on bigger datasets or with a low support. For simplicity, we can categorize these existing compression techniques used in frequent itemset mining into three groups: (i) vertical compression (Zaki, 1999, 2003); (ii) horizontal compression (Han et al., 2000); and (iii) vertical tid compression (Shenoy et al., 2000).

Vertical Compression

This uses a vertical bit vector to represent the presence and absence of an item in the dataset, and adopts a lossless compression. For example, VIPER introduces a novel compression technique known as skinning based on the Golomb encoding scheme (Shenoy et al., 2000). The skinning process divides the run of 0s and the run of 1s divided into groups of size $W0$ and $W1$ respectively, where W is the weight. Each of the full groups is represented in the encoded bit vector as a single 'weight' bit set to 1. The last partial group is represented by a count field that stores the binary equivalent of the remaining length. However, it achieves an order magnitude compression ratio over the vertical tid-based approach in a best-case scenario, but fails to compress; rather, it causes expansion when the user-specified support is less then 0.02% (Zaki, 2003).

Figure 3. (a) Transaction dataset; (b) an example of FP-tree

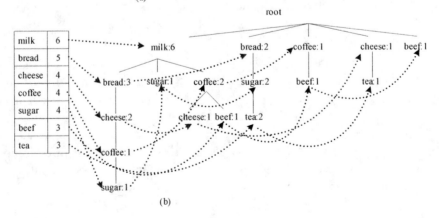

Transaction #	Item Purchased
1	bread, milk, toothpaste
2	bread, cheese, milk,
3	cereal, coffee, cheese, milk
4	beef, coffee, milk
5	bread, sugar, tea
6	milk, potatoes, sugar
7	cheese, tea
8	bread, coffee, cheese, milk, pasta, sugar
9	beef, coffee, pasta
10	bread, sugar, tea
11	rice, soap, toy
12	battery, beef, potatoes, rice

(a)

(b)

Horizontal Compression

A tree-based data structure can be used to compress a horizontal dataset. For example, the FP-tree aims to compress the horizontal dataset into a compact FP-tree structure. At the first dataset scan, it discovers all frequent 1-itemsets, and then during the second dataset scan, it discards all frequent 1-itemsets and constructs the FP-tree. All items in the FP-tree are ordered in descending order based on their support frequency as shown in Figure 3. Since most occurring items are close to the root of the FP-tree, it is presumed that the FP-tree will be able to keep the dataset as condensed as possible (Geothals, 2003). The hypothesis behind this is quite simple: *items that occur most often in a dataset often form the longest frequent itemsets; therefore, keeping them closer to the root minimizes the number of branches in the FP-tree.* Finally, it generates all frequent itemsets using this compressed FP-tree structure. Consequently, this not only solves the multiple dataset scan problem, but it is also able to generate support of frequent itemsets without any intermediate candidate itemset.

Although the above technique is able to compress the dataset when most of the transactions have the same prefix items, the problem with this approach is the amount of main memory needed to hold the entire compact FP-tree as shown in Figure 3. In fact, the size of the FP-tree often becomes massive if the number of attributes after the first iteration is large. In addition, it causes expansion rather than compression, if the dataset is sparse (El-Hajj & Zaiane, 2003). Thus, the inability to hold the entire FP-tree structure in the main memory subsequently affects its performance. Alternatively, in order to perform a mining task using the above technique, one can think of the prefix B++ tree technique. Indeed, such a technique can hold the FP-tree, but involves secondary disk access, and subsequently increases the I/O cost and therefore is not suitable in many cases (El-Hajj & Zaiane, 2003). As a result, it achieves and retains performance improvement only when the user-specified support is high or the dataset is small.

Vertical tid Compression

The vertical tid dataset stores only those tids of items that are frequent after the first iteration, thus enabling the elimination of those items that are unable to generate frequent itemsets. During support enumeration, it uses a vertical dataset layout and intersects tids. For example, the éclat algorithm intersects the tidset of the current level and finds common tids among different items, then uses the tidset to find the support of frequent itemsets in the next level. Since at every level this method intersects the tids of those items that are common, the number of intermediate tidsets becomes very large, especially in a dense dataset. To overcome this drawback, as well as to further compress the dense dataset, an alternative approach using diffset (Zaki, 2003) has been proposed. The diffset stores only those tids of a particular item where that item is absent, rather the entire tid where that itemset appears. And subsequently, it gains a good compression ratio if the user-specified support is greater than 50%. However, when the support is low—that is, less than 50%—the diffset technique may not be able to compress the dataset, because the number of diffsets is larger than the actual tids (i.e., number of times each of the items occurs in the transaction). Regardless of above optimization technique, both éclat and déclat algorithms need to store the dataset (i.e., tidset or diffset) in the main memory (Geothals, 2003), thus paying off significantly if the vertical dataset exceeds the main memory capacity.

Since all of the abovementioned compression techniques heavily depend on user-specified support and/or dataset characteristics, these techniques often do not allow us to enhance main memory utilization. However, from the above discussion, it is apparent that main memory is one of the key resources and all frequent itemset generation methods are indeed main memory bound. Due to limited main memory capacity, the frequent itemset mining algorithms often experience a performance bottleneck, particularly when performing the mining task on a large dataset. It is impossible to improve performance of frequent itemset mining methods without enhancing the main memory utilization. Thus, the problem can be expressed as: how to enhance main memory utilization to improve the performance of the frequent itemset mining methods.

From the above discussions, it is clear that main memory is one of the key resources to improve performance of association rule mining. However, due to a limited main memory capacity, the mining algorithms experience a performance bottleneck particularly when performing the mining task on a large dataset. To enhance main memory capacity, in this chapter we propose an algorithm that uses a bit-oriented approach to compress a vertical tid dataset. The proposed technique keeps track of the difference between two tids and converts the differences into a bit format, and finally, stores these bits into a bit vector in an efficient way, so the resultant bit vector has only a few unused bits.

The Proposed Technique

To increase the performance of association rule mining, it is necessary to exploit main memory efficiently without exceeding its capacity; otherwise the performance will be affected regardless of different efficient techniques. In order to achieve this goal, in this section we introduce an efficient main memory enhancement technique known as dif-bits. The proposed technique uses a vertical dataset layout to compress the dataset because it allows us to perform an intersection between itemsets in order to find the support of all frequent itemsets. As mentioned above, we can represent the vertical dataset in two different ways: (i) vertical bitmap, and (ii) vertical tidset. Let us first analyze each of the vertical dataset representations and compute the amount of main memory needed by them in order to observe the drawbacks of these techniques, and subsequently find every means of enhancing the main memory utilization for vertical mining methods.

The vertical bitmaps vector needs to register both the absence and presence of an item in a transaction; it will reduce the dataset size when the dataset is dense or the user-specified support is high. In other words, if all items of the dataset occur many times, that is, if the bitmap vector has more '1's than '0's, subsequently the size of the vertical bitmaps is smaller than the dataset size. Conversely, if it has more '0's than '1's when the dataset is sparse or user-specified support is low, the size of the vertical bitmaps will exceed the original dataset size. The total number of bits we require to retain the whole dataset in the main memory can be calculated using the following formulas:

$$I = \sum_{1}^{n} n_1 + \sum_{1}^{n} n_0 \tag{1}$$

$$T_{BV} = \sum_{1}^{N} I \tag{2}$$

where I is an item, $n1$ and $n0$ are the number of transactions, item I is present and absent, and T is the total number of bits we need to hold N number of items in the main memory.

The vertical tids is an alternative representation of vertical bit vectors. Each item of this representation has a list, consisting of all transaction IDs where that item appears. Each item only represents the transaction ID where it appears, and perhaps needs less memory compared to vertical bit vectors when dataset is sparse and/or when the user specified support is low. However, this representation becomes more expensive in terms of space if user-specified support is more than 3.33%, because each of the tid stores in a list (i.e., transaction number where it appears) of a particular item as a positive integer. The most common representation of a positive integer is a string of bits consisting of 32 bits (i.e., integers in most architectures require 32 bits). On the other hand, when support is 3.33%, it implies that every item in the bit vector will have a true bit on average after every 32-bits interval. Thus any support greater than 3.33% always implies that every item in the bit vector will have true bit less than 32-bit intervals. In addition, more main memory spaces are needed if the dataset has more transactions than the highest integer representation of a 32-bit architecture. The total number of bits needed to hold vertical tids in main memory can be computed using the following formulas:

$$I = n * 32 \tag{3}$$

$$T_{TID} = \sum_{1}^{N} I \tag{4}$$

where I is the item and TTID is the total number of bits we need to hold all N number of items in the main memory.

Observation

The vertical mining methods keep initial tidset or diffset datasets in the main memory where each item is associated with a corresponding tidset/diffset. Since elements of tidset/diffset are stored as integers, 32 bits are needed to represent where an item appears regardless of the number of transactions that that particular dataset has. For example, if a dataset has 10 million transactions, and in order to hold each occurrence of an item to its corresponding tidset or diffset, 32 bits are needed. On the contrary, if the dataset has only 100,000 transactions, then to hold the tidset/diffset of the same item, the same number of bits are still needed to represent where that appeared.

However, when the dataset is small, one can reduce a significant amount of space from the tidset or diffset of an item, if bits are used instead of an integer to represent where that item appeared. The rationale behind this is very simple: if the size of the dataset is small, this implies that the total number of transactions of that dataset is also less. On the other hand, if the elements of tidset or diffset of an item of that dataset is still kept as an integer, then it is obvious that each of the tids of an item will occupy 32 bits in the main memory even though many of these 32 bits are unused. On the contrary, if the last transaction ID of a dataset is converted to binary format, and the size of that binary number (i.e., how many bits required to represent that tid) is used instead of an integer to represent the tid into the corresponding tidset/diffset, then a smaller dataset can be accommodated within a small amount of main memory. For simplicity, we name this representation as tid-bits. For example, consider Figure 4 where the dataset has only 1 million transactions per item and has occurred at tid {5, 20, 100, 99999 and 1000000}. Suppose the elements of a tidset/diffset of an item are kept as an integer as shown in Figure 4a, then to represent each element of tidset/diffset will require 32 bits. Since the binary representation of the last transaction ID of that dataset is 20 bits long (i.e., if we convert the 1,000,000 to binary format), then we convert every tid of that dataset into a corresponding binary number such that each binary number is 20 bits long and store these bits in the tidset/diffset instead of integer. This produces 12 bits less space in the main memory for every element of the tidset/diffset as shown in Figure 4b.

Figure 4. (a) Naïve approach – tid stored as integer and (b) tid-bits – representation of tid into bits

Integer	Corresponding bits (naive)
5	0 0 0 0 0 0 0 0 0 0 0 0 0 0 0 0 0 0 0 0 0 0 0 0 0 0 0 0 0 1 0 1
20	0 0 0 0 0 0 0 0 0 0 0 0 0 0 0 0 0 0 0 0 0 0 0 0 0 0 0 1 0 1 0 0
100	0 0 0 0 0 0 0 0 0 0 0 0 0 0 0 0 0 0 0 0 0 0 0 0 0 1 1 0 0 1 0 0
99999	0 0 0 0 0 0 0 0 0 0 0 0 0 0 1 1 0 0 0 0 1 1 0 1 0 0 1 1 1 1 1 1
1000000	0 0 0 0 0 0 0 0 0 0 0 0 1 1 1 1 0 1 0 0 0 0 1 0 0 1 0 0 0 0 0 0

(a)

Integer	Corresponding bits (tid-bits)
5	0 0 0 0 0 0 0 0 0 0 0 0 0 0 0 0 0 1 0 1
20	0 0 0 0 0 0 0 0 0 0 0 0 0 0 0 1 0 1 0 0
100	0 0 0 0 0 0 0 0 0 0 0 0 0 1 1 0 0 1 0 0
99999	0 0 0 1 1 0 0 0 0 1 1 0 1 0 0 1 1 1 1 1
1000000	1 1 1 1 0 1 0 0 0 0 1 0 0 1 0 0 0 0 0 0

(b)

Converting any tid into a binary number with a specific length, or vice versa, is quite straightforward; one can do it on the fly without any performance degradation. Nevertheless, tid-bits representation requires less than 32 bits to hold a word, and therefore it becomes less expensive in terms of space compared with the bit vectors, if the user-specified support is less than $(100/n)\%$, where n is the number of bits when converting the last transaction ID into a bit format. To illustrate the above rationale more clearly, let us consider the following example.

Suppose a dataset has 1,000 items and 1 million transactions with an average transaction size of 20. Now, we will calculate number of bits required to hold this dataset in the main memory using the abovementioned three different techniques: vertical bitmaps, vertical tidset is naïve, and tid-bits approaches. Firstly, we employ Formula 2 and calculate the total number of bits required in vertical bitmaps which is equal to 1,000,000,000 bits. Secondly, using Formula 4 we find that the naïve vertical tids approach needs 640,000,000 bits. Finally, to find the total number of bits, we need to hold the entire vertical tidset dataset in tid-bits format. We first convert the last transaction ID of that dataset into bits; that is, in this case we convert 1,000,000 to its corresponding bit and find the number of bits associated with it. Here, to represent the last transaction ID into corresponding bits, we need a maximum of 20 bits; therefore, we can accommodate any word that is any tid of this dataset within 20 bits. And, to hold the entire dataset, we need only 400,000,000 bits—in fact, 16 times less memory than with the naïve vertical tidset approach.

From the above example, it is clear that tid-bits require fewer bits than the other two vertical representations. However, we have not yet used any user-specified support, and hence one may think that this calculation may not be appropriate in the presence of user-specified support. In this regard, we would like to mention here that tid-bits require less space than vertical tids no matter what the user-specified support is, because the tid-bits approach is able to accommodate each element of the vertical tidset dataset within 20 bits; in comparison, the naïve approach needs 32 bits. In contrast, with the bitmap vector, less space is required as long as the user-specified support is less than 100/20 = 5%. Indeed, below 5% support, the bitmap vector will, on average, need more than 20 bits (i.e., theoretically it will find the occurrence of an item on average after each 20 transactions).

Methodology

Since the amount of main memory needed to store tidset/diffset dataset in the main memory relies on the number of bits that are required to hold each of the elements in the tidset/diffset, we need to find an alternative approach that requires a minimal number of bits to store each tid of an item; subsequently, all frequent itemset generation methods that use vertical dataset layout will be able to be handle larger datasets or low support thresholds. As mentioned above, the algorithms that use a vertical tid dataset layout such as éclat and déclat face the biggest challenge and are often unable to complete support enumeration of frequent itemsets if the intermediate results of the vertical tid lists exceed the main memory limits. Thus, storing vertical tid lists in an efficient way that accommodates the tidset dataset and all intermediate tid lists into main memory, allows us to employ intersect-based algorithms such as éclat and déclat on a bigger dataset or low support threshold.

As seen in the previous section, naïve tid-bits need the same number of bits when the bit representation of the last transaction ID of a dataset needs 32 bits, consequently indicating that the tid-bits are not scalable in terms of the number of transactions. To overcome this drawback, in this section we propose a technique that does not depend on the number of transactions, as is the case with the tid-bits. Subsequently, it has the advantage of being able to accommodate tids in the main memory without exceeding its capacity. In addition, as we shall discuss in detail, the proposed technique always requires fewer bits than the tid-bits approach because it does not merely convert the tid into bits; rather, it finds the difference between two tids and stores that difference in the bit format.

Before we embark on the details of our proposed algorithm, it is important to explain why we need a specific number of bits for all tids (i.e., equal to the bit representation of the last tid of a dataset) in the bit-tid approach. For example, when a dataset has 100,000 transactions, we need 17 bits for each entry, and it increases up to 20 bits when the dataset has 1,000,000 transactions, although we can accommodate the first 100,000 transactions within 17 bits. However, we cannot have a different number of bits (i.e., size) for different tids, because when we convert each entry to the bit vector to find its corresponding tid, we need to read a specific number of bits for every entry; otherwise it is difficult to convert these bits to their corresponding tids.

Figure 5. Bit representation of tids: (a) without padding (b) with padding

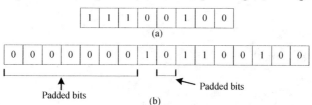

For example, an item that occurs in the 1st and 100th transactions of a dataset has converted its tids into a bit format (i.e., 1 and 1100100) and put these bits directly into a vector as shown in Figure 5a. However, such an insertion causes ambiguity when we try to convert entries of that vector to its corresponding tids, as we will not know how many tids there are, or how many bits each entry has. Thus, we are unable to obtain the tid values of each entry of that vector. To overcome such ambiguity, we can use only a specific number of bits for all entries regardless of the exact bit size of each individual entry. And if we encounter a bit representation of a tid that is less than that number, then we pad it with '0' as shown in Figure 5b. Therefore, we know the exact size (i.e., number of bits) of each entry as well as the number of entries.

Since in the naïve tid-bits approach, the number of bits (i.e., to hold each entry) required to represent each tid increases as the number of transactions increases in the dataset, we can achieve scalability only when we are able to find alternative approaches where the number of bits required to represent a tid do not rely on the number of transactions in the dataset. On the other hand, the above goal raises a question: how can we store elements of tidset/diffset in a binary format so that the number of bits associated with each tid remains constant regardless of the number of transactions in the dataset?

Dif-Bits

In order to address the aforementioned issue, here we propose an enhancement technique that compresses elements of tidset/diffset in an efficient way so that the number of bits associated with each tid does not increase as the number of transactions increases. The proposed technique does not convert any tid into a bit format on the fly as it does with the tid-bit. Rather, during the dataset reading, it finds the difference between current (i.e., transaction number of current reading position) and previous (i.e., the transaction number where this item appears last time) tids of every item and converts that difference into a bit format. For simplicity, we called the bit representation of each of those differences dif-bits. Finally, it places these dif-bits into a bit vector. The analogy behind this can be described in the following property:

- **Property 1:** The difference between two tids is always smaller than their largest tid.

- **Rationale:** Suppose $T1$ and $T2$ are two tids of an item 'A', the difference between those two tids is $D = T2 - T1$. Since the value of D is the subtraction of two tids, it is always smaller than $T2$.

Since the difference of two tids is always smaller than the original tid when the other tid is subtracted, subsequently this implies that the dif-bits also have fewer bits compared with the number of bits, we need to represent the original tid. In addition, the dif-bits store the difference between the two tids, and the size of the dif-bits does not rely on the number of transactions, rather on how frequently that item appears in the dataset. Thus, regardless of the number of transactions, the size of each dif-bit is always minimal. For a better understanding, let us consider the following example.

Consider the dataset in Figure 6a, where item bread appears in the $\{1^{st}, 2^{nd}, 5^{th}, 8^{th},$ and $10^{th}\}$ transactions. To store these tids in the initial dataset using the naïve tidset approach, we need at least $32 \times 5 = 160$ bits in the main memory. Let us now find the difference of every following two tids for each item. For example, item bread first appears in the transaction ID 1, so the difference is the current transaction ID and transaction ID where item bread appeared previously equal to $1 = 1-0$, then it appears in transaction 2 and the difference is $1 = 2-1$; this process continues for all transactions where the item bread appears. Since all of those difference values shown in Figure 6b are in the integer format, in order to retain those differences in the main memory, we still need 160 bits. Let us now convert each of those differences into

Figure 6a. Dataset

Item	Transaction #
bread	1, 2, 5, 8, 10
battery	12
beef	4, 9, 12
cheese	2, 3, 7, 8
cereal	3
coffee	3, 4, 8, 9
milk	1, 2, 3, 4, 6, 8
pasta	8, 9
potatoes	6, 12
rice	11, 12
soap	11
sugar	5, 6, 8, 10
tea	5, 7, 10
toothpaste	1
toy	11

(a)

Figure 6b. Difference between two tids

Item	Tid Difference
bread	1, 1, 3, 3, 2
battery	12
beef	4, 5, 3
cheese	2, 1, 4, 1
cereal	3
coffee	3, 1, 4, 1
milk	1, 1, 1, 1, 2, 2
pasta	8, 1
potatoes	6, 6
rice	11, 1
soap	11
sugar	5, 1, 2, 2
tea	5, 2, 3
toothpaste	1
toy	11

(b)

Figure 6c. Corresponding dif-bits in bit vector

Item	Dif bits
bread	1 1 1 1 1 1 1 0
battery	1 1 0 0
beef	1 0 0 1 0 1 1 1
cheese	1 0 1 1 0 0 1
cereal	1 1
coffee	1 1 1 1 0 0 1
milk	1 1 1 1 1 0 1 0
pasta	1 0 0 0 1
potatoes	1 1 0 1 1 0
rice	1 0 1 1 1
soap	1 0 1 1
sugar	1 0 1 1 1 0 1 0
tea	1 0 1 1 0 1 1
toothpaste	1
toy	1 0 1 1

(c)

corresponding binary format and insert them into the bit vector. To illustrate each element of the bit vector, and the total number bits needed to hold each of those elements, let us analyze Figure 6c. Suppose that we consider the item bread from the above dataset; the dif-bits of that item in the main memory can be accommodated within 8 bits, compared with 160 bits if we took the naïve tidset approach.

The above example clearly illustrates that if dif-bits are used rather than the original tid value in the bit vector, then the size of the vector will be reduced significantly; subsequently, this implies that the bit vector can accommodate a greater number of transactions or intermediate vertical results. Perhaps it is worth mentioning that the dif-bits method needs only 32 bits when the difference between the two tids of an item is more than 2.3 billion. But, it is quite uncommon for an item to occur in the dataset after such a long interval. Nevertheless, if any item does occur in the dataset after such a long interval, the corresponding item support is also very low.

For example, if an item always appears in the dataset after 2.1 billion transactions, its support must be less than 4.6×10-8%. Indeed, it is apparent that association rule mining algorithms rarely, or never, use such a small minimum support threshold for generating frequent itemsets; thus, the proposed technique never requires 32 bits to store dif-bits no matter how big the dataset is!

Inserting dif-bits into a bit vector reduces its size as discussed above. However, there is a problem associated with it—that is, how to convert each difference value of an item from the bit vector to its original tids format. Because the proposed dif-bits method converts the difference of two tids and inserts them into the bit vector as a binary format, neither knows the exact number of bits associated with each of the differences, nor the total number of dif-bits entries that have been inserted in the bit vector. As mentioned earlier, it is difficult to convert each entry of the bit vector into the original tids if the size of the entry is unknown. Thus, the proposed dif-bits method is unable to convert entries of the bit vector to the corresponding tids. To alleviate this, we have modified our proposed dif-bits technique. To indicate the size of each dif-bits entry, n number of bits are inserted in the bit vector for every entry before inserting the original difference of the two tids, where 'n' specifies the number of bits required to convert the difference of two tids into bit format. For simplicity, we name the n number of bits padding bits. Therefore, when we convert each entry from the bit vector, we know the exact size of the difference if we read the n number of bits in advance for every entry. For example, let us consider the item bread from the dataset as shown in the Figure 6a. Suppose 3 bits are inserted to specify the exact length of each before inserting the original dif-bits in the bit vector as depicted in Figure 7. Since each of the dif-bits entries of the bit vector first defined the size of the corresponding dif-bits, then reading those 3 bits in advance will define the exact number of bits associated with the corresponding dif-bits entry.

Since inserting padding bits in advance for every dif-bits entry incurs some overhead, one may raise a question about the efficiency of our proposed technique. In this regard we argue that the size of padding bits is very small. For example, if the padding bits size is equal to 5, then we can insert any entry of dif-bits in the bit

Figure 7. Dif-bits with padding bits

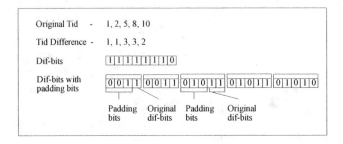

Table 1. Dif-bits and the corresponding padding bits

Difference in Decimal	Dif-bits	Padding Bits Describing the Size of Dif-bits
1	1	0 0001
7	111	0 0011
31	1 1111	0 1010
1023	11 1111 1111	1 0000
65535	1111 1111 1111 1111	1 0000
2097151	1 1111 1111 1111 1111 1111	1 0101
1073741823	11 1111 1111 1111 1111 1111 1111 1111	1 1110
2147483647	111 1111 1111 1111 1111 1111 1111 1111	1 1111

vector that has 31 bits as illustrated in Table 1 (original tid values are subtracted by 1). However, from our previous discussion we can conclude that there is rarely the need for 31 bits because a dif-bits entry with 31 bits represents a difference of two tids of an item that occurs in the dataset after 2.1 billion transactions.

Nevertheless, we can further reduce the length of dif-bits entry if we remove the leftmost bit from every dif-bits entry. Since the leftmost bit of dif-bits is always '1', an elimination of this bit from the dif-bits will not have any impact. Additionally, when we convert each dif-bits entry to its corresponding difference, we just reassemble that entry, simply adding a true bit that is '1' at the same position (i.e., leftmost), thereby obtaining the original dif-bits.

To illustrate this more clearly, consider the following example: suppose the size of padding bits of every dif-bits entry is 5 and a difference between two tids of a particular item is 9. Thus the corresponding dif-bits entry is equal to '1001'. The dif-bits entry has 4 bits, and therefore the padding bit of that entry is constructed as '00100', indicating the size of the dif-bits. However, suppose we remove the leftmost bits from that dif-bits entry, thus that particular entry now becomes '001', which has only 3 bits. Hence the corresponding padding bits become '00011'. During insertion of that dif-bits entry into the corresponding bit vector, we put padding bits '00011' and then the dif-bits '001' into the bit vector rather than padding bits '00100' and dif-bits '1001', and subsequently reduce 1 bit from each dif-bits entry.

Finally, when we convert that dif-bits entry, we first read the padding bits '00011', which informs us of the exact number of bits associated with that corresponding dif-bits entry; in this case, place 1 after the padding bits, read the remaining 3 bits, and obtain the original dif-bits value '1001'.

The length of the padding bits could further be reduced if we divide the length of dif-bits into several partitions rather inserting the exact padding bits of a dif-bits entry into the bit vector. Since the insertion of an exact padding bit size for each dif-bits entry requires 5 bits, using those 5 bits we can represent any dif-bit which is 31 bits long. To reduce the size of padding bits, we can divide 31 bits into 8 different partitions; and to represent 8 different partitions, we need only 3 bits such as '000', '001', '010', '011', '100', '101', '110', and '111'. Each of those partitions specifies the length of a particular dif-bits entry, meaning number of bits associated with any particular partition. For example, padding bits '000' can assign to hold those dif-bits entries that have less than or equal to 4 bits, similarly padding bits '001' for those dif-bits that have 8 bits, and so on. If a particular dif-bits entry has fewer bits than the number of bits assigned to that particular partition, then it first finds the difference between the partition length and exact size of that dif-bits entry, and it skips that many leftmost bits of that particular partition. For example, suppose the dif-bits entry is equal to '111011', which has 6 bits, and the corresponding partition length is equal to 8. To insert that dif-bits entry of that particular partition, it first skips 2 leftmost bits of that partition, then inserts the dif-bits entry starting from 3rd index position of that partition.

Algorithm

The dif-bits algorithm consists of two parts: (i) inserting dif-bits into the bit vector, and (ii) reading dif-bits from the bit vector. In the first part, it reads dataset and inserts the dif-bits into the corresponding bit vector. The pseudo code of the first phase—that is, inserting dif-bits into the bit vector—is shown in the following algorithm. The sketch of the dif-bits insertion method is as follows:

- **Step 1:** It reads the dataset and finds the difference between each item when it subtracts the current tid from the previous tid of an item when it last appeared. For example, suppose the last time that an item appeared was in the 3rd transaction, and now it appears in the current transaction that is 10th. Then it subtracts the current transaction that is 10 from the previous transaction tid 3 and finds the difference.

```
input: Dataset (D), Items (I) and Minimum Support (s);
output: Set of Bit Vectors F;
1. for all t ∈ T in D
2.    for all i ∈ I in t
// i_c ← current tid i_p ← previous tid
3.              D_i ← I_c - I_p;
4.              i_p ← I_c;
5.              b ← integerToBits(D_i);
6.              n ← findDifbitsSize(b);
7.              c ← findPaddingSize(n);
8.              addBitvector(c,b);
9.       end for;
10. end for;
```

- **Step 2:** In this step, it first converts those differences of each item found at step 1 from integer to binary format as shown in line 5. For example, suppose it currently reads transaction number 10, which has 4 items, and finds the corresponding difference value which is in this case 2, 8, 2, and 9. It converts each of those difference values to bits format: '10', '1000', '10', and '1001'.

It then finds each dif-bits entry's length, meaning the exact number of bits needed to represent each of the dif-bits entries, as shown in the line 6 in the above algorithm.

Once it finds the exact size of each dif-bits entry, it constructs the corresponding padding bits using one of the two approaches described in previous sections as shown in line 7. Suppose in this case we are using fixed-length padding bits and its length is set to 5. Thus it constructs the following padding bits from the above differences '00001', '00011', '00001', and '00011'.

Finally, in the bit vector associated with each item of that transaction, it inserts their corresponding padding bits and dif-bits entry after removing leftmost bits from each dif-bits entry, thereby dif-bits entries become '0', '00', '0', and '01'.

The second part of the dif-bits algorithm mainly describes how we read each of the dif-bits entries from the bit vector and convert them to the original tid where that item appeared. The pseudo code of our proposed reading is shown in the following algorithm. Let us discuss the dif-bits reading algorithm.

- **Step 1:** At first, it reads the padding bits of each dif-bits entry and subsequently finds the length of the next dif-bits entry. For example, if it reads the padding bits as '00100', then from those padding bits it finds the length of the dif-bits of the next entry and in this scenario it is 4.

Algorithm 2: Reading dif-bits entry from bit vector

```
input: A bit Vectors (V), Range (r);
output: Set of Tids (T);
1. t=0;
2. for all e∈V
3.    n←readDifBitsSize (e);
4.    d←readDifBits (n);
5.    no←convertToInteger (d);
6.    t←t+no;
7. end for;
```

- **Step 2:** Then it reads as many bits from the bit vector and converts them back to the original difference. Finally, it finds the exact tid by summing up that difference value with the previous tid. For example, suppose the dif-bits of the current entry is equal to '101', then the current difference is 5. Let us say that the previous tid of this item is equal to 5. Then it adds that difference value to the previous tid and finds the current tid: 10 = 5+5.

- **Property 2:** The compression ratio increases as the support of an item increases.

- **Rationale:** When the support increases, the density of an item in the dataset also increases. Consequently it decreases the dif-bits size because the average difference between two tids also reduces. For example, when an item has 0.1% support, then on an average that item appears in the dataset after an interval of 1,000 transactions. Therefore, to hold each of the differences (i.e., dif-bits size), we need 10 bits excluding the padding bits. However, if the item support increases up to 0.5%, then on an average the item appears in the dataset every 200 transactions. Thus, the average dif-bits size also reduces to 8 bits.

Mining Frequent Itemset with Dif-Bits Technique

In this section we will illustrate an example in order to show how our proposed dif-bits method described in the previous section allows us to generate all frequent itemsets with minimal amounts of main memory space. Since the dif-bits compress the vertical tidset dataset, first we will show the initial tidset/diffset in dif-bits format, then dif-bits approached is used to hold intermediate results during the frequent itemset generation process. Finally we will outline the amount of memory the proposed dif-bits method occupies during frequent itemset generation process.

Given the dataset (taken from Zaki & Gouda, 2003) shown in Figure 8, we are interested to find all frequent itemsets that have appeared at least three times in the dataset. Though both éclat and déclat algorithms intersect on vertical tidset or diffset dataset to generate frequent itemset, while performing intersection between the tidset of two itemsets, the éclat algorithm finds the common tids, whereas the déclat algorithm finds uncommon tids. For example, the éclat algorithm shown in Figure 8a intersects the tidset of items 'A' and 'C' and finds the common tids of 'A C' = {1, 3, 4, 5}. On the contrary, the déclat algorithm shown in Figure 9a subtracts the tidset of item 'A' from 'C' and finds only uncommon tids—that is, $A - C$ = {}. Since both of the above algorithms generate frequent itemset using two separate techniques, in the following example we apply our proposed dif-bits techniques to both of those algorithms. In addition, we also show how our proposed dif-bits technique accomplished the frequent itemset generation task with minimal main memory consumption.

Figure 8a. Éclat algorithm (a) naïve and (b) dif-bits approach

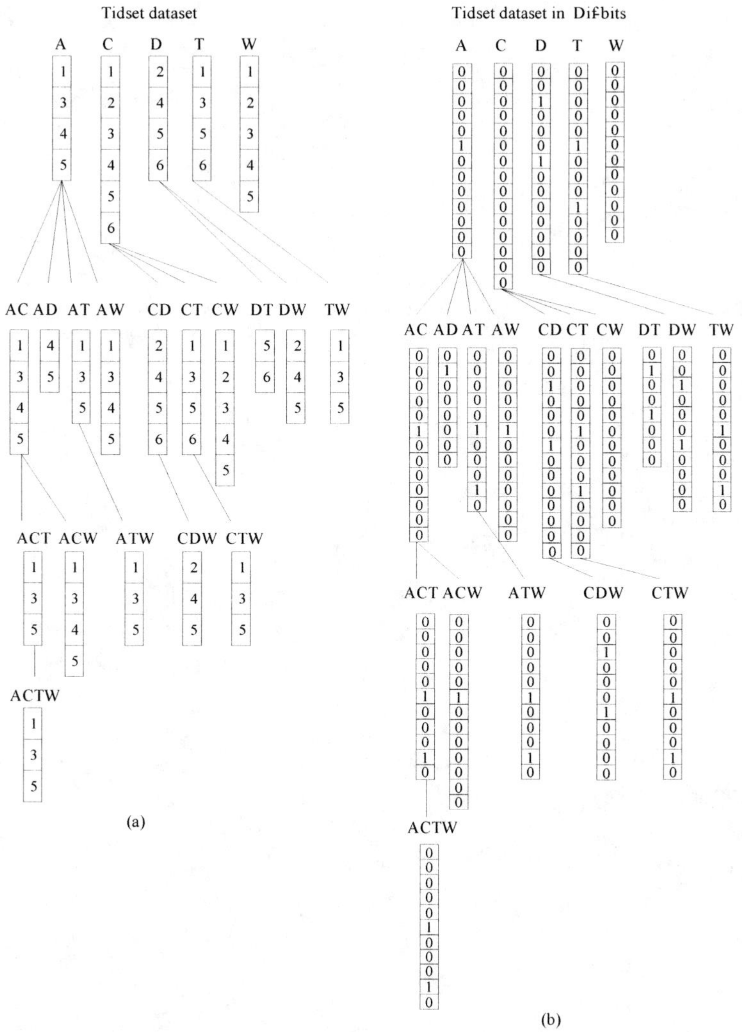

Tidset dataset

A	C	D	T	W
1	1	2	1	1
3	2	4	3	2
4	3	5	5	3
5	4	6	6	4
	5			5
	6			

AC AD AT AW   CD CT CW   DT DW   TW

AC	AD	AT	AW	CD	CT	CW	DT	DW	TW
1	4	1	1	2	1	1	5	2	1
3	5	3	3	4	3	2	6	4	3
4		4	5	5	5	3		5	5
5		5		6	6	4			
						5			

ACT ACW   ATW   CDW CTW

ACT	ACW	ATW	CDW	CTW
1	1	1	2	1
3	3	3	4	3
5	4	5	5	5
	5			

ACTW

ACTW
1
3
5

(a)

Tidset dataset in Dif-bits

(b)

The examples shown in Figures 8 and 9 illustrate initial datasets and all intermediate vertical lists in dif-bits and the naïve approaches of éclat and déclat algorithms. The dif-bits-based approach shown in Figures 8b and 9b use 3 bits (i.e., padding bits) to indicate the size of the next dif-bits entry. Although the dif-bits approach generates the frequent itemset in the same manner as it intersects the dif-bits of one class with another and subsequently finds the corresponding itemset support, during intersects it reads those dif-bits and converts them into the original tids. For example, suppose dif-bits items 'A' and 'C' intersect as shown in Figure 8b. It reads the padding bit of 'A', which is '000' indicating that item 'A' appeared in the 1st transaction, then

Figure 9. Déclat algorithm. (a) Naïve, and (b) dif-bits approach

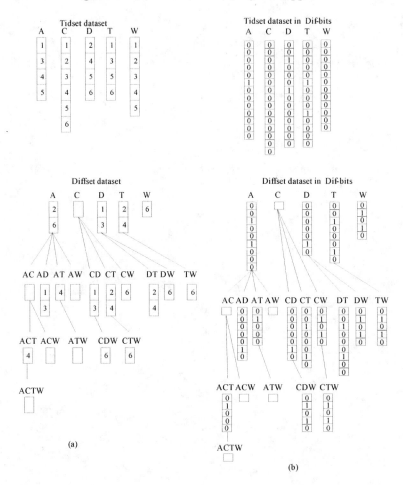

(a)

(b)

it reads the first dif-bits entry of item '*C*', which is also '000' meaning that item '*C*' also appeared in the 1st transaction. Since both of the items appear in the 1st transaction, then the first dif-bits entry of itemset '*A C*' is also '000'. The process continues until there are no more dif-bits entries in item '*A*'.

Let us now examine the amount of main memory the dif-bits approach requires during the frequent itemset generation. As we can see from Figure 8a, the tidset dataset has 23 entries and the éclat algorithm holds the entire dataset in the main memory to generate all frequent itemsets. To hold that dataset, it requires $23 \times 32 = 736$ bits, in contrast to the dif-bits which is able to hold it within 68 bits. To hold all intermediate vertical tid lists, including the tidset dataset, the éclat algorithm requires 2,432 bits. On the other hand, the dif-bits approach needs only 251 bits. Similarly, if we consider the déclat algorithm that uses the vertical diffset dataset (however, please note that it can generate frequent itemsets from a tidset dataset), it has only 7 entries. To hold that dataset in the main memory, at least 7×32 = 224 bits are required. However, the proposed dif-bits approach is able to accommodate the entire dataset within 30 bits. In addition, the déclat algorithm stores 23 tids—that is, 23×32 = 736 bits, including the diffset dataset to accomplish the frequent itemset generation task, while the dif-bits approach needs only 65 bits, although it stores the same number of tids. The above example clearly illustrates that the proposed dif-bits method significantly compresses the tidset or diffset dataset as well as all intermediate vertical lists. Thus, by incorporating the dif-bits-based method in the éclat or déclat algorithm, the main memory utilization will obviously be enhanced; subsequently, this allows those algorithms to generate frequent itemsets from bigger datasets that the naïve approach of those algorithms is unable to perform because of the main memory constraint.

Performance Evaluation

We have done an extensive performance study on our proposed technique to confirm our analysis of its effectiveness. Four datasets are chosen for this evaluation study. Table 2 shows the characteristics of each dataset that is used in our evaluation. It describes the number of items, the average size of each transaction, and the number of transactions of each dataset. The "Cover Type" and "Connect-4" dataset are taken from the UC Irvine Machine Learning Dataset Repository (Blake & Mertz, 1998). The "T40I10D100K" dataset was generated using the IBM dataset generator and obtained from Goethals and Zaki, (2003). Finally, the "Kosarakare" is a real dataset containing (anonymized) click-stream data of a Hungarian online news portal that has been made publicly available by the FIMI workshop organizers (Goethals & Zaki, 2003).

When we put dif-bits into a bit vector, we put n number of bits prior to dif-bits insertion in order to specify the size of that dif-bits. However, when choosing the value of n, we have two alternatives: exact size and range. The former specifies the exact size of a dif-bits; hence, the size of n never goes beyond 5, since by using 5

Table 2. Dataset characteristics

Name	Transaction Size avg.	Number of Distinct Items	Number of Records
Cover Type	55	120	581012
Connect-4	43	130	67557
T40I10D100K	40	1000	100000
Kosarak	8	41000	990000

bits we can represent a number up to 32 bits long. The latter approach specifies a dif-bits size, and therefore the size of n becomes smaller. For example, 32 bits can be divided into four groups (i.e., 1-8, 9-16, etc.), and to represent each group we need 2 bits only. Furthermore, during the insertion, a particular range value that is suitable for a dif-bits size is found and placed before the dif-bits. Since the latter approach needs fewer bits, in the performance evaluation we adopt the range approach.

Dif-Bits vs. Tid

In the first experimentation, we evaluate the efficiency of our proposed method by comparing it with the tid-based approaches. It is worth mentioning that this tid-based approach uses a well-known vertical dataset layout and has been used in many different association rule mining algorithms (Zaki, 1999, 2003; Doug et al., 2001; Shenoy et al., 2000). These algorithms discover frequent itemsets in two phases: at first it stores tids of all items separately in the main memory, then it intersects the tids of one item with those of other items and finds the exact support. However, if

Figure 10. Comparison dif-bits vs. tid

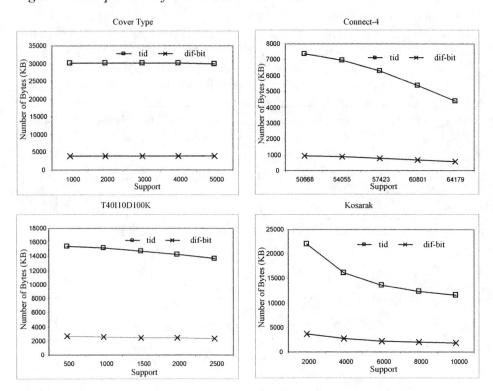

the dataset is large, in order to perform the first task, these algorithms require large amounts of main memory; otherwise they will be unable to finish the mining task (Goethals, 2003).

Because the aim of this experiment is to find out the total amount of memory that each of the approaches consumes, we are keen to know only how much memory space those tid-based algorithms (Zaki, 2003) need in order to complete the first phase. In Figure 10, we plot a detailed comparison between dif-bits (our proposed method) and tid. It shows how much memory each of the approaches takes at different support thresholds.

A number of observations can be made based on the performance results depicted in Figure 10. First, it is clear that the dif-bits approach always requires less memory than the tidset regardless of the dataset characteristics. The average size of dif-bits is 3-7 times smaller than the corresponding tidset approach used by the traditional vertical mining method éclat. With the dif-bits approach, every time an item appears in the transaction, it finds the difference of two tids—that is, between where it appeared the last time and the current the transaction; it converts that difference into bit format and puts those bits into a bit vector. Therefore, it often requires fewer bits to represent a difference value. In contrast, as mentioned earlier, the tidset approach requires 4 bytes (i.e., 32 bits) to represent each of the tids in the tidset (i.e., each appearance), hence requiring more memory.

Secondly, the average compression ratio of the dif-bits approach increases as the minimum support threshold increases. In fact, this characteristic is not surprising, but is rather expected because items having a higher support threshold appear in the dataset frequently and the average difference between two tids is also decreasing, thereby requiring fewer bits to represent a difference. For example, in kosarak dataset, when minimum support threshold is 500, the compression ratio is 3.1, whereas the ratio increases up to 3.9 at minimum support threshold 4,000.

Finally, since the compression ratio at low support threshold is more that 2.9 as depicted in Figure 10, this further confirms that the dif-bits is able to compress regardless of the support threshold or the dataset characteristic.

Dif-Bits vs. Compressed Bit Vector

VIPER (Shenoy et al., 2000) proposed an algorithm that uses a compression technique to compress the bit vector rather than the tid. In this section, we will compare this approach with our proposed dif-bits approach. In a customer transaction dataset, customers may not purchase the same item in a consecutive manner, and hence the authors assume that the bit representation of such dataset has many '0's and only a few '1's. Due to this assumption, the authors mentioned that the simple RLE (Run Length Encoding) is not appropriate for compressing the bit vectors of this kind of dataset. Hence, they developed an alternative approach known as Skinning based on an innovative encoding scheme. A detailed explanation of this approach is beyond the scope of this chapter, but can be obtained from Shenoy et al. (2000). However, in recent years, Zaki and Gouda (2003) presented a study illustrating that the best and worst compression ratio can be achieved from the abovementioned Skinning technique. The best compression ratio of the Skinning technique can be calculated using the following formula:

$$C_b \geq \frac{1}{0.03 + \dfrac{1}{8192 * \text{min\_sup}}} \tag{5}$$

Thus, the compression ratio in the best case is 32 when the minimum support is 0.1%. However, the best case assumes that all the $n1$ $1s$ come before the $n0$ (i.e., number 0- in the bit vector) $0s$. Indeed, such an assumption is quite uncommon and happens infrequently. On the other hand, in a worst case scenario, the compression ratio can be calculated using the following formula:

$$C_w \geq \frac{1}{0.34 + \dfrac{1}{8192 * \text{min\_sup}}} \tag{6}$$

The maximum compression ratio reaches 2.91 asymptotically when the support is 0.1%. However, in the worst case scenario, the Skinning technique fails to compress when the minimum support is less than 0.02%. To show the actual compression ratio achieved by the VIPER algorithms, we took the following statistics from Shenoy et al. (2000). Table 3 depicts the original size of the T10I4D100M dataset in tidset and the snakes format. From the table, it is clear that the snake format requires 2.90 times less memory than the corresponding tidset.

In contrast, the dif-bits technique required five to eight times less memory than the tid approach, as shown in the previous experiment (refer to Figure 10). Thus, the proposed dif-bits method is a better compression technique than VIPER. In addition, in a worst case scenario, when support is low, VIPER fails to compress; rather, it

Table 3. Dataset format size

Data Representation Format	Disk Space
Snakes	135MB
TidSet	392MB

expands (Zaki, 2003). On the other hand, the dif-bits technique never causes an expansion, no matter how low the user-specified support is. Indeed, such characteristic clearly exhibits the effectiveness of our proposed dif-bit technique.

Discussion

The dif-bits technique finds the difference of the two tids of an item, converts that into binary format, and finally inserts them into the bit vector. Since the difference of two tids is always smaller than the original tid value, the binary representation of the corresponding difference will also be smaller in size. Because the insertion of the difference value directly to the bit vector does not allow us to convert them to the corresponding tid, a specific number of padding bits need to be inserted before the dif-bits are inserted into the bit vector. However, the size of the padding bits is small, so the number of bits required to insert the difference of two tids along with the padding bits is also small.

Despite difference being kept in the bit vector, converting them back to the original tids value is quite simple and can be done on the fly. To convert them to the original tid, at first it reads the padding bits, finds the exact number of bits associated with the next dif-bits entry, then it reads that number of bits and converts them to the corresponding integer. Finally, it adds that integer to the previous tid to find the exact transaction ID where that item appeared.

The vertical mining method holds the initial dataset, and the intermediate results in the main memory. On the other hand, the dif-bits technique is able to hold the tidset/diffset and intermediate results within small amounts of main memory. Therefore, if vertical mining methods used the dif-bits approach instead of the naïve integer approach to hold those initial tidset/diffset dataset and intermediate results into the corresponding dif-bits, then during the mining process, less main memory space will be required.

Conclusion

Main memory is one of the important resources that can be used to improve the performance of association rule mining. However, due to restricted main memory capacity, mining algorithms often experience a performance bottleneck when performing a mining task on a large dataset. Since association mining algorithms inherently depend on the amount of main memory when that amount is not sufficient, then these algorithms will be unable to finish the mining task. Therefore, we critically need efficient memory enhancement techniques to make any mining algorithm complete the mining task on large datasets. To achieve this goal, in this chapter we present a technique known as dif-bits, which obtains a good compression ratio regardless of dataset characteristics or user-specified support. The performance evaluation confirms that the proposed algorithm needs only a small amount of memory compared with other compression techniques previously used for association rule mining.

Note

4 bytes for frequent itemset and 4 bytes for the support

References

Agrawal, R., Imielinski, T., & Swami, A.N. (1993). Mining association rules between sets of items in large databases. In *Proceedings of the ACM SIGMOD International Conference on Management of Data* (pp. 207-216).

Agrawal, R., & Srikant, R. (1994). Fast algorithms for mining association rules in large database. In *Proceedings of the 20ᵗʰ International Conference on Very Large Databases*, Santiago, Chile (pp. 407-419).

Ashoka, S., Edward, O., & Shamkant, N.B. (1995). An efficient algorithm for mining association rules in large databases. In *Proceedings of the 21ˢᵗ International Conference on Very Large Databases*, Zurich, Switzerland (pp. 432-444).

Blake, C.L., & Mertz, C.J. (1998). *UCI repository of machine learning databases*. Retrieved from www.ics.uci.edu/~mlearn/MLRepository.html

Doug, B., Manuel, C., & Johannes, G. (2001). MAFIA: A maximal frequent itemset algorithm for transactional databases. In *Proceedings of the International Conference on Data Engineering* (pp. 443-452).

El-Hajj, M., & Zaiane, O.R. (2003). Inverted matrix efficient discovery of frequent items in large datasets in the context of interactive mining. In *Proceedings of the 9ᵗʰ ACM SIGKDD International Conference of Knowledge Discovery and Data Mining*. ACM Press.

Geothals, B. (2003). Memory efficient association mining. In *Proceedings of the ACM Symposium of Applied Computing*.

Goethals, B. (n.d.). *Survey on frequent pattern mining*. Finland: University of Helsinki.

Goethals, B., & Zaki, M.J. (2003). *FIMI repository*. Retrieved from http://fimi. cs.helsinki.fi/fimi03/

Han, J., Pei, J., & Yin, Y. (2000). Mining frequent patterns without candidate generation. In *Proceedings of ACM SIGMOD International Conference on Management of Data* (pp. 1-12).

Jong, P.S., Ming-Syan, C., & Philip, Y.S. (1995). An effective hash-based algorithm for mining association rules. In *Proceedings of the 1995 ACM SIGMOD International Conference on Management of Data*, San Jose, CA (pp. 175-186).

Shenoy, P., Haritsa, J.R., Sudarshan, S., Bhalotia, G., Bawa, M., & Shah, D. (2000). Turbo-charging vertical mining of large databases. In *Proceedings of the ACM SIGMOD International Conference Management of Data*.

Zaki, M.J. (1999). Parallel and distributed association mining: A survey. *IEEE Concurrency*, (October-December).

Zaki, M.J. (2000). Scalable algorithms for association mining. *IEEE Transactions on Knowledge and Data Engineering, 12*(2), 372-390.

Zaki, M.J., & Gouda, K. (2003). Fast vertical mining using diffsets. In *Proceedings of the 9th ACM SIGKDD International Conference of Knowledge Discovery and Data Mining*. ACM Press.

Section III

Data Mining in Bioinformatics

Chapter VII

A Tutorial on Hierarchical Classification with Applications in Bioinformatics

Alex Freitas, University of Kent, UK

André C.P.L.F. de Carvalho, University of São Paulo, Brazil

Abstract

In machine learning and data mining, most of the works in classification problems deal with flat classification, where each instance is classified in one of a set of possible classes and there is no hierarchical relationship between the classes. There are, however, more complex classification problems where the classes to be predicted are hierarchically related. This chapter presents a tutorial on the hierarchical classification techniques found in the literature. We also discuss how hierarchical classification techniques have been applied to the area of bioinformatics (particularly the prediction of protein function), where hierarchical classification problems are often found.

Introduction

Classification is one of the most important problems in machine learning (ML) and data mining (DM). In general, a classification problem can be formally defined as:

Given a set of training examples composed of pairs $\{x_i, y_i\}$, find a function f(x) that maps each x_i to its associated class y_i, i = 1, 2, ..., n, where n is the total number of training examples.

After training, the predictive accuracy of the classification function induced is evaluated by using it to classify a set of unlabeled examples, unseen during training. This evaluation measures the generalization ability (predictive accuracy) of the classification function induced.

The vast majority of classification problems addressed in the literature involves flat classification, where each example is assigned to a class out of a finite (and usually small) set of classes. By contrast, in hierarchical classification problems, the classes are disposed in a hierarchical structure, such as a tree or a directed acyclic graph (DAG). In these structures, the nodes represent classes. Figure 1 illustrates the difference between flat and hierarchical classification problems. To keep the example simple, Figure 1b shows a tree-structured class hierarchy. The more complex case of DAG-structured class hierarchies will be discussed later. In Figure 1, each node—except the root nodes—is labeled with the number of a class. In Figure 1b, class 1 is divided into two sub-classes, 1.1 and 1.2, and class 3 is divided into three

Figure 1. An example of flat vs. hierarchical classification

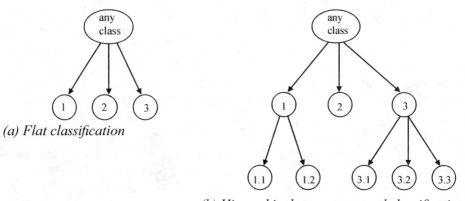

(a) Flat classification

(b) Hierarchical, tree-structured classification

sub-classes. The root nodes are labeled "any class" to denote the case where the class of an example is unknown. Figure 1 clearly shows that flat classification problems are actually a particular case of hierarchical classification problems where there is a single level of classes—that is, where no class is divided into sub-classes.

In the flat classification problem of Figure 1a, there is a single level of classes to be assigned to an example, but the class hierarchy of Figure 1b offers us more flexibility to specify at which level of the hierarchy a class will be assigned to an example.

For instance, one could require that an example should be assigned to a leaf, most specific, class. In the case of Figure 1b, this means that the candidate classes to be assigned to this example are 1.1, 1.2, 2, 3.1, 3.2, and 3.3. At first glance, by defining that only leaf classes can be assigned to an example, we are implicitly transforming the hierarchical classification problem into a flat one, since we could use a flat classification algorithm to solve it. Note, however, that in this case the flat classification algorithm would ignore valuable information in the structure of the class hierarchy. For instance, the fact that class 1.1 is more similar to class 1.2 than to class 3.1. By contrast, a truly hierarchical classification algorithm will take into account the structure of the class hierarchy. Even if we require the hierarchical algorithm to perform class assignments at the leaf level, the algorithm exploits the structure of the class hierarchy to look for a more accurate classification function.

On the other hand, we could be more flexible and allow the hierarchical classification algorithm to classify an example at any appropriate level, depending on the predictive power of the available data. For instance, an example could be reliably classified as having the specific class 1.1, while perhaps another example could only be reliably classified as having the general class 1.

Note that in general, class assignments at internal nodes can be carried out in a more reliable manner than class assignments at leaf nodes, because discriminating between the most specific classes at leaf nodes is more difficult than discriminating between the more general classes at internal nodes and, as a related factor, the number of examples per leaf node tends to be considerably smaller than the number of examples per internal node. On the other hand, class assignments at the leaf node tend to be more useful than class assignments at internal nodes, because the former provides more information about the class of an example. This trade-off between the reliability of a class assignment and its usefulness is common in hierarchical classification problems.

This chapter also presents applications of concepts and methods of hierarchical classification to problems in bioinformatics, at present one of the most important groups of DM applications. The application of DM techniques to bioinformatics is a very active research area, and it is not feasible to address the entire area in a single book chapter. Hence, this chapter focuses on a particular kind of bioinformatics problem, namely the prediction of protein function.

Proteins are large molecules that execute nearly all of the functions of a cell in a living organism (Alberts et al., 2002). They consist essentially of long sequences of amino acids, which fold into structures that usually minimize energy. Proteins can fold into a large number of structures, where different structures are usually associated with different functions. Due to the progress in genome sequencing technology, the number of proteins with known sequence has grown exponentially in the last few years. Unfortunately, the number of proteins with known structure and function has grown at a substantially lower rate. The reason for this is that, in general, determining the structure of a protein is much more difficult, time consuming, and expensive than determining its sequence. The main database with information about protein structures is the Protein Data Bank (PDB), which contains information related to experimentally determined structures. The doubling time for the number of experimentally determined protein structures available in the PDB has been recently calculated as 3.31 years, which, although impressive, represents a considerably slower growth than the doubling time for the number of sequences in the GenBank, which is just 1.4 years (Higgs & Attwood, 2005).

There are several motivations to investigate the application of concepts and methods of hierarchical classification to the prediction of protein function. First, proteins have a large diversity of functions, which can be categorized in many different ways. This naturally gives rise to hierarchical classification problems where the classes to be predicted are arranged in a tree-like or a DAG-like structure.

Furthermore, bearing in mind that the ultimate goal of DM is to discover useful knowledge, the prediction of protein function can potentially lead to better treatment and diagnosis of diseases, design of more effective medical drugs, and so forth, constituting an important and much needed application of DM in the context of intelligent systems for human health improvement. An additional, related motivation is that the contents of all the major protein databases are freely available on the Web. Thus, DM researchers do not have to face the problems of data privacy and restricted data access found in commercially oriented DM applications.

Another motivation to focus this chapter on hierarchical classification applied to the prediction of protein function is that this is still a relatively new, under-explored research area, where there are many opportunities for further research and improvement of current practice. For instance, the vast majority of works on hierarchical classification for the prediction of protein function are still using a conventional measure of predictive accuracy for flat classification problems. In principle, it would be more effective to use a measure of predictive accuracy tailored for hierarchical classification problems, as will be discussed later.

It should be noted that recently, there has been extensive research on hierarchical classification, but the majority of that research has been oriented to text mining, rather than bioinformatics (see, e.g., the survey of Sun, Lim, & Ng, 2003b). On the other hand, a large amount of work has been lately published reporting the use of

DM techniques in bioinformatics. However, the majority of this research focuses on the analysis of gene expression data (Slonim, Tamayo, Mesirov, Golub, & Lander, 2000; Jiang, Tang, & Zhang, 2004), which is very different from the problem of predicting protein function addressed in this chapter. Given the aforementioned exponential growth of protein sequence data available in biological databases and the important role of effective protein function predictions in improving understanding, diagnosis, and treatment of diseases, it is timely to focus on the problem of protein function prediction.

To summarize, this chapter has two main contributions. First, it presents a comprehensive tutorial on hierarchical classification, discussing the main approaches and different techniques developed for solving these problems. Second, it discusses how concepts and methods from hierarchical classification have been applied to a very challenging and important DM problem in bioinformatics, namely the prediction of protein function.

The remainder of this chapter is organized as follows. The second section presents a gentle introduction to the problem of protein function prediction for data miners who are not familiar with molecular biology. The third section describes several approaches for categorizing hierarchical classification problems. The fourth section covers different hierarchical classification methods, including methods based on transforming a hierarchical classification problem into one or more flat classification problems. The fifth section reviews several works on hierarchical classification applied to the prediction of protein function. Finally, the sixth section presents the conclusions and future research directions.

An Overview of Protein Function Prediction

Proteins are large molecules consisting of long sequences (or chains) of amino acids, also called polypeptide chains, which fold into a number of different structures and perform nearly all of the functions of a cell in a living organism.

We can distinguish four levels of organization in the structure of a protein (Alberts et al., 2002). The primary sequence of a protein consists of its linear sequence of amino acids. The secondary structure consists of α helices (helical structures formed by a subsequence of amino acids) and β sheets (subsequences of amino acids folded to run approximately side by side with one another). The tertiary structure consists of the three-dimensional organization of the protein. Some proteins also have a quaternary structure, a term used to refer to the complete structure of protein molecules formed as a complex of more than one polypeptide chain. These four levels of protein structure are illustrated in Figure 2, adapted from Lehninger, Nelson, and Cox (1998). The leftmost part of the figure shows part of a sequence of amino acids—each one with its name abbreviated by three letters. This part of the sequence forms an α helix—an element of secondary structure, as shown in the second part of the figure. This α helix is part of the larger tertiary structure, as shown in the third part of the figure. Finally, the rightmost part of the figure shows two polypeptide chains assembled into a larger quaternary structure.

In addition to these four levels of organization, there is a unit of organization named protein domain, which seems particularly important for the prediction of protein functions. A protein domain consists of a substructure produced by some part of a polypeptide chain that can fold, independently from other parts of the chain, into a compact, stable structure. Therefore, protein domains can be regarded as "higher-level building blocks" from which proteins are built. The term "higher-level" has been used to distinguish protein domains from the lower-level, fundamental building blocks of proteins, namely the amino acids composing its primary sequence. To see the importance of protein domains, it has been argued that protein domains, rather than genes, are the fundamental units of evolution (Nagl, 2003). The presence of one or more protein domains in a given polypeptide chain is often a useful clue to predict that protein's function, since different domains are often associated with different functions.

The most used approach to predict the function of a new protein given its primary sequence consists of performing a similarity search in a protein database. Such a

Figure 2. Four levels of structure in a protein

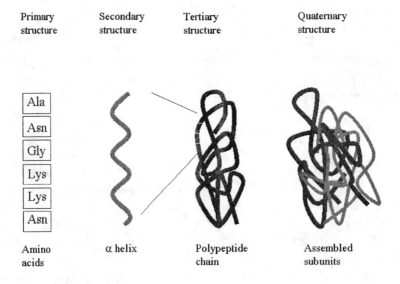

Primary structure	Secondary structure	Tertiary structure	Quaternary structure
Amino acids	α helix	Polypeptide chain	Assembled subunits

database contains proteins for which we know both their sequence and function. In essence, the program finds the protein whose sequence is most similar to the sequence of the new protein. If the similarity is higher than a threshold, the function of the selected protein is transferred to the new protein. This method will be hereafter referred to as *similarity-based protein function prediction* and is illustrated in Figure 3.

The similarity between a new protein and each protein in the database is usually computed by measuring the similarity between the sequences of amino acids of the two proteins, which involves performing some kind of alignment between these two amino acid sequences (Higgs & Attwood, 2005).

A very simple example of this kind of alignment is shown in Figure 4. Note that in Figure 4b a gap, denoted by the symbol "–" was inserted into the fifth position of the second sequence, which had the effect of sliding the subsequence "VACFW" to the right. This allows the system to detect that the two sequences have the same amino acids at their last five positions. Comparing the sequences in Figure 4b in a position-wise fashion, there are only two differences between them: a difference in the amino acid at the second position and the presence of a gap at the fifth position in the bottom sequence. Intuitively, this can be considered a high similarity, much larger than the similarity of two randomly chosen sequences of the same size, since each position could contain any of the 20 amino acids. Intuitively, this high similarity would suggest that the two sequences are homologous, in the sense that they evolved from a common ancestor (Higgs & Attwood, 2005) and the difference between them could be explained by just two mutations: first, a mutation in the second position, which either changed an A to a K or a K to an A (there is no way of knowing which was the case by just comparing the two sequences), and second, a mutation in the

Figure 3. Overview of similarity-based protein function prediction

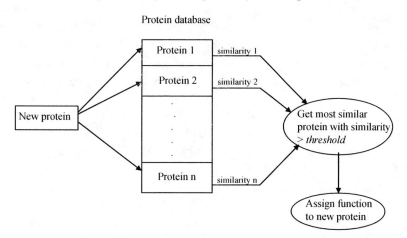

Figure 4. Example of alignment between two amino acid sequences

DACAPVACFW	DACAPVACFW
DKCAVACFW	DKCA–VACFW
(a) before alignment	(b) after alignment

fifth position, where either a P was inserted into the top sequence or a P was deleted at the bottom sequence (again, we do not know which was the case).

From an ML and DM perspective, the similarity-based protein function prediction method can be regarded as an instance of the Instance-Based Learning (IBL) or Nearest Neighbor paradigm (Aha, Kibler, & Albert, 1991; Aha, 1992), sometimes called "lazy learning" (Aha, 1997). The latter term is sometimes used because in this paradigm, learning is delayed to the moment when a new test instance is to be classified, rather than first learning a model from the training data and then using the model to classify a new test instance. The main difference between the similarity-based protein function prediction method and the majority of conventional IBL algorithms is that, in the latter, the measure of distance (the dual of similarity) between two instances is usually simpler, involving a generic distance measure, such as the well-known Euclidean distance or another distance measure suitable for the target problem (Liao, Zhang, & Mount, 1998). More precisely, in conventional IBL algorithms, the distance measure usually is computed between two instances with the same number of attributes, and the distance between the values of a given attribute in two instances is usually computed in a straightforward manner, say by the subtraction of two numbers in the case of numeric attributes.

By contrast, when comparing two protein sequences, matters are considerably more complicated. The two sequences being compared usually have different lengths, so that they first have to be aligned, as illustrated in Figure 4. Alignments are often performed by using a dynamic programming algorithm that finds alignments with optimal scores. However, the results of the algorithm will, of course, depend on several parameters of the heuristic scoring function. One such parameter, for instance, is how much an alignment score should be penalized for each gap. Another parameter involves how to compute the similarity between two different amino acids. The naïve approach of assigning a similarity score of 1 to two identical amino acids and a similarity score of 0 to any pair of distinct amino acids is not effective, because it ignores the well-established fact that some kinds of amino acids are more similar to each other than others. In order to take this aspect into account, the computation of the similarity between two amino acid values is usually based on a matrix M, where each entry $M_{i,j}$ represents the similarity score between amino acid i and amino acid j. Such matrices are generally constructed from data involving sets of proteins believed to be homologous (because they have sequence similarity higher than a certain threshold). However, it should be noted that the construction of such matrices is a heuristic process, depending on both assumptions associated with the evolutionary model used and the data available at the time the amino acid distance matrix is constructed.

In any case, despite the complexity of measuring the similarity between the amino acid sequences of two proteins, we emphasize that the similarity-based protein function prediction method can still be considered as an instance of the IBL paradigm. In particular, it has the following core IBL properties: (a) the "training phase" of the method is very simple, consisting of storing known-function proteins in a large database; and (b) in the "testing phase," the protein database is directly used as a "classification model" by assigning the new protein to the functional class(es) of the most similar protein(s) stored in the protein database, as long as the similarity is above a threshold value.

One advantage of this method—which is inherent to virtually all IBL methods—is that the simplicity of its training phase makes it naturally incremental. That is, as more and more proteins with known function are added to the database, the training set—and so the classification model—is immediately expanded, which should in principle increase the predictive accuracy of new functional predictions.

Although this method is very useful in several cases, it also has some limitations, as follows. First, it is well known that two proteins might have very similar sequences and perform different functions, or have very different sequences and perform the same or similar function (Syed & Yona, 2003; Gerlt & Babbitt, 2000). Second, the proteins being compared may be similar in regions of the sequence that are not determinants of their function (Schug, Diskin, Mazzarelli, Brunk, & Stoeckert, 2002). Third, the prediction of function is based only on sequence similarity, ignoring many relevant biochemical properties of proteins (Karwath & King, 2002; Syed & Yona, 2003).

In order to mitigate these problems, another approach consists of inducing from protein data a classification model, so that new proteins can be classified by the model. In this approach, instead of computing similarities between pairs of sequences, each protein is represented by a set of attributes. The learning algorithm induces a model that captures the most relevant relationships between the attributes and the functional classes in the training dataset. As long as the examples in the training dataset being mined have the same number of attributes, as usual in most ML and DM classification problems, this approach opens up the opportunity to use a large variety of classification algorithms for the prediction of protein function.

Additionally, if the induced classification model is expressed in a comprehensible representation—say, as a set of rules, a decision tree or perhaps a Bayesian network—it can also be shown to a biologist, to give her/him new insights regarding relationships between the sequence, the biochemical properties, and the function of proteins, as well as possibly to suggest new biological experiments. The induced model approach also has the advantage that it can predict the function of a new protein even in the absence of a sequence similarity measure between that protein and other proteins with known function (King, Karwath, Clare, & Dehaspe, 2001).

In the remainder of this chapter, we will assume the use of this framework of classification model induction, unless mentioned otherwise. In any case, it should be emphasized that the induced model-based approach aims mainly at complementing—rather than replacing—the conventional similarity-based approach for protein function prediction. Ideally, both approaches should be used in practice.

Since the focus of this chapter is on hierarchical classes, the issue of how to create predictor attributes to represent proteins is not directly related to the focus of this chapter. However, the choice of predictor attributes is crucial to any classification task, so it is worth briefly mentioning here some predictor attributes previously used in the literature to predict protein function:

a. **Attributes directly derived from protein sequence:** for instance, composition percentage of each of the 20 amino acids and the 400 possible pairs of possible amino acids (Syed & Yona, 2003; King et al., 2001), molecular weight, average hydrophobicity, average isoeletric point, and so forth

b. **Attributes predicted from the sequence by using some computational method:** this includes predicted attributes based on the secondary structure (Syed & Yona, 2003; Jensen et al., 2002; Karwath & King, 2002) and post-translational modifications, for example, glycosylation (Gupta & Brunak, 2002; Stawiski, Mandel-Gutfreund, Lowenthal, & Gregoret, 2002)

c. **Attributes obtained from biological databases:** for instance, UniProt/SwissProt contains information about tissue specificity, organism, and domain/motifs associated with proteins (whose details can be obtained by following links to databases like PRODOM and PROSITE). As another example, predictor attributes based on protein-protein interaction data can be derived from the Database of Interacting Proteins (DIP) (Jensen et al., 2002) or other data sources (Hendlich, Bergner, Gunther, & Klebe, 2003; Deng, Zhang, Mehta, Chen, & Sun, 2002)

Categorizing Hierarchical Classification Problems

In order to understand hierarchical classification problems, the first step is to categorize those problems according to relevant criteria. Intuitively, this categorization should be useful in the design of a new algorithm for hierarchical classification—that is, the algorithm should be tailored for the specific characteristics of the target hierarchical classification problem. Several relevant criteria for this categorization are described next. Note that in this section, we analyze the structure of hierarchical classification *problems,* regardless of the kind of algorithm used to solve them. An analysis of the structure of hierarchical classification *algorithms* will be presented in the next section.

Categorization Based on the Structure of the Class Hierarchy

In general, there are two main types of structure for a class hierarchy, namely a *tree structure* and *a direct acyclic graph (DAG) structure.* These structures are illustrated in Figures 5 and 6, respectively. In these figures, each node represents a class—identified by the number inside the node—and the edges between the nodes represent the corresponding super-class and sub-class relationships. Figures 5 and 6 show just a two-level class hierarchy, to keep the pictures simple. In both figures, the root node corresponds to "any class," denoting a total absence of knowledge about the class of an object. The main difference between the tree structure and the DAG structure is that in a tree structure, each class node has at most one parent, while in a DAG structure, each class node can have more than one parent.

In the tree structure of Figure 5, each node is labeled with the number (ID) of its corresponding class. The root node is considered to be at level 0, and the level of any other node is given by the number of edges linking that node to the root node. Nodes at the first level have just one digit, whereas nodes at the second level have two digits: the first digit identifies the parent class (at the first level), and the second digit identifies the subclass at the second level, as a child of the parent class.

In the context of protein functional classification, a typical example of a class hierarchy structured as a tree is the functional classification of enzymes. Enzymes are proteins specialized in catalyzing (or accelerating) chemical reactions (Alberts et

Figure 5. Example of a class hierarchy specified as a tree structure

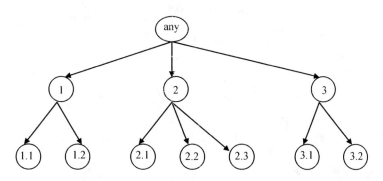

al., 2002; Dressler & Potter, 1991). Each enzyme is assigned to a class according to its EC code, which specifies the chemical reaction catalyzed by enzymes. The EC code consists of a series of four digits, where the first digit specifies the most general class of the enzyme and the fourth digit the most specific one. For instance, the EC code 1.1.1.1 specifies the class Alcohol Dehydrogenase.

The notation for the labels of class nodes in Figure 6 is similar to the notation in Figure 5. The main difference occurs for nodes with multiple parents, namely the nodes 1-2.1 and 2-3.1 at the second level of the class hierarchy. In this notation, the parent classes are specified by not just a single digit, but rather two digits before the class level-delimiter ".", that is, one digit for each of the parent classes. Hence, in the class number 1-2.1, the notation "1-2" indicates that this node has parent classes 1 *and* 2, and the "1" after the "." indicates that this is the first child class of those two parent classes considered as a whole (rather than each parent class individually).

In the context of protein functional classification, a typical example of a class hierarchy structured as a DAG is the gene ontology (GO), a relatively recent approach for classifying gene/protein functions (GO Consortium, 2000; Lewis, 2004; Camon et al., 2003). GO consists of three categories of functions, namely biological process, molecular function, and cellular component, which are implemented as three independent ontologies. GO has important advantages when compared with previous schemes for classifying protein functions. It specifies a well-defined, common, controlled vocabulary for describing protein functions. Hence, it improves the interoperability of genomic databases and provides a generic framework for protein functional classification. In addition, it is a *pan-organism* classification—that is, it can potentially be applied to all organisms, contributing to the unification of biology. The use of GO and its associated DAG structure are increasingly popular in the protein function prediction literature (Jensen, Gupta, Staerfeldt, & Brunak, 2003; King, Foulger, Weight, White, & Roth, 2003; Laegreid, Hvidsten, Midelfart, Komorowski, & Sandvik, 2003; Thomas et al., 2003). In addition, several other bioinformatics ontologies have lately been developed based on some basic ideas

Figure 6. Example of a class hierarchy specified as a DAG (direct acyclic graph)

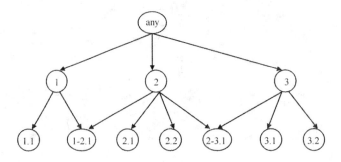

from GO, particularly the use of a DAG structure to represent the class hierarchy. Two examples are the cell type ontology (Bard, Rhee, & Ashburner, 2005) and the mammalian phenotype ontology (Smith, Goldsmith, & Eppig, 2004).

Categorization Based on the Hierarchical Level of Predicted Classes

Two main groups of problems can be distinguished according to this criterion. First, in some problems, all examples must be assigned to classes that are leaf nodes in the class hierarchy. We will refer to this group of problems as *mandatory leaf-node prediction* problems. Note that, in the case of a tree structure, when the system assigns a leaf class to an example, the system is also implicitly assigning to that example a unique class at each internal (non-leaf) level of the class hierarchy.

For instance, if the system predicts that the EC code of an enzyme is 2.1.3.1, the system is effectively predicting not only the enzyme's class at the fourth level, but also the enzyme's classes at the first three levels. However, this is not necessarily true in the case of a DAG structure, where a leaf node can have more than one parent.

Second, in some problems, examples can be assigned to classes that are either leaf nodes or internal nodes in the class hierarchy. We will refer to these problems as *optional leaf-node prediction* problems. In this case, the system has autonomy to decide, depending on the predictive power of the available data, how deep in the hierarchy the predicted class should be for each example.

For instance, although some enzymes could be easily classified by the system at the level of the fourth EC code digit (leaf class), for other enzymes the system could be much less confident about a fourth-level (most specific) prediction and decide to make a prediction only at the second, or perhaps first, level of the class hierarchy.

Of course, ideally, this decision should take into account not only the confidence in the predictions at different levels, but also their relative usefulness to the user. In general, the more specific (the deeper in the class hierarchy) a prediction is, the more it tends to be useful to the user, but the more difficult the prediction tends to be.

This holds particularly true for a tree structure, where the prediction of a leaf class subsumes the prediction of its parent classes, as mentioned earlier. The difficulty of prediction usually increases with the depth of the tree because the number of examples per class node in a deep level of the classification tree tends to be much smaller than in a shallow level, which means there is less data to support the discovery of a reliable classification model.

The situation is more complex in the DAG structure, where a class node can have more than one parent. In this case, it is actually possible that a class node has more examples than each of its parent class nodes. For instance, suppose that class C is a child of the classes P_1 and P_2; class P_1 has 100 examples, 70 of which also belong to its child class C; class P_2 has 50 examples, 40 of which also belong to its child class C. In this case, class C has 110 examples, a number larger than the number of examples in each of the parent classes P_1 and P_2. Thus, other things being equal, with respect to the number of examples per class, it might be easier to predict the more specific class C than any of its more generic parent classes P_1 and P_2 individually. In practice, however, even in a DAG, it is usually the case that the predictive accuracy decreases with an increase in the depth (specificity) of the prediction. For instance, Pal and Eisenberg (2005) obtained "...about 85% correct assignments at ontology depth 1 and 40% at depth 9."

Before we proceed, we must make a note about the terminology used in this subsection. The proposed terms *mandatory leaf-node prediction* and *optional leaf-node prediction* correspond to the types of class hierarchy named *virtual category tree (or DAG)* and *real category tree (or DAG)* by Sun and Lim (2001) and Sun et al. (2003b). In this chapter, we prefer the new terminology introduced in this subsection because it intuitively has a more direct meaning.

Categorization Based on the Predictive Performance Measure

There are several alternatives for measuring the predictive performance of a classification algorithm. A recent paper by Caruana and Niculescu-Mizil (2004) discusses nine different measures of predictive performance in the context of standard, flat classification problems. A discussion of conventional measures of predictive performance for flat classification is out of the scope of this chapter, since this topic is well covered in the mentioned paper and in data mining textbooks (Witten & Frank, 2005; Tan, Steinbach, & Kumar, 2006). Here we are rather interested in the orthogonal problem of how to take the class hierarchy into account when measuring predictive performance. We can identify at least four different ways of measuring predictive performance in hierarchical classification. Each of these is discussed in one of the following four subsections. Related discussions on predictive performance measures for hierarchical classification can also be found in Blockeel, Bruynooghe, Dzeroski, Ramon, and Struyf (2002) and Sun and Lim (2001).

Uniform Misclassification Costs

In this category of predictive performance measure, all misclassification costs are the same (say, unitary cost) for all possible values of the predicted class and the true class of an example—regardless of the level of the predicted and the true classes in the hierarchy.

Note that uniform misclassification costs can be straightforwardly employed both in *mandatory leaf-node prediction* problems, where all examples must be assigned to classes that are leaf nodes in the class hierarchy, and in *optional leaf-node prediction* problems, where examples can be assigned to internal or leaf class nodes. In the latter, we simply compare the class predicted for an example with the true class of the example at the same level of the predicted class, of course. For instance, if the system has assigned an enzyme to the EC code 3.1, we just have to compare this class (predicted at level 2 of the class hierarchy) with the true class of this enzyme at the second level, which effectively ignores the enzyme's true classes at the third and fourth levels.

However, the use of uniform misclassification costs in optional leaf-node prediction problems is not recommended, because it ignores the fact that the prediction of deeper-level classes tends to be more difficult than the prediction of shallower-level classes (particularly for tree-structured class hierarchies), as discussed earlier. In addition, a misclassification at a deep class level will mislead the user relatively little, by comparison with a misclassification at a shallow class level. Hence, other things being equal, misclassification costs at shallower levels of the classification tree should be larger than misclassification costs at deeper levels of the classification tree.

Note also that, even when all classes are predicted at the same level of the class hierarchy, the uniform misclassification costs approach is usually not the ideal approach for measuring predictive performance in hierarchical classification problems. This occurs because it ignores the fact that classes that are closer to each other in the hierarchy (say, "sibling" classes) are normally more similar to each other than classes that are further away to each other in the hierarchy (say, "cousin" classes) (Koller & Sahami, 1997). For instance, if the true second-level class of an enzyme is 2.1, misclassifying it as its sibling class 2.2 should have a smaller misclassification cost than misclassifying it as its cousin class 3.2. This introduces the motivation for another measure of predictive performance, discussed in the next subsection.

Distance-Based Misclassification Costs

This category of predictive performance measure consists of assigning, to each misclassification, a cost that is proportional to the distance between the example's predicted class and the example's true class in the hierarchy. This category can be further sub-divided into two sub-categories. In the first one, the distance between two classes can be measured in the same way, regardless of the level (depth) of these two classes in the hierarchy. This will be called *depth-independent distance-based misclassification costs.* The typical approach in this sub-category consists of defining the distance between two nodes in the class hierarchy as the number of edges in the shortest path connecting them. We stress that by "path" we mean here a sequence of *undirected* edges—that is, we do not take into account the original direction of each of the edges in the graph for the purpose of finding paths between two nodes. For instance, the distance between classes 1.1 and 3.2 in the tree-structured hierarchy of Figure 5 is 4. In a tree, the computation of this distance is very simple. If we consider only paths where each edge is used at most once, there is exactly one path between each pair of distinct nodes in the tree.

The situation is more complex in a DAG, where there can be multiple paths (each of them without edge duplication) between a pair of nodes. For instance, there are several paths between the class nodes 1-2.1 and 2-3.1 in Figure 6. More precisely, using the notation $<n_1, n_2>$ to denote an edge linking node n_1 and node n_2, we can observe the following paths between nodes 1-2.1 and 2-3.1 in Figure 6:

a. <1-2.1, 1$>$, <1, any$>$, $<$any, 3$>$, <3, 2-3.1$>$

b. <1-2.1, 1$>$, <1, any$>$, $<$any, 2$>$, <2, 2-3.1$>$

c. <1-2.1, 2$>$, <2, any$>$, $<$any, 3$>$, <3, 2-3.1$>$

d. <1-2.1, 2$>$, <2, 2-3.1$>$

Using the common definition of distance between two class nodes as the number of edges in the shortest path connecting these nodes, the distance in the previous example would be equal to 2, corresponding to the number of edges in the path (d).

This predictive performance measure has the advantage of simplicity, but it has the disadvantage of not taking into account that fact that, in many problems, misclassification costs at higher levels of the class hierarchy tend to be higher than misclassification costs at lower levels of the tree. For instance, suppose an example has leaf class 1.1.1.1 in a four-level hierarchy and the predicted class for this example is 1.1.1.4. The distance between the true class and the predicted class for this example is 2, since they are sibling classes separated by two edges—their common parent class is 1.1.1. Now suppose that the same example is assigned just to the internal, second-level class 1.2—assuming an *optional leaf-node prediction* problem. Again, the distance between the true class (1.1) and the predicted class (1.2) is 2. However, intuitively, the latter misclassification should have a larger cost than the former, because an error in the second-level (fairly general) class of an enzyme is much less forgivable than an error in the fourth-level (very specific) class of an enzyme. To overcome this deficiency, we should use another category of distance-based misclassification costs, where the cost of a misclassification depends on both the distance between the predicted and true classes and their depth in the class hierarchy. This will be called *depth-dependent distance-based misclassification costs*. If this measure is adopted, when computing the distance of a path, we can consider weighted edges, where deeper edges have smaller weights than shallower edges (Blockeel et al., 2002). The distance between two nodes can be computed as the shortest weighted path between these two nodes.

Semantics-Based Misclassification Costs

This category of predictive performance measures is based on a determination of class similarity that is independent of the distance of the classes in the hierarchy. The measure of similarity is supposed to be based on some notion of "semantics" of the classes, which is independent of the structure of the class hierarchy. This approach has been proposed, in the context of text mining—more precisely document classification—by Sun and Lim (2001) and Sun, Lim, and Ng (2003a). In this context, each class of documents is represented by a feature vector derived by adding up the features vectors of all documents belonging to that class. Then, the similarity between two classes is computed by some measure of similarity between their corresponding vectors (the cosine measure, often used in information retrieval, was proposed by the authors).

In the context of bioinformatics—particularly protein functional classification—the idea of a predictive performance measure based on class similarity independent from distance in the class hierarchy might be somewhat controversial. On one hand, presumably, the class hierarchy of several protein functional classifications—such as the EC code for enzymes—was constructed based on extensive biological knowledge, and its structure is already supposed to reflect some notion of the semantics of the classes, so that the distance between classes in the hierarchy should be considered when measuring predictive performance. On the other hand, it is interesting to observe that, once a measure of class similarity (independent of class distance in the hierarchy) has been precisely defined and its value computed for each pair of classes, this could, in principle, be used to construct another class hierarchy by using, say, a hierarchical clustering algorithm. This new hierarchical classification—rather than the original one—could then be given to the DM algorithm, whose predictive performance could then be evaluated by taking into account the distances between classes in the new hierarchy. This approach seems very under-unexplored in the literature about hierarchical classification. It could potentially shed a new light into some existing biological hierarchical-classification problems.

Hierarchical Misclassification Cost Matrix

This category of predictive performance measures consists of explicitly specifying the cost associated with each possible misclassification, by using a hierarchical misclassification cost matrix. This type of matrix is a generalization of the well-known misclassification cost matrix for standard flat classification (Witten & Frank, 2005).

There are different ways of making this generalization. Let us start with a hierarchical misclassification cost matrix for *mandatory leaf-node prediction,* whose matrix structure is illustrated in Figure 7. To keep the figure simple, there are only two classes at the first level of this matrix. Each of these classes has only two subclasses at the second level. However, the matrix in Figure 7 can be straightforwardly extended to represent a larger number of class levels and larger numbers of classes per level. Note that in the simple structure of Figure 7, although the structure is hierarchical, the misclassification costs are specified only at the level of the leaf class nodes. In the main diagonal the misclassification costs are zero, as usual, since the cells along that diagonal represent correct classifications. In the other cells, the misclassification costs are labeled $a,\ldots,l$, and each of these values is assumed to be larger than zero. It is trivial to look up the matrix in Figure 7 to determine a misclassification cost in the case of a mandatory leaf-node prediction problem. For instance, if the class predicted for an example is 2.1 and the true class of that example is 1.1, this wrong prediction has a misclassification cost of g.

Note that, although the basic structure of the matrix in Figure 7 is quite simple, in general it is flexible enough to implement the previously discussed categories of predictive performance measures as particular cases, with a proper specification of the misclassification costs $a,\ldots,l$ for each category. This can be shown as follows:

- To obtain *uniform misclassification costs,* all the costs $a,\ldots,l$ are set to the same value

- To obtain *distance-based misclassification costs,* where the costs are given by the number of edges in the hierarchical classification tree—so that the costs associated with sibling class nodes are equal to 2 and the costs associated with cousin class nodes are equal to 4—the costs should be set as follows: $a = d = i = l = 2$ and $b = c = e = f = g = h = j = k = 4$

Figure 7. Structure of a hierarchical misclassification cost matrix for mandatory leaf-node prediction

			True Class			
			1		2	
			1.1	1.2	2.1	2.2
Predicted Class	1	1.1	0	a	b	c
		1.2	d	0	e	f
	2	2.1	g	h	0	i
		2.2	j	k	l	0

- To obtain *semantics-based misclassification costs,* the costs $a,...,l$ are simply set to the corresponding values of semantic distance between each pair of classes

Recall that the discussion so far has assumed the context of a mandatory leaf-node prediction problem. If the target problem is *optional leaf-node prediction,* the scenario becomes more complex. In this new scenario, it seems natural to extend the matrix in Figure 7 in order to represent hierarchical misclassification costs involving non-leaf classes. This leads to the more complex hierarchical misclassification cost matrix shown in Figure 8. In that matrix, the notation ".*" refers to a wild card denoting any class at the second level. For instance, the notation "1.*" for a predicted class means that class 1 was predicted at the first, non-leaf level and no class was predicted at the second, leaf level. The misclassification costs involving at least one first-level, non-leaf class (i.e., a row or column with the wild care ".*") are denoted by upper case letters, while the misclassification costs involving only second-level, leaf classes are denoted by lower case letters (using the same notation as the simpler matrix of Figure 7). For instance, the cell at the intersection of the 1.* row and the 1.* column represents the misclassification cost A of predicting class 1 at the first level and making no prediction at the second level, when the true class at the first level is 1 and the true class at the second level is unknown. Note that intuitively this cost should be larger than zero, to take into account the lack of prediction for the second-level class. The cost zero should be reserved only for the cases where both the predicted and the true classes at the second level are known to be equal. As another example of the use of the ".*" notation, the cell at the intersection of

Figure 8. Structure of a hierarchical misclassification cost matrix for optional leaf-node prediction

| | | | True Class | | | | | |
| | | | 1 | | | 2 | | |
			1.*	1.1	1.2	2.*	2.1	2.2
Predicted Class	1	1.*	A	B	C	D	E	F
		1.1	G	0	a	H	b	c
		1.2	I	d	0	J	e	f
	2	2.*	K	L	M	N	O	P
		2.1	Q	g	h	R	0	i
		2.2	S	j	k	T	l	0

the 2.* row and the 1.2 column specifies the misclassification cost M of predicting class 2 at the first level and making no prediction at the second level, when the true class is known to be 1.2.

Categorizing Hierarchical Classification Approaches

Transforming a Hierarchical Classification Problem into a Flat Classification Problem

A standard flat classification problem can be regarded as a particular case (or a degenerated case) of a hierarchical classification problem where none of the classes to be predicted has super-classes or sub-classes. Hence, a simple, somewhat naïve way to "solve" a hierarchical classification problem consists of transforming it into a flat classification problem, and then applying one of the very many flat classification algorithms available to solve the new problem.

Consider, for instance, the tree-structured class hierarchy in Figure 5. We could transform the hierarchical classification problem associated with this figure into the problem of predicting classes only at the first level (i.e., most general classes) of the hierarchy. In this case, however, we would miss the opportunity of making more specific predictions at the second level of the hierarchy, which in principle would be more useful, providing more knowledge to the user. Alternatively, one could transform the original hierarchical classification problem into the problem of predicting only classes at the second level (i.e., the leaf classes) of the hierarchy. As mentioned earlier, by predicting classes at the leaves of the hierarchy, we are implicitly predicting the classes at higher levels (internal nodes). In this case, however, we would miss the opportunity of predicting classes at higher levels of the hierarchy, which presumably can be predicted with more confidence than classes at lower, deeper levels, as also previously discussed.

Hierarchical Class Predictions Using Flat Classification Algorithms

One way of avoiding the missed opportunities discussed in the previous subsection consists of transforming the original hierarchical classification problem into a set of flat classification problems, more precisely one flat classification problem for each level of the class hierarchy, and then using a flat classification algorithm to solve each of these problems *independently*. For instance, in the case of Figure 5, the associated hierarchical classification problem would be transformed into two problems, namely predicting the classes at the first level and predicting the classes at the second level. A flat classification algorithm would then be applied to each of these two problems independently, that is, each of the two runs of the algorithm would ignore the result of the other run.

Note that, in this case, in principle each of the two runs of the classification algorithm would be associated with its own measure of predictive performance, since the two independent runs effectively correspond to two distinct flat classification problems. In other words, the multiple runs of the classification algorithm are independent both in the training phase and in the test phase (classification of new, previously unknown, examples).

One problem with this approach is that there is no guarantee that the classes predicted by the independent runs at different class levels will be compatible with each other. For instance, still referring to the simple hypothetical example of class hierarchy in Figure 5, it is possible, in principle, to have a situation where the classifier at level 1 assigns a test example to class 1, while the classifier at level 2 assigns the example to class 2.1, which is clearly incompatible with the first-level prediction.

A more sophisticated approach to hierarchical class predictions consists of having multiple runs of a classification algorithm in such a way that results from independent training runs are used together during the test phase. Thus, there is a single measure of predictive performance on the test set associated with the results of all the training runs. To summarize, in this approach the multiple runs of the classification algorithm are independent during training, but integrated or dependent during the test phase.

The most common way of implementing this approach consists of training a different classification model for each node of the class hierarchy. Typically, each trained classification model is a binary classifier that decides, for each test example, whether or not the example should be assigned the class associated with the corresponding classification node. Note that this approach can be implemented in a way that naturally allows a test example to be assigned to more than one class at any level of the hierarchy, if the example satisfies the conditions of the corresponding binary classifiers.

In passing, notice that this is a straightforward approach to implement a multi-label classifier—that is, a classifier that has the autonomy to assign one or more classes to each example, rather than the conventional single-label classifiers that assign just one class to an example. Multi-label classification is out of the scope of this chapter, but a more detailed discussion about how to integrate multi-label classification and hierarchical classification into a single algorithm can be found in Blockeel et al. (2002).

In any case, if we do not want to allow an example to be assigned to more than one class at each level of the class hierarchy, this constraint can be easily incorporated in the classification procedure during the test phase, by forcing the procedure to assign a test example only to the most likely class at each level of the class hierarchy.

Big-Bang vs. Top-Down Hierarchical Classification

Probably the most important watershed to categorize truly hierarchical classification algorithms is the distinction between the *big-bang* and the *top-down* approaches. The main characteristics of these approaches are as follows (Sun & Lim, 2001; Sun et al., 2003a).

In the big-bang approach, a single (relatively complex) classification model is built from the training set, taking into account the class hierarchy as a whole during a single run of the classification algorithm. When used during the test phase, each test example is classified by the induced model, a process that can assign classes at potentially every level of the hierarchy to the test example. An example of the big-bang approach in the context of text mining can be found in Sasaki and Kita (1998), whereas an example of this approach in the context of bioinformatics—the focus of this chapter—will be discussed in the next section.

In the top-down approach, in the training phase, the class hierarchy is processed one level at a time, producing one or more classifiers for each class level. In the test phase, each example is classified in a top-down fashion, as follows. First, the test example is assigned to one or more classes by the first-level classifier(s). Then the second-level classifier(s) will assign to this example one or more sub-classes of the class(es) predicted at the first level, and so on, until the example's class(es) is(are) predicted at the deepest possible level.

In order to produce a hierarchical set of classifiers in the top-down approach, we can either train a single classifier per class level or train multiple classifiers per level. In the former case, we use a multi-class classification algorithm. Thus, at each class level, we build a classifier that predicts the class(es) of an example at that level. In the latter case, we typically train a binary classifier at each class node. Therefore, for each test example and for each class level, we present the example to each of the binary classifiers at that level. As a result, the test example will be assigned to one or more classes at each level, and this information will be taken into account in the next level, as previously explained.

The top-down approach has the advantage that each classification model (built either for a class level or a single class node) is induced to solve a more modular, focused classification problem, by comparison with the big-bang approach, where a more complex classification model has to be built by considering the entire class hierarchy at once. The modular nature of the top-down approach is also exploited in the test phase, where the classification of an example at a given class level guides its classification at the next level. However, the more modular nature of the top-down approach does not guarantee that this approach will have a better predictive performance than the big-bang approach. In particular, the top-down approach has the disadvantage that, if a test example is misclassified at a certain level, it tends to be misclassified at all the deeper levels of the hierarchy. The probability that this kind of error occurs can be reduced by using a procedure that tries to recover from misclassifications in a shallower level of the class tree (for a discussion of procedures to address this kind of problem, see Dumais & Chen, 2000; Sun, Lim, & Ng, 2004).

A Review of Works Addressing Hierarchical Classification Problems in Protein Functional Classification

Table 1 summarizes key aspects of previous works addressing hierarchical classification problems in the context of the prediction of protein functional classes. The second column of this table indicates the broad category of class hierarchy, either tree-structured or DAG-structured, and the specific protein functional classification scheme addressed in each work. The third column indicates whether the predictions made by the system are flat or hierarchical. If they are hierarchical, the column also indicates which class level(s) is(are) predicted. The fourth column points out whether the classification algorithm being used is a flat or a hierarchical algorithm. Note that for flat predictions, the classification algorithm is always flat. However, in the case of hierarchical predictions, the classification algorithm can be either flat (see "Hierarchical Class Predictions Using Flat Classification Algorithms" of the previous section) or hierarchical (see "Big-Bang vs. Top-Down Hierarchical Classification" of the previous section).

As can be observed in Table 1, there are several works involving tree-structured class hierarchies where *the original hierarchical classification problem is transformed into a flat classification problem.* Two examples of this approach are mentioned in Table 1:

- Jensen et al. (2002) and Weinert and Lopes (2004) predict only classes at the first level of the previously discussed EC code for enzymes.

- Jensen et al. (2002) predict only classes at the first level of Riley's hierarchical classification scheme. This scheme was originally defined for *E. coli* bacteria (Riley, 1993), but it has been modified to describe protein functions in other organisms.

Table 1. Review of works involving hierarchical classification of protein functions

Work	Kind of Class Hierarchy	Flat or Hierarchical Class Predictions?	Hierarchical or Flat classification Algorithm?
Jensen et al., 2002	Tree: Riley's scheme, EC code	Flat; only first class level	Flat artificial neural network
Weinert & Lopes, 2004	Tree: EC code	Flat; only first class level	Flat artificial neural network
Clare & King, 2001	Tree: MIPS	Flat; all class levels, but just one level at a time	Flat decision-tree induction algorithm
Clare & King, 2003	Tree: MIPS	Hierarchical; all class levels	Hierarchical (big-bang) decision-tree induction algorithm, compared with flat decision-tree induction algorithm
Holden & Freitas, 2005	Tree: EC code	Hierarchical; all class levels	Hierarchical rule set (top-down) discovered using many runs of a flat hybrid particle swarm/ant colony optimization algorithm
Holden & Freitas, 2006	Tree: GPCR classes	Hierarchical; first four class levels	Hierarchical rule set (top-down) discovered using many runs of a flat hybrid particle swarm/ant colony optimization algorithm
Jensen et al., 2003	DAG: GO	Hierarchical; learnability-based prediction, potentially at any class level	Flat artificial neural network
Laegreid et al., 2003	DAG: GO	Hierarchical, learnability-based prediction, potentially at any class level	Flat rough set-based rule induction and genetic algorithms; class hierarchy used to create flat training sets in data pre-processing
Tu, Yu, Guo, & Li, 2004	DAG: GO	Hierarchical; learnability-based prediction of child classes given their parent class	Flat artificial neural network; class hierarchy used to create flat training sets in data pre-processing
King et al., 2003	DAG: GO	Deep, specific levels; predictions based on other known classes for the same protein	Flat decision-tree induction algorithm and hierarchical Bayesian networks

Let us now turn to *hierarchical class predictions using a flat classification algorithm*. In the context of tree-structured class hierarchies, the approach of predicting each level of the hierarchy independently from the other levels—that is, by running a separate flat classification algorithm for each level—is found in Clare and King (2001), where it was the only hierarchical classification approach used, and in Clare and King (2003), where it was compared with a more sophisticated approach based on a hierarchical version of the well-known C4.5 algorithm, as will be discussed later in this section.

Turning to DAG-structured hierarchical classes, Table 1 mentions several works—in particular Jensen et al. (2003), Laegreid et al. (2003), and Tu et al. (2004)—where classes can be predicted at potentially any level of the previously discussed gene ontology (GO) using a flat classification algorithm—although in practice the actual number of predicted classes is relatively small. Let us first review the strategies used by these works to achieve such flexibility, and next discuss their limitations concerning the actual number of classes predicted.

In Jensen et al. (2003), a flat artificial neural network (ANN) was trained for each GO class at a time. It seems that parent-child relationships between classes were virtually ignored during the ANN training, since each run of the ANN treated the current class as the positive class and apparently considered all the other classes—regardless of their position in the class hierarchy—as negative classes.

Laegreid et al. (2003) predicts GO classes using a combination of a rough set-based rule induction algorithm and a genetic algorithm (GA). However, these algorithms do not directly cope with the DAG-structured class hierarchy of GO. Rather, the class hierarchy is used just to pre-process the data into suitable flat classification training sets, as follows. The genes in the original training set were grouped into 23 high-level GO classes. For genes whose most specific annotated class was below the level of the target classes, the more specific classes were ignored. This corresponds to generalizing each of the specific classes to one of the general classes at the level of the target 23 classes. As a result, 23 groups of genes were created, each group associated to one of the 23 classes. Thus, each group was considered as a training set to the combined technique. As a result, a set of rules was discovered for each of the 23 classes—that is, each rule predicts a single class.

Note that in both Jensen et al. (2003) and Laegreid et al. (2003), the essential result of the training phase is one classification model for each of the GO training classes. The basic difference is the nature of the classification model, which is an ANN in Jensen et al. (2003) and a set of rules in Laegreid et al. (2003). However, at a high level of abstraction, we can ignore this difference and focus on the important point: in both works, a classification model was built for each class, one class at a time. Consequently, when a new example in the test set needs to be classified, we can simply apply each of the classification models (each of them associated with a predicted class at potentially any level in the hierarchy) to that test example, and then assign to the test example the best class(es) among the classes predicted by the classification models, based on some measure of confidence in the prediction made by these models. That is why classification models trained for flat classification were able to assign a new test example to potentially any class at any level of the GO hierarchy.

The work of Tu et al. (2004) also uses a flat-classification ANN as the classification algorithm. However, unlike the work of Jensen et al. (2003), where the class hierarchy seems to have been virtually ignored, the work of Tu et al. (2004) applied the ANN in a way that clearly takes into account the parent-child relationships between classes. A set with a parent GO class and its child sub-classes was called by the authors a classification space. At each classification space, a flat-classification ANN was trained to predict the child class for an example that was known to belong to the parent class. This is what the authors called "further prediction," because in order to predict child classes at a given level n, it is necessary to know their parent class at level $n - 1$ (where $n \geq 2$). Note that this is in contrast with the works of Jensen et al. (2003) and Laegreid et al. (2003), which do not require the parent class of a protein to be known in order to predict its corresponding child class.

Observe also that in both Laegreid et al. (2003) and Tu et al. (2004), the structure of the class hierarchy—that is, parent-child class relationships—was essentially used to create flat training sets in a kind of data pre-processing step for the application of a flat classification algorithm.

We now turn to limitations in the actual number of GO classes predicted in the works of Jensen et al. (2003), Laegreid et al. (2003), and Tu et al. (2004). To understand these limitations, we first must bear in mind that the prediction of GO classes is particularly challenging. As discussed earlier, GO classes are arranged in a DAG, and the number of GO classes is very high (more than 13,000), referring to an extremely diverse set of gene/protein functions. As a result, it is not surprising that many works, like Jensen et al. (2003), Laegreid et al. (2003), and Tu et al. (2004), follow an approach that can be named *learnability-based prediction,* a term explicitly introduced by Tu et al. (2004). The basic idea is to focus on the prediction of the classes which are "more learnable,"—that is, which can be predicted with reasonable accuracy (given the available predictor attributes) and whose prediction is considered interesting and non-trivial. Let us briefly discuss how this approach has been used in the previously mentioned works.

Jensen et al. (2003) initially tried to predict 347 GO classes, but this number was significantly reduced later in two stages:

a.   The majority of the 347 classes was discarded either because they could not be predicted with reasonable accuracy or because they represented trivial classes whose prediction was not interesting—this reduced the number of classes to be predicted to 26.

b.   A number of classes was discarded to avoid redundancy with respect to other classes, which finally left only 14 GO classes to be predicted.

As another example of the use of the learnability-based prediction approach, Tu et al. (2004) considered 44 classification spaces, containing in total 131 classes, including both parent and child classes. The final set of learnable classes was reduced to just 14 classification spaces, containing in total 45 classes, again including both parent and child classes. In addition, as mentioned earlier, Laegreid et al. (2003) focused on predicting only 23 general classes of the GO hierarchy.

Let us now discuss two works making *hierarchical predictions based on either the big-bang or the top-down approach.*

Clare and King (2003) modified the well-known C4.5 decision-tree induction algorithm to perform hierarchical classification. This modification was not described in detail in the paper, but the basic idea seems to be that the entropy formula—used to decide which attribute will be selected for a given node in the decision tree being built—was weighted. This weighting took into account the facts that shallower (more general) classes tend to have lower entropy than deeper (more specific) classes, but more specific classes are preferred—since they provide more biological knowledge about the function of a protein. The predictive accuracy of the hierarchical version of C4.5 was compared with the predictive accuracy obtained applying the standard C4.5 separately to each class level. The hierarchical version of C4.5 obtained mixed results in terms of predictive accuracy, outperforming the standard C4.5 in some cases, but being outperformed by the latter in other cases. Since the hierarchical version of C4.5 apparently considered the entire class hierarchy during its training and produced a hierarchical classification model in a single run of the algorithm, this work can be considered an example of the big-bang approach.

By contrast, an example of the top-down approach is found in Holden and Freitas (2005). This work applied a new hybrid particle swarm optimization/ant colony optimization (PSO/ACO) algorithm to the prediction of the EC code of enzymes. In addition, Holden and Freitas (2006) applied a slightly improved version of the PSO/ACO algorithm to the prediction of G-Protein-Coupled-Receptor (GPCR) classes. Since in both works the hierarchical classification method used has essentially the same basic structure, our discussion hereafter will refer only to the work of Holden and Freitas (2005), for the sake of simplicity.

In this work the top-down approach was used mainly for the creation of the training sets used by the PSO/ACO algorithm and for the classification of the examples in the test set, as follows. During its training, the PSO/ACO algorithm was run once for each internal (non-leaf) node of the tree hierarchy. At each internal node, the PSO/ACO discovered a set of rules discriminating among all the classes associated with the child nodes of this internal node. For instance, at the root node, the algorithm discovered rules discriminating among the first-level classes $1, 2, \ldots, k_0$, where k_0 is the number of first-level classes (child nodes of the root node). At the node corresponding to class 1, the algorithm discovered rules discriminating among the second-level classes $1.1, 1.2, \ldots, k_1$, where k_1 is the number of child classes of the class 1, and so on. The class hierarchy was used to select a specific set of positive and negative examples for each run of the PSO, containing only the examples directly relevant for that run. For instance, the algorithm run corresponding to class node 1—that is, discovering rules to discriminate among classes 1.1, 1.2,..., k_1—used only examples belonging to classes 1.1, 1.2,..., k_1. During that run of the algorithm, when evaluating a rule predicting, say, class 1.1, examples of this class were considered positive examples, and examples of its sibling classes 1.2, 1.3..., k_1 were considered negative examples.

This approach produces a hierarchical set of rules, where each internal node of the hierarchy is associated with its corresponding set of rules. When classifying a new example in the test set, the example is first classified by the rule set associated with the root node. Next, it is classified by the rule set associated with the first-level node whose class was predicted by the rule set at the root ("zero-th") level, and so on, until the example reaches a leaf node and is assigned the corresponding fourth-level class. For instance, suppose the example was assigned to class 1 by the rule set associated with the root node. Next, the example will be classified by the rule set associated with the class node 1, in order to have its second-level class predicted, and so on, until the complete EC code is assigned to the example. This top-down approach for classification of test examples exploits the hierarchical nature of the discovered rule set, but it has the drawback that, if an example is misclassified at level l, then clearly the example will also be misclassified at all levels deeper than l.

In addition, note that in Holden and Freitas (2005), the class hierarchy was used during training just to produce compact sets of positive and negative examples associated with the run of the PSO/ACO algorithm at each node, but the algorithm itself was essentially a flat classification algorithm. That is, each time the algorithm was run, it was solving a flat classification problem, and it is just the many runs of the algorithm—one run for each internal node of the class hierarchy—that produces the hierarchical rule set.

Hence, this work can be considered as a borderline between hierarchical prediction using a top-down hierarchical classification method and hierarchical prediction using a flat classification algorithm. In this chapter we categorize it mainly as belonging to the former group of methods, mainly because it produces a hierarchical rule set that is used to classify test examples according to the top-down approach. Besides, it systematically creates a hierarchical rule set covering the entire class hierarchy. These characteristics are in contrast with methods that are more typical examples of the approach of hierarchical prediction with a flat classification algorithm, such as predicting classes at each level of hierarchy independently from other levels (as in Clare & King, 2001) or using a flat classification algorithm to predict just a relatively small subset of the class hierarchy (as in Jensen et al., 2003; Laegreid et al., 2003; Tu et al., 2004).

Finally, let us discuss the work of King et al. (2003) for the prediction of GO classes. First of all, this work is quite different from the other works predicting GO classes shown in Table 1, with respect to the predictor attributes used to make the prediction. In this work, when predicting whether or not a particular GO term g should be assigned to a gene, the set of predictor attributes consists of all the other terms annotated for this gene, except the terms that are ancestors or descendants of the term g in the GO DAG. By contrast, the other works predicting GO classes mentioned in Table 1 address the more usual problem of predicting GO classes based on a set of predictor attributes, which do not involve any previously annotated GO term.

Since the work of King et al. (2003) requires a gene to have a set of GO term annotations different from the GO term g currently being predicted, this work can be said to perform a kind of "further prediction," a term that was also used to describe the work of Tu et al. (2004). One important difference is that in Tu et al. (2004), the prediction of a new term requires knowledge of the parent of that term in the GO DAG, while in King et al. (2003), the prediction of a new term g requires knowledge of any other term, except the ancestors and descendants of g in the GO DAG.

Concerning the algorithms, King et al. (2003) investigated two algorithms. One was essentially a flat-classification decision-tree induction algorithm. The other, a Bayesian network algorithm, can be called a hierarchical algorithm in the sense of directly taking the class hierarchy into account when generating the Bayesian network. This was achieved by ordering the attributes (random variables for the Bayesian network algorithm) in a way compatible with the GO DAG; more precisely, using an ordering $A_1, ..., A_m$—where m is the number of attributes—in which attribute A_i comes before attribute A_j whenever A_i is a parent of A_j in the GO DAG. Once one of these orderings is found—there are in general many orderings satisfying the mentioned property, and the authors did not try to find the optimal one—it is taken into account in the construction of the Bayesian network.

Conclusion and Future Research

This chapter has two main contributions. The first one is to present a tutorial on hierarchical classification, discussing how to categorize hierarchical classification problems and hierarchical classification algorithms. The second contribution of this chapter is to present a review of a number of works applying hierarchical classification techniques to protein function prediction—an important Bioinformatics problem.

Let us now list the main conclusions of the discussion presented in this chapter, followed by corresponding suggested research directions.

First, in hierarchical classification the misclassification costs tend to vary significantly across different levels of the hierarchy and even across the same level. This is an under-explored topic in the literature on hierarchical classification of protein functions. In general, the works mentioned in Table 1 employ a simple approach to measure predictive accuracy, assuming uniform misclassification costs. We would like to point out that it is important to use a measure of predictive accuracy tailored for hierarchical classification problems, such as distance-based misclassification costs or a measure based on a hierarchical misclassification cost matrix. The use of these measures is expected to be a significant improvement over the current situation of using a simple predictive accuracy measure that ignores the class hierarchy.

Second, when the target hierarchical classification problem is categorized as optional leaf-node prediction, the hierarchical classification algorithm has autonomy to decide how deep in the class hierarchy should be the most specific class assigned to an example. This decision should, in principle, be based on at least two factors, namely:

a.   How much confidence the algorithm has in different class predictions at different levels of the class hierarchy—recall that, in general, the deeper the class level, the more difficult the prediction is, and so the less confident the algorithm will tend to be in the prediction.

b.   The usefulness of different class predictions at different levels of the class hierarchy—recall that, in general, the deeper the level of a predicted class, the more useful the prediction tends to be to the user.

This trade-off between confidence and usefulness of class predictions at different levels of a class hierarchy is still very under-explored in the literature, and a future research direction would be to try to develop methods for quantifying this trade-off and coping with it during the construction of the classification model. Since maximizing prediction confidence and maximizing prediction usefulness tend to be conflicting objectives, perhaps the use of a multi-objective classification algorithm based on the concept of Pareto dominance would be useful here. The reader is referred to Deb (2001) for a comprehensive review of the concept of Pareto dominance and to Freitas (2004) for a review of the motivation for the use of this concept in data mining.

Third, as a particularly important special case of the general trade-off between confidence and usefulness just discussed, we identify the challenging problem of predicting functional classes of the gene ontology—a class hierarchy in the form of a DAG. As discussed in the latter part of this chapter, several works in this area focus on predicting classes in just a relatively small subset of the GO DAG, rather than all classes in the entire DAG, and in particular focus on classes that are more "learnable"—characterizing the so-called "learnability-based prediction framework." The basic idea of this framework consists of predicting classes which are more learnable and whose prediction is more interesting, which is conceptually similar to the idea of trying to maximize the confidence and the usefulness of the predictions made by the hierarchical classification algorithm. The need for this learnability-based framework is clearly understandable, since the GO DAG contains more than 13,000 class nodes and, in a given bioinformatics application, the user may very well be interested in predicting a relatively small set of GO functional classes. However, it should be pointed out that, in the literature in general, the precise determination of which GO functional classes should be predicted in the learnability-based framework is usually done in an ad-hoc fashion, being very much dependent on the user's intuition. There is a need to develop more formal and effective methods to determine how to quantify the degree of learnability and interestingness of nodes in the GO class hierarchy. This is an important and challenging research direction.

References

Aha, D.W., Kibler, D., & Albert, M.K. (1991). Instance-based learning algorithms. *Machine Learning, 6,* 37-66.

Aha, D.W. (1992). Tolerating noisy, irrelevant and novel attributes in instance-based learning algorithms. *International Journal of Man-Machine Studies, 36,* 267-287.

Aha, D.W. (1997). *Artificial Intelligence Review—Special Issue on Lazy Learning, 11,* 1-5.

Alberts, B., Johnson, A., Lewis, J., Raff, M., Roberts, K., & Walter, P. (2002). *The molecular biology of the cell* (4th ed.). Garland Press.

Bard, J., Rhee, S.Y., & Ashburner, M. (2005). An ontology for cell types. *Genome Biology 2005, 6*(2), Article R21.

Blockeel, H., Bruynooghe, M., Dzeroski, S., Ramon, J., & Struyf, J. (2002). Hierarchical multi-classification. KDD-2002 Workshop Notes: In *Proceedings of MRDM 2002—Workshop on Multi-Relational Data Mining* (pp. 21-35).

Camon, E., Magrane, M., Barrel, D., Binns, D., Fleischmann, W., Kersey, P., Mulder, N., Oinn, T., Maslen, J., Cox, A., & Apweiler, R. (2003). The Gene Ontology Annotation (GOA) project: Implementation of GO in Swiss-Prot, TrEMBL and InterPro. *Genome Research.*

Caruana, R., & Niculescu-Mizil, A. (2004). Data mining in metric space: An empirical analysis of supervised learning performance criteria. In *Proceedings of the 6th ACM SIGMOD International Conference on Knowledge Discovery and Data Mining (KDD-2004)* (pp. 69-78). ACM Press.

Clare, A., & King, R.D. (2001). Knowledge discovery in multi-label phenotype data. In *Proceedings of the 5th European Conference on Principles and Practice of Knowledge Discovery and Data Mining (PKDD-2001)* (LNAI 2168, pp. 42-53).

Clare, A., & King, R.D. (2003). Predicting gene function in *Saccharomyces Cerevisiae. Bioinformatics, 19*(Suppl. 2), ii42-ii49.

Deb, K. (2001). *Multi-objective optimization using evolutionary algorithms*. New York: John Wiley & Sons.

Deng, M., Zhang, K., Mehta, S., Chen, T., & Sun, F. (2002). Prediction of protein function using protein-protein interaction data. In *Proceedings of the IEEE Computer Society Bioinformatics Conference (CSB '02)* (pp. 947-960).

Dressler, D., & Potter, H. (1991). *Discovering enzymes*. Scientific American Library.

Dumais, S., & Chen, H. (2000). Hierarchical classification of Web content. In *Proceedings of the SIGIR-00 23rd ACM International Conference on Research and Development in Information Retrieval* (pp. 256-263). ACM Press.

Freitas, A.A. (2004). A critical review of multi-objective optimization in data mining: A position paper. *ACM SIGKDD Explorations, 6*(2), 77-86.

Gerlt, J.A., & Babbitt, P.C. (2000). Can sequence determine function? *Genome Biology, 1*(5), 1-10.

Gene Ontology Consortium. (2000). Gene ontology: Tool for the unification of biology. *Nature Genetics, 25,* 25-29.

Gupta, R., & Brunak, S. (2002). Prediction of glycosylation across the human proteome and the correlation to protein function. In *Proceedings of the Pacific Symposium on Biocomputing (PSB-2002)* (pp. 310-322).

Hendlich, M., Bergner, A., Gunther, J., & Klebe, G. (2003). Relibase: Design and development of a database for comprehensive analysis of protein-ligand interactions. *Journal of Molecular Biology, 326,* 607-620.

Higgs, P.G., & Attwood, T.K. (2005). *Bioinformatics and molecular evolution*. Blackwell.

Holden, N., & Freitas, A.A. (2005). A hybrid particle swarm/ant colony algorithm for the classification of hierarchical biological data. In *Proceedings of the 2005 IEEE Swarm Intelligence Symposium* (pp. 100-107).

Holden, N., & Freitas, A.A. (2006). Hierarchical classification of G-Protein-Coupled Receptors with a PSO/ACO algorithm. *To appear in Proceedings of the 2006 IEEE Swarm Intelligence Symposium*.

Jensen, L.J., Gupta, R., Blom, N., Devos, D., Tamames, J., Kesmir, C., et al. (2002). Prediction of human protein function from post-translational modifications and localization features. *Journal of Molecular Biology, 319,* 1257-1265.

Jensen, L.J., Gupta, R., Staerfeldt, H.-H., & Brunak S. (2003). Prediction of human protein function according to gene ontology categories. *Bioinformatics, 19*(5), 635-642.

Jiang, D., Tang, C., & Zhang, A. (2004). Cluster analysis for gene expression data: A survey. *IEEE Transactions on Knowledge and Data Engineering, 16*(11), 1370-1386.

Karwath, A., & King, R.D. (2002). Homology induction: The use of machine learning to improve sequence similarity searches. *BMC Bioinformatics, 3*(11).

King, R.D., Karwath, A., Clare, A., & Dehaspe, L. (2001). The utility of different representations of protein sequence for predicting functional class. *Bioinformatics, 17*(5), 445-454.

King, O.D., Foulger, R.E., Weight, S.D., White, J.V., & Roth, F.P. (2003). Predicting gene function from patterns of annotation. *Genome Research, 13,* 896-904.

Koller, D., & Sahami, M. (1997). Hierarchically classifying documents using very few words. In *Proceedings of the 14th International Conference on Machine Learning* (ICML-1997) (pp. 170-178). San Francisco: Morgan Kaufmann.

Laegreid, A., Hvidsten, T.R., Midelfart, H., Komorowski, J., & Sandvik, A.K. (2003). Predicting gene ontology biological process from temporal gene expression patterns. *Genome Research, 13,* 965-979.

Lenhinger, A.L., Nelson, D.L., & Cox, M.M. (1998). *Principles of biochemistry with an extended discussion of oxygen-binding proteins* (2nd ed.) New York: Worth Publishers.

Lewis, S.E. (2004). Gene ontology: Looking backwards and forwards. *Genome Biology 2004, 6*(1), Article 103.

Liao, T.W., Zhang, Z., & Mount, C.R. (1998). Similarity measures for retrieval in case-based reasoning systems. *Applied Artificial Intelligence, 12,* 267-288.

Nagl, S.B. (2003). Molecular evolution. In C.A. Orengo, D.T. Jones, & J.M. Thornton (Eds.), *Bioinformatics: Genes, proteins, computers* (pp. 1-17).

Pal, D., & Eisenberg, D. (2005). Inference of protein function from protein structure. *Protein Structure, 13,* 121-130.

Riley, M. (1993). Functions of the gene products of *Eschirichia coli. Microbiological Reviews, 57,* 862-952.

Sasaki, M., & Kita, K. (1998). Rule-based text categorization using hierarchical categories. In *Proceedings of the IEEE International Conference on Systems, Man and Cybernetics* (pp. 2827-2830). IEEE Press.

Schug, J., Diskin, S., Mazzarelli, J., Brunk, B.P., & Stoeckert, C.J. Jr. (2002). Predicting gene ontology functions from ProDom and CDD protein domains. *Genome Research, 12,* 648-655.

Slonim, D.K., Tamayo, P., Mesirov, J.P., Golub, T.R., & Lander, E.S. (2000). Class prediction and discovery using gene expression data. In *Proceedings of the 4th Annual International Conference on Computational Molecular Biology (RECOMB)*, Tokyo, Japan (pp. 263-272). Universal Academy Press.

Smith, C.L., Goldsmith, C.A.W., & Eppig, J.T. (2004). The mammalian phenotype ontology as a tool for annotating, analyzing and comparing phenotypic information. *Genome Biology, 6*(1), Article R7.

Stawiski, E.W., Mandel-Gutfreund, Y., Lowenthal, A.C., & Gregoret, L.M. (2002). Progress in predicting protein function from structure: Unique features of O-glycosidases. In *Proceedings of the 2002 Pacific Symposium on Biocomputing* (pp. 637-648).

Sun, A., & Lim, E.-P. (2001). Hierarchical text classification and evaluation. In *Proceedings of the 1ˢᵗ IEEE International Conference on Data Mining* (pp. 521-528). IEEE Computer Society Press.

Sun, A., Lim, E.-P., & Ng, W.-K. (2003a). Performance measurement framework for hierarchical text classification. *Journal of the American Society for Information Science and Technology, 54*(11), 1014-1028.

Sun, A., Lim, E.-P., & Ng, W.-K. (2003b). Hierarchical text classification methods and their specification. In A.T.S. Chan, S.C.F. Chan, H.V. Leong, & V.T.Y. Ng. (Eds.), *Cooperative internet computing* (pp. 236-256). Kluwer.

Sun, A., Lim, E.-P., & Ng, W.-K. (2004). Blocking reduction strategies in hierarchical text classification. *IEEE Transactions on Knowledge and Data Engineering, 16*(10), 1305-1308.

Syed, U., & Yona, G. (2003). Using a mixture of probabilistic decision trees for direct prediction of protein function. In *Proceedings of the 2003 Conference on Research in Computational Molecular Biology* (RECOMB-2003) (pp. 289-300).

Tan, P.N., Steinbach, M., & Kumar, V. (2006). *Introduction to data mining.* Addison-Wesley.

Thomas, P.D., Kejariwal, A., Campbell, M.J., Mi, H., Diemer, K., Guo, N., et al. (2003). PANTHER: A browsable database of gene products organized by biological function, using curated protein family and subfamily classification. *Nucleic Acids Research, 31*(1), 334-341.

Tu, K., Yu, H., Guo, Z., & Li, X. (2004). Learnability-based further prediction of gene functions in gene ontology. *Genomics, 84,* 922-928.

Weinert, W.R., & Lopes, H.S. (2004). Neural networks for protein classification. *Applied Bioinformatics, 3*(1), 41-48.

Witten, I.H., & Frank, E. (2005). *Data mining: Practical machine learning tools with Java implementations* (2ⁿᵈ ed.). San Francisco: Morgan Kaufmann.

Chapter VIII

Topological Analysis and Sub-Network Mining of Protein-Protein Interactions

Daniel Wu, Drexel University, USA

Xiaohua Hu, Drexel University, USA

Abstract

In this chapter, we report a comprehensive evaluation of the topological structure of protein-protein interaction (PPI) networks, by mining and analyzing graphs constructed from the popular data sets publicly available to the bioinformatics research community. We compare the topology of these networks across different species, different confidence levels, and different experimental systems used to obtain the interaction data. Our results confirm the well-accepted claim that the degree distribution follows a power law. However, further statistical analysis shows that residues are not independent on the fit values, indicating that the power law model may be inadequate. Our results also show that the dependence of the average clustering coefficient on the vertices degree is far from a power law, contradicting many published results. For the first time, we report that the average vertex density exhibits a strong powder law dependence on the vertices degree for the networks studied, regardless of species, confidence levels, and experimental systems. We also present an efficient and accurate approach to detecting a community in a protein-protein interaction network from a given seed protein. Our experimental results show strong structural and functional relationships among member proteins within each of the communities identified by our approach, as verified by MIPS complex catalog database and annotations.

Introduction

Proteins are important players in executing the genetic program. When carrying out a particular biological function or serving as molecular building blocks for a particular cellular structure, proteins rarely act individually. Rather, biological complexity is encapsulated in the structure and dynamics of the combinatorial interactions among proteins as well as other biological molecules (such as DNA and RNA) at different levels, ranging from the simplest biochemical reactions to the complex ecological phenomena (Barabasi & Oltvai, 2004). Therefore, one of the key challenges in the post-genomic era is to understand these complex molecular interactions that confer the structure and dynamics of a living cell.

Traditionally, knowledge about protein-protein interactions (PPIs) has been accumulated from the so-called small-scale biochemical and biophysical studies. The results obtained through these small-scale experiments are considered to be reliable and become the foundation of our understanding of the complex bio-molecular interaction networks. Recent years, however, have seen a tremendous increase in the amount of data about protein-protein interactions attributed to the development of high-throughput data collection techniques. On one hand, the collection of this high volume of data provides a great opportunity for further investigations, including those employing computational approaches for modeling, and thus understanding the structure and dynamics of the complex biological systems. On the other hand, the data available are still incomplete and appear to be noisy, posting a great challenge for further analysis. Nonetheless, analyzing these PPI data is widely believed to be important and may provide valuable insights into proteins, protein complexes, signaling pathways, cellular processes, and even complex diseases (Bork et al., 2004).

Modeling protein-protein interactions often takes the form of graphs or networks, where vertices represent proteins and edges represent the interactions between pairs of proteins. Research on such PPI networks has revealed a number of distinctive topological properties, including the "small-world effect," the power-law degree distribution, clustering (or network transitivity), and the community structure (Girvan & Newman, 2002).

These topological properties, shared by many biological networks, appear to be of biological significance. One example of such biological relevance is the correlation reported between gene knock-out lethality and the connectivity of the encoded protein (Jeong, Mason, Barabasi, & Oltvai, 2001). Correlation is also found between the evolutionary conservation of proteins and their connectivity (Fraser et al., 2002; Fraser et al., 2003; Wuchty, 2004). Not surprisingly, topological information has been exploited in the predictive functional assignment of uncharacterized proteins and the theoretical modeling for the evolution of PPI networks (Pei & Zhang, 2005; Valente, Cusick, Fagerstrom, Hill, & Vidal, 2005; Bu et al., 2003; Hu, 2005; Hu et al., 2004).

In this chapter, we present a comprehensive evaluation of the topological structure of PPI networks across different species. We also introduce a novel and efficient approach, which exploits the network topology, for mining the PPI networks to detect a protein community from a given seed. We begin with a review of related work, followed by a description of the data sets and metrics we use to analyze the topological structure of PPI networks. We then present the algorithm for detecting a protein community from a seed. Finally, we report our findings and conclude the chapter with a discussion.

Background

We can study the topological properties of networks either globally or locally. Global properties describe the entire network to provide a birds-eye view of a given network. While useful, global properties in general are not capable of describing the intricate differences among different networks. Especially when data about networks are incomplete and noisy, such as PPI networks, the ability of global properties to accurately describe a given network suffers. On the contrary, local properties study only parts of the entire networks. They measure local sub-graphs or patterns. In regard to studying incomplete and noisy networks, local properties have one obvious advantage in that they may describe these networks more accurately because sub-graphs in these networks are believed more likely to be complete than the whole graph.

Most research in the area of network topological analysis thus far has been focused on such properties as network diameters, degree distribution, clustering co-efficient, and the community structure.

The diameter of a network is the average distance between any two vertices in the network. The distance between two vertices is measured by the shortest path lengths between these two vertices. Despite their large sizes, many real-world networks, such as biological and social networks, have small diameters. The so-called "small-world" property refers to such small diameters in the network. The "small-world" model was first proposed by Watts and Strogatz (1998), who started a large area of research related to the small-world topology.

The degree (or connectivity) of a vertex v is the number of edges connecting v to other vertices in the network. The degree distribution, denoted as $P(k)$, is defined as the probability that a given vertex v in an undirected graph has exact degree of k. $P(k)$ has been used to characterize the distribution of degrees in a network.

In their pioneering work, Barabasi and Albert (1999) discovered a highly heterogeneous PPI network with non-Poisson, scale-free degree distribution in the yeast. The signature of scale-free networks, as opposed to random networks, is that the degrees of vertices are distributed following a power-law:

$$P(k) \sim k^{-\gamma},$$

where $P(k)$ is the probability of a vertex having a degree of k and $\gamma > 0$. The power law degree distribution has been observed in many real-world networks such as the World Wide Web, and social and biological networks including PPI networks of *S. cerevisiae, H. pylori, E. coli, C. elegans*, and *D. melanogaster* (Uetz et al., 2000; Rain et al., 2001; Butland et al., 2005; Walhout et al., 2000; Li et al. 2004; Giot et al., 2004). Therefore, since its emergence, the scale-free network model has been widely adopted.

In network analysis, the term "clustering" is used exchangeable with "network transitivity" to describe the phenomenon of an increased probability of two vertices being adjacent if both share a common neighbor—that is, if a vertex A is connected to vertex B, and vertex C is also connected to vertex B, then there is a heightened probability that A has a direct connection to C. Clustering property is normally measured by the clustering coefficient, which is the average probability that two neighbors of a given vertex are adjacent. Formally, the clustering coefficient of vertex v, denoted as C_v (Barabasi & Albert, 1999), is defined by:

$$C_v = \frac{E_v}{n(n-1)/2},$$

where n is the number of neighboring vertices of v, E_v is the actual number of edges among these n neighboring vertices, and $n(n-1)/2$ is the maximal possible number of edges among these n vertices. The clustering coefficient is a local topological property measuring local group cohesiveness. A corresponding global measurement for characterizing a network in this regard can be quantified by averaging the clustering coefficient over all vertices in the network, as defined by:

$$< C >= \frac{1}{n}\sum_{v} C_{v},$$

$<C>$ provides a statistical view of local group cohesiveness over the entire network. In addition, a network can also be characterized quantitatively by the clustering coefficient distribution which is defined by:

$$C(k) = \frac{1}{n_{k}}\sum_{v} C_{v}, \forall v \mid d_{v} = k,$$

where n_{k} is the number of vertices with degree k, and d_{v} is the degree of vertex v. It has been shown that the clustering coefficient distribution is also following a power law (Spirin & Mirny, 2003; Yook, Oltvai, & Barabasi, 2004; Colizza, Flammini, Maritan, & Vespignani, 2005), that is:

$$C(k) \sim k^{\beta}, \beta > 0.$$

A recent work by Ng and Huang (2004) carries out a study on two topological properties, degree distribution and diameter, of PPI networks across six different species. Their work confirms the popular scale-free topology across different species based on these two measurements.

Even though the scale-free network model is well adopted, whether the power-law behavior is applicable to all PPI networks is still up to challenges. Thomas, Cannings, Monk, and Cannings (2003) found that the degree distribution in a human PPI network does not follow a power law. They argued that the current belief of power-law connectivity distribution may reflect a behavior of a sampled sub-graph. Since we only have an incomplete and low coverage sample of an entire protein interactome, the behavior in a sampled sub-graph does not necessarily imply the same behavior for the whole graph. Therefore, they called for the attention of importance to assess the accuracy of the observed degree distribution in reference to the full proteome.

From a different angle, Tanaka et al. (2005) recently reported that some PPI networks do not follow power law if using a rank-degree plot instead of regularly used frequency-degree plot.

Colizza et al. (2005) also evaluated three PPI networks constructed from three different yeast data sets. Although they observe that the degree distribution follows a power law, only one of the three networks exhibits approximate power law behavior for the clustering coefficient. Soffer and Vazquez (2004) find that the power law dependence of the clustering coefficient is to some extent caused by the degree correlations of the networks, with high-degree vertices preferentially connecting with low-degree vertices.

Community structure is another property common to many networks. Although there is no formal definition for the community structure in a network, it often loosely refers to the gathering of vertices into groups such that the connections within groups are denser than connections between groups (Girvan & Newman, 2002). The study of community structure in a network is closely related to the graph partitioning in graph theory and computer science. It also has close ties with the hierarchical clustering in sociology (Newman, 2003). Recent years have witnessed an intensive activity in this field, partly due to the dramatic increase in the scale of networks being studied.

Because communities are believed to play a central role in the functional properties of complex networks (Newman, 2003), the ability to detect communities in networks could have practical applications. Studying the community structure of biological networks is of particular interest and challenging, given the high data volume and the complex nature of interactions. In the context of biological networks, communities might represent structural or functional groupings. They can be synonymous with molecular modules, biochemical pathways, gene clusters, or protein complexes. Being able to identify the community structure in a biological network may help us to understand better the structure and dynamics of biological systems.

Many algorithms for detecting community structure in networks have been proposed. They can be roughly classified into two categories, divisive and agglomerative. The divisive approach takes the route of recursive removal of vertices (or edges) until the network is separated into its components or communities, whereas the agglomerative approach starts with isolated individual vertices and joins together small communities. One important algorithm (the GN algorithm) is proposed by Girvan and Newman (2002). The GN algorithm is based on the concept of betweenness, a quantitative measure of the number of shortest paths passing through a given vertex (or edge). The vertices (or edges) with the highest betweenness are believed to play the most prominent role in connecting different parts of a network. The GN algorithm detects communities in a network by recursively removing these high betweenness vertices (or edges). It has produced good results and is well adopted by different authors in studying various networks (Newman, 2003). However, it has a major disadvantage, which is its computational cost. For sparse networks with n vertices, the GN algorithm is of $O(n^3)$ time. Various alternative algorithms have been proposed (Newman, 2004a, 2004b; Newman & Girvan, 2004; Donetti & Munoz, 2004; White & Smyth, 2005), attempting to improve either the quality of the community structure or the computational efficiency.

The GN algorithm has been applied to a number of metabolic networks from different organisms to detect communities that relate to functional units in the networks

(Holme, Huss, & Jeong, 2003). It has also been adapted to analyze a network of gene relationships as established by co-occurrence of gene names in published literature and to detect communities of related genes (Wilkinson & Huberman, 2004).

One goal of our work here is to address a slightly different question about the community structure in a PPI network—that is, what is the community a given protein (or proteins) belongs to? We are motivated by two main factors. Firstly, due to the complexity and modularity of biological networks, it is more feasible computationally to study a community containing one or a few proteins of interest. Secondly, sometimes the whole community structure of the network may not be our primary concern. Rather, we may be more interested in finding the community that contains a protein (or proteins) of interest.

Hashimoto et al. (2004) have used a similar approach to growing genetic regulatory networks from seed genes. Their work is based on probabilistic Boolean networks, and sub-networks are constructed in the context of a directed graph using both the coefficient of determination and the Boolean function influence among genes. The similar approach is also taken by Flake, Lawrence, Giles, and Coetzee (2002) to find highly topically related communities in the Web based on the self-organization of the network structure and on a maximum flow method.

Related works also include those that predict co-complex proteins. Jansen, Lan, Qian, and Gerstein (2002) use a procedure integrating different data sources to predict the membership of protein complexes for individual genes based on two assumptions: first, the function of any protein complex depends on the functions of its subunits; and second, all sub-units of a protein complex share certain common properties. Bader and Hogue (2003) report a Molecular Complex Detection (MCODE) clustering algorithm to identify molecular complexes in a large protein interaction network. MCODE is based on local network density—a modified measure of the clustering coefficient. Bu et al. (2003) use a spectral analysis method to identify the topological structures such as quasi-cliques and quasi-bipartites in a protein-protein interaction network. These topological structures are found to be biologically relevant functional groups. In our previous work, we developed a spectral-based clustering method using local density and vertex neighborhood to analyze the chromatin network (Bu et al., 2003; Hu, 2005). Two recent works along this line of research are based on the concept of network modularity introduced by Hartwell, Hopfield, Leibler, and Murray (1999). The works of Spirin and Mirny (2003) and Rives and Galitski (2003) both used computational analyses to cluster the yeast PPI network and discovered that molecular modules are densely connected with each other but sparsely connected with the rest of the network.

Method

We intuitively model a protein-protein interaction network as a simple graph, meaning that it is undirected, unweighted, and without self-loops. Each vertex of the graph represents a protein and each edge represents an interaction between the two proteins connected by it.

Data Sets

We analyze the topology of PPI networks using the species-specific data set which includes *E. coli, H. pylori, S. cerevisiae, D. melanogaster, C. elegans, M. musculus,* and *H. sapiens* PPI networks. The data sets were downloaded from the Database for Interacting Proteins (DIP) (Salwinski et al., 2004). To test our algorithm, we use a data set of interactions for *Saccharomyces cerevisae* downloaded from the General Repository for Interaction Datasets (GRID) (Breitkreutz, Stark, & Tyers, 2003). The GRID database contains all published large-scale interaction datasets as well as available curated interactions. The GRID yeast data set we downloaded has 4,907 proteins and 17,598 interactions.

Measurements of Network Topology

The basic properties are measured for each PPI network, including:

1.   The number of proteins, measured by the number of vertices
2.   The number of interactions, measured by the number of edges
3.   The number of connected components within the network
4.   The size of the largest (or giant) component, measured by the size of the largest connected sub-graph

We also measure three degree-related metrics: the maximum degree (k_{max}), the average degree ($<k>$), defined as:

$$<k> = \frac{2|E|}{n},$$

where $|E|$ is the total number of edges and n is the total number of vertices, and the degree distribution $(P(k))$, which is the frequency of a vertex having degree k in the network.

The diameter of a network $<l>$ is defined as the average distance between any two vertices. The distance between two vertices is defined as the number of edges along their shortest path.

For a vertex i, we adopt the definition of the clustering coefficient C_v from Uetz, et al. (2000) as defined above. A global measurement related to this is the average clustering coefficient $<C>$, also defined earlier on. Assuming the same degree distribution, we adopt the following definition to obtain an average clustering coefficient of a random network (Newman, 2003):

$$< C_{rand} >= \frac{(<k^2> - <k>)^2}{n<k>^3}.$$

We also calculate a local property called vertex density $<D>$. The definition of vertex density is inspired by Bader and Hogue (2003), who define a local density by expanding the definition of the clustering coefficient for vertex v to include v itself in the formula when calculating C_v.

All statistical analyses are performed using an SPSS software package.

The Algorithm

Notation

An undirected graph $G = (V, E)$ is composed of two sets, vertices V and edges E. An edge e is defined as a pair of vertices (u, v) denoting the direct connection between vertices u and v. The graphs we use in this chapter are undirected, unweighted, and simple—meaning no self-loops or parallel edges.

For a subgraph $G' \subset G$ and a vertex i belonging to G', we define the in-community degree for vertex i, $k_i^{in}(G')$, to be the number of edges connecting vertex i to other vertices belonging to G' and the out-community degree, $k_i^{out}(G')$, to be the number of edges connecting vertex i to other vertices that are in G but do not belong to G'.

In our algorithm, we adopt the quantitative definitions of community defined by Radicchi, Castellano, Cecconi, Loreto, and Parisi (2004). In this definition, a subgraph G' is a community in a strong sense, if for each vertex i in G', its in-community degree is greater than out-community degree. More formally, G' is a community in a strong sense if:

$$K_i^{in}(G') > K_i^{out}(G'), \forall i \in G', G' \subset G.$$

In a weak sense, if the sum of all degrees within G' is greater than the sum of all degrees from G' to the rest of the graph...that is, G' is a community in a weak sense if

$$\sum_i K_i^{in}(G') > \sum_i K_i^{out}(G'), i \in G', G' \subset G.$$

Alorithm 1. CommBuilder(G, s, f)

1: $G(V, E)$ is the input graph with vertex set V and edge set E.

2: s is the seed vertex, f is the affinity threshold.

3: $N \leftarrow \{$Adjacency list of $s \} \cup \{s\}$

4: $C \leftarrow$ FindCore(N)

5: $C' \leftarrow$ ExpandCore(C, f)

6: **return** C'

7: FindCore(N)

8:     **for each** $v \in N$

9:         calculate $k_v^{in}(N)$

10:     **end for**

11:     $Kmin \leftarrow$ min $\{ k_v^{in}(N), v \in N \}$

12:     $Kmax \leftarrow$ max $\{ k_v^{in}(N), v \in N \}$

13:     **if** $Kmin = Kmax$ **then return** N

14:     **else return** FindCore($N - \{v\}, k_v^{in}(N) = Kmin$)

15: ExpandCore(C, f)

16:     $D \leftarrow \bigcup_{(v,w) \in E, v \in C, w \notin C} \{v, w\}$

17:     $C' \leftarrow C$

18:     **for each** $t \in D$ **and** $t \notin C$

19:         calculate $k_v^{in}(D)$

20:         calculate $k_t^{out}(D)$

21:     **if** $k_v^{in}(D) > k_t^{out}(D)$ **or** $k_v^{in}(D)/|D| > f$ **then** $C' \leftarrow C' \cup \{t\}$

22:     **end for**

23:     **if** $C' = C$ **then return** C

24:     **else return** ExpandCore(C', f)

The Algorithm

The algorithm, called *CommBuilder,* accepts the seed protein *s*, gets the neighbors of *s*, finds the core of the community to build, and expands the core to find the eventual community. See Algorithm 1.

The two major components of *CommBuilder* are *FindCore* and *ExpandCore*. In fact, *FindCore* performs a naïve search for maximum clique from the neighborhood of the seed protein by recursively removing vertices with the lowest in-community degree until all vertices in the core set have the same in-community degree.

The algorithm performs a breadth-first expansion in the core expanding step. It first builds a candidate set containing the core and all vertices adjacent to each vertex in the core. It then adds to the core a vertex that either meets the quantitative definition of community in a strong sense or the fraction of in-community degree over a relaxed affinity threshold *f* of the size of the core. The affinity threshold is 1 when the candidate vertex connects to each of vertices in the core set. This threshold provides flexibility when expanding the core, because it is too strict requiring every expanding vertex to be a strong sense community member.

The *FindCore* is a heuristic search for a maximum complete subgraph in the neighborhood N of seed s. Let K be the size of N, then the worst-case running time of *FindCore* is $O(k^2)$. The *ExpandCore* part costs in worst case approximately $|V|$ + $|E|$ + overhead. $|V|$ accounts for the expanding of the core, at most all vertices in V—minus what are already in the core—would be included. $|E|$ accounts for calculating the in- and out-degrees for the candidate vertices that are not in the core but in the neighborhood of the core. The overhead is caused by recalculating the in- and out-degrees of neighboring vertices every time the *FindCore* is recursively

Table 1. PPI networks of different species

Species	Proteins	Interactions	#components	Giant Component(*)
E. Coli	1,640	6,658	200	1,396 (85.1%)
H. Pylori	702	1,359	9	686 (97.7%)
S. Cerevisiae (Core)	2,614	6,379	66	2,445 (93.5%)
D. Melanogaster	7,441	22,636	52	7,330 (98.5%)
C. Elegans	2,629	3,970	99	2,386 (90.8%)
M. Musculus	327	274	79	49 (15.0%)
H. Sapiens	1,059	1,318	119	563 (53.2%)

* Number inside the parentheses: percentage of the size of the giant component in the entire network

called. The number of these vertices is dependent on the size of the community we are building and the connectivity of the community to the rest of the network, but not the overall size of the network.

Results

Basic Properties of the PPI Networks

Table 1 lists the basic properties of all PPI networks used for our analysis. The sizes of networks vary significantly across species, indicating the varied status in data collecting and documenting for the specific data source and virtually our understanding of PPI for these organisms. Table 1 shows the small sizes of so-called giant components for *H. sapiens* and *M. musculus,* meaning that we have a fairly large number of unconnected small sub-graphs in these two networks.

Average Global Topological Properties of PPI Networks

In Table 2, we report the average global topological properties of PPI networks. Across species, PPI networks all exhibit small values of average degree and diameters, even though the absolute values differ significantly. Also, except for *C. elegans,* PPI networks for all other species have larger average clustering coefficient comparing to the corresponding random clustering coefficient, indicating a non-random and hierarchical structure within these networks. Contrary to the average clustering coefficient, the average vertex density shows much lesser variability across species.

Table 2. Average global topological properties of PPI networks

NETWORK	K_{max}	$<k>$	$<l>$	$<D>$	$<C>$	$<C_{rand}>$
E. coli	152	8.12	3.73	0.7053	0.5889	0.1168
H. pylori	54	3.87	4.14	0.4514	0.0255	0.0403
S. cerevisiae (Core)	111	4.88	5.00	0.5609	0.2990	0.0103
D. melanogaster	178	6.08	4.39	0.3920	0.0159	0.0097
C. elegans	187	3.02	4.81	0.4885	0.0490	0.0462
M. musculus	12	1.68	3.57	0.6082	0.1011	0.0062
H. sapiens	33	2.49	6.80	0.5703	0.1658	0.0098

Figure 1. Degree distribution P(k) of PPI networks across species

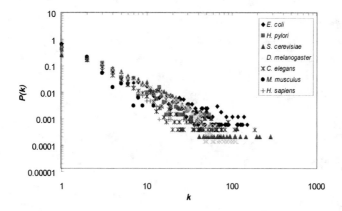

Figure 2. Residuals vs. fit values

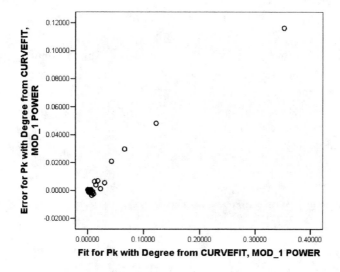

Degree Distribution

Degree distribution *P(k)* is the probability that a selected protein has exactly degree *k*. We evaluate the distribution of degrees $P(k)$ as a function of *k*. Figure 1 shows the degree distribution for the networks across different species. The log-log plot clearly demonstrates the power law dependence of $P(k)$ on degree *k*. For our analysis, we select to use directly the raw data, instead of following Uetz, et al. (2000) with

Table 3. Statistical analysis of PPI networks

NETWORKS	$\gamma\dagger$ (R^2)	$\alpha\dagger$ (R^2)	$\beta\dagger$ (R^2)
E. coli	1.355 (0.882)	0.562 (0.656)	0.536 (0.756)
H. pylori	1.651 (0.899)	0.495 (0.373)	0.826 (0.985)
D. melanogaster	1.945 (0.923)	3.050 (0.311)	0.836 (0.989)
S. cerevisiae (Core)	1.977 (0.911)	0.893 (0.721)	0.759 (0.867)
C. elegans	1.599 (0.839)	0.625 (0.362)	0.833 (0.976)
M. musculus	2.360 (0.931)	0.598 (0.431)*	0.689 (0.965)
H. sapiens	2.025 (0.931)	0.657 (0.190)*	0.626 (0.699)

† $P(k) \sim k^\gamma$, $C(k) \sim k^\alpha$, $D(k) \sim k^\beta$

* $p > 0.05$

exponential cutoff. The results of statistical analysis are listed in Table 3. Without exponential cutoff, our regression analysis yields power law exponents γ between 1.36 and 2.36, in fairly good agreement with previously reported results.

Even though the regression analysis and figures clearly show strong power-law degree distribution, we want to conduct further statistical analysis to test if the power law model adequately captures all the features in the testing data. Using SPSS software package, we create a scatter plot of residues by fit values for the power law model. The result is shown in Figure 2, which clearly indicates a pattern in the data that is not captured by the power law model. This means that the power law is a model that has excellent fit statistics, but has poor residuals, indicating the inadequacy of the model.

The Average Clustering Coefficient Distribution

We have shown results of average clustering coefficient for PPI networks in a previous section. We now take a closer look at the distribution of the clustering coefficient by averaging the clustering coefficient over vertices with degree k, $C(k)$, as defined above.

The results, as shown in Figure 3, indicate that while *E. coli* and *S. cerevisiae* (also shown in Table 3) PPI networks show somewhat weak power law distribution, networks of other species do not follow a power law. Regression analysis shows that there is no statistical significance for fitting a power law for networks from *M. musculus* and *H. sapiens*. Even though the remaining networks from *H. pylori*, *D. melanogaster*, and *C. elegans* have p values less than 0.05, the values of R^2 are fairly low.

Figure 3. Average clustering coefficient C(k) as a function of degree k in PPI net-works across different species

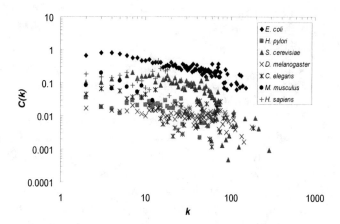

Figure 4. Average vertex density D(k) as a function of degree k in PPI networks across different species

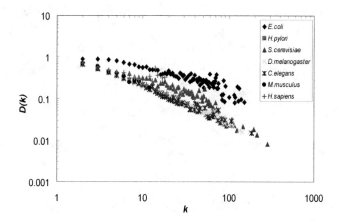

The Average Vertex Density Distribution

We evaluate the distribution of the average vertex density over the vertices with degree k. The results for the vertex density spectrum ($D(k)$ over degree k) display consistent power law behavior for all the networks (Figure 4).

Protein Communities

We applied our algorithm against the network built from the downloaded data set as described earlier in this chapter. The average running time for finding a community of around 50 members is about 20 minutes.

Because there is no alternative approach to our method, we decided to compare the performance of our algorithm to the work on predicting protein complex membership by Asthana, King, Gibbons, and Roth (2004), who reported results of queries with four complexes using probabilistic network reliability (we will refer to their work as the PNR method in the following discussion). Four communities are identified by CommBuilder, using one protein as seed from each of the query complexes used by the PNR method. The seed protein is selected randomly from the "core" protein set. The figures for visualizing the identified communities are created using Pajek (Batagelj & Mrvar, 1998). The community figures are extracted from the network we build using the above mentioned data set, omitting connections and proteins outside the detected community. The proteins in each community are annotated with a brief description obtained from the MIPS complex catalog database (Mewes et al., 2002), as shown in Tables 4-7. As a comparison, we use *Complexpander,* an implementation of the PNR method (Asthana et al., 2004) and available at *http://llama.med. harvard.edu/Software.html,* to predict co-complex using the core protein set that contains the same seed protein used by *CommBuilder.* For all our queries when using *Complexpander,* we select the option to use the MIPS complex catalog database. We record in Tables 4-7 the ranking of the members in our identified communities that also appear in the co-complex candidate list predicted by *Complexpander.*

Figure 5. The SAGA-SRB community. The seed protein is TAF6 (dark dot).

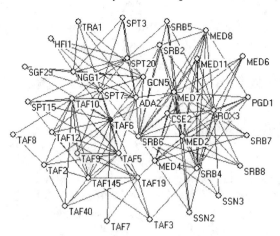

The first community, shown in Figure 5, is identified using TAF6 (in red) as seed. TAF6 is a component of the SAGA complex, which is a multifunctional co-activator that regulates transcription by RNA polymerase II (Wu, Ruhlmann, Winston, & Schultz, 2004). The SAGA complex is listed in MIPS complex catalog as a known cellular complex consisting of 16 proteins. As shown in Table 4, the community identified by our algorithm contains 39 members, including 14 of the 16 SAGA complex proteins listed in MIPS (indicated by an asterisk in the *Alias* column). The community also contains 14 of 21 proteins listed in MIPS as Kornberg's mediator (SRB) complex. The rest of the proteins in the community are either TATA-binding proteins or transcription factor IID (TFIID) subunits or SRB related. TFIID is

Table 4. The SAGA-SRB community

Protein[a]	Alias	Description	Rank
YDR448w	ADA2[b]	general transcriptional adaptor or co-activator	1
YNR010w	CSE2[c]	subunit of RNA polymerase II mediator complex	
YGR252w	GCN5[b]	histone acetyltransferase	2
YPL254w	HFI1[b]	transcriptional coactivator	3
YMR112c	MED11[c]	mediator complex subunit	
YDL005c	MED2[c]	transcriptional regulation mediator	20
YOR174w	MED4[c]	transcription regulation mediator	23
YHR058c	MED6[c]	RNA polymerase II transcriptional regulation mediator	
YOL135c	MED7[c]	member of RNA Polymerase II transcriptional regulation mediator complex	21
YBR193c	MED8[c]	transcriptional regulation mediator	24
YDR176w	NGG1[b]	general transcriptional adaptor or co-activator	10
YGL025c	PGD1[c]	mediator complex subunit	37

Table 4. continued

YBL093c	ROX3[c]	transcription factor	
YCL010c	SGF29[b]	SAGA associated factor	43
YER148w	SPT15	TATA-binding protein TBP	15
YOL148c	SPT20[b]	member of the TBP class of SPT proteins that alter transcription site selection	4
YDR392w	SPT3[b]	general transcriptional adaptor or co-activator	13
YBR081c	SPT7[b]	involved in alteration of transcription start site selection	5
YHR041c	SRB2[c]	DNA-directed RNA polymerase II holoenzyme and Kornberg's mediator (SRB) subcomplex subunit	
YER022w	SRB4[c]	DNA-directed RNA polymerase II holoenzyme and Kornberg's mediator (SRB) subcomplex subunit	27
YGR104c	SRB5[c]	DNA-directed RNA polymerase II holoenzyme and Kornberg's mediator (SRB) subcomplex subunit	
YBR253w	SRB6[c]	DNA-directed RNA polymerase II suppressor protein	19
YDR308c	SRB7[c]	DNA-directed RNA polymerase II holoenzyme and Kornberg's mediator (SRB) subcomplex subunit	46
YCR081w	SRB8	DNA-directed RNA polymerase II holoenzyme and Srb10 CDK subcomplex subunit	

Table 4. continued

ORF	Gene	Description	
YDR443c	SSN2	DNA-directed RNA polymerase II holoenzyme and Srb10 CDK subcomplex subunit	
YPL042c	SSN3	cyclin-dependent CTD kinase	
YGR274c	TAF1	TFIID subunit (TBP-associated factor), 145 kD	14
YDR167w	TAF10[b]	TFIID and SAGA subunit	7
YML015c	TAF11	TFIID subunit (TBP-associated factor), 40 kD	18
YDR145w	TAF12[b]	TFIID and SAGA subunit	8
YML098w	TAF13	TFIID subunit (TBP-associated factor), 19 kD	17
YCR042c	TAF2	component of TFIID complex	22
YPL011c	TAF3	component of the TBP-associated protein complex	50
YBR198c	TAF5[b]	TFIID and SAGA subunit	9
YGL112c	TAF6[b]	TFIID and SAGA subunit	
YMR227c	TAF7	TFIID subunit (TBP-associated factor), 67 kD	
YML114c	TAF8	TBP associated factor 65 kDa	
YMR236w	TAF9[b]	TFIID and SAGA subunit	11
YHR099w	TRA1[b]	component of the Ada-Spt transcriptional regulatory complex	12

[a] *The open reading frame (ORF) name is used.*

[b] *Proteins belong to SAGA complex listed in MIPS.*

[c] *Proteins belong to SRB complex listed in MIPS.*

a complex involved in initiation of RNA polymerase II transcription. SAGA and TFIID are structurally and functionally correlated, make overlapping contributions to the expression of RNA polymerase II transcribed genes. SRB complex is a mediator that conveys regulatory signals from DNA-binding transcription factors to RNA polymerase II (Guglielmi et al., 2004). In addition, 27 of the top 50 potential co-complex proteins (9 of the top 10), not including the seed proteins, predicted by *Complexpander* are in the identified community.

The second community is discovered using NOT3 as seed (Figure 6 and Table 5). NOT3 is a known component protein of the CCR4-NOT complex, which is a global regulator of gene expression and involved in such functions as transcription regulation and DNA damage responses. The MIPS complex catalog lists five proteins for NOT complex and 13 proteins (including the five NOT complex proteins) for CCR4

Figure 6. The CCR4-NOT community. The seed protein is NOT3 (in red).

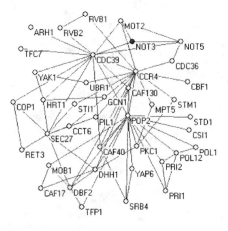

Table 5. The CCR4-NOT community

Protein[a]	Alias	Description	Rank
YDR376w	ARH1	mitochondrial protein putative ferredoxin-NADP+ reductase	38
YGR134w	CAF130[c]	CCR4 associated factor 130 kDa	8
YJR122w	CAF17[b]	CCR4 associated factor	
YNL288w	CAF40[c]	CCR4 associated factor 40 kDa	9
YJR060w	CBF1	centromere binding factor 1	
YAL021c	CCR4[bc]	transcriptional regulator	3
YDR188w	CCT6[c]	component of chaperonin-containing T-complex (zeta subunit)	30

Table 5. continued

YDL165w	CDC36 [bc]	transcription factor	40
YCR093w	CDC39 [bc]	nuclear protein	1
YDL145c	COP1 [c]	coatomer complex alpha chain of secretory pathway vesicles	11
YMR025w	CSI1	subunit of the Cop9 signalosome, involved in adaptation to pheromone signaling	46
YGR092w	DBF2 [b]	ser/thr protein kinase related to Dbf20p	6
YDL160c	DHH1 [b]	DExD/H-box helicase, stimulates mRNA decapping	17
YGL195w	GCN1 [c]	translational activator	26
YOL133w	HRT1	Skp1-Cullin-F-box ubiquitin protein ligase (SCF) subunit	
YIL106w	MOB1 [b]	required for completion of mitosis and maintenance of ploidy	10
YER068w	MOT2 [bc]	transcriptional repressor	2
YGL178w	MPT5	multi-copy suppressor of POP2	
YIL038c	NOT3 [bc]	general negative regulator of transcription, subunit 3	
YPR072w	NOT5 [bc]	component of the NOT protein complex	5
YGR086c	PIL1	long chain base-responsive inhibitor of protein kinases Phk1p and Phk2p, acts along with Lsp1p to down-regulate heat stress resistance	
YBL105c	PKC1	ser/thr protein kinase	
YNL102w	POL1 [c]	DNA-directed DNA polymerase alpha, 180 KD subunit	32
YBL035c	POL12 [c]	DNA-directed DNA polymerase alpha, 70 KD subunit	28
YNR052c	POP2 [bc]	required for glucose derepression	4
YIR008c	PRI1 [c]	DNA-directed DNA polymerase alpha 48kDa subunit (DNA primase)	34

Table 5. continued

YKL045w	PRI2 [c]	DNA-directed DNA polymerase alpha, 58 KD subunit (DNA primase)	31
YPL010w	RET3	coatomer complex zeta chain	39
YDR190c	RVB1	RUVB-like protein	29
YPL235w	RVB2 [c]	RUVB-like protein	21
YGL137w	SEC27 [c]	coatomer complex beta chain (beta-cop) of secretory pathway vesicles	7
YER022w	SRB4	DNA-directed RNA polymerase II holoenzyme and Kornberg's mediator (SRB) subcomplex subunit	44
YOR047c	STD1	dosage-dependent modulator of glucose repression	
YOR027w	STI1	stress-induced protein	
YLR150w	STM1	specific affinity for guanine-rich quadruplex nucleic acids	
YOR110w	TFC7 [c]	TFIIIC (transcription initiation factor) subunit, 55 kDa	25
YDL185w	TFP1 [c]	encodes 3 region protein, which is self-spliced into TFP1p and PI-SceI	27
YGR184c	UBR1	ubiquitin-protein ligase	
YJL141c	YAK1	ser/thr protein kinase	
YDR259c	YAP6	transcription factor of a fungal-specific family of bzip proteins	

[a] *The open reading frame (ORF) name is used.*

[b] *Proteins belong to CCR4-NOT complex listed in MIPS.*

[c] *Proteins considered part of a complex involved in transcription and DNA/chromatin structure maintenance.*

complex. The CCR4-NOT community identified is composed of 40 members. All five NOT complex proteins listed in MIPS and 11 of the 13 CCR4 complex proteins are members of the community. POL1, POL2, PRI1, and PRI2 are members of the DNA polymerase alpha (I) – primase complex, as listed in MIPS. RVB1, PIL1, UBR1, and STI1 have been grouped together with CCR4, CDC39, CDC36, and POP2 by systematic analysis (Ho et al , 2002). The community also contains 20 out of 26 proteins of a complex that is probably involved in transcription and DNA/chromatin structure maintenance (Gavin, et al., 2002).

Figure 7. The RFC community. The seed protein is RFC2 (in red).

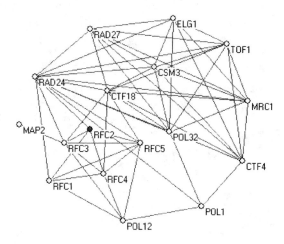

Table 6. The RFC community

Protein[a]	Alias	Description	Rank
YMR048w	CSM3[c]	protein required for accurate chromosome segregation during meiosis	
YMR078c	CTF18[c]	required for accurate chromosome transmission in mitosis and maintenance of normal telomere length	6
YPR135w	CTF4[c]	DNA-directed DNA polymerase alpha-binding protein	
YOR144c	ELG1[c]	protein required for S phase progression and telomere homeostasis, forms an alternative replication factor C complex important for DNA replication and genome integrity	7
YBL091c	MAP2	methionine aminopeptidase, isoform 2	
YCL061c	MRC1[c]	mediator of the replication checkpoint	
YNL102w	POL1[c]	DNA-directed DNA polymerase alpha, 180 kD subunit	19
YBL035c	POL12[c]	DNA-directed DNA polymerase alpha, 70 kD subunit	5
YJR043c	POL32[c]	polymerase-associated gene, third (55 kDa) subunit of DNA polymerase delta	
YER173w	RAD24[c]	cell cycle checkpoint protein	1

Table 6. Continued

YKL113c	RAD27[c]	ssDNA endonuclease and 5'-3'exonuclease	
YOR217w	RFC1[bc]	DNA replication factor C, 95 kD subunit	8
YJR068w	RFC2[bc]	DNA replication factor C, 41 kD subunit	
YNL290w	RFC3[bc]	DNA replication factor C, 40 kDa subunit	2
YOL094c	RFC4[bc]	DNA replication factor C, 37 kDa subunit	4
YBR087w	RFC5[bc]	DNA replication factor C, 40 kD subunit	3
YNL273w	TOF1[c]	topoisomerase I interacting factor 1	

[a] *The open reading frame (ORF) name is used.*

[b] *Proteins belong to RFC complex listed in MIPS.*

[c] *Proteins listed in the functional category of DNA recombination and DNA repair or cell cycle checkpoints in MIPS.*

The third community is identified by using RFC2 as the seed (Figure 7 and Table 6). RFC2 is a component of the RFC (replication factor C) complex, the "clamp loader," which plays an essential role in DNA replication and DNA repair. The community identified by our algorithm has 17 members. All five proteins of RFC complex listed in the MIPS complex catalog database are members of this community, as shown in Table 6. All but one member in this community are in the functional category of DNA recombination and DNA repair or cell cycle checkpoints according to MIPS. This community also includes the top eight ranked proteins predicted by *Complexpander.*

We use ARP3 as seed to identify the last community (Figure 5). ARP2/ARP3 complex acts as multi-functional organizer of actin filaments. The assembly and maintenance of many actin-based cellular structures likely depend on functioning ARP2/ARP3 complex (Machesky & Gould, 1999). The identified community contains all seven proteins of the ARP2/ARP3 complex listed in MIPS (see Table 7). Not including the seed (ARP3), these proteins represent the top six ranked proteins predicted by *Complexpander.* As indicated in Table 7, there are 14 members belonging to the same functional category of budding, cell polarity, and filament formation, according to MIPS.

Figure 8. The ARP2/ARP3 community. The seed protein is ARP3 (in black).

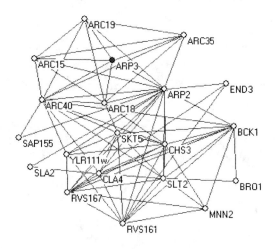

Table 7. The ARP2/ARP3 community

Protein[a]	Alias	Description	Rank
YLR111w	YLR111w	hypothetical protein	
YIL062c	ARC15[bc]	subunit of the ARP2/3 complex	1
YLR370c	ARC18[b]	subunit of the ARP2/3 complex	4
YKL013c	ARC19[bc]	subunit of the ARP2/3 complex	3
YNR035c	ARC35[b]	subunit of the ARP2/3 complex	5
YBR234c	ARC40[bc]	ARP2/3 protein complex subunit, 40 kilodalton	6
YDL029w	ARP2[bc]	actin-like protein	2
YJR065c	ARP3[b]	Actin-related protein	
YJL095w	BCK1[c]	ser/thr protein kinase of the MEKK family	
YPL084w	BRO1	required for normal response to nutrient limitation	
YBR023c	CHS3[c]	chitin synthase III	
YNL298w	CLA4[c]	ser/thr protein kinase	
YNL084c	END3[c]	required for endocytosis and cytoskeletal organization	
YBR015c	MNN2	type II membrane protein	
YCR009c	RVS161[c]	protein involved in cell polarity development	

Table 7. continued

YDR388w	RVS167[c]	reduced viability upon starvation protein
YFR040w	SAP155[c]	Sit4p-associated protein
YBL061c	SKT5[c]	protoplast regeneration and killer toxin resistance protein
YNL243w	SLA2[c]	cytoskeleton assembly control protein
YHR030c	SLT2[c]	ser/thr protein kinase of MAP kinase family

[a] *The open reading frame (ORF) name is used.*

[b] *Proteins belong to ARP2/ARP3 complex listed in MIPS.*

[c] *Proteins listed in the functional category of budding, cell polarity, and filament formation in MIPS.*

Discussion and Future Work

In this chapter, we used the graph theory and statistical approaches to analyze the topological structure of protein-protein interaction networks across different species. We have shown the polarity on data and perhaps knowledge about the PPI networks at the "omics" level across a variety of species.

Our results confirmed that PPI networks have small diameters and small average degrees. All networks we evaluated display power law degree distribution. However, further statistical analysis indicates an inadequacy of such a model in capturing certain features in the data. We strongly believe that further investigation into this issue may shed some new light on our understanding of PPI networks.

Most of the networks we evaluated also reveal a larger clustering coefficient, indicating the non-random structure of the networks. However, the values of the clustering coefficient varied significantly across different species. This may result from the incompleteness and noise of the data, since there are significant differences in the clustering coefficient between networks with different confidence levels (Wu & Hu, 2006). In addition, networks consisting of interactions detected from different experimental systems differed significantly in the values of the clustering coefficient (Wu & Hu, 2006). The spectrum of the average clustering coefficient over the vertices degree k fails to exhibit scale-free behavior in most of the networks evaluated.

One interesting finding of this chapter is the power law distribution of the average vertex density over the vertex degree k, consistent across all networks from different species. This power law distribution is not susceptible to either biases of different experimental systems or noise in data (Wu & Hu, 2006). The difference between the clustering coefficient and the vertex density in calculation is the introduction of a new k into the formula. The clustering coefficient measures the network transitivity in the neighborhood of a vertex, whereas the vertex density reflects the network connectivity inside the locality of the neighborhood of a vertex. Our finding indicates that the vertex density distribution may be a better measurement to provide hints on the existence of a hierarchical organization in the PPI networks. A decaying $D(k)$ function may indicate a hierarchy in which low-degree proteins in general belong to well-interconnected communities (high vertex density), and high-degree proteins (hubs) are the cores connecting many proteins that have no direct interactions (low vertex density). The intriguing part of this finding is also related to a new definition introduced by Soffer and Vazquez (2004) to eliminate degree correlation bias. They argue that the dependence of the clustering coefficient with degree k is partially due to this bias. The new definition they propose actually makes the power law behavior disappear. On the contrary, we did not observe the power law distribution of $C(k)$ over degree k, but the power law behavior appears when we modify the $C(k)$ to $D(k)$. We expect this information will be helpful because we have already seen the application of vertex density in Bader and Hogue (2003) and in detecting a protein community reported here.

We present an efficient approach for growing a community from a given seed protein. It uses topological property of community structure in a network and takes advantage of local optimization in searching for the community comprising the seed protein. Due to the complexity and modularity of biological networks, it is more desirable and computationally more feasible to model and simulate a network of smaller size. Our approach builds a community of manageable size and scales well to large networks. Its usefulness is demonstrated by the experimental results that all the four communities identified reveal strong structural and functional relationships among member proteins. It provides a fast and accurate way to find a community comprising a protein or proteins with known functions or of interest. For those community members that are not known to be part of a protein complex or a functional category, their relationship to other community members may deserve further investigation which in turn may provide new insights.

Although we do not explicitly use our approach to the prediction of co-complexed proteins, the results of comparing with the PNR method developed by Asthana et al. (2004) have shown that the communities identified by our approach do include the top-ranked candidates of co-complexed proteins. Compared to the methods in predicting co-complexed proteins, our approach can discover a community rather than a single complex. In the context of this discussion, the notion of a community can be a complex, but it can also be a functional group consisting of several complexes, such as the SAGA/SRB community (Figure 1). This may not be always desirable. However, it does provide benefits of delineating the structure-function relationships beyond a single complex. In this spirit, one part of our future work is to further explore the relaxation threshold (f), aiming to identify either a more tightly connected community under a strict expanding condition or a more loosely connected community under a relaxed condition so that we could study interactions of different strengths within a community.

Our approach does not consider the quality of data in our downloaded data set. By using the strong sense definition of community (Radicchi et al., 2004), we could to some degree reduce the noises. However, to improve the quality of an identified community, we have to take into account the quality of data, and that is another part of our future work. One possible way is to use the probabilities assigned to individual protein pairs as used by Jansen et al. (2002), Radicchi et al. (2004), Bader (2003), and Bader, Chaudhuri, Rothberg, and Chant (2004).

Acknowledgment

This research work is supported in part by the NSF Career grant (NSF IIS 0448023), NSF CCF 0514679, and the Pennsylvania Department of Health Tobacco Settlement Formula Grant (#240205, 240196).

References

Asthana, S., King, O.D., Gibbons, F.D., & Roth, F.P. (2004). Predicting protein complex membership using probabilistic network reliability. *Genome Res, 14*, 1170-1175.

Bader, G.D., & Hogue, C.W. (2003). An automated method for finding molecular complexes in large protein interaction networks. *BMC Bioinformatics, 4*, 2.

Bader, J.S. (2003). Greedily building protein networks with confidence. *Bioinformatics, 19*(15), 1869-1874.

Bader, J.S., Chaudhuri, A., Rothberg, J.M., &Chant, J. (2004). Gaining confidence in high-throughput protein interaction networks. *Nat Biotech, 22*(1), 78-85.

Barabasi, A.-L., & Albert, R. (1999). Emergence of scaling in random networks. *Science, 286*, 509-512.

Barabasi, A.-L., & Oltvai, Z.N. (2004). Network biology: Understanding the cell's functional organization. *Nat. Rev. Genet, 5*, 101-114.

Batagelj, V., & Mrvar, A. (1998). Pajek: Program for large network analysis. *Connections, 21*, 47-57.

Bork, P., Jensen, L.J., von Mering, C., Ramani, A.K., Lee, I., & Marcotte, E.M. (2004). Protein interaction networks from yeast to human. *Curr. Opin. Struct. Biol, 14,* 292-299.

Breitkreutz, B.-J., Stark, C., & Tyers, M. (2003). The GRID: The General Repository for Interaction Datasets. *Genome Biology, 4,* R23.

Bu, D., Zhao, Y., Cai, L., Xue, H., Zhu, X., Lu, H., Zhang, J., Sun, S., Ling, L., Zhang, N., Li, G., & Chen, R. (2003). Topological structure analysis of the protein-protein interaction network in budding yeast. *Nucleic Acids Res, 31,* 2443-2450.

Butland, G., et al. (2005). Interaction network containing conserved and essential protein complexes in *Escherichia coli. Nature, 433,* 531-537.

Colizza, V., Flammini, A., Maritan, A., & Vespignani, A. (2005). Characterization and modeling of protein-protein interaction networks. *Physica A, 352,* 1-27.

Donetti, L., & Munoz, M.A. (2004). Detecting network communities: A new systematic and efficient algorithm. *Journal of Stat. Mech,* P10012.

Flake, G.W., Lawrence, S.R., Giles, C.L., & Coetzee, F.M. (2002). Self-organization and identification of Web communities. *IEEE Computer, 35,* 66-71.

Fraser, H.B. et al. (2002). Evolutionary rate in the protein interaction network. *Science, 296,* 750.

Fraser, H.B. et al. (2003). A simple dependence between protein evolution rate and the number of protein-protein interactions. *BMC Evol. Biol, 3,* 11.

Gavin, A.-C. et al (2002). Functional organization of the yeast proteome by systematic analysis of protein complexes. *Nature, 415,* 141-147.

Giot, L. et al. (2004). A protein interaction map of *Drosophila melanogaster. Science, 302,* 1727-1736.

Girvan, M., & Newman, M.E.J. (2002). Community structure in social and biological networks. In *Proceedings of the National Academy of Science USA 99* (pp. 7821-7826).

Guglielmi, B., van Berkum, N.L., Klapholz, B., Bijma, T., Boube, M., Boschiero, C., Bourbon, H.M., Holstege, F.C.P., & Werner, M. (2004). A high-resolution protein interaction map of the yeast Mediator complex. *Nucleic Acids Res, 32,* 5379-5391.

Hartwell, L.H., Hopfield, J.J., Leibler, S., & Murray, A.W. (1999). From molecular to modular cell biology. *Nature, 402,* C47-C52.

Hashimoto, R.F., Kim, S., Shmulevich, I., Zhang, W., Bittner, M.L., & Dougherty, E.R. (2004). Growing genetic regulatory networks from seed genes. *Bioinformatics, 20*(8), 1241-1247.

Ho, Y. et al. (2002). Systematic identification of protein complexes in *Saccharomyces cerevisiae* by mass spectrometry. *Nature, 415,* 180-183.

Holme, P., Huss, M., & Jeong, H. (2003). Sub-network hierarchies of biochemical pathways. *Bioinformatics, 19*(4), 532-538.

Hu, X. (2005). Mining and analyzing scale-free protein-protein interaction network. *International Journal of Bioinformatics Research and Application, 1*(1), 81-101.

Hu, X., Yoo, I., Song, I.-Y., Song, M., Han, J., & Lechner, M. (2004, October 7-8). Extracting and mining protein-protein interaction network from biomedical literature. In *Proceedings of the 2004 IEEE Symposium on Computational Intelligence in Bioinformatics and Computational Biology* (IEEE CIBCB 2004), San Diego, CA.

Jansen, R., Lan, N., Qian, J., & Gerstein, M. (2002). Integration of genomic data-sets to predict protein complexes in yeast. *Journal of Structural Functional Genomics, 2,* 71-81.

Jeong, H., Mason, S.P., Barabasi, A.-L., & Oltvai, Z.N. (2001). Lethality and centrality in protein networks. *Nature, 411,* 41-42.

Li, S. et al. (2004). A map of the interactome network of the metazoan *C. elegans. Science, 303,* 540-543.

Machesky, L.M., & Gould, K.L. (1999). The ARP2/3 complex: A multifunctional actin organizer. *Curr. Opin. Cell Biol, 11,* 117-121.

Mewes, H.W., Frishman, D., Guldener, U., Mannhaupt, G., Mayer, K., Mokrejs, M., Morgenstern, B., Munsterkotter, M., Rudd, S., & Weil, B. (2002). MIPS: A database for genomes and protein sequences. *Nucleic Acids Res, 30,* 31-34.

Newman, M.E.J. (2004). Detecting community structure in networks. *Eur. Phys. Journal B, 38,* 321-330.

Newman, M.E.J. (2004). Fast algorithm for detecting community structure in networks. *Phys. Rev. E, 69,* 066133.

Newman, M.E.J., & Girvan, M. (2004). Finding and evaluating community structure in networks. *Phys. Rev. E, 69,* 026113.

Newman, M.E.J. (2003). Random graphs as models of networks. In S. Bornholdt, & H.G. Schuster (Eds.), *Handbook of graphs and networks: From the genome to the Internet* (pp. 35-68). Berlin: Wiley-VCH.

Newman, M.E.J. (2003). The structure and function of complex networks. *SIAM Review, 45*(2), 167-256.

Ng, K.-L., & Huang, C.-H. (2004). A cross-species study of the protein-protein interaction networks via the random graph approach. In *Proceedings of the 4th IEEE Symposium on Bioinformatics and Bioengineering (BIBE'04).*

Pei, P., & Zhang, A. (2005, August 8-11). A topological measurement for weighted protein interaction network. In *Proceedings of CSB2005,* Stanford, CA.

Radicchi, F., Castellano, C., Cecconi, F., Loreto, V., & Parisi, D. (2004). Defining and identifying communities in networks. In *Proceedings of the National Academy of Science USA 101* (pp. 2658-2663).

Rain, J.C. et al. (2001). The protein-protein interaction map of *Helicobacter pylori. Nature, 409,* 211-215.

Rives, A.W., & Galitski, T. (2003). Modular organization of cellular networks. *Proceedings of the National Academy of Science USA 100* (pp. 1128-1133).

Salwinski, L., Miller, C.S., Smith, A.J., Pettit, F.K., Bowie, J.U., & Eisenberg, D. (2004). The database of interacting proteins: 2004 update. *NAR, 32.*

Soffer, S., & Vazquez, A. (2004). Clustering coefficient without degree correlations. biases.arXiv:cond-mat/0409686.

Spirin, V., & Mirny, L. (2003). Protein complexes and functional modules in molecular networks. In *Proceedings of the National Academy of Science USA 100* (pp. 1128-1133).

Tanaka, R., Yi, T.-M, & Doyle, J. (2005). Some protein interaction data do not exhibit power law statistics. arXiv:q-bio.MN/0506038.

Thomas, A., Cannings, R., Monk, N.A.M., & Cannings, C. (2003). On the structure of protein-protein interaction networks. *Biochem Soc Trans, 31,* 1491-1496.

Uetz, P. et al. (2000). A comprehensive analysis of protein-protein interactions in *Saccharomyces cerevisiae. Nature, 403,* 623-627.

Valente, A.X.C.N., Cusick, M.E., Fagerstrom, R.M., Hill, D.E., & Vidal, M. (2005). Yeast protein interactome topology provides framework for coordinated-functionality. arXiv:q-bio.MN/0505006.

Walhout, A.J.M., Sordella, R., Lu, X.W., Hartley, J.L., Temple, G.F., Brasch, M.A., Thierry-Mieg, N., & Vidal, M. (2000). Protein interaction mapping in *C. elegans* using proteins involved in vulval development. *Science, 287,* 116-122.

Watts, D.J., & Strogatz, S.H. (1998). Collective dynamics of "small world" networks. *Nature, 393,* 440-442.

White, S., & Smyth, P. (2005). A spectral clustering approach to finding communities in graphs. In *Proceedings of the SIAM International Conference on Data Mining 2005,* Newport Beach, CA.

Wilkinson, D., & Huberman, B.A (2004). A method for finding communities of related genes. In *Proceedings of the National Academy of Science USA 101* (suppl. 1, pp. 5241-5248).

Wu, D., & Hu, X. (2006, April 23-27). Mining and analyzing the topological structure of protein-protein interaction networks. In *Proceedings of the 2006 ACM Symposium on Applied Computing (Bioinformatics Track),* Dijon, France.

Wu, P.Y., Ruhlmann, C., Winston, F., & Schultz, P. (2004). Molecular architecture of the *S. cerevisiae* SAGA complex. *Mol. Cell, 15,* 199-208.

Wuchty, S. (2004). Evolution and topology in the yeast protein interaction network. *Genome Research, 14,* 1310-1314.

Yook, S.-H., Oltvai, Z.N., & Barabasi, A.-L. (2004) Functional and topological characterization of protein interaction networks. *Proteomics, 4,* 928-942.

Section IV

Data Mining Techniques

Chapter IX

Introduction to Data Mining Techniques via Multiple Criteria Optimization Approaches and Applications

Yong Shi, University of the Chinese Academy of Sciences, China & University of Nebraska at Omaha, USA

Yi Peng, University of Nebraska at Omaha, USA

Gang Kou, University of Nebraska at Omaha, USA

Zhengxin Chen, University of Nebraska at Omaha, USA

Abstract

This chapter provides an overview of a series of multiple criteria optimization-based data mining methods, which utilize multiple criteria programming (MCP) to solve data mining problems, and outlines some research challenges and opportunities for the data mining community. To achieve these goals, this chapter first introduces the basic notions and mathematical formulations for multiple criteria optimization-based classification models, including the multiple criteria linear programming model, multiple criteria quadratic programming model, and multiple criteria fuzzy linear programming model. Then it presents the real-life applications of these models in credit card scoring management, HIV-1 associated dementia (HAD) neuronal damage and dropout, and network intrusion detection. Finally, the chapter discusses research challenges and opportunities.

Introduction

Data mining has become a powerful information technology tool in today's competitive business world. As the sizes and varieties of electronic datasets grow, the interest in data mining is increasing rapidly. Data mining is established on the basis of many disciplines, such as machine learning, databases, statistics, computer science, and operations research. Each field comprehends data mining from its own perspective and makes its distinct contributions. It is this multidisciplinary nature that brings vitality to data mining. One of the application roots of data mining can be regarded as statistical data analysis in the pharmaceutical industry. Nowadays the financial industry, including commercial banks, has benefited from the use of data mining. In addition to statistics, decision trees, neural networks, rough sets, fuzzy sets, and vector support machines have gradually become popular data mining methods over the last 10 years. Due to the difficulty of accessing the accuracy of hidden data and increasing the predicting rate in a complex large-scale database, researchers and practitioners have always desired to seek new or alternative data mining techniques. This is a key motivation for the proposed multiple criteria optimization-based data mining methods.

The objective of this chapter is to provide an overview of a series of multiple criteria optimization-based methods, which utilize the multiple criteria programming (MCP) to solve classification problems. In addition to giving an overview, this chapter lists some data mining research challenges and opportunities for the data mining community. To achieve these goals, the next section introduces the basic notions and mathematical formulations for three multiple criteria optimization-based classification models: the multiple criteria linear programming model, multiple criteria quadratic programming model, and multiple criteria fuzzy linear programming model. The third section presents some real-life applications of these models, including credit card scoring management, classifications on HIV-1 associated dementia (HAD) neuronal damage and dropout, and network intrusion detection. The chapter then outlines research challenges and opportunities, and the conclusion is presented.

Multiple Criteria Optimization-Based Classification Models

This section explores solving classification problems, one of the major areas of data mining, through the use of multiple criteria mathematical programming-based methods (Shi, Wise, Luo, & Lin, 2001; Shi, Peng, Kou, & Chen, 2005). Such methods have shown its strong applicability in solving a variety of classification problems (e.g., Kou et al., 2005; Zheng et al., 2004).

Classification

Although the definition of classification in data mining varies, the basic idea of classification can be generally described as to "predicate the most likely state of a categorical variable (the class) given the values of other variables" (Bradley, Fayyad, & Mangasarian, 1999, p. 6). Classification is a two-step process. The first step constructs a predictive model based on training dataset. The second step applies the predictive model constructed from the first step to testing dataset. If the classification accuracy of testing dataset is acceptable, the model can be used to predicate unknown data (Han & Kamber, 2000; Olson & Shi, 2005).

Using the multiple criteria programming, the classification task can be defined as follows: *for a given set of variables in the database, the boundaries between the classes are represented by scalars in the constraint availabilities*. Then, the standards of classification are measured by minimizing the total overlapping of data and maximizing the distances of every data to its class boundary simultaneously. Through the algorithms of MCP, an "optimal" solution of variables (so-called classifier) for the data observations is determined for the separation of the given classes. Finally, the resulting classifier can be used to predict the unknown data for discovering the hidden patterns of data as possible knowledge. Note that MCP differs from the known support vector machine (SVM) (e.g., Mangasarian, 2000; Vapnik, 2000). While the former uses multiple measurements to separate each data from different classes, the latter searches the minority of the data (support vectors) to represent the majority in classifying the data. However, both can be generally regarded as in the same category of optimization approaches to data mining.

In the following, we first discuss a generalized multi-criteria programming model formulation, and then explore several variations of the model.

A Generalized Multiple Criteria Programming Model Formulation

This section introduces a generalized multi-criteria programming method for classification. Simply speaking, this method is to classify observations into distinct groups based on two criteria for data separation. The following models represent this concept mathematically:

Given an r-dimensional attribute vector $a=(a_1,...a_r)$, let $A_i=(A_{i1},...,A_{ir})\in R^r$ be one of the sample records of these attributes, where $i=1,...,n$; n represents the total number of records in the dataset. Suppose two groups G_1 and G_2 are predefined. A boundary scalar b can be selected to separate these two groups. A vector $X = (x_1,...,X_r)^T \in R^r$ can be identified to establish the following linear inequations (Fisher, 1936; Shi et al., 2001):

- $A_i X < b, \forall A_i \in G_1$
- $A_i X \geq b, \forall A_i \in G_2$

To formulate the criteria and complete constraints for data separation, some variables need to be introduced. In the classification problem, $A_i X$ is the score for the ith data record. Let α_i be the overlapping of two-group boundary for record A_i (external measurement) and β_i be the distance of record A_i from its adjusted boundary (internal measurement). The overlapping α_i means the distance of record A_i to the boundary b if A_i is misclassified into another group. For instance, in Figure 1 the "black dot" located to the right of the boundary b belongs to G_1, but it was misclassified by the boundary b to G_2. Thus, the distance between b and the "dot" equals α_i. Adjusted boundary is defined as $b-\alpha^*$ or $b+\alpha^*$, while α^* represents the maximum of overlapping (Freed & Glover, 1981, 1986). Then, a mathematical function $f(\alpha)$ can be used to describe the relation of all overlapping α_i, while another mathematical function $g(\beta)$ represents the aggregation of all distances β_i. The final classification accuracies depend on simultaneously minimizing $f(\alpha)$ and maximizing $g(\beta)$. Thus, a generalized bi-criteria programming method for classification can be formulated as:

(Generalized Model) *Minimize $f(\alpha)$* and *Maximize $g(\beta)$*

Subject to:

$$A_i X - \alpha_i + \beta_i - b = 0, \ \forall \ A_i \in G_1,$$
$$A_i X + \alpha_i - \beta_i - b = 0, \ \forall \ A_i \in G_2,$$

where A_i, $i = 1, \ldots, n$ are given, X and b are unrestricted, and $\alpha = (\alpha_1, \ldots \alpha_n)^T$, $\beta = (\beta_1, \ldots \beta_n)^T$; α_i, $\beta_i \geq 0$, $i = 1, \ldots, n$.

All variables and their relationships are represented in Figure 1. There are two groups in Figure 1: "black dots" indicate G_1 data objects, and "stars" indicate G_2 data objects. There is one misclassified data object from each group if the boundary scalar b is used to classify these two groups, whereas adjusted boundaries $b - \alpha^*$ and $b + \alpha^*$ separate two groups without misclassification.

Based on the above generalized model, the following subsection formulates a multiple criteria linear programming (MCLP) model and a multiple criteria quadratic programming (MCQP) model.

Multiple Criteria Linear and Quadratic Programming Model Formulation

Different forms of $f(\alpha)$ and $g(\beta)$ in the generalized model will affect the classification criteria. Commonly $f(\alpha)$ (or $g(\beta)$) can be component-wise and non-increasing (or non-decreasing) functions. For example, in order to utilize the computational power of some existing mathematical programming software packages, a sub-model can be set up by using the norm to represent $f(\alpha)$ and $g(\beta)$. This means that we can assume $f(\alpha) = \|\alpha\|_p$ and $g(\beta) = \|\beta\|_q$. To transform the bi-criteria problems of the generalized model into a single-criterion problem, we use weights $w_\alpha > 0$ and $w_\beta > 0$ for $\|\alpha\|_p$ and $\|\beta\|_q$, respectively. The values of w_α and w_β can be pre-defined in the

Figure 1. Two-group classification model

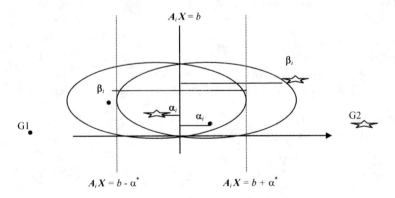

process of identifying the optimal solution. Thus, the generalized model is converted into a single criterion mathematical programming model as:

Model 1: *Minimize $w_\alpha \|\alpha\|_p - w_\beta \|\beta\|_q$*

Subject to:

$$A_i X - \alpha_i + \beta_i - b = 0, \ \forall \ A_i \in G_1,$$
$$A_i X + \alpha_i - \beta_i - b = 0, \ \forall A_i \in G_2,$$

where A_i, $i = 1, \ldots, n$ are given, X and b are unrestricted, and $\alpha = (\alpha_1, \ldots, \alpha_n)^T$, $\beta = (\beta_1, \ldots \beta_n)^T$; $\alpha_i, \beta_i \geq 0$, $i = 1, \ldots, n$.

Based on Model 1, mathematical programming models with any norm can be theoretically defined. This study is interested in formulating a linear and a quadratic programming model. Let $p = q = 1$, then $\|\alpha\|_1 = \sum_{i=1}^{n} \alpha_i$ and $\|\beta\|_1 = \sum_{i=1}^{n} \beta_i$. Let $p = q = 2$, then $\|\alpha\|_2 = \sum_{i=1}^{n} \alpha_i^2$ and $\|\beta\|_2 = \sum_{i=1}^{n} \beta_i^2$. The objective function in Model 1 can now be an MCLP model or MCQP model.

Model 2: MCLP

Minimize $w_a \sum_{i=1}^{n} \alpha_i - w_\beta \sum_{i=1}^{n} \beta_i$

Subject to:

$$A_i X - \alpha_i + \beta_i + b = 0, \ \forall A_i \in G_1,$$
$$A_i X + \alpha_i - \beta_i - b = 0, \ \forall A_i \in G_2,$$

where A_i, $i = 1, \ldots, n$ are given, X and b are unrestricted, and $\alpha = (\alpha_1, \ldots \alpha_n)^T$, $\beta = (\beta_1, \ldots \beta_n)^T$; $\alpha_i, \beta_i \geq 0$, $i = 1, \ldots, n$.

Model 3: MCQP

Minimize $w_a \sum_{i=1}^{n} \alpha_i^2 - w_\beta \sum_{i=1}^{n} \beta_i^2$

Subject to:

$$A_i X - \alpha_i + \beta_i - b = 0, \ \forall A_i \in G_1,$$
$$A_i X + \alpha_i - \beta_i - b = 0, \ \forall A_i \in G_2,$$

where A_i, $i = 1, \ldots, n$ are given, X and b are unrestricted, and $\alpha = (\alpha_1, \ldots, \alpha_n)^T$, $\beta = (\beta_1, \ldots, \beta_n)^T$; $\alpha_i, \beta_i \geq 0$, $i = 1, \ldots, n$.

Remark 1

There are some issues related to MCLP and MCQP that can be briefly addressed here:

1. In the process of finding an optimal solution for MCLP problem, if some β_i is too large with given $w_\alpha > 0$ and $w_\beta > 0$ and all α_i relatively small, the problem may have an unbounded solution. In the real applications, the data with large β_i can be detected as "outlier" or "noisy" in the data preprocessing, which should be removed before classification.

2. Note that although variables X and b are unrestricted in the above models, $X = 0$ is an "insignificant case" in terms of data separation, and therefore it should be ignored in the process of solving the problem. For $b = 0$, however, may result a solution for the data separation depending on the data structure. From experimental studies, a pre-defined value of b can quickly lead to an optimal solution if the user fully understands the data structure.

3. Some variations of the generalized model, such as MCQP, are NP-hard problems. Developing algorithms directly to solve these models can be a challenge. Although in application we can utilize some existing commercial software, the theoretical-related problem will be addressed in later in this chapter.

Multiple Criteria Fuzzy Linear Programming Model Formulation

It has been recognized that in many decision-making problems, instead of finding the existing "optimal solution" (a goal value), decision makers often approach a "satisfying solution" between upper and lower aspiration levels that can be represented by the upper and lower bounds of acceptability for objective payoffs, respectively (Charnes & Cooper, 1961; Lee, 1972; Shi & Yu, 1989; Yu, 1985). This idea, which has an important and pervasive impact on human decision making (Lindsay & Norman 1972), is called the decision makers' goal-seeking concept. Zimmermann (1978) employed it as the basis of his pioneering work on FLP. When FLP is adopted to classify the 'good' and 'bad' data, a fuzzy (satisfying) solution is used to meet a threshold for the accuracy rate of classifications, although the fuzzy solution is a near optimal solution.

According to Zimmermann (1978), in formulating an FLP problem, the objectives (*Minimize* $\Sigma_i \alpha_i$ and *Maximize* $\Sigma_i \beta_i$) and constraints ($A_i X = b + \alpha_i - \beta_i$, $A_i \in$ G; $A_i X$

$= b - \alpha_i + \beta_i, A_i \in B)$ of the generalized model are redefined as fuzzy sets F and X with corresponding membership functions $\mu_F(x)$ and $\mu_X(x)$ respectively. In this case the fuzzy decision set D is defined as $D = F \cup X$, and the membership function is defined as $\mu_D(x) = \{\mu_F(x), \mu_X(x)\}$. In a maximal problem, x_1 is a "better" decision than x_2 if $\mu_D(x_1) \geq \mu_D(x_2)$. Thus, it can be considered appropriately to select x^* such that $\max\limits_x \mu_D(x) = \max\limits_x \min\{\mu_F(x), \mu_X(x)\} = \min\{\mu_F(x^*), \mu_X(x^*)\}$ is the maximized solution.

Let y_{1L} be *Minimize* $\Sigma_i \alpha_i$ and y_{2U} be *Maximize* $\Sigma_i \beta_i$, then one can assume that the value of *Maximize* $\Sigma_i \alpha_i$ to be y_{1U} and that of *Minimize* $\Sigma_i \beta_i$ to be y_{2L}. If the "upper bound" y_{1U} and the "lower bound" y_{2L} do not exist for the formulations, they can be estimated. Let $F_1\{x: y_{1L} \leq \Sigma_i \alpha_i \leq y_{1U}\}$ and $F_2\{x: y_{2L} \leq \Sigma_i \beta_i \leq y_{2U}\}$ and their membership functions can be expressed respectively by:

$$\mu_{F_1}(x) = \begin{cases} 1, & \text{if } \Sigma_i \alpha_i \geq y_{1U} \\ \dfrac{\Sigma_i \alpha_i - y_{1L}}{y_{1U} - y_{1L}}, & \text{if } y_{1L} < \Sigma_i \alpha_i < y_{1U} \\ 0, & \text{if } \Sigma_i \alpha_i \leq y_{1L} \end{cases}$$

and $$\mu_{F_2}(x) = \begin{cases} 1, & \text{if } \Sigma_i \beta_i \geq y_{2U} \\ \dfrac{\Sigma_i \beta_i - y_{2L}}{y_{2U} - y_{2L}}, & \text{if } y_{2L} < \Sigma_i \beta_i < y_{2U} \\ 0, & \text{if } \Sigma_i \beta_i \leq y_{2L} \end{cases}$$

Then the fuzzy set of the objective functions is $F = F_1 \cap F_2$, and its membership function is $\mu_F(x) = \min\{\mu_{F_1}(x), \mu_{F_2}(x)\}$. Using the crisp constraint set $X = \{x: A_i X = b + \alpha_i - \beta_i, A_i \in G; A_i X = b - \alpha_i + \beta_i, A_i \in B\}$, the fuzzy set of the decision problem is , and its membership function is .

Zimmermann (1978) has shown that the "optimal solution" of $\max\limits_x \mu_D(x) = \max\limits_x \min\{\mu_{F_1}(x), \mu_{F_2}(x), \mu_X(x)\}$ is an efficient solution of a variation of the generalized model when $f(\alpha) = \Sigma_i \alpha_i$ and $g(\beta) = \Sigma_i \beta_i$. Then, this problem is equivalent to the following linear program (He, Liu, Shi, Xu, & Yan, 2004):

Model 4: FLP

Maximize ξ

Subject to:
$$\xi \leq \frac{\Sigma_i \alpha_i - y_{1L}}{y_{1U} - y_{1L}}$$

$$\xi \leq \frac{\Sigma_i \beta_i - y_{2L}}{y_{2U} - y_{2L}}$$

$$A_i X = b + \alpha_i - \beta_i, A_i \in G,$$

$$A_i X = b - \alpha_i + \beta_i, A_i \in B,$$

where $A_i, y_{1L}, y_{1U}, y_{2L}$ and y_{2U} are known, X and b are unrestricted, and $\alpha_i, \beta_i, \xi \geq 0$. Note that Model 4 will produce a value of ξ with $1 > \xi \geq 0$. To avoid the trivial solution, one can set up $\xi > \varepsilon \geq 0$, for a given ε. Therefore, seeking *Maximum* ξ in the FLP approach becomes the standard of determining the classifications between 'good' and 'bad' records in the database. A graphical illustration of this approach can be seen from Figure 2; any point of hyper plane $0 < \xi < 1$ over the shadow area represents the possible determination of classifications by the FLP method. Whenever Model 4 has been trained to meet the given thresholdτ, it is said that the better classifier has been identified.

A procedure of using the FLP method for data classifications can be captured by the flowchart of Figure 2. Note that although the boundary of two classes b is the unrestricted variable in Model 4, it can be presumed by the analyst according to the structure of a particular database. First, choosing a proper value of b can speed up solving Model 4. Second, given a thresholdτ, the best data separation can be selected from a number of results determined by different b values. Therefore, the parameter b plays a key role in this chapter to achieve and guarantee the desired accuracy rateτ. For this reason, the FLP classification method uses b as an important control parameter as shown in Figure 2.

Real-life Applications Using Multiple Criteria Optimization Approaches

The models of multiple criteria optimization data mining in this chapter have been applied in credit card portfolio management (He et al., 2004; Kou, Liu, Peng, Shi, Wise, & Xu, 2003; Peng, Kou, Chen, & Shi, 2004; Shi et al., 2001; Shi, Peng, Xu, & Tang, 2002; Shi et al., 2005), HIV-1-mediated neural dendritic and synaptic damage treatment (Zheng et al., 2004), network intrusion detection (Kou et al., 2004a; Kou, Peng, Chen, Shi, & Chen. 2004b), and firms bankruptcy analyses (Kwak, Shi, Eldridge, & Kou, 2006). These approaches are also being applied in other ongoing real-life data mining projects, such as anti-gene and antibody analyses, petroleum

Figure 2. A flowchart of the fuzzy linear programming classification method

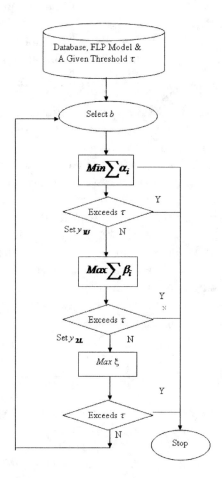

drilling and exploration, fraud management, and financial risk evaluation. In order to let the reader understand the usefulness of the models, the key experiences in some applications are reported as below.

Credit Card Portfolio Management

The goal of credit card accounts classification is to produce a "blacklist" of the credit cardholders; this list can help creditors to take proactive steps to minimize charge-off loss. In this study, credit card accounts are classified into two groups:

'good' or 'bad'. From the technical point of view, we need first construct a number of classifiers and then choose one that can find more bad records. The research procedure consists of five steps. The first step is *data cleaning*. Within this step, missing data cells and outliers are removed from the dataset. The second step is *data transformation*. The dataset is transformed in accord with the format requirements of MCLP software (Kou & Shi, 2002) and LINGO 8.0, which is a software tool for solving nonlinear programming problems (LINDO Systems Inc.). The third step is *datasets selection*. The training dataset and the testing dataset are selected according to a heuristic process. The fourth step is *model formulation and classification*. The two-group MCLP and MCQP models are applied to the training dataset to obtain optimal solutions. The solutions are then applied to the testing dataset within which class labels are removed for validation. Based on these scores, each record is predicted as either bad (bankrupt account) or good (current account). By comparing the predicted labels with original labels of records, the classification accuracies of multiple-criteria models can be determined. If the classification accuracy is acceptable by data analysts, this solution will be applied to future unknown credit card records or applications to make predictions. Otherwise, data analysts can modify the boundary and attributes values to get another set of optimal solutions. The fifth step is *results' presentation*. The acceptable classification results are summarized in tables or figures and presented to end users.

Credit Card Dataset

The credit card dataset used in this chapter is provided by a major U.S. bank. It contains 5,000 records and 102 variables (38 original variables and 64 derived variables). The data were collected from June 1995 to December 1995, and the cardholders were from 28 states of the United States. Each record has a class label to indicate its credit status: either 'good' or 'bad'. 'Bad' indicates a bankruptcy credit card account and 'good' indicates a good status account. Among these 5,000 records, 815 are bankruptcy accounts and 4,185 are good status accounts. The 38 original variables can be divided into four categories: balance, purchase, payment, and cash advance. The 64 derived variables are created from the original 38 variables to reinforce the comprehension of cardholders' behaviors, such as times over-limit in last two years, calculated interest rate, cash as percentage of balance, purchase as percentage to balance, payment as percentage to balance, and purchase as percentage to payment. For the purpose of credit card classification, the 64 derived variables were chosen to compute the model since they provide more precise information about credit cardholders' behaviors.

Experimental Results of MCLP

Inspired by the k-fold cross-validation method in classification, this study proposed a heuristic process for training and testing dataset selections. Standard k-fold cross-validation is not used because the majority-vote ensemble method used later on in this chapter may need hundreds of voters. If standard k-fold cross-validation was employed, k should be equal to hundreds. The following paragraph describes the heuristic process.

First, the bankruptcy dataset (815 records) is divided into 100 intervals (each interval has eight records). Within each interval, seven records are randomly selected. The number of seven is determined according to empirical results of k-fold cross-validation. Thus 700 'bad' records are obtained. Second, the good-status dataset (4,185 records) is divided into 100 intervals (each interval has 41 records). Within each interval, seven records are randomly selected. Thus the total of 700 'good' records is obtained. Third, the 700 bankruptcy and 700 current records are combined to form a training dataset. Finally, the remaining 115 bankruptcy and 3,485 current accounts become the testing dataset. According to this procedure, the total possible combinations of this selection equals $(C_8^7 \times C_{41}^7)^{100}$. Thus, the possibility of getting identical training or testing datasets is approximately zero. The across-the-board thresholds of 65% and 70% are set for the 'bad' and 'good' class, respectively. The values of thresholds are determined from previous experience. The classification results whose predictive accuracies are below these thresholds will be filtered out.

The whole research procedure can be summarized using the following algorithm:

Algorithm 1

Input: The data set $A = \{A_1, A_2, A_3, \ldots, A_n\}$, boundary b

Output: The optimal solution, $X^* = (x_1^*, x_2^*, x_3^*, \ldots, x_{64}^*)$, the classification score MCLPi

Step 1: Generate the Training set and the Testing set from the credit card data set.

Step 2: Apply the two-group MCLP model to compute the optimal solution $X^* = (x_1^*, x_2^*, \ldots, x_{64}^*)$ as the best weights of all 64 variables with given values of control parameters (b, α^*, β^*) in Training set.

Step 3: The classification score $MCLP_i = Ai \, X^*$ against of each observation in the Training set is calculated against the boundary b to check the performance measures of the classification.

Step 4: If the classification result of Step 3 is acceptable (i.e., the found performance measure is larger or equal to the given threshold), go to the next step. Otherwise, arbitrarily choose different values of control parameters (b, α^*, β^*) and go to Step 1.

Step 5: Use $X^* = (x_1^*, x_2^*, \ldots, x_{64}^*)$ to calculate the MCLP scores for all A_i in the Testing set and conduct the performance analysis. If it produces a satisfying classification result, go to the next step. Otherwise, go back to Step 1 to reformulate the Training Set and Testing Set.

Step 6: Repeat the whole process until a preset number (e.g., 999) of different X^* are generated for the future ensemble method.

End.

Using Algorithm 1 to the credit card dataset, classification results were obtained and summarized. Due to the space limitation, only a part (10 out of the total 500 cross-validation results) of the results is summarized in Table 1 (Peng et al., 2004). The columns "Bad" and "Good" refer to the number of records that were correctly classified as "bad" and "good," respectively. The column "Accuracy" was calculated using correctly classified records divided by the total records in that class. For instance, 80.43% accuracy of Dataset 1 for bad record in the training dataset was calculated using 563 divided by 700 and means that 80.43% of bad records were correctly classified. The average predictive accuracies for bad and good groups in the training dataset are 79.79% and 78.97%, and the average predictive accuracies for bad and good groups in the testing dataset are 68% and 74.39%. The results demonstrated that a good separation of bankruptcy and good status credit card accounts is observed with this method.

Table 1. MCLP credit card accounts classification

Cross Validation	Training Set (700 Bad +700 Good)				Testing Set (115 Bad +3485 Good)			
	Bad	Accuracy	Good	Accuracy	Bad	Accuracy	Good	Accuracy
DataSet 1	563	80.43%	557	79.57%	78	67.83%	2575	73.89%
DataSet 2	546	78.00%	546	78.00%	75	65.22%	2653	76.13%
DataSet 3	564	80.57%	560	80.00%	75	65.22%	2550	73.17%
DataSet 4	553	79.00%	553	79.00%	78	67.83%	2651	76.07%
DataSet 5	548	78.29%	540	77.14%	78	67.83%	2630	75.47%
DataSet 6	567	81.00%	561	80.14%	79	68.70%	2576	73.92%
DataSet 7	556	79.43%	548	78.29%	77	66.96%	2557	73.37%
DataSet 8	562	80.29%	552	78.86%	79	68.70%	2557	73.37%
DataSet 9	566	80.86%	557	79.57%	83	72.17%	2588	74.26%
DataSet 10	560	80.00%	554	79.14%	80	69.57%	2589	74.29%

Improvement of MCLP Experimental Results with Ensemble Method

In credit card bankruptcy predictions, even a small percentage of increase in the classification accuracy can save creditors millions of dollars. Thus it is necessary to investigate possible techniques that can improve MCLP classification results. The technique studied in this experiment is majority-vote ensemble. An ensemble consists of two fundamental elements: a set of trained classifiers and an aggregation mechanism that organizes these classifiers into the output ensemble. The aggregation mechanism can be an average or a majority vote (Zenobi & Cunningham, 2002). Weingessel, Dimitriadou, and Hornik (2003) have reviewed a series of ensemble-related publications (Dietterich, 2000; Lam, 2000; Parhami, 1994; Bauer & Kohavi, 1999; Kuncheva, 2000). Previous research has shown that an ensemble can help to increase classification accuracy and stability (Opitz & Maclin, 1999). A part of MCLP's optimal solutions was selected to form ensembles. Each solution will have one vote for each credit card record, and final classification result is determined by the majority votes. Algorithm 2 describes the ensemble process:

Algorithm 2

Input: The data set $A = \{A_1, A_2, A_3, \ldots, A_n\}$, boundary b, a certain number of solutions, $X^* = (x_1^*, x_2^*, x_3^*, \ldots, x_{64}^*)$

Output: The classification score $MCLP_i$ and the prediction P_i

Step 1: A committee of certain odd number of classifiers X^* is formed.

Step 2: The classification score $MCLPi = A_i X^*$ against each observation is calculated against the boundary b by every member of the committee. The performance measures of the classification will be decided by majorities of the committee. If more than half of the committee members agreed in the classification, then the prediction P_i for this observation is successful, otherwise the prediction is failed.

Step 3: The accuracy for each group will be computed by the percentage of successful classification in all observations.

End.

The results of applying Algorithm 2 are summarized in Table 2 (Peng et al., 2004). The average predictive accuracies for bad and good groups in the training dataset are 80.8% and 80.6%, and the average predictive accuracies for bad and good groups in the testing dataset are 72.17% and 76.4%. Compared with previous results, ensemble

Table 2. MCLP credit card accounts classification with ensemble

Ensemble Results	Training Set (700 Bad data+700 Good data)				Testing Set (115 Bad data+3485 Good data)			
No. of Voters	Bad	Accuracy	Good	Accuracy	Bad	Accuracy	Good	Accuracy
9	563	80.43%	561	80.14%	81	70.43%	2605	74.75%
99	565	80.71%	563	80.43%	83	72.17%	2665	76.47%
199	565	80.71%	566	80.86%	83	72.17%	2656	76.21%
299	568	81.14%	564	80.57%	84	73.04%	2697	77.39%
399	567	81.00%	567	81.00%	84	73.04%	2689	77.16%

technique improves the classification accuracies. Especially for bad records classification in the testing set, the average accuracy increased 4.17%. Since bankruptcy accounts are the major cause of creditors' loss, predictive accuracy for bad records is considered to be more important than for good records.

Experimental Results of MCQP

Based on the MCQP model and the research procedure described in previous sections, similar experiments were conducted to get MCQP results. LINGO 8.0 was used to compute the optimal solutions. The whole research procedure for MCQP is summarized in Algorithm 3:

Algorithm 3

Input: The data set $A = \{A_1, A_2, A_3, \ldots, A_n\}$, boundary b

Output: The optimal solution, $X^* = (x_1^* x_2^*, x_3^*, \ldots, x_{64}^*)$, the classification score $MCQP_i$

Step 1: Generate the Training set and Testing set from the credit card data set.

Step 2: Apply the two-group MCQP model to compute the compromise solution $X^* = (x_1^*, x_2^*, \ldots, x_{64}^*)$ as the best weights of all 64 variables with given values of control parameters (b, α^*, β^*) using LINGO 8.0 software.

Step 3: The classification score $MCQP_i = A_i X^*$ against each observation is calculated against the boundary b to check the performance measures of the classification.

Step 4: If the classification result of Step 3 is acceptable (i.e., the found performance measure is larger or equal to the given threshold), go to the next step. Otherwise, choose different values of control parameters (b, α^*, β^*) and go to Step 1.

Step 5: Use $X^* = (x_1^*, x_2^*, ..., x_{64}^*)$ to calculate the MCQP scores for all A_i in the test set and conduct the performance analysis. If it produces a satisfying classification result, go to the next step. Otherwise, go back to Step 1 to reformulate the Training Set and Testing Set.

Step 6: Repeat the whole process until a preset number of different X^* are generated.

End.

A part (10 out of the total 38 results) of the results is summarized in Table 3.

The average predictive accuracies for bad and good groups in the training dataset are 86.61% and 73.29%, and the average predictive accuracies for bad and good groups in the testing dataset are 81.22% and 68.25%. Compared with MCLP, MCQP has lower predictive accuracies for good records. Nevertheless, bad group classification accuracies of the testing set using MCQP increased from 68% to 81.22%, which is a remarkable improvement.

Improvement of MCQP with Ensemble Method

Similar to the MCLP experiment, the majority-vote ensemble discussed previously was applied to MCQP to examine whether it can make an improvement. The results are represented in Table 4. The average predictive accuracies for bad and good groups in the training dataset are 89.18% and 74.68%, and the average predictive

Table 3. MCQP credit card accounts classification

Cross Validation	Training Set (700 Bad data+700 Good data)				Testing Set (115 Bad data+3485 Good data)			
	Bad	Accuracy	Good	Accuracy	Bad	Accuracy	Good	Accuracy
DataSet 1	602	86.00%	541	77.29%	96	83.48%	2383	68.38%
DataSet 2	614	87.71%	496	70.86%	93	80.87%	2473	70.96%
DataSet 3	604	86.29%	530	75.71%	95	82.61%	2388	68.52%
DataSet 4	616	88.00%	528	75.43%	95	82.61%	2408	69.10%
DataSet 5	604	86.29%	547	78.14%	90	78.26%	2427	69.64%
DataSet 6	614	87.71%	502	71.71%	94	81.74%	2328	66.80%
DataSet 7	610	87.14%	514	73.43%	95	82.61%	2380	68.29%
DataSet 8	582	83.14%	482	68.86%	93	80.87%	2354	67.55%
DataSet 9	614	87.71%	479	68.43%	90	78.26%	2295	65.85%
DataSet 10	603	86.14%	511	73.00%	93	80.87%	2348	67.37%

Table 4. MCQP credit card accounts classification with ensemble

Ensemble Results	Training Set (700 Bad data+700 Good data)				Testing Set (115 Bad data+3485 Good data)			
No. of Voters	Bad	Accuracy	Good	Accuracy	Bad	Accuracy	Good	Accuracy
3	612	87.43%	533	76.14%	98	85.22%	2406	69.04%
5	619	88.43%	525	75.00%	95	82.61%	2422	69.50%
7	620	88.57%	525	75.00%	97	84.35%	2412	69.21%
9	624	89.14%	524	74.86%	100	86.96%	2398	68.81%
11	625	89.29%	525	75.00%	99	86.09%	2389	68.55%
13	629	89.86%	517	73.86%	100	86.96%	2374	68.12%
15	629	89.86%	516	73.71%	98	85.22%	2372	68.06%
17	632	90.29%	520	74.29%	99	86.09%	2379	68.26%
19	628	89.71%	520	74.29%	100	86.96%	2387	68.49%

accuracies for bad and good groups in the testing dataset are 85.61% and 68.67%. Compared with previous MCQP results, majority-vote ensemble improves the total classification accuracies. Especially for bad records in testing set, the average accuracy increased 4.39%.

Experimental Results of Fuzzy Linear Programming

Applying the fuzzy linear programming model discussed earlier in this chapter to the same credit card dataset, we obtained some FLP classification results. These results are compared with the decision tree, MCLP, and neural networks (see Tables 5 and 6). The software of decision tree is the commercial version called C5.0 (C5.0 2004), while software for both neural network and MCLP were developed at the Data Mining Lab, University of Nebraska at Omaha, USA (Kou & Shi, 2002).

Table 5. Learning comparisons on balanced 280 records

Decision Tree	T_g	T_b	Total
Good	*138*	2	140
Bad	13	**127**	140
Total	151	129	**280**
Neural Network	T_g	T_b	Total
Good	**116**	24	140
Bad	14	**126**	140
Total	130	150	**280**
MCLP	T_g	T_b	Total
Good	**134**	6	140
Bad	7	*133*	140
Total	141	139	**280**
FLP	T_g	T_b	Total
Good	**127**	13	140
Bad	13	**127**	140
Total	140	140	**280**

Table 6. Comparisons on prediction of 5,000 records

Decision Tree	T_g	T_b	Total
Good	**2180**	2005	4185
Bad	141	**674**	815
Total	2321	2679	**5000**
Neural Network	$T_g T$	b	Total
Good	**2814**	1371	4185
Bad	176	**639**	815
Total	2990	2010	**5000**
MCLP	$T_g T$	b	Total
Good	*3160*	1025	4185
Bad	484	**331**	815
Total	3644	1356	**5000**
FLP	$T_g T$	b	Total
Good	**2498**	1687	4185
Bad	113	*702*	815
Total	2611	2389	**5000**

Note that in both Table 5 and Table 6, the columns T_g and T_b respectively represent the number of good and bad accounts identified by a method, while the rows of good and bad represent the actual numbers of the accounts.

Classifications on HIV-1-Mediated Neural Dendritic and Synaptic Damage USING MCLP

The ability to identify neuronal damage in the dendritic arbor during HIV-1-associated dementia (HAD) is crucial for designing specific therapies for the treatment of HAD. A two-class model of multiple criteria linear programming (MCLP) was proposed to classify such HIV-1 mediated neuronal dendritic and synaptic damages. Given certain classes, including treatments with brain-derived neurotrophic factor (BDNF), glutamate, gp120, or non-treatment controls from our in vitro experimental systems, we used the two-class MCLP model to determine the data patterns between classes in order to gain insight about neuronal dendritic and synaptic damages under different treatments (Zheng et al., 2004). This knowledge can be applied to the design and study of specific therapies for the prevention or reversal of neuronal damage associated with HAD.

Database

The data produced by laboratory experimentation and image analysis was organized into a database composed of four classes (G1-G4), each of which has nine attributes. The four classes are defined as the following:

- **G1:** Treatment with the neurotrophin BDNF (brain-derived neurotrophic factor, 0.5 ng/ml, 5 ng/ml, 10 ng/mL, and 50 ng/ml), this factor promotes neuronal cell survival and has been shown to enrich neuronal cell cultures (Lopez et al., 2001; Shibata et al., 2003).

- **G2:** Non-treatment, neuronal cells are kept in their normal media used for culturing (Neurobasal media with B27, which is a neuronal cell culture maintenance supplement from Gibco, with glutamine and penicillin-streptomycin).

- **G3:** Treatment with glutamate (10, 100, and 1,000 □M). At low concentrations, glutamate acts as a neurotransmitter in the brain. However, at high concentrations, it has been shown to be a neurotoxin by over-stimulating NMDA receptors. This factor has been shown to be upregulated in HIV-1-infected macrophages (Jiang et al., 2001) and thereby linked to neuronal damage by HIV-1 infected macrophages.

- **G4:** Treatment with gp120 (1 nanoM), an HIV-1 envelope protein. This protein could interact with receptors on neurons and interfere with cell signaling leading to neuronal damage, or it could also indirectly induce neuronal injury through the production of other neurotoxins (Hesselgesser et al., 1998; Kaul, Garden, & Lipton, 2001; Zheng et al., 1999).

The nine attributes are defined as:

- $x1$ = The number of neurites

- $x2$ = The number of arbors

- $x3$ = The number of branch nodes

- $x4$ = The average length of arbors

- $x5$ = The ratio of neurite to arbor

- $x6$ = The area of cell bodies

- $x7$ = The maximum length of the arbors

- $x8$ = The culture time (during this time, the neuron grows normally and BDNF, glutamate, or gp120 have not been added to affect growth)

- $x9$ = The treatment time (during this time, the neuron was growing under the effects of BDNF, glutamate, or gp120)

The database used in this chapter contained 2,112 observations. Among them, 101 are on G1, 1,001 are on G2, 229 are on G3, and 781 are on G4.

Comparing with the traditional mathematical tools in classification, such as neural networks, decision tree, and statistics, the two-class MCLP approach is simple and direct, free of the statistical assumptions, and flexible by allowing decision makers to play an active part in the analysis (Shi, 2001).

Results of Empirical Study Using MCLP

By using the two-class model for the classifications on {G1, G2, G3, and G4}, there are six possible pairings: G1 vs. G2; G1 vs. G3; G1 vs. G4; G2 vs. G3; G2 vs. G4; and G3 vs. G4. In the cases of G1 vs. G3 and G1 vs. G4, we see these combinations would be treated as redundancies, therefore they are not considered in the pairing groups. G1 through G3 or G4 is a continuum. G1 represents an enrichment of neuronal cultures, G2 is basal or maintenance of neuronal culture, and G3/G4 are both damage of neuronal cultures. There would never be a jump between G1 to G3/G4 without traveling through G2. So, we used the following four two-class pairs: G1 vs. G2; G2 vs. G3; G2 vs. G4; and G3 vs. G4. The meanings of these two-class pairs are:

- G1 vs. G2 shows that BDNF should enrich the neuronal cell cultures and increase neuronal network complexity—that is, more dendrites and arbors, more length to dendrites, and so forth.

- G2 vs. G3 indicates that glutamate should damage neurons and lead to a decrease in dendrite and arbor number including dendrite length.

- G2 vs. G4 should show that gp120 causes neuronal damage leading to a decrease in dendrite and arbor number and dendrite length.

- G3 vs. G4 provides information on the possible difference between glutamate toxicity and gp120-induced neurotoxicity.

Given a threshold of training process that can be any performance measure, we have carried out the following steps:

Algorithm 4

Step 1: For each class pair, we used the Linux code of the two-class model to compute the compromise solution $X^* = (x_1^*,..., x_9^*)$ as the best weights of all nine neuronal variables with given values of control parameters (b, α^*, β^*).

Step 2: The classification score $MCLP_i = A_i X^*$ against of each observation has been calculated against the boundary b to check the performance measures of the classification.

Step 3: If the classification result of Step 2 is acceptable (i.e., the given performance measure is larger or equal to the given threshold), go to Step 4. Otherwise, choose different values of control parameters (b, α^*, β^*) and go to Step 1.

Step 4: For each class pair, use $X^* = (x_1^*,..., x_9^*)$ to calculate the MCLP scores for all A_i in the test set and conduct the performance analysis.

According to the nature of this research, we define the following terms, which have been widely used in the performance analysis as:

TP (True Positive) = the number of records in the first class that has been classified correctly

FP (False Positive) = the number of records in the second class that has been classified into the first class

TN (True Negative) = the number of records in the second class that has been classified correctly

FN (False Negative) = the number of records in the first class that has been classified into the second class

Then we have four different performance measures:

$$\text{Sensitivity} = \frac{TP}{TP+FN}$$

$$\text{Positive Predictivity} = \frac{TP}{TP+FP}$$

$$\text{False-Positive Rate} = \frac{FP}{TN+FP}$$

$$\text{Negative Predictivity} = \frac{TN}{FN+TN}$$

The "positive" represents the first-class label while the "negative" represents the second-class label in the same class pair. For example, in the class pair {G1 vs. G2}, the record of G1 is "positive" while that of G2 is "negative." Among the above four measures, more attention is paid to sensitivity or false-positive rates because both measure the correctness of classification on class-pair data analyses. Note that in a given a class pair, the sensitivity represents the corrected rate of the first class, and one minus the false positive rate is the corrected rate of the second class by the above measure definitions.

Considering the limited data availability in this pilot study, we set the across-the-board threshold of 55% for sensitivity [or 55% of (1- false positive rate)] to select the experimental results from training and test processes. All 20 of the training and test sets, over the four class pairs, have been computed using the above procedure. The results against the threshold are summarized in Tables 7 to 10. As seen in these tables, the sensitivities for the comparison of all four pairs are higher than 55%, indicating that good separation among individual pairs is observed with this method. The results are then analyzed in terms of both positive predictivity and negative predictivity for the prediction power of the MCLP method on neuron injuries. In Table 7, G1 is the number of observations predefined as BDNF treatment, G2 is the number of observations predefined as non-treatment, N1 means the number of observations classified as BDNF treatment, and N2 is the number of observations classified as non-treatment. The meanings of other pairs in Tables 8 to 10 can be similarly explained. In Table 7 for {G1 vs. G2}, both positive predictivity and negative predictivity are the same (61.80%) in the training set. However, the negative

Table 7. Classification results with G1 vs. G2

Training	N1	N2	Sensitivity	Positive	False Positive	Negative
G1	55 (TP)	34 (FN)	61.80%	61.80%	38.20%	61.80%
G2	34 (FP)	55 (TN)				
Test	N1	N2	Sensitivity	Positive	False Positive	Negative
G1	11 (TP)	9 (FN)	55.00%	3.78%	30.70%	98.60%
G2	280 (FP)	632 (TN)				

Table 8. Classification results with G2 vs. G3

Training	N2	N3	Sensitivity	Positive	False	Negative
G2	126 (TP)	57 (FN)	68.85%	68.48%	31.69%	68.68%
G3	58 (FP)	125 (TN)				
Test	N2	N3	Sensitivity	Positive	False	Negative
G2	594 (TP)	224 (FN)	72.62%	99.32%	8.70%	15.79%
G3	4 (FP)	42 (TN)				

Table 9. Classification results with G2 vs. G4

Training	N2	N4	Sensitivity	Positive	False Positive	Negative
G2	419(TP)	206 (FN)	67.04%	65.88%	34.72%	66.45%
G4	217 (FP)	408 (TN)				
Test	N2	N4	Sensitivity	Positive	False Positive	Negative
G2	216 (TP)	160 (FN)	57.45%	80.90%	32.90%	39.39%
G4	51 (FP)	104 (TN)				

Table 10. Classification results with G3 vs. G4

Training	N3	N4	Sensitivity	Positive	False	Negative
G3	120(TP)	40 (FN)	57.45%	80.90%	24.38%	75.16%
G4	39 (FP)	121 (TN)				
Test	N3	N4	Sensitivity	Positive	False	Negative
G3	50 (TP)	19 (FN)	72.46%	16.78%	40.00%	95.14%
G4	248 (FP)	372 (TN)				

predictivity of the test set (98.60%) is much higher than that of the positive predictivity (3.78%). The prediction of G1 in the training set is better than that of the test set, while the prediction of G2 in test outperforms that of training. This is due to the small size of G1. In Table 3 for {G2 vs. G3}, the positive predictivity (68.48%) is almost equal to the negative predictivity (68.68%) of the training set. The positive predictivity (99.32%) is much higher than the negative predictivity (15.79%) of the test set. As a result, the prediction of G2 in the test set is better than in the training set, but the prediction of G3 in the training set is better than in the test set.

The case of Table 9 for {G2 vs. G4} is similar to that of Table 8 for {G2 vs. G3}. We see that the separation of G2 in test (80.90%) is better than in training (65.88%), while the separation of G4 in training (66.45%) is better than in test (39.39%). In the case of Table 10 for {G3 vs. G4}, the positive predictivity (80.90%) is higher than the negative predictivity (75.16%) of the training set. Then, the positive predictivity (16.78%) is much lower than the negative predictivity (95.14%) of the test set. The prediction of G3 in training (80.90%) is better than that of test (16.78%), and the prediction of G4 in test (95.14%) is better than that of training (75.16%).

In summary, we observed that the predictions of G2 in test for {G1 vs. G2}, {G2 vs. G3}, and {G2 vs. G4} is always better than those in training. The prediction of G3 in training for {G2 vs. G3} and {G3 vs. G4} is better than those of test. Finally, the prediction of G4 for {G2 vs. G4} in training reverses that of {G3 vs. G4} in test. If we emphasize the test results, these results are favorable to G2. This may be due to the size of G2 (non-treatment), which is larger than all other classes. The classification results can change if the sizes of G1, G3, and G4 increase significantly.

Network Intrusion Detection

Network intrusions are malicious activities that aim to misuse network resources. Although various approaches have been applied to network intrusion detection, such as statistical analysis, sequence analysis, neural networks, machine learning, and artificial immune systems, this field is far from maturity, and new solutions are worthy of investigation. Since intrusion detection can be treated as a classification problem, it is feasible to apply a multiple-criterion classification model to this type of application. The objective of this experiment is to examine the applicability of MCLP and MCQP models in intrusion detection.

KDD99 Dataset

The KDD-99 dataset provided by DARPA was used in our intrusion detection test. The KDD-99 dataset includes a wide variety of intrusions simulated in a military network environment. It was used in the 1999 KDD-CUP intrusion detection contest. After the contest, KDD-99 has become a de facto standard dataset for intrusion detection experiments. Within the KDD-99 dataset, each connection has 38 numerical variables and is labeled as normal or attack. There are four main categories of attacks: denial-of-service (DOS), unauthorized access from a remote machine (R2L), unauthorized access to local root privileges (U2R), surveillance and other probing. The training dataset contains a total of 24 attack types, while the testing dataset contains an additional 14 types (Stolfo, Fan, Lee, Prodromidis, & Chan, 2000). Because the number of attacks for R2L, U2R, and probing is relatively small, this experiment focused on DOS.

Experimental Results of MCLP

Following the heuristic process described in this chapter, training and testing datasets were selected: first, the 'normal' dataset (812,813 records) was divided into 100 intervals (each interval has 8,128 records). Within each interval, 20 records were randomly selected. Second, the 'DOS' dataset (247,267 records) was divided into 100 intervals (each interval has 2,472 records). Within each interval, 20 records were randomly selected. Third, the 2,000 normal and 2,000 DOS records were combined to form a training dataset. Because KDD-99 has over 1 million records, and 4,000 training records represent less than 0.4% of it, the whole KDD-99 dataset is used for testing. Various training and testing datasets can be obtained by repeating this process. Considering the previous high detection rates of KDD-99 by other methods, the across-the-board threshold of 95% was set for both normal and DOS. Since training dataset classification accuracies are all 100%, only testing dataset (10 out of the total 300 results) results are summarized in Table 11 (Kou et al., 2004a). The average predictive accuracies for normal and DOS groups in the testing dataset are 98.94% and 99.56%.

Improvement of MCLP with Ensemble Method

The majority-vote ensemble method demonstrated its superior performance in credit card accounts classification. Can it improve the classification accuracy of network intrusion detection? To answer this question, the majority-vote ensemble was applied to the KDD-99 dataset. Ensemble results are summarized in Table 12 (Kou et al., 2004a). The average predictive accuracies for normal and DOS groups in the testing dataset are 99.61% and 99.78%. Both normal and DOS predictive accuracies have been slightly improved.

Table 11. MCLP KDD-99 classification results

Cross Validation	Testing Set (812813 Normal + 247267 Dos)			
	Normal	Accuracy	DOS	Accuracy
DataSet 1	804513	98.98%	246254	99.59%
DataSet 2	808016	99.41%	246339	99.62%
DataSet 3	802140	98.69%	245511	99.29%
DataSet 4	805151	99.06%	246058	99.51%
DataSet 5	805308	99.08%	246174	99.56%
DataSet 6	799135	98.32%	246769	99.80%
DataSet 7	805639	99.12%	246070	99.52%
DataSet 8	802938	98.79%	246566	99.72%
DataSet 9	805983	99.16%	245498	99.28%
DataSet 10	802765	98.76%	246641	99.75%

Table 12. MCLP KDD-99 classification results with ensemble

Number of Voters	Normal	Accuracy	DOS	Accuracy
3	809567	99.60%	246433	99.66%
5	809197	99.56%	246640	99.75%
7	809284	99.57%	246690	99.77%
9	809287	99.57%	246737	99.79%
11	809412	99.58%	246744	99.79%
13	809863	99.64%	246794	99.81%
15	809994	99.65%	246760	99.79%
17	810089	99.66%	246821	99.82%
19	810263	99.69%	246846	99.83%

Experimental Results of MCQP

A similar MCQP procedure used in credit card accounts classification was used to classify the KDD-99 dataset. A part of the results is summarized in Table 13 (Kou et al., 2004b). These results are slightly better than MCLP.

Improvement of MCQP with Ensemble Method

The majority-vote ensemble was used on MCQP results, and a part of the outputs is summarized in Table 14 (Kou et al., 2004b). The average predictive accuracies for normal and DOS groups in the testing dataset are 99.86% and 99.82%. Although

Table 13. MCQP KDD-99 classification results

Cross Validation	Testing Set(812813 Normal + 247267 Dos)			
N	ormal	Accuracy	DOS A	ccuracy
DataSet 1	808142	99.43%	245998	99.49%
DataSet 2	810689	99.74%	246902	***99.85%***
DataSet 3	807597	99.36%	246491	99.69%
DataSet 4	808410	99.46%	246256	99.59%
DataSet 5	810283	99.69%	246090	99.52%
DataSet 6	809272	99.56%	246580	99.72%
DataSet 7	806116	***99.18%***	246229	99.58%
DataSet 8	808143	99.43%	245998	99.49%
DataSet 9	811806	***99.88%***	246433	99.66%
DataSet 10	810307	99.69%	246702	99.77%

Table 14. MCQP KDD-99 classification results with ensemble

NO of Voters N	ormal	Accuracy	DOS A	ccuracy
3	810126	99.67%	246792	99.81%
5	811419	99.83%	246930	***99.86%***
7	811395	99.83%	246830	99.82%
9	811486	99.84%	246795	99.81%
11	812030	99.90%	246845	99.83%
13	812006	99.90%	246788	99.81%
15	812089	99.91%	246812	99.82%
17	812045	99.91%	246821	99.82%
19	812069	99.91%	246817	99.82%
21	812010	99.90%	246831	99.82%
23	812149	***99.92%***	246821	99.82%
25	812018	99.90%	246822	99.82%

the increase in classification accuracy is small, both normal and DOS predictive accuracies have been improved compared with previous 99.54% and 99.64%.

Research Challenges and Opportunities

Although the above multiple criteria optimization data mining methods have been applied in the real-life applications, there are number of challenging problems in mathematical modeling. While some of the problems are currently under investigation, some others remain to be explored.

Variations and Algorithms of Generalized Models

Given Model 1, if $p=2$, $q=1$, it will become a convex quadratic program which can be solved by using some known convex quadratic programming algorithm. However, when $p=1$, $q=2$, Model 1 is a concave quadratic program; and when $p=2$, $q=2$, we have Model 3 (MCQP), which is an indefinite quadratic problem. Since both concave quadratic programming and MCQP are NP-hard problems, it is very difficult to find a global optimal solution. We are working on both cases for developing direct algorithms that can converge to local optima in classification (Zhang, Shi, & Zhang, 2005).

Kernel Functions for Data Observations

The generalized model in the chapter has a natural connection with known support vector machines (SVM) (Mangasarian, 2000; Vapnik, 2000) since they both belong to the category of optimization-based data mining methods. However, they differ from ways to identify the classifiers. As we mentioned before, while the multiple criteria optimization approaches in this chapter use the overlapping and interior distance as two standards to measure the separation of each observation in the dataset, SVM selects the minority of observations (support vectors) to represent the majority of the rest of the observations. Therefore, in the experimental studies and real applications, SVM may have a high accuracy in the training set, but a lower accuracy in the testing result. Nevertheless, the use of kernel functions in SVM has shown its efficiency in handling nonlinear datasets. How to adopt kernel functions into the multiple criteria optimization approaches can be an interesting research problem. Kou, Peng, Shi, and Chen (2006) explored some possibility of this research direction. The basic idea is outlined.

First, we can rewrite the generalized model (Model 1) similar to the approach of SVM. Suppose the two-classes G_1 and G_2 are under consideration. Then, a $n \times n$ diagonal matrix Y, which only contains +1 or -1, indicates the class membership. A -1 in row i of matrix Y indicates the corresponding record $A_i \in G_1$, and a +1 in row i of matrix Y indicates the corresponding record $A_i \in G_2$. The constraints in Model 1, $A_i X = b + \alpha_i - \beta_i$, $\forall A_i \in G_1$ and $A_i X = b - \alpha_i + \beta_i$, $\forall A_i \in G_2$, are converted as: $Y(<A \cdot X> - eb) = \alpha - \beta$, where $e = (1,1,...,1)^T$, and $\beta = (\beta_1,...,\beta_n)^T$. In order to maximize the distance

$$\frac{2}{\|X\|_2}$$

between the two adjusted bounding hyper planes, the function $\frac{1}{2}\|X\|_2$ should also be minimized. Let $s = 2$, $q = 1$, and $p = 1$, then a simple quadratic programming (SQP) variation of Model 1 can be built as:

Model 5: SQP

Minimize $-\frac{1}{2}\|X\|_2 + w_\alpha \sum_{i=1}^{n} \alpha_i - w_\beta \sum_{i=1}^{n} \beta_i$

Subject to $Y(<A \cdot X> - eb) = \alpha - \beta$, where $e = (1,1,...,1)^T$, $\alpha = (\alpha_1,...,\alpha_n)^T$ and $\beta = (\beta_1,...,\beta_n)^T \geq 0$.

Using Lagrange function to represent Model 5, one can get an equivalent of the Wolfe dual problem of Model 5 expressed as:\

Model 6: Dual of SQP

Maximize $-\frac{1}{2} \sum_{i=1}^{n} \sum_{j=1}^{n} \xi_i y_i \xi_j y_j (A_i \cdot A_j) + \delta \sum_{i=1}^{n} \xi_i$

Subject to $\sum_{i=1}^{n} \xi_i y_i = 0$, $w_\beta \leq \xi_i \leq w_\alpha$,

where $w_\beta < w_\alpha$ are given, $1 \leq i \leq n$.

The global optimal solution of the primal problem if Model 5 can be obtained from the solution of the Wolfe dual problem: $X^* = \sum_{i=1}^{n} \xi_i^* y_i A_i$, $b^* = y_j - \sum_{i=1}^{n} \xi^* y_i (A_i \cdot A_j)$.

As a result, the classification decision function becomes:

$$sgn((\mathbf{X}^* \cdot B) - b^*) \begin{cases} > 0, B \in G_1 \\ \leq 0, B \in G_2 \end{cases},$$

We observe that because the form $(A_i \cdot A_j)$ of Model 6 is inner product in the vector space, it can be substituted by a positive semi-definite kernel $K(A_i, A_j)$ without affecting the mathematical modeling process. In general, a kernel function refers to a real-valued function on $\chi \times \chi$ and for all $A_i, A_j \in \chi$. Thus, Model 6 can be easily transformed to a nonlinear model by replacing $(A_i \cdot A_j)$ with some positive semi-definite kernel function $K(A_i, A_j)$. Use of kernel functions in multiple criteria optimization approaches can extend its applicability to linear inseparable datasets. However, there are some theoretical difficulties to directly introduce kernel function to Model 5. How to overcome them deserves a careful study. Future studies may be done on establishing a theoretical guideline for selection of a kernel that is optimal in achieving a satisfactory credit analysis result. Another open problem is to study the subject of reducing computational cost and improving algorithm efficiency for high dimensional or massive datasets.

Choquet Integrals and Non-Additive Set Function

Considering the r-dimensional attribute vector $a = (a_1,...,a_r)$ in the classification problem, let $P(a)$ denote the power set of a. We use $f(a_1),...,f(a_r)$ to denote the values of each attribute in an observation. The procedure of calculating a Choquet integral can be given as (Wang & Wang, 1997):

$$\int f \, d\mu = \sum_{j=1}^{r} [f(a_j') - f(a_{j-1}')] \times \mu(\{a_1', a_2',...,a_r'\}),$$

where $\{a_1', a_2',..., a_r'\}$ is a permutation of $a = (a_1,...,a_r)$. Such that $f(a_0') = 0$ and $f(a_1'),..., f(a_r')$ is non-decreasingly ordered such that: $f(a_1) \leq ... \leq f(a_r)$. The non-additive set function is defined as: $\mu: P(a) \rightarrow (-\infty, +\infty)$, where $\mu(\varnothing) = 0$. We use μ_i to denote set function μ, where $i = 1,...,2^r$.

Introducing the Choquet measure into the generalized model of an section refers to the utilization of Choquet integral as a representative of the left-hand side of the constraints in Model 1. This variation for non-additive data mining problem is (Yan, Wang, Shi, & Chen, 2005):

Model 7: Choquet Form

Minimize $f(\alpha)$ and $g(\beta)$ Maximize

Subject to:

$\int f\, d\mu - \alpha_i + \beta_i - b = 0, \ \forall A_i \in G_1,$

$\int f\, d\mu + \alpha_i - \beta_i - b = 0, \ \forall A_i \in G_2,$

where $\int f\, d\mu$ denotes the Choquet integral with respect to a signed fuzzy measure to aggregate the attributes of a observation f, b is unrestricted, and $\alpha = (\alpha_1,...,\alpha_n)^T$, $\beta = (\beta_1,...,\beta_n)^T$; $\alpha_i, \beta_i \geq 0$, $i = 1,..., n$.

Model 7 results in the replacement of a linear combination of all the attributes $A_i X$ in the left-hand side of constraints with the Choquet integral representation $\int f\, d\mu$. The number of parameters, denoted by μ_i, increases from r to 2^r (r is the number attributes). How to determine the parameters through linear programming framework is not easy. We are still working on this problem and shall report the significant results.

Conclusion

As Usama Fayyad pointed out at the KDD-03 Panel, data mining must attract the participation of the relevant communities to avoid re-inventing wheels and bring the field an auspicious future (Fayyad, Piatetsky-Shapiro, & Uthurusamy, 2003). One relevant field to which data mining has not attracted enough participation is optimization. This chapter summarizes a series of research activities that utilize multiple criteria decision-making methods to classification problems in data mining. Specifically, this chapter describes a variation of multiple criteria optimization-based models and applies these models to credit card scoring management, HIV-1 associated dementia (HAD) neuronal damage and dropout, and network intrusion detection as well as the potential in various real-life problems.

Acknowledgments

Since 1998, this research has been partially supported by a number of grants, including First Data Corporation, USA; DUE-9796243, the National Science Foundation of USA; U.S. Air Force Research Laboratory (PR No. E-3-1162); National Excellent Youth Fund #70028101, Key Project #70531040, #70472074, National Natural Science Foundation of China; 973 Project #2004CB720103, Ministry of Science and Technology, China; K.C. Wong Education Foundation (2001, 2003), Chinese Academy of Sciences; and BHP Billiton Co., Australia.

References

Bradley, P.S., Fayyad, U.M., & Mangasarian, O.L. (1999). Mathematical programming for data mining: Formulations and challenges. *INFORMS Journal on Computing, 11*, 217-238.

Bauer, E., & Kohavi, R. (1999). an empirical comparison of voting classification algorithms: Bagging, boosting, and variants. *Machine Learning, 36*, 105-139.

C 5.0. (2004). Retrieved from http://www.rulequest.com/see5-info.html

Charnes, A., & Cooper, W.W. (1961). *Management models and industrial applications of linear programming* (vols. 1 & 2). New York: John Wiley & Sons.

Dietterich, T. (2000). *Ensemble methods in machine learning.* In Kittler & Roli (Eds.), Multiple classifier systems (pp. 1-15). Berlin: Springer-Verlag (Lecture Notes in Pattern Recognition 1857).

Fayyad, U.M., Piatetsky-Shapiro, G., & Uthurusamy, R. (2003). Summary from the KDD-03 Panel: Data mining: The next 10 years. *ACM SIGKDD Explorations Newsletter, 5*(2), 191-196.

Fisher, R.A. (1936). The use of multiple measurements in taxonomic problems. *Annals of Eugenics, 7*, 179-188.

Freed, N., & Glover, F. (1981). Simple but powerful goal programming models for discriminant problems. *European Journal of Operational Research, 7*, 44-60.

Freed, N., & Glover, F. (1986). Evaluating alternative linear programming models to solve the two-group discriminant problem. *Decision Science, 17*, 151-162.

Han, J.W., & Kamber, M. (2000). *Data mining: Concepts and techniques.* San Diego: Academic Press.

He, J., Liu, X., Shi, Y., Xu, W., & Yan, N. (2004). Classifications of credit cardholder behavior by using fuzzy linear programming. *International Journal of Information Technology and Decision Making, 3*, 633-650.

Hesselgesser, J., Taub, D., Baskar, P., Greenberg, M., Hoxie, J., Kolson, D.L., & Horuk, R. (1998). Neuronal apoptosis induced by HIV-1 gp120 and the Chemokine SDF-1alpha mediated by the Chemokine receptor CXCR4. *Curr Biol, 8*, 595-598.

Kaul, M., Garden, G.A., & Lipton, S.A. (2001). Pathways to neuronal injury and apoptosis in HIV-associated dementia. *Nature, 410*, 988-994.

Kou, G., & Shi, Y. (2002). *Linux-based Multiple Linear Programming Classification Program: (Version 1.0.)* College of Information Science and Technology, University of Nebraska-Omaha, USA.

Kou, G., Liu, X., Peng, Y., Shi, Y., Wise, M., & Xu, W. (2003). Multiple criteria linear programming approach to data mining: Models, algorithm designs and software development. *Optimization Methods and Software, 18*, 453-473.

Kou, G., Peng, Y., Yan, N., Shi, Y., Chen, Z., Zhu, Q., Huff, J., & McCartney, S. (2004a, July 19-21). Network intrusion detection by using multiple-criteria linear programming. In *Proceedings of the International Conference on Service Systems and Service Management*, Beijing, China.

Kou, G., Peng, Y., Chen, Z., Shi, Y., & Chen, X. (2004b, July 12-14). A multiple-criteria quadratic programming approach to network intrusion detection. In *Proceedings of the Chinese Academy of Sciences Symposium on Data Mining and Knowledge Management*, Beijing, China.

Kou, G., Peng, Y., Shi, Y., & Chen, Z. (2006). *A new multi-criteria convex quadratic programming model for credit data analysis.* Working Paper, University of Nebraska at Omaha, USA.

Kuncheva, L.I. (2000). Clustering-and-selection model for classifier combination. In *Proceedings of the 4th International Conference on Knowledge-Based Intelligent Engineering Systems and Allied Technologies* (KES'2000).

Kwak, W., Shi, Y., Eldridge, S., & Kou, G. (2006). Bankruptcy prediction for Japanese firms: Using multiple criteria linear programming data mining approach. In *Proceedings of the International Journal of Data Mining and Business Intelligence*.

Jiang, Z., Piggee, C., Heyes, M.P., Murphy, C., Quearry, B., Bauer, M., Zheng, J., Gendelman, H.E., & Markey, S.P. (2001). Glutamate is a mediator of neurotoxicity in secretions of activated HIV-1-infected macrophages. *Journal of Neuroimmunology, 117*, 97-107.

Lam, L. (2000). *Classifier combinations: Implementations and theoretical issues.* In Kittler & Roli (Eds.), Multiple classifier systems (pp. 78-86). Berlin: Springer-Verlag (Lecture Notes in Pattern Recognition 1857).

Lee, S.M. (1972). *Goal programming for decision analysis.* Auerbach.

Lindsay, P.H., & Norman, D.A. (1972). *Human information processing: An introduction to psychology.* New York: Academic Press.

LINDO Systems Inc. (2003). *An overview of LINGO 8.0.* Retrieved from http://www.lindo.com/cgi/frameset.cgi?leftlingo.html;lingof.html

Lopez, A., Bauer, M.A., Erichsen, D.A., Peng, H., Gendelman, L., Shibata, A., Gendelman, H.E., & Zheng, J. (2001). The regulation of neurotrophic factor activities following HIV-1 infection and immune activation of mononuclear phagocytes. In *Proceedings of Soc. Neurosci. Abs.*, San Diego, CA.

Mangasarian, O.L. (2000). Generalized support vector machines. In A. Smola, P. Bartlett, B. Scholkopf, & D. Schuurmans (Eds.), Advances in large margin classifiers (pp. 135-146). Cambridge, MA: MIT Press.

Olson, D., & Shi, Y. (2005). *Introduction to business data mining*. New York: Mc-Graw-Hill/Irwin.

Opitz, D., & Maclin, R. (1999). Popular ensemble methods: An empirical study. *Journal of Artificial Intelligence Research, 11*, 169-198.

Parhami, B. (1994). *Voting algorithms. IEEE Transactions on Reliability, 43*, 617-629.

Peng, Y., Kou, G., Chen, Z., & Shi, Y. (2004). Cross-validation and ensemble analyses on multiple-criteria linear programming classification for credit cardholder behavior. In *Proceedings of ICCS 2004* (pp. 931-939). Berlin: Springer-Verlage (LNCS 2416).

Shi, Y., & Yu, P.L. (1989). *Goal setting and compromise solutions*. In B. Karpak & S. Zionts (Eds.), Multiple criteria decision making and risk analysis using microcomputers (pp. 165-204). Berlin: Springer-Verlag.

Shi, Y. (2001). *Multiple criteria and multiple constraint levels linear programming: Concepts, techniques and applications*. NJ: World Scientific.

Shi, Y., Wise, W., Luo, M., & Lin, Y. (2001). *Multiple criteria decision making in credit card portfolio management*. In M. Koksalan & S. Zionts (Eds.), Multiple criteria decision making in new millennium (pp. 427-436). Berlin: Springer-Verlag.

Shi, Y, Peng, Y., Xu, W., & Tang, X. (2002). Data mining via multiple criteria linear programming: Applications in credit card portfolio management. *International Journal of Information Technology and Decision Making, 1*, 131-151.

Shi, Y, Peng, Y., Kou, G., & Chen, Z. (2005). Classifying credit card accounts for business intelligence and decision making: A multiple-criteria quadratic programming approach. *International Journal of Information Technology and Decision Making, 4*, 581-600.

Shibata, A., Zelivyanskaya, M., Limoges, J., Carlson, K.A., Gorantla, S., Branecki, C., Bishu, S., Xiong, H., & Gendelman, H.E. (2003). Peripheral nerve induces macrophage neurotrophic activities: Regulation of neuronal process outgrowth, intracellular signaling and synaptic function. *Journal of Neuroimmunology, 142*, 112-129.

Stolfo, S.J., Fan, W., Lee, W., Prodromidis, A., & Chan, P.K. (2000). Cost-based modeling and evaluation for data mining with application to fraud and intrusion detection: Results from the JAM project. In *Proceedings of the DARPA Information Survivability Conference*.

Vapnik, V.N. (2000). T*he nature of statistical learning theory* (2nd ed.). New York: Springer.

Wang, J., & Wang, Z. (1997). Using neural network to determine Sugeno measures by statistics. *Neural Networks, 10*, 183-195.

Weingessel, A., Dimitriadou, E., & Hornik, K. (2003, March 20-22). An ensemble method for clustering. In *Proceedings of the 3rd International Workshop on Distributed Statistical Computing*, Vienna, Austria.

Yan, N., Wang, Z., Shi, Y., & Chen, Z. (2005). *Classification by linear programming with signed fuzzy measures*. Working Paper, University of Nebraska at Omaha, USA.

Yu, P.L. (1985). *Multiple criteria decision making: Concepts, techniques and extensions*. New York: Plenum Press.

Zenobi, G., & Cunningham, P. (2002). An approach to aggregating ensembles of lazy learners that supports explanation. *Lecture Notes in Computer Science, 2416*, 436-447.

Zhang, J., Shi, Y., & Zhang, P. (2005). S*everal multi-criteria programming methods for classification*. Working Paper, Chinese Academy of Sciences Research Center on Data Technology & Knowledge Economy and Graduate University of Chinese Academy of Sciences, China.

Zheng, J., Thylin, M., Ghorpade, A., Xiong, H., Persidsky, Y., Cotter, R., Niemann, D., Che, M., Zeng, Y., Gelbard, H. et al. (1999). Intracellular CXCR4 signaling, neuronal apoptosis and neuropathogenic mechanisms of HIV-1-associated dementia. J*ournal of Neuroimmunology, 98*, 185-200.

Zheng, J., Zhuang, W., Yan, N., Kou, G., Erichsen, D., McNally, C., Peng, H., Cheloha, A., Shi, C., & Shi, Y. (2004). Classification of HIV-1-mediated neuronal dendritic and synaptic damage using multiple criteria linear programming. *Neuroinformatics, 2*, 303-326.

Zimmermann, H.-J. (1978). Fuzzy programming and linear programming with several objective functions. *Fuzzy Sets and Systems, 1*, 45-55.

Chapter X

Linguistic Rule Extraction from Support Vector Machine Classifiers

Xiuju Fu, Institute of High Performance Computing, Singapore

Lipo Wang, Nanyang Technological University, Singapore

GihGuang Hung, Institute of High Performance Computing, Singapore

Liping Goh, Institute of High Performance Computing, Singapore

Abstract

Classification decisions from linguistic rules are more desirable compared to complex mathematical formulas from support vector machine (SVM) classifiers due to the explicit explanation capability of linguistic rules. Linguistic rule extraction has been attracting much attention in explaining knowledge hidden in data. In this chapter, we show that the decisions from an SVM classifier can be decoded into linguistic rules based on the information provided by support vectors and decision function. Given a support vector of a certain class, cross points between each line, which is extended from the support vector along each axis, and an SVM decision hyper-curve are searched first. A hyper-rectangular rule is derived from these cross points. The hyper-rectangle is tuned by a tuning phase in order to exclude those out-class data points. Finally, redundant rules are merged to produce a compact rule set. Simultaneously, important attributes could be highlighted in the extracted rules. Rule extraction results from our proposed method could follow SVM classifier decisions very well. We compare the rule extraction results from SVM with RBF kernel function and linear kernel function. Experiment results show that rules extracted from SVM with RBF nonlinear kernel function are with better accuracy than rules extracted from SVM with linear kernel function. Comparisons between our method and other rule extraction methods are also carried out on several benchmark data sets. Higher rule accuracy is obtained in our method with fewer number of premises in each rule.

Introduction

Rule extraction (Bologna & Pellegrini, 1998; Fu, Ong, Keerthi, Hung, & Goh, 2004; Hruschka & Ebecken, 1999; McGarry, Wermter, & MacIntyre, 1999; Saito & Nakano, 1998; Tsukimoto, 2000) can increase perceptibility and help human beings better understand decisions of learning models in data mining applications. Rule extraction can also help refine initial domain knowledge since irrelevant or redundant attributes tend to be absent in extracted rules. In future data collections, labor cost can be reduced by skipping redundant or irrelevant attributes. In addition, active attributes can be shown in rules extracted which facilitate classification decision making. Those attributes which are more active compared to others can be highlighted in linguistic rules. On the contrary, other classification models usually are opaque in identifying active attributes.

Rule extraction techniques are usually based on machine learning methods such as neural networks, support vector machines, genetic algorithms (GAs), statistical methods, rough sets, decision trees, and fuzzy logic.

For a data set with tens or hundreds of attributes and thousands of data patterns, it is hard to identify the roles of the attributes in classifying new patterns without any aid from learning models. For example, neural networks can be trained on these training samples to abstract essences and store the learned essential knowledge as parameters in the network. However, though essential knowledge has been captured and embedded in the trained neural network, humans cannot tell exactly why a new pattern is classified to a class, which is sometimes referred to as "black-box" characteristics of neural networks. In the medical domain, a disjunctive explanation given as a rule "If medical measurement A is $a1$, and medical measurement B is $b1$,..., then conclusion" is preferable to a complex mathematical decision function hidden in neural networks.

Rule extraction from neural networks has been an active research topic in recent years. In early rule extraction work, Gallant (1998) used trained neural networks to develop an expert-system engine and interpret the knowledge embedded in neural network models by IF-THEN rules. More than a decade had passed. The capability of rule extraction (Hofmann et al., 2003; Setiono, Leow, & Zurada, 2002; Tan & Lim, 2004) had been shown for delivering comprehensible descriptions on data concepts from complex machine learning models.

GA has been widely used for practical problem solving and for scientific modeling. With the capability in searching for desirable solutions in the problem space, GA has been employed for extracting rules from neural networks. Fukumi and Akamatsu (1998) used GA to prune the connections in neural networks before extracting rules. Hruschka and Ebecken (2000) proposed clustering genetic algorithm (CGA) to cluster the activation values of the hidden units of a trained neural network. Rules were then extracted based on the results from CGA. Ishibuchi and Nii (1996; with Murata, 1997) used GA to obtain concise rules by selecting important members from the rules extracted from a neural network.

Decision trees are often combined together with neural networks in both pedagogical and decompositional rule extraction approaches (Sato & Tsukimoto, 2001; Setiono & Liu, 1996). In the decompositional approach proposed in Sato and Tsukimoto (2001), neural networks are first trained to extract the essential relationship between the input and output. The relationship is thus embedded in interconnected weights and hidden neurons of trained neural networks. Then decision trees are applied to decompose the relationship between inputs and hidden neurons, as well as the relationship between hidden neurons and outputs. The results from decision trees are combined together to deliver rules.

In recent years, support vector machine (SVM) (Burges, 1998; Joachims, 2000) has attracted a lot of interest for its capability in solving classification and regression problems. Successful applications of SVM have been reported in various areas, including but not limited to areas in communication, time series prediction, and bioinformatics. In many applications, it is desirable to know not only the classification decisions, but also what leads to the decisions. However, SVMs offer little insight into the reasons why SVM has made its final results. It is a challenging task to develop a rule extraction algorithm (Nunez, Angulo, & Catala, 2002) in order to reveal knowledge embedded in trained SVMs and represent the classification decisions based on SVM classification results by linguistic rules.

In this chapter, we propose a rule extraction algorithm RulExSVM (rule extraction from support vector machines) for revealing the relationships between attributes and class labels through linguistic rules. The extracted rules are in IF-THEN forms with hyper-rectangular boundaries. Rules are generated directly based on information of support vectors. Given a support vector of a certain class, cross points between lines, along each axis, extended from the support vector and SVM decision hyper-curves are found. A hyper-rectangular rule is derived from these cross points. Out-class data points, which do not have the same class label with the support vector, are detected. The hyper-rectangle is tuned by a tuning phase in order to exclude those out-class data points. Finally rules are merged to obtain a more compact rule set.

In this chapter, SVM is briefly introduced, and the rule extraction algorithm RulExSVM is described. Two examples are presented for illustrating the rule extraction algorithm, then more experimental results are offered, followed by the chapter's conclusion.

Support Vector Machine Classifiers

Given a two-class data set with a set of pattern $\{X_i, y_i\}_{i=1}^{N}$, where $X_i = \{x_{i1}, x_{i2}, ..., x_{in}\}$ $\in R^n$, $y_i \in \{1, -1\}$, and N is the number of patterns. The support vector machine classifier can be considered as a quadratic cost function for solving the following optimization problem:

Minimize:

$$\sum_i \alpha_i - \frac{1}{2}\sum_{i,j}\alpha_i \alpha_j y_i y_j K(X_i, X_j)$$
(1)

subject to:

$$0 \leq \alpha_i \leq C,$$
(2)

$$\sum_i \alpha_i y_i = 0.$$
(3)

$K(X_i, X_j)$ is the kernel function. $K(X_i, X_j) = \phi(X_i \cdot X_j)$, $\phi(X_i)$ maps X_i into a higher dimensional space. C is called the regularization constant. Each data point X_i is with a α_i. The data points with $0 < \alpha_i \leq C$ are support vectors, such as the data points $\{A, B, C, D, E, F, G, I, J\}$ shown in Figure 1 (SVM kernel function is nonlinear). Support vector i with $\alpha_i = C$ falls into the region between two separating hyper-curves. See points I and J in Figure 1.

*Figure 1. Separating hyper-curves, support vectors, and the decision function (©
2005 IEEE). We thank the IEEE for allowing the reproduction of this figure, which
first appeared in Fu et al. (2004).*

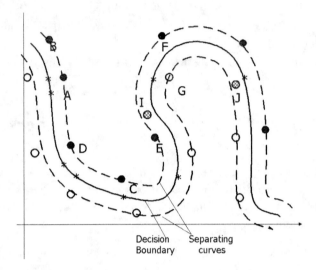

Based on the solution of the above optimization problem (Vapnik, 1995), a decision
function is determined using the α_i so obtained:

$$f(X)= \sum_{i=1}^{N_s}\alpha_i y_i K(S_i , X)+ b \qquad (4)$$

S_i represents the ith support vector and N_S is the number of support vectors.

Rule Extraction

In this section, we describe the rule extraction procedure for a two-class data set.
Based on the trained SVM classifier, support vectors of class 1 are used for generating
rules for class 1. The rule extraction method described later can be easily extended
to multi-class problems. In the rule extraction algorithm, the current class processed
is referred to as class 1. All the other classes are referred to as class 2.

Let us consider an example in the two-dimensional space. SVM classifier is with
RBF nonlinear kernel function. In Figure 2, black points are the support vectors of
class 1, and white points are the support vectors of class 2. For each axis, a line,

*Figure 2: Cross points (© 2005 IEEE). We thank the IEEE for allowing the repro-
duction of this figure, which first appeared in Fu et al., 2004)*

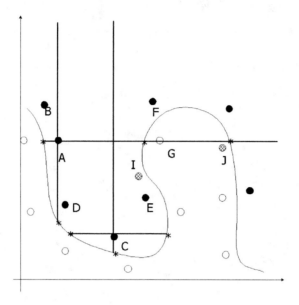

parallel to the axis, starting from a support vector of class 1, is extended in two
directions. The cross points between the line and the "decision boundary" can be
obtained. The decision boundary refers to the line with $f(X) = 0$. As an example, for
support vectors A and C, cross points between the extended lines and the decision
boundary are shown in Figure 2. Based on these cross points, the initial boundaries
of the hyper-rectangular rules can be obtained and shown as rectangles with dashed
lines in Figures 3a and 3b for support vectors A and C, respectively.

The rule extraction algorithm from SVM, RulExSVM, consists of three phases,
initial, tuning, and pruning phases. In the initial phase, given a support vector of
class 1, a rule with hyper-rectangular boundary is generated based on the information
provided by the support vector and the decision boundary. In the tuning phase, the
initial rule is tuned towards the direction improving the rule accuracy for classifying data. The two phases are stated as below. In the following description of our
rule extraction method, SVM classifiers are assumed with RBF kernel functions.
The rule extraction procedure based on SVM classifiers with linear kernel functions
could be easily figured out accordingly.

Figure 3a. Initial rule generated based on support vector A; Figure 3b. Initial rule generated based on support vector C (© 2005 IEEE). We thank the IEEE for allowing the reproduction of this figure, which first appeared in Fu et al., 2004)

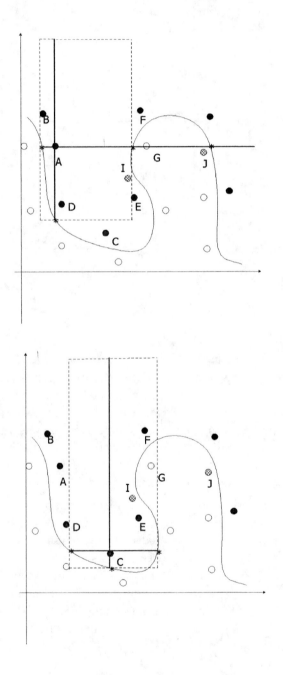

The Initial Phase for Generating Rules

In this section, how to calculate initial hyper-rectangular rules for a two-class data set is stated in detail. The following notation is used. A_i is the support vector set of class i: $i = \{1,2\}$. N_i is the number of support vectors of class i: $N_S = N_1 + N_2$. $S_m = \{s_{m1}, s_{m2},...,s_{mn}\}$ is the mth support vector of class 1. $X = \{x_1, x_2,...,x_n\}$ is a pattern of data. Note that all attributes of data points are normalized between [0,1].

The rule with hyper-rectangular boundary derived from a support vector S_m of class 1 can be represented by points included in the rule region:

$$\{X : s_{ml} + \overline{\lambda}_l \geq \overline{x}_l \geq s_{ml} + \underline{\lambda}_l, l = 1,...,n\} \tag{5}$$

subject to $1 \geq \overline{\lambda}_l \geq -1$ and $1 \geq \underline{\lambda}_l \geq -1$.

Let:

$$L_l = s_{ml} + \underline{\lambda}_l \tag{6}$$

and

$$H_l = s_{ml} + \overline{\lambda}_l \tag{7}$$

where H_l and L_l give the upper and lower limits of the hyper-rectangular rule along the lth dimension. Based on the decision function $f(X)$, L_l and H_l are determined in the following procedure.

Given the solution of a SVM determined by equation 4 and the corresponding axis l, the rule deriving from support vector S_m can be generated as follows:

1. Set $l = 1$, l refers to dimension l.

2. Let $X(\lambda) = S_m + \lambda e_p$ where e_l is a unit vector with all zero elements except the lth element. Define $\tilde{f}(\lambda):= f(X(\lambda))$ as given by Equation 4. Find all possible roots of $\tilde{f}(\lambda)$ with $1 \geq \lambda \geq -1$ by the Newton's method. Let $V_l = \{\tilde{\lambda}_1, \tilde{\lambda}_2...,\tilde{\lambda}_{kl}\}$ be the set of these k_l roots of $\tilde{f}(\lambda)$.

3. Determine H_l and L_l. There are several cases to be considered:

   a. $k_l = 0$. This means that there is no cross point between the line extended from S_m along dimension l and the decision boundary. Hence $H_l = 1$ and $L_l = 0$.

b. $k_l = 1$:

If $\tilde{\lambda}_1 < 0$, $L_l = (s_{ml} + \tilde{\lambda}_1)$, and $H_l = 1$, else $L_l = 0$, and $H_l = (s_{ml} + \tilde{\lambda}_1)$.

c. $k_l = 2$. Assume $\tilde{\lambda}_1 < \tilde{\lambda}_2$:

if $\tilde{\lambda}_1 > 0$, then $L_l = 0$, and $H_l = (s_{ml} + \tilde{\lambda}_1)$

if $\tilde{\lambda}_1 < 0$ and $\tilde{\lambda}_2 > 0$, then $L_l = (s_{ml} + \tilde{\lambda}_1)$, and $H_l = (s_{ml} + \tilde{\lambda}_1)$

if $\tilde{\lambda}_2 < 0$, then $L_l = (s_{ml} + \tilde{\lambda}_2)$, and $H_l = 1$.

d. $k_l > 2$. Assume $\tilde{\lambda}_1 < \tilde{\lambda}_2 < ... < \tilde{\lambda}_{kl}$:

if $\tilde{\lambda}_1 > 0$, then $L_l = 0$, and $H_l = (s_{ml} + \tilde{\lambda}_1)$

if $\tilde{\lambda}_1 < 0$ and $\tilde{\lambda}_{kl} > 0$, then there exists an index j with $\tilde{\lambda}_j < 0 < \tilde{\lambda}_{j+1}$. Hence, $L_l = (s_{ml} + \tilde{\lambda}_j)$, and $H_l = (s_{ml} + \tilde{\lambda}_{j+1})$

if $\tilde{\lambda}_{kl} < 0$, then $L_l = (s_{ml} + \tilde{\lambda}_k)$, and $H_l = 1$.

4. $l = l + 1$, if $l \leq n$, go to Step 2, else end

The Tuning Phase for Rules

The tuning phase of the RulExSVM method is implemented after an initial rule is generated. The rules generated in the initial phase rely on support vectors and the decision function. Hence it is possible for data points from the other class to lie within the rule regions. It is therefore necessary to redefine the rule by adjusting H_l and L_l to exclude those data points. There are many choices of l varying from 1 to n to achieve the adjustment. We then wish to adjust so that the volume of the tuned hyper-rectangular rule is largest for the various choices of l. The implementation steps of RulExSVM are as follows:

1.   Randomly choose a support vector S_m from A1 and invoke the initial phase with S_m as an input. If A1 is empty, then stop.

2.   Search all samples of class 2 which are included in the rule region. Let the collection of all such points be Q with cardinality $|Q|$. If $|Q| > 0$, then randomly choose a sample from Q, and go to Step 3, otherwise, remove S_m from A1 and go to Step 1.

3.   Adjust the hyper-rectangular rule so that the sample point is outside of the rule region, and that the remaining volume of the rule region is the largest among the possible n dimensions. Go to Step 2.

The Pruning Phase for Rules

Rules that classify data patterns from different classes may overlap with each other since rules extracted are independent during initialization and tuning phases. If a rule region is totally overlapped by another, it would be considered redundant. The pruning phase removes such redundant rules from the rule set. The pruning procedure is as follows: (1) find the data points that fall into each rule region; (2) if the set of points in a rule region is a subset of points covered by another rule, the rule is removed; (3) repeat the pruning to remove all redundant rules.

An Illustrative Example

In this section, we present an example applying RulExSVM. The data set is a binary-class data set. For a multiple-class data set with M classes, rule extraction is carried out for M binary-class data sets—that is, one-against-all policy is employed for extracting rules for each class. When training SVM classifiers and extracting rules, we normalize all the attributes to the interval [0, 1]. In the expression of rules, the attributes will be transformed to their original ranges.

The breast cancer data set (Mangasarian & Wolberg, 1990) obtained from the University of Wisconsin Hospitals, Madison, from Dr. William H. Wolberg, has nine discrete attributes. The original range of the discrete attributes is the interval [1, 10].

RulExSVM extracts rules based on trained SVM classifiers. The parameters of SVM $\{\sigma, C\}$ are determined using 5-fold cross-validation.

Choose a support vector S_m of class 1 randomly; Newton's method is employed to find the initial rule derived from this support vector. In order to reduce the calculation time of Newton's method when searching the cross points between lines extending from the selected support vector along each axis and the decision boundary of support vector machine, a set of values $\{0, 0.05, 0.1, 0.15, ..., 0.9, 0.95, 1.0\}$ are taken from the interval [0, 1]. Then calculate the values of $\tilde{f}(\lambda)$ (Equation 4) subject to that λ equals to each of the 21 values. In the results of $\tilde{f}(\lambda)$, we are to find two neighbors $\{\lambda | \lambda_1, \lambda_2\}$ whose signs of $\tilde{f}(\lambda)$ are different. Let $\lambda = (\lambda_1 + \lambda_2)/2$. If signs of all of $\tilde{f}(\lambda)$'s are the same, λ equals the value which corresponds to the smallest $\tilde{f}(\lambda)$. This λ serves as the starting point for Newton's method to find the solutions of $\tilde{f}(\lambda) = 0$.

We obtained seven rules for breast cancer data set based on SVM classifier with RBF kernel function. The rule accuracy for classification is 97.51%. These rules describe the Benign case, and the Malign case is the default class. The character-istics of the Malign class are considered as the ones opposite to those presented in the rule set.

In Setiono (2000), 2.9 rules were generated with accuracy 94.04%. Higher rule accuracy is obtained by our method, though the number of rules is higher. It is also observed in our rule set that the rule accuracy is obtained without the contribution of attributes 2, 5, 7. When we use the attributes {1, 3, 4, 6, 8, 9} presented in the rule set as the inputs to SVM, we can obtain the same classification result as that obtained by using the whole original attributes as inputs to SVM. It shows that these three attributes are not active in determining class labels. The point is that an advantage of rule decisions over SVM decision though the accuracy of black-box SVM classifiers is usually higher than the accuracy of rules.

Experimental Results

Data sets Mushroom, Breast Cancer, and Wine are used to demonstrate the proposed method. These data sets could be obtained from the UCI database (Murphy & Aha, 1994). The characteristics of data sets used here are shown in Table 1. Discrete and numerical attributes can be found in data sets.

In Table 2, the number of support vectors in SVM classifiers for separating each class from other classes is shown, together with classification accuracy based on trained SVM classifiers. The classification results from SVM classifiers with linear and nonlinear kernel functions are listed together in Table 2. The information of rules extracted based on SVM classifiers with nonlinear kernel functions (RBF kernel functions) are shown in Table 3. Rule results based on SVM classifiers with linear kernel functions are shown in Table 4. The number of premises of each rule is calculated on average. In Table 4, the fidelity shows that rules extracted match SVM classifiers well.

In the experiments, only support vectors are used for generating initial rules and tuning rules by considering training data points. In Table 5, time (seconds) consumed

Table 1. Characteristics of data sets used

Data Sets	Patterns	Numeric Attributes	Discrete Attributes	Classes
Mushroom	8,124	0	22	2
Wine	178	13	0	3
Breast Cancer	683	0	9	2

for training SVM classifiers and extracting rules is presented. The rule extraction program is written in C.

In Setiono (2000), rules were obtained for the Mushroom data set with two rules and 98.12% accuracy. For the Mushroom data set, seven rules with 100% accuracy are obtained by the RulExSVM method.

Table 2. SVM classification results

Data Sets	SVM Accuracy	
	RBF Kernel	**Linear Kernel**
Mushroom	100%	98.67%
Wine	99.3%	97.22%
Breast Cancer	97.8%	97.25%

Table 3. Rule extraction results from SVM classifiers with RBF kernel

Data Sets	Rule Accuracy	Number of Rules	Premises per Rule	Fidelity
Mushroom	100%	7	3.33	100%
Wine	99.3%	6	4.3	99.3%
Breast Cancer	97.51%	7	5.3	99.27%

Table 4. Rule extraction results from SVM classifiers with linear kernel

Data Sets	Rule Accuracy	Number of Rules	Premises per Rule	Fidelity
Mushroom	99.08%	6	7.67	97.75%
Wine	100%	4	7	97.22%
Breast Cancer	94.2%	4	8	95.64%

Table 5. SVM training time and time spent for rule extraction (CPU 1.3GHZ)

Data Sets	RBF Kernel (seconds)		Linear Kernel (seconds)	
	SVM Training	**Rule Extraction**	**SVM Training**	**Rule Extraction**
Mushroom	3.16	24.04	0.78	12.96
Wine	0.03	0.3	0.03	0.06
Breast Cancer	0.07	0.22	0.04	0.15

Discussion and Conclusion

Training a learning model is considered a prior step to discovering hidden information from data sets. The proposed rule extraction method RulExSVM is composed of three main components: first, based on the trained SVM classifier, initial rules are determined by calculating cross points between support vectors and the decision boundary along each axis; second, rules are tuned based on the criterion that excludes data points of other classes from the rule region, and keep the rule region as large as possible; third, the rules that are overlapped completely by other rules will be pruned. In this work, we explore rule extraction from SVM classifiers with linear kernel functions and nonlinear RBF kernel functions. The rule extraction procedure reported here could be easily extend to SVM with other types of kernel functions.

An example is presented to illustrate how our proposed rule-extraction algorithm RulExSVM works. Our method could be used to extract rules from data sets with discrete or continuous attributes. It is observed that some attributes might not be present in extracted rules. And the roles of present attributes are highlighted in rules. Rule extraction results are more understandable than the decision from SVM classifiers because attributes that make a contribution in classifying data samples are observable. For high-dimensional data, the number of rules extracted might be too many. However, it is worthwhile to extract rules since important attributes might be found in rules. And even though there might be only a few interesting rules in the rule set, it is worthwhile to extract rules since domain experts such as doctors might get valuable information by observing objects covered by those interesting rules. On the other hand, Tables 3 and 4 shows that the fidelity of our rule extraction results corresponding to SVM classification decisions is high. For evaluating a rule extraction algorithm, high rule accuracy is a criterion, but not the only one. Since rules are extracted based on SVM classifiers, it is expected that rule extraction procedure could explain the black-box decision in a linguistic way and reflect the performance of SVM classifiers well. The fidelity is also an important criterion to evaluate rule extraction algorithms.

Rules extracted by our algorithm have hyper-rectangular decision boundaries, which is desirable due to its explicit perceptibility. Rule extraction results from the proposed method could follow SVM classifier decisions very well. Comparisons between the proposed method and other rule extraction methods show that higher rule accuracy is obtained in our method with a fewer number of premises in each rule. We believe that rule extraction from SVM classifiers is useful for putting SVM into more practical data mining applications.

References

Bologna, G., & Pellegrini, C. (1998). Constraining the MLP power of expression to facilitate symbolic rule extraction. In *Proceedings of the IEEE World Congress on Computational Intelligence* (Vol. 1), 146-151.

Burges, C.J.C. (1998). A tutorial on support vector machines for pattern recognition. *Data Mining and Knowledge Discovery, 2*(2), 955-974.

Fu, X.J., Ong, C.J., Keerthi, S.S., Hung, G.G., & Goh, L.P. (2004). Extracting the knowledge embedded in support vector machines. In *Proceedings of the IEEE International Joint Conference on Neural Networks, 1*, (pp. 25-29).

Fukumi, M., & Akamatsu, N. (1998). Rule extraction from neural networks trained using evolutionary algorithms with deterministic mutation. In *Proceedings of the 1998 IEEE International Joint Conference on Computational Intelligence, 1*, (pp. 686-689).

Gallant, S.I. (1998). Connectionist expert systems. *Communications of the ACM, 31*, 152-169.

Hofmann, A., Schmitz, C., & Sick, B. (2003). Rule extraction from neural networks for intrusion detection in computer networks. In *Proceedings of the IEEE International Conference on Systems, Man and Cybernetics, 2*, (pp. 1259-1265).

Hruschka, E.R., & Ebecken, N.F.F. (1999). Rule extraction from neural networks: Modified RX algorithm. In *Proceedings of the International Joint Conference on Neural Networks, 4*, (pp. 2504-2508).

Hruschka, E.R., & Ebecken, N.F.F. (2000). Applying a clustering genetic algorithm for extracting rules from a supervised neural network. In *Proceedings of the IEEE-INNS-ENNS International Joint Conference on Neural Networks, 3*, (pp. 407-412).

Ishibuchi, H., & Nii, M. (1996). Generating fuzzy if-then rules from trained neural networks: Linguistic analysis of neural networks. In *Proceedings of the IEEE International Conference on Neural Networks, 2*, (pp. 1133-1138).

Ishibuchi, H., Nii, M., & Murata, T. (1997). Linguistic rule extraction from neural networks and genetic-algorithm-based rule selection. In *Proceedings of the International Conference on Neural Networks, 4*, (pp. 2390-2395).

Joachims, T. (2000). Estimating the generalization performance of an SVM efficiently. In *Proceedings of the 17th International Conference on Machine Learning (ICML)*. San Francisco: Morgan Kaufmann.

McGarry, K.J., Wermter, S., & MacIntyre, J. (1999). Knowledge extraction from radial basis function networks and multilayer perceptrons. In *Proceedings of the International Joint Conference on Neural Networks, 4*, (pp. 2494-2497).

Mangasarian, O.L., & Wolberg, W.H. (1990). Cancer diagnosis via linear programming. *SIAM News, 23*(5), 1-18.

Murphy, P.M., &. Aha, D.W. (1994). *UCI repository of machine learning databases.* Irvine, CA: University of California, Department of Information and Computer Science.

Nunez, H., Angulo, C., & Catala, A. (2002). Rule extraction from support vector machines. In *Proceedings of the European Symposium on Artificial Neural Networks* (pp. 107-112). Bruges, Belgium: D-Side.

Saito, K., & Nakano, R. (1998). Medical diagnostic expert system based on PDP Model. In *Proceedings of the IEEE International Conference on Neural Networks, 1,* 255-262.

Sato, M., & Tsukimoto, H. (2001). Rule extraction from neural networks via decision tree induction. In *Proceedings of the International Joint Conference on Neural Networks, 3,* 1870-1875.

Setiono, R. (2000). Extracting M-of-N rules from trained neural networks. *IEEE Transactions on Neural Networks, 11*(2), 512-519.

Setiono, R., & Liu, H. (1996). Symbolic representation of neural networks. *Computer, 29,* 71-77.

Setiono, R., Leow, L.W., & Zurada, J.M. (2002). Extraction of rules from artificial neural networks for nonlinear regression. *IEEE Transactions on Neural Networks, 13*(3), 564-577.

Tan, S.C., & Lim, C.P. (2004). Application of an adaptive neural network with symbolic rule extraction to fault detection and diagnosis in a power generation plant. *IEEE Transactions on Energy Conversion, 19,* 369-377.

Tsukimoto, H. (2000). Extracting rules from trained neural networks. *IEEE Transactions on Neural Networks, 11,* 377-389.

Vapnik, V. (1995). *The nature of statistical learning theory.* New York: Springer-Verlag.

Chapter XI

Graph-Based Data Mining

Wenyuan Li, Nanyang Technological University, Singapore

Wee-Keong Ng, Nanyang Technological University, Singapore

Kok-Leong Ong, Deakin University, Australia

Abstract

With the most expressive representation that is able to characterize the complex data, graph mining is an emerging and promising domain in data mining. Meanwhile, the graph has been well studied in a long history with many theoretical results from various foundational fields, such as mathematics, physics, and artificial intelligence. In this chapter, we systematically reviewed theories and techniques newly studied and proposed in these areas. Moreover, we focused on those approaches that are potentially valuable to graph-based data mining. These approaches provide the different perspectives and motivations for this new domain. To illustrate how the method from the other area contributes to graph-based data mining, we did a case study on a classic graph problem that can be widely applied in many application areas. Our results showed that the methods from foundational areas may contribute to graph-based data mining.

Introduction

The advances in data mining and the rising needs of modern applications helped researchers realize the limitations of traditional attribute-value and item-set representations in domains such as networks, Web analysis, text mining, biology, and chemistry. Consequently, this motivated new directions in data mining with emphasis on alternative (and more expressive) representations. In mathematics, the graph is one of the most generic topological structures that has, in the last few years, became the basis of graph mining—an active research direction within the KDD community. Without any surprises, the emerging complexity of data in the domains that we cited above is why graphs are becoming the preferred representation. It has the following advantages:

- **Expressiveness of real-life data sets:** Most data in the real world can be expressed naturally as graphs. Examples include the hypertexts from the World Wide Web, the Internet networks, and social networks (e.g., networks for fund-transfers in stock markets, switches in telephone-calls, relationships between the actors and their co-starred movies, scientists and their coauthored papers, maps from city streets, biological networks from gene sequences and metabolism, circuits and even program structures constructed by the compiler, etc). These examples demonstrate the range of applications for which the graph representation is the appropriate abstraction.

- **Profound foundations:** Graph theories have been extensively studied for hundreds of years in mathematics, and techniques of graphs have been explored in artificial intelligence since the early days of computer science. As a consequence, many important and useful properties of graphs were proven. In recent years, there is also an increasing interest in the field of theoretical physics to use the graph as the foundation for understanding the statistical properties of real-world networks (Albert, 2001; Newman, 2004). The foundations developed in these fields eventually built a foundation for graph mining research.

With the graph being the best understood and most widely applied representation in computer science, it is not difficult to appreciate the opportunities that the graph brought to the data mining community. As a result, we see an emerging domain called graph mining in the KDD community. The fundamental objective of graph mining is to provide new principles and efficient algorithms to discover topological patterns in graph data.

Basics of Graphs

Mathematically, a graph G is represented as a triple $G=(V, E, f)$, where V is a set of vertices, E is a set of edges connecting some vertex pairs in V, and f is a mapping f: $E \rightarrow V \times V$. With the different settings of V and E, we can get different graphs, such as *tree* (or acyclic graph), *bipartite graph*, *complete graph*, *k-regular graph*, and so forth (Brandstädt, Le, & Spinrad, 1999). Some basic concepts of the graph include:

- **Degree:** The number of edges connected to a vertex $v \in V$, denoted as $d(v)$. If the graph is a directed graph, there is an in-degree and an out-degree for a vertex.

- **Walk:** A sequence of vertices $(v_0, v_1,...,v_s)$ with $\{v_{i-1}, v_i\} \in E(G)$ for all $1 \leq i \leq s$. A *path* is a walk with no repeated vertices. A *cycle* is a path that the first and final vertices are the same. A *tour* is a cycle that includes every vertex. The *length* of a walk, a path, or a cycle is number of its edges.

- **Distance:** For two vertices u and v, the *distance* between u to v is the minimum length of any path from u to v. The *diameter* of a graph is the maximum distance between any two vertices of G.

- **Induced subgraph:** A subset of the vertices of a graph G together with any edges whose endpoints are both in this subset.

- **Connected graph:** A graph that there is a path from every vertex to every other vertex in the graph. A graph that is not connected consists of a set of *connected components*, which are maximal connected subgraphs.

- **Weighted graph:** A graph, each edge of which is associated with numbers (*weights*) generally representing a distance or cost.

Graph invariants can be used to quantitatively characterize the topological structure of a graph. If two graphs are topologically identical, then they have identical graph invariants. The number and the degree of vertices are examples of graph invariants. In some applications, graph invariants are used to reduce the search space and, in other cases, solve graph isomorphism problems. The solutions to these classic graph problems eventually form the building blocks for many graph applications, to which we only list some of the notable ones in Table 1 for space reasons. The readers can refer to Sedgewick (2001, p. 72) for a comprehensive list.

Generally, the graph is represented as an adjacency matrix. It is a V-by-V array of Boolean (real) values with the entry in row u and column v defined to be 1 (weight of the edge) if there is an edge connecting vertex u and v in the graph (weighted graph), and to be 0 otherwise. As a result of this representation, graphs are closely related to matrix theory.

Table 1. Some difficult graph problems

Hamilton Tour	Is there a tour that uses each vertex exactly once? This is NP-hard.
Maximum Clique	Given a clique that is an induced sub-graph with its every vertex connected to every other vertex, what is size of the largest clique in a given graph? This is NP-hard.
Graph Cut	What is the minimum number of edges (or vertices) whose removal will separate a graph into two disjoint parts? This is also known as the edge (vertex) connectivity problem. It is a difficult problem solved in some algorithms (Sedgewick, 2001, p. 68).
Independent Set	What is the size of the largest subset of the vertices of a graph with the property that no two vertices are connected by an edge? This problem is also NP-hard.
Traveling Salesperson	Is there a minimum-length cycle through all the vertices of a weighted graph? This is a famous problem in computer science that is NP-hard.
Isomorphism	Are two given graphs identical by renaming their vertices? This is a NP-hard problem. Efficient algorithms are known for this problem for many special types of graphs, but the difficulty of the general problem remains open (Sedgewick, 2001, p. 71).

For some applications of graphs, there is a need to compare the similarity of two graphs. Hence, several measures of similarity have been considered in the literature. Many of them involve edge transformations such as edge rotations, edge slides, and edge jumps, where the class of graphs involved is that of a fixed size or a subclass thereof (Chartrand, Kubicki, & Schultz, 1998).

There are also some meaningful metrics for characterizing graph structures that emerged from the field of social network analysis that further provides practical insights to the nature of graphs. They include centrality, betweenness, reciprocity, reachability, prestige, balance, cohesiveness, and equivalence.

Theories for Graphs

The main contributors of graph theories are mathematics and physics. The mathematicians consider mathematical aspects of graphs purely in its abstract and mathematical representation, whereas the physicians focused mainly on the mechanics of complex networks in the real world, as in how they emerge, evolve, and impact the understanding of complex systems.

There is a long history of graph theory in mathematics that originates from the 18th century in the work of Leonhard Euler. Since the middle of the 20th century, graph theory has evolved greatly from a statistical and algorithmic standpoint. The theory of random graphs was founded by Paul Erdős and Alféd Rényi, after Erdős discovered that probabilistic methods are useful in tackling problems in graph theory (Erdős & Rényi, 1959, 1960), leading to the construction of the Erdős- Rényi model.

In practice however, data is usually difficult to describe using random graphs as they are more clustered exhibiting the small-world and power-law phenomenon. Since random graphs do not capture these characteristics, a different model known as the power-law random graph was proposed (a.k.a., scale-free random graph) (Bollobás, 2001; Aiello, Chung, & Lu, 2000). In this model, the degree distribution is a constraint, but all other respects are random. In other words, the edges connect randomly to selected vertices, but the degree distribution is restricted by the power-law.

A comprehensive theory with given degree distribution was developed by Newman, Watts, and Strogatz (2001) using a generating function to calculate a variety of quantities on large graphs with arbitrary degree distribution. Some of its properties were discussed in Gkantsidis, Mihail, and Saberi (2003), and Chung, Lu, and Vu (2003). As the power-law and the small-world phenomena become established over the years, they are also becoming the theoretical basis for graphs exhibiting these two properties.

Graph theory also has close relationships with other mathematical areas, of which two of them are matrix theory and linear algebra. They have been effective methods for graphs that are regular and symmetric, for example, in the analysis of adjacency matrices of graphs. As a matter of fact, both matrix theory and linear algebra form the basis of spectral graph theory. In spectral graph theory, the eigenvalues are closely related to almost all major invariants of a graph, linking one extremal property to another. Therefore, eigenvalues play a central role in our fundamental understanding of graphs (Chung, 1997).

As mentioned, various networks from the real world are natural prototypes of graphs. It is therefore natural that there have been several works in physics reporting the mechanics of real-world networks that later form an important component of graph theories. In the last several years, the field of statistical physics has made several important observations on some massive networks. The study of statistical mechanics of complex networks soon became an active field responsible for understanding the essence of these networks.

Consequently, two amazing phenomena in complex networks become the hallmark of complex systems—the power-law and the small-world phenomena. They are pervasive in complex networks of all forms, for example, human language (Ferrer & Solé, 2001), networks of scientific collaborators (Newman, 2001), WWW (Watts & Strogatz, 1998), metabolic network (Wagner & Fell, 2000), software architecture (Valverde & Solé, 2003), and electronic circuits (Ferrer, Janssen, & Solé, 2001). Recently, the analysis of co-authorship relationships from the notable conferences (SIGMOD, PODS, VLDB, and ICDE) also showed that this graph has features of a small world (*http://database.cs.ualberta.ca/coauthorship*) (Nascimento, Sander,

& Pound, 2003). The implication of these works revealed that the small-world phenomenon has great importance in many applications.

One of them is the observation that individuals in the network have only limited local information about the global network, and therefore, finding short paths between two individuals is a non-trivial decentralized search effort (Kleinberg, 2000; Watts, Dodds, & Newman, 2002; Dodds, Muhamad, & Watts, 2003; Granovetter, 2003). Moreover, recent research shows that the small-world and power-law phenomena are two coexisting properties of complex networks (Solé, Cancho, Montoya, & Valverde, 2002; Ravasz & Barabási, 2003). The hierarchical organization model was then proposed to simultaneously capture these two properties (Ravasz & Barabási, 2003; Barabási, Deszo, Ravasz, Yook, & Oltvai, 2004). One of the applications of the coexisting two properties is the growing and navigating of the Web by local content (Menczer, 2002). The other application is in halting viruses from spreading in scale-free networks (Dezso & Barabási, 2002). A more direct application is the link analysis of the graph by exploiting these two properties (Hackathorn, 2003).

Perspectives of Graphs

Different perspectives of understanding graphs have been proposed to solve different problems in various domains. In most cases, these perspectives were motivated out of the need to solve some real-world problems—often these solutions being application or domain dependent. In this section, we shall briefly introduce the different perspectives from their origins and application domains. This is different from the survey that Washio and Motoda (2003, pp. 63-67) conducted in terms of understanding how they originate, how their nature is, and what potential values they possess. Our presentation should be more meaningful for the readers to understand the essence of these perspectives. In addition, we attempt to introduce some potential methods that have not been applied to any real-world problems, as we believe they would be the promising research directions for graph mining in the near future.

Graph Theories in Mathematics

Spectral graph theory is a component of spectral analysis that originates from mathematics. It is the study of relationships between a graph and the eigenvalues of matrices (such as the adjacency matrix) that is naturally associated to a graph (Chung, 1997). The set of eigenvectors of a graph is another component of spectral analysis which has been successfully applied to link analysis of the Web for improving information retrieval (Lawrence, Sergey, Rajeev, & Terry, 1999; Kleinberg, 1998) and data clustering (Shi & Malik, 2000; Ng, Jordan, & Weiss, 2001). While several applications of spectral analysis have been introduced (Ding, He, & Zha, 2001), there remain many open problems in networks with large-scale and random properties. Many of these problems, we believe, can be solved by random graph theories.

Graph Theories in Physics

In addition to random graph theories, the integration of statistical physics and information theory has also provided abundant materials and fertile sources of new ideas to solving complex network problems. Here, we introduce three theories from this domain that we believe will be significant contributors to solving complex network problems.

Mean field (MF) methods are deterministic methods that make use of tools such as Taylor expansions and convex relaxations to approximate or bound quantities of interest. The main idea is to focus on one particle and assume that the most important contribution to the interactions of such particle with its neighboring particles is determined by the mean field due to the neighboring particles. The *cellular automata (CA) model* was conceived by Ulam and Von Neumann in the 1940s to provide a formal framework for investigating the behavior of complex and extended systems (Von Neumann, 1966). A cellular automaton consists of a grid of cells, each of which can be in one of a finite number of k possible states, updated in discrete time steps according to a local interaction rule. This rule (also known as the transition function or interaction rule) normally operates on each of the cells. Hence, the state of any single cell is determined by the previous states of the cells in its neighborhood (Wolfram, 1984; Toffoli & Margolus, 1987). The *Markov random field (MRF) theory* is a branch of probability theory for analyzing the spatial or contextual dependencies of physical phenomena. It is used in visual labeling to establish probabilistic distributions of interacting labels. MRF provides a convenient and consistent way of modeling spatially correlated features. This is achieved through characterizing mutual influences among such entities using MRF probabilities. MRF has been extensively applied in image processing and computer vision (Li, 1995). All these methods have potential value in establishing an insight to the understanding and to the modeling of the characteristics of graphs. To date, the MRF has been applied in graph mining (Domingos & Richardson, 2001).

Traditional Artificial Intelligence (AI)

Since the beginning of computer science, artificial intelligence investigates the intelligent search algorithms in graphs. These search algorithms are categorized into three different types based on their strategies.

- **Branch and Bound Strategy**—Includes best-first search, and depth-first and branch-and-bound algorithms.

- **Greedy and Local Strategy**—Designed to iteratively improve the objective function by searching for better solutions in a local neighborhood of the current solution.

- **Stochastic-Based Strategy**—Includes genetic algorithm and simulated annealing algorithm.

The above graph problems are typically solved by these search algorithms. Another important research field in AI is the neural network (NN), which itself is a graph-based model. There are many types of neural networks, such as back-propagation NN, bidirectional associative memory (BAM), and so forth. NN has been applied in many fields, including data mining. Its natural representation of graphs makes it a good candidate for graph mining representations.

Data Mining and Machine Learning

Kernel methods, especially support vector machines (SVMs), have become popular tools in machine learning. They are computationally attractive because of the low cost in computing the feature map. Research in kernel methods has recently turned towards kernel functions defined on graphs (Gärtner, 2003). This is a new area for knowledge discovery in graphs. In traditional data mining, there are major works on discovering useful patterns or knowledge in large and real-world graphs. An example of this is the AGM (Apriori-based Graph Mining) system (Inokuchi, Washio, & Motoda, 2003). The basic principle of AGM is similar to the Apriori algorithm for basket analysis. It finds frequent substructures, and thus the problem of finding frequent itemsets is generalized to frequent subgraphs. After AGM, a family of graph-based data mining based on similar principles is also proposed. This includes the SUBDUE system (Cook & Holder, 2000), a faster version of SUBDUE called FARMER (Nijssen & Kok, 2001), the MolFea approach to find characteristic paths from graph data (Raedt & Kramer, 2001), and the ANF (Palmer, Gibbons, & Faloutsos, 2002), which is a fast and scalable tool for analyzing massive graphs in the real world.

Social Network Analysis (SNA)

Aimed at uncovering the interaction pattern of people, and based on the intuition that these patterns are important features of the lives of the individuals who displayed them, academics in the social sciences observe networks of people using socio-metric techniques and have been developing a set of techniques to provide both visual and mathematical analysis of human relationships. It is now becoming mainstream due to better techniques for tracing relationships. Research in this area now focuses on mining a relationship of graphs among customers for marketing. Relationships among customers are of potential marketing tools in many businesses. Discovering potential customers for effective business objectives and network values for virus marketing were proposed in the last three years (Ong, Ng, & Lim, 2002; Domingos & Richardson, 2001). Models and processes in analysis of the customer relationships have also been proposed, including the MRF model, independent cascade model, and linear threshold model (Domingos & Richardson, 2001; Kempe, Kleinberg, & Tardos, 2003).

A Case Study of the Graph Problem

In this section, we focus on a case study to show how a classic graph problem is solved in mathematical methods. It is the problem of finding the heavy subgraph in a weighted graph. The heavy subgraph refers to a subset of vertices that are highly connected with strong ties (measured by the edge weights) with each other. This concept is very useful in many areas. For example, in Bioinformatics, there are many biological networks where a heavy subgraph may reveal important functional modules of genes or proteins. For simplifying and formulating the task of finding the heavy subgraph, it was conventionally formulated as the Heaviest k-Subgraph Problem (k-HSP). It is one of the typical combinatorial maximization problems in the graph theory. Given an undirected graph $G=(V,E)$ with non-negative edge weights—that is, $w_{ij} \geq 0$ for all edges $(v_i, v_j) \in E$. The k-HSP is to find a subset of k vertices $V' \in V$ so that the total edge weight of its subgraph induced by V' is maximized. When all edge weights are 0 or 1, k-HSP becomes the Densest k-Subgraph Problem (k-DSP).

To mathematically formulate the k-HSP, we first introduce the characterization vector of a subgraph:

Definition 1: (*Characterization Vector of Subgraph*): Given a graph $G=(V,E)$ and its subgraph $S=(V',E')$ (i.e., $V' \in V$ and $E' \in E$), the characterization vector of the subgraph S, i.e., $x^S = (x_1^S, x_2^S, ..., x_n^S)^T$, is defined as follows,

$$x_i^S = \begin{cases} 1, & \text{if } v_i \in V' \\ 0, & \text{otherwise} \end{cases} \quad \text{for } i = 1, 2, ..., n \tag{1}$$

In general, the traditional formulation k-HSP is based on the characterization vector of the subgraph; it considers the following quadratic function, also called as the *Lagrangian* of G.

$$L(x) = x^T W x = \sum_{i=1}^{n} \sum_{j=1}^{n} w_{ij} x_i x_j \tag{2}$$

The straightforward meaning of $L(x)$ is the sum of edge weights in the subgraph. Therefore, the k-HSP based on L function can be given as follows (Billionnet, 2005):

$$(Q1) \begin{cases} \text{maximize} & L(x) = x^T W x \\ \text{subject to} & \sum_{i=1}^{n} x_i = k, \text{ and } x_i \in \{0,1\} \text{ for } i = 1, 2, \ldots, n \end{cases} \tag{3}$$

With the formulation ($Q1$), we can establish the connection between the k-HSP and optimization problem if the parameter k is given. There has been the well-studied theoretical result in the classic problem of finding the largest clique in the unweighted graph. Because the largest clique can be viewed as the special case of k-HSP to some extent, we extend this theoretical result to the context of HSP. Motzkin and Straus (1965) established a remarkable connection between the largest clique problem in unweighted graph and the quadratic programming problem. Let the $n \times n$ symmetric matrix W be the adjacency matrix of the unweighted graph $G=(V,E)$ and $x^S = (x_1^S, x_2^S, \ldots, x_n^S)^T \in \{0,1\}^n$ be the characterization vector of a subgraph $S=(V',E')$. Correspondingly, we denote the normalized x^S to be $y^S = (y_1^S, y_2^S, \ldots, y_n^S)^T = \text{norm}(x^S)$. Equation (1) in Definition 1 can be rewritten as:

$$y_i^S = \begin{cases} 1/|V'|, & \text{if } v_i \in V' \\ 0, & \text{otherwise} \end{cases} \tag{4}$$

This means y^S is subject to $y^S \in \Delta$, where Δ is a superplane in n-dimensional Euclidean space:

$$\Delta = \left\{ x \in R^n \mid \sum_{i=1}^{n} x_i = 1, \text{and } x_i \geq 0 \ (i = 1, 2, \ldots, n) \right\} \tag{5}$$

Based on the normalization of the characterization vector of a subgraph y^S, a strong relationship between the largest clique S and its associated vector y^S can be established by the following theorem:

Theorem 1 (*Motzkin-Straus*): A clique S of G is maximum, if and only if its normalized characterization vector $y^S = \text{norm}(x^S)$ is a global maximizer of L on Δ, where x^S is the characterization vector of the subgraph $S=(V',E')$ in G, and the function L is defined in Equation (2).

If y^* is a global maximizer of L on Δ, Motzkin and Straus also proved the clique number of G is related to $L(y^*)$ by the following formula:

$$\omega(G) = \frac{1}{1 - L(y^*)}$$

The Motzkin-Straus theorem points out a new way in continuous domain to solve the graph problem of the discrete domain. Although the Motzkin-Straus theorem is proven in the context of the unweighted graph, it is also reasonable to extend the idea of normalized characterization vector of the subgraph $y^S = \text{norm}(x^S)$ to the weighted graph for finding heavy subgraph to optimize $L(y)$ where y is normalized. In this methodology, we do not add the parameter k to the optimization conditions, while the coordinates of y represent a kind of ranking values by indicating the degree the corresponding vertices belong to the heavy subgraph. Thus we re-formulate the HSP without the parameter k as follows:

$$(Q2)\begin{cases} \text{maximize} \quad L(y) = y^T W y \\ \text{subject to} \quad \sum_{i=1}^{J} y_i = 1, \text{ and } 0 \leq y_i \leq 1 \quad \text{for } i = 1,2,\ldots,n \end{cases} \tag{6}$$

After obtaining the solution y^* of $(Q2)$, we sort elements of y^* in decreasing order and select vertices corresponding to the first k largest values to form a subgraph. For simplicity, the elements of y^* are called the ranking values associated with vertices. Based on the intuitive explanation of the Motzkin-Straus theorem, we argue that this subgraph generated by the first k ranking values is also a reasonable approximation solution to the HSP.

For comparison with the reformulation of HSP $(Q2)$, we employed the solution of the formulation $(Q1)$ and the solution of $(Q2)$ by using a free software "LPSolve" (available at *http://groups.yahoo.com/group/lp_solve*), which is a widely used

Figure 1. Solutions of different problem formulations in a 40-vertex graph. The graph is represented in the form of the adjancency matrix.

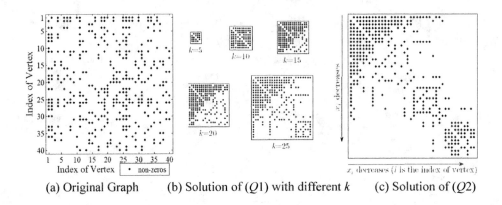

(a) Original Graph   (b) Solution of (*Q*1) with different *k*   (c) Solution of (*Q*2)

mixed integer programming solver and is implemented in C on many different platforms. Please note that the solution of (*Q*1) is the exact one and that of (*Q*2) is the approximate one. Next, we illustrate the solutions of (*Q*1) and (*Q*2) with a simple example.

In the example graph shown in Figure 1a, we obtained the exact solution of the formulation (*Q*1) with *k*=5,10,15,20,25. These five different heavy subgraphs are

Table 2. The average computation time for the problem formulations (Q1) and (Q2) on five randomly generated weighted graphs with 40 vertices. Here, the sparsity is to measure if a graph is sparse or not. Therefore, it only counts the number of edges whose weights are zero and does not consider the edges with non-zero weights. Given a graph G=(V,E) and n=|V|, the sparsity of G is (m-|E|)/m, where m=n(n-1)/2 is the edge number of the complete graph with the same V.

	(*Q*1)			(*Q*2)		
Sparsity:	0.75	0.5	0.25	0.75	0.5	0.25
k=10	31.9 (s)	235.7(s)	262.7(s)			
k=15	152.5(s)	5822.4(s)	15558.5(s)	0.0103(s)	0.0320(s)	0.0364(s)
k=20	51.1(s)	5129.5(s)	42477.6(s)			

shown in Figure 1b. It is clearly seen that they are really the heaviest subgraphs among all the subgraphs with the same size. However, it took a long time to get the result even in this small 40-vertex graph. The average computation time of five randomly generated 40-vertex graphs of ($Q1$) solutions is shown in Table 1. On the contrary, the formulation ($Q2$) does not need the parameter k and the continuous relaxation of the variables; its solution can be quickly sorted to collect the heavy subgraph to the left-top corner of the sorted adjancency matrix as shown in Figure 1c. We can observe that the sorted adjacency matrix in Figure 1c can clearly characterize the value distribution, and therefore the heavy subgraphs with different sizes can be simultaneously observed. For example, we found that all five subgraphs are aligned to the left-top corner of the sorted adjacency matrix in Figure 1c. It makes the discovery of the heavy subgraphs very efficient.

Conclusion

Due to the complex properties of real-world data, the graph is one of the most expressive representations and is suitable for characterizing such complex data types. In that sense, graphs have great potential for discovering knowledge via KDD methods (while borrowing from other related domains by the virtue of its universality and foundation) that previous techniques may fail. We believe graph-based data mining is a new area full of challenging and exciting directions.

References

Aiello, W., Chung, F., & Lu, L. (2000). A random graph model for massive graphs. In *Proceedings of the 32nd Annual ACM Symposium on Theory of Computing (STOC)* (pp. 171-180).

Albert, R. (2001). *Statistical mechanics of complex networks*. PhD thesis, University of Notre Dame, USA.

Barabási, A.-L., Deszo, Z., Ravasz, E., Yook, S.H., & Oltvai, Z.N. (2004). Scale-free and hierarchical structures in complex networks. In *Sitges Proceedings on Complex Networks*.

Billionnet, A. (2005). Different formulations for solving the heaviest k-subgraph problem. *Information Systems and Operational Research, 43*(3), 171-186.

Bollobás, B. (2001). *Random graphs* (2nd ed.). Cambridge: Cambridge University Press.

Brandstädt, A., Le, V.B., & Spinrad, J.P. (1999). Graph classes: A survey. In *SIAM Monographs on Discrete Mathematics and Applications*. Philadelphia: Society for Industrial and Applied Mathematics (SIAM).

Chartrand, G., Kubicki, G., & Schultz, M. (1998). Graph similarity and distance in graphs. *Aequationes Mathematicae, 55*(1-2), 129-145.

Chung, F. (1997). Spectral graph theory. *CBMS Regional Conference Series in Mathematics* (No. 92). American Mathematical Society.

Chung, F., Lu, L., & Vu, V. (2003). The spectra of random graphs with given expected degrees. In *Proceedings of the National Academy of Sciences, 100*(11), 6313-6318.

Cook, D.J., & Holder, L.B. (2000). Graph-based data mining. *IEEE Intelligent Systems, 15*(2), 32-41.

Dezso, Z., & Barabási, A.-L. (2002). Halting viruses in scale-free networks. *Physical Review E, 65,* 055103.

Ding, C., He, X., & Zha, H. (2001). A spectral method to separate disconnected and nearly-disconnected Web graph components. In *Proceedings of the 7th ACM SIGKDD International Conference on Knowledge Discovery and Data Mining* (pp. 275-280).

Dodds, P.S., Muhamad, R., & Watts, D.J. (2003). An experimental study of search in global social networks. *Science, 301,* 827-829.

Domingos, P., & Richardson, M. (2001). Mining the network value of customers. In *Proceedings of the 7th ACM SIGKDD International Conference on Knowledge Discovery and Data Mining* (pp. 57-66).

Erdős, P., & Rényi, A. (1959). On random graphs. *Publicationes Mathematicae, 6,* 290-297.

Erdős, P., & Rényi, A. (1960). On the evolution of random graphs. *Publication of the Mathematical Institute of the Hungarian Academy of Sciences, 5,* 17-61.

Ferrer, R., Janssen, C., & Solé, R.V. (2001). Topology of technology graphs: Small-world patterns in electronic circuits. *Physical Review E, 64,* 046119.

Ferrer, R., & Solé, R.V. (2001). The small-world of human language. In *Proceedings of the Royal Society of London Series B—Biological Sciences* (Vol. 268, pp. 2261-2265).

Gärtner, T. (2003). A survey of kernels for structured data. *ACM SIGKDD Explorations Newsletter, 5*(1), 49-58.

Gkantsidis, C., Mihail, M., & Saberi, A. (2003). Conductance and congestion in power law graphs. *Proceedings of the International Conference on Measurement and Modeling of Computer Systems (ACM SIGMETRICS 2003)* (pp. 148-159).

Granovetter, M. (2003). Ignorance, knowledge, and outcomes in a small world. *Science, 301,* 773-774.

Hackathorn, R. (2003). The link is the thing. *DB Review.*

Inokuchi, A., Washio, T., & Motoda, H. (2003). Complete mining of frequent patterns from graphs: Mining graph data. *Machine Learning, 50*(3), 321-354.

Kempe, D., Kleinberg, J.M., & Tardos, E. (2003). Maximizing the spread of influence through a social network. In *Proceedings of the 9th ACM SIGKDD International Conference on Knowledge Discovery and Data Mining* (pp. 137-146).

Kleinberg, J.M. (1998). Authoritative sources in a hyperlinked environment. In *Proceedings of the 9th Annual ACM-SIAM Symposium Discrete Algorithms* (pp. 668-677). New York: ACM Press.

Kleinberg, J. (2000). Navigation in a small world. *Nature, 406,* 845.

Lawrence, P., Sergey, B., Rajeev, M., & Terry, W. (1999). *The PageRank citation ranking: Bringing order to the Web.* Technical Report, Stanford Digital Library Technologies Project, USA.

Li, S.Z. (1995). *Markov random field modeling in computer vision.* Springer-Verlag.

Menczer, F. (2002). Growing and navigating the small-world Web by local content. *Proceedings of the National Academy of Sciences, 99*(22), 14014-14019.

Motzkin, T.S., & Straus, E.G. (1965). Maxima for graphs and a new proof of a theorem of Turán. *Canadian Journal of Mathematics, 17*(4), 533-540.

Nascimento, M.A., Sander, J., & Pound, J. (2003). Analysis of SIGMOD's co-authorship graph. *ACM SIGMOD Record, 32*(3).

Newman, M.E.J. (2003). The structure and function of complex networks. *SIAM Review, 45*(2), 167-256.

Newman, M.E.J. (2001). The structure of scientific collaboration networks. *Proceedings of the National Academy of Sciences, 98*(2), 404-409.

Newman, M.E.J., Strogatz, S.H., & Watts, D.J. (2001). Random graphs with arbitrary degree distributions and their applications. *Physical Review E, 64,* 026118.

Ng, A., Jordan, M., & Weiss, Y. (2001). On spectral clustering: Analysis and an algorithm. *Proceedings of Advances in Neural Information Processing Systems 14 (NIPS)* (pp. 849-856).

Nijssen, S., & Kok, J.N. (2001). Faster association rules for multiple relations. In *Proceedings of the 17th International Joint Conference on Artificial Intelligence (IJCAI)* (pp. 891-896).

Ong, K.-L., Ng, W.-K., & Lim, E.-P. (2002). Mining relationship graphs for effective business objectives. In *Proceedings of the 6th Pacific-Asia Conference on Knowledge Discovery and Data Mining* (pp. 561-566).

Palmer, C.R., Gibbons, P.B., & Faloutsos, C. (2002). ANF: A fast and scalable tool for data mining in massive graphs. In *Proceedings of the 8th ACM SIGKDD International Conference on Knowledge Discovery and Data Mining* (pp. 81-90).

Raedt, L.D., & Kramer, S. (2001). The level-wise version space algorithm and its application to molecular fragment finding. In *Proceedings of the 17th International Joint Conference on Artificial Intelligence (IJCAI)* (pp. 853-862).

Ravasz, E., & Barabási, A.-L. (2003). Hierarchical organization in complex networks. *Physical Review E, 67,* 026112.

Sedgewick, R. (2001). *Algorithms in C, part 5: Graph algorithms* (3rd ed.). Addison-Wesley.

Shi, J., & Malik, J. (2000). Normalized cuts and image segmentation. *IEEE Transactions on Pattern Analysis and Machine Intelligence,* 888-905.

Solé, R.V., Cancho, R.F., Montoya, J.M., & Valverde, S. (2002). Selection, tinkering and emergence in complex networks. *Complexity, 8*(1), 20-33.

Toffoli, T., & Margolus, N. (1987). *Cellular automata machines.* Cambridge, MA: MIT Press.

Valverde, S., & Solé, R.V. (2003). Hierarchical small worlds in software architecture. *IEEE Transactions in Software Engineering.*

Von Neumann, J. (1966). *Theory of self-reproducing automata.* Champaign-Urbana, IL: University of Illinois Press.

Wagner, A., & Fell, D. (2000). *The small world inside large metabolic networks.* Technical Report 00-07-041, Santa Fe Institute, USA.

Washio, T., & Motoda, H. (2003). State of the art of graph-based data mining. *ACM SIGKDD Explorations Newsletter, 5*(1), 59-68.

Watts, D.J., & Strogatz, S.H. (1998). Collective dynamics of small-world networks. *Nature, 393,* 440-442.

Watts, D.J., Dodds, P.S., & Newman, M.E.J. (2002). Identity and search in social networks. *Science, 296,* 1302-1305.

Wolfram, S. (1984). Cellular automata as models of complexity. *Nature, 311,* 419-
424.

Chapter XII

Facilitating and Improving the Use of Web Services with Data Mining

Richi Nayak, Queensland University, Australia

Abstract

Web services have recently received much attention in businesses. However, a number of challenges such as lack of experience in estimating the costs, lack of service innovation and monitoring, and lack of methods for locating appropriate services are to be resolved. One possible approach is by learning from the experiences in Web services and from other similar situations. Such a task requires the use of data mining to represent generalizations on common situations. This chapter examines how some of the issues of Web services can be addressed through data mining.

Introduction

Web services have received much attention in recent years (Clark, 2002; Kearney et al., 2002; Booth et al., 2004). By allowing applications residing in disparate systems to communicate, Web services create myriad opportunities for implementing new business models based on the offering and consumption of services. However, despite its apparent benefits, businesses are slow in the widespread adoption of Web services (Chen, 2003). This is largely due to the many issues relating to the technology, as well as the lack of experience in this area. These issues span across the entire development process, from initial planning through to final implementation. Additionally, as the number of Web services increases, it becomes increasingly important to provide a scalable infrastructure of registries that allows both developers and end users to perform service discovery. One possible approach to overcome these problems is by learning from the experiences in Web services and from other similar situations. Such a task leans itself towards the use of models that represent generalizations on common situations. The high volume of data accumulated from Web services activities is an excellent source for building these models. What is needed therefore is an automated mechanism to perform this task. This is where data mining (DM) plays an important role.

But what are the sorts of knowledge that can be extracted to alleviate the above problems? What data is available for data mining? How can we extract the useful information from this data? Since this is an innovative application area, what are some of the issues and challenges that we may have to face and resolve? These are the questions this chapter attempts to answer. In this chapter, first we explain the Web services enabling technologies and issues affecting data mining. Next, we recommend a set of applications that can leverage problems concerned with the planning, development, and maintenance of Web services. We also summarize some of the existing works that have been conducted for the mutual benefits of Web services and data mining technologies. We end the chapter by discussing the future of these two widely adopted technologies.

Web Services Environment

Web services emerged from the fields of distributed computing and the Web. Web services operate with existing Internet protocols to provide Web-based access, easy integration, and service reusability by using loosely coupled connections, and vendor, platform, and language independent protocols (Systinet Corp, 2002; Booth et al., 2004). Web services enable applications residing in disparate systems to communicate and produce interesting interactions. Based on the existing Web protocols and eXtensible Markup Language (XML) standards (Yergeau, Bray, Paoli, Sperberg-McQueen, & Maler, 2004), the Web services architecture makes it possible for businesses to use small pieces of software as services to compose complex operations that facilitate its business processes, using the Internet as the underlying infrastructure.

Enabling Technologies

Web services are implemented by a set of core technologies that provide the mechanisms for communication, description, and discovery of services. The standards that provide these functionalities are simple object access protocol (SOAP), Web Services Description Language (WSDL), and universal description, discovery, and integration (UDDI) (Vasudevan, 2001; Curbera et al., 2002). These XML-based standards use common Internet protocols for the exchange of service requests and responses. Figure 1 shows the relationship of these technologies as a standards stack for Web services.

When a service provider creates a new service, it describes the service using WSDL. WSDL defines a service in terms of the messages to be exchanged between services and how they can be bound by specifying the location of the service with a URL. To make the service available to service consumers, the service provider registers the service in a UDDI registry by supplying the details of the service provider, the category of the service, and technical details on how to bind to the service. The UDDI registry will then maintain pointers to the WSDL description and to the service. When a service consumer wants to use a service, it queries the UDDI registry to find a service that matches its needs and obtains the WSDL description of the service, as well as the access point of the service. The service consumer uses the WSDL description to construct a SOAP message to be transported over HTTP with which to communicate with the service.

Figure 1. Web services standards stack

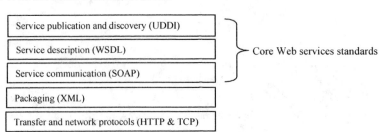

Since HTTP is used, traffic for Web services is directed to Web servers. As a result, all communications between Web services pass through the Web server. Since Web servers store access request information in Web server access logs, all interactions between Web services will thus be recorded, similar to the human-server interactions that are prevalent on the Web now. Web server access logs recording site access have been a rich source for discovering the browsing behavior of site visitors (Wang, Huang, Wu, & Zhang, 1999; Srivastava, Cooley, Deshpande, & Tan, 2000; Nayak, 2002). In a similar manner, logs that record Web service access can be mined for Web service usage patterns by organizations. With the huge volume of access, the amounts of logs that can be collected make a feasible source for mining operations.

Issues in Web Services

Cost Planning

Chen (2003) performed an analysis on factors that are affecting the adoption of Web services. Among the identified decision criteria that hold constant across all cases are financial considerations. Costs that can be saved both in the short and long term are one of the major reasons that businesses can justify their investments in a new technology. Therefore, unless businesses have an idea of how much they should spend on Web services, and on the foreseeable savings, they will be indecisive on the adoption of Web services. The enabling technologies of Web services are only concerned with the technicalities, and do not have any provision for the planning of costs and savings that can gained.

Answering to this is the cost and performance model for Web services investment (Larsen & Bloniarz, 2000). The model helps businesses assess the costs in terms of the functionalities required and increases in target performance. For each assessment area, three levels of service (modest, moderate, and elaborate) are defined in order to identify the most profitable option. Worksheets setting out the details of each of these areas are used as aids for estimating the figures.

Although the model provides tools for estimating costs, it does not take into consideration that many businesses may not have any experience in Web services and thus find the estimation difficult in the first place. Furthermore, it does not provide any indications of whether the benefits from the proposed project match those of competitors' projects that are similar. That is, there is no measure on the effectiveness at which a business can deploy Web services. If a business can find out that other similar projects cost less but yield the same returns, then it may consider outsourcing the project instead of developing it in-house.

A distinctive characteristic of DM is that the outputs are generalizations of the inputs (Fayyad, Piatesky-Shapiro, Smyth, & Uthurusamy, 1996). This makes it an ideal tool for benchmarking, especially in predictive modeling operations. Using the derived models and rules, an analysis can feed in experimental data and get results that represent what the majority would get if the data were real. Based on this, if models representing Web services deployment costs can be built, then businesses intending to adopt Web services can make use of these models both for estimating the cost of their deployment, as well as deciding whether outsourcing them is more feasible than developing them in-house.

Service Discovery

The discovery of services requires seven steps (Hoschek, 2002): description, presentation, publication, request, discovery, brokering, and execution. Description is the process of defining metadata for a service, such as the interfaces it offers, the operations and arguments for an interface, and the binding of network protocols and endpoints. Presentation is concerned with mechanisms that allow the retrieval of the service descriptions. This requires a means of uniquely identifying a service in a global scale. Publication makes a service known to interested clients via the use of a registration system. Request and discovery involves a user formulating a request for a service, while discovery involves searching the registry for candidate services that implement the requested functions. Brokering and execution are concerned with the scheduling and allocation of resources for the execution of the services.

WSDL and the UDDI are two standards designed for the description, presentation, publication, request, and discovery of Web services. However, they have limitations in addressing the problem. The UDDI especially has drawn much criticism. Although WSDL facilitates the description of the service parameters, messages to be exchanged between applications, and how to connect to the services, it provides little clue to the service consumer as to what the service does. The only parts of the description that may give hints on the functionalities of a service are the name attributes of the parameters, messages, and operations. This lack of semantics led to the development of DARPA Agent Markup Language (DAML)-based languages (http://www.daml.org/services/) for service description, where service capability matching is based on the inputs, outputs, preconditions, and effects, and ontology is used to encode the relationship between concepts (McIlraith, Son, & Zeng, 2001; Paolucci, Kawamura, Payne, & Sycara, 2002). However, with the current state of Web services, we are still a long way from automatic service matching. For now, the manual discovery of services will have to suffice, and effort is needed to improve its efficiency.

Similar to WSDL descriptions, the UDDI does not make use of semantic information to describe and discover services based on their capabilities (Paolucci et al., 2002). Apart from the text descriptions, there is no provision for specifying the capabilities of the service. The categorization of businesses and services—that is, the "yellow pages"—is also of little help in the discovery of suitable services (Newcomer, 2002). The classification schemes used—NAICS and UNSPSC—were designed for the broad-based classification of industries, products, and services. There is little or no differentiation between products or services in the same line of business. These schemes do not provide the specificity needed for service discovery. Furthermore, searching in UDDI is restricted to keyword matching on names, locations, business, bindings, and tModels (unique identifiers for reusable concepts). There is no provision for inference or flexible match on the keywords, which means service providers and requesters must choose the names and description of services very precisely when using the UDDI in order to be found.

Normally, developers have to search the service from tens or hundreds of service entries in UDDI. This process is very time consuming and can be considered as loss of profits in terms of business. As the single most pervasive source for the discovery of Web services, there is a great need to address the shortcomings of the UDDI. A most intuitive way to help alleviate the situation is by predicting what a service requester may be looking for and suggesting services accordingly. This can be done by extracting common behaviors of users searching the UDDI by mining the user query logs. Thus data mining can help Web search engines to find high-quality Web pages and enhances Web click stream analysis.

Application of Data Mining in Web Services

The benefits of the data mining applications can be seen as those that deliver business value and those that have technical value (Nayak & Tong, 2002). Data mining applications can be used by management to assist in making strategic decisions or by human resource personnel in maximizing staffing levels while minimizing costs. More specifically, data mining can be used to provide insights on the planning of Web services deployment via "Web services cost and savings prediction," and how costs on staffing for the monitoring of services can be optimized via "performance monitoring." Data mining applications can also be used by technical staff in devising new services or in services that their organization can use via "services innovations and recommendations."

Web Services Cost and Savings Prediction

It is difficult for businesses to gauge the costs and savings of a Web service deployment with having little or even no experience in deployments. However, businesses can learn from the experiences of similar organizations and get a good approximation of these values from the data collected by research firms such as Nemertes (Johnson, 2003).

Value prediction is suitable in this instance to model the investment vs. return functions for the prediction of figures for costs and savings. Regression techniques derive the predicted continuous values obtained from functions that best fit the case (Devore, 1995). For predicting the costs, the input data required consists of, for each deployment, the number of staff members involved, the time it took, and the complexity of the deployment. The complexity of the deployment can be quantified in terms of the lines of code used in the programs, and the annual revenue from the operations that the deployment oversees. The costs of the proposed deployment can be predicted based on these parameters.

Once the costs are known, prospective savings can be predicted. Using inputs such as the cost of the deployment, and the original and new cost of the operation, savings can be determined. Having determined the costs and the savings that can be gained, the return of investment for Web services deployments can be calculated based on these figures. Businesses can then identify the size of Web services deployment that is best suited for them and turn the discovered insights into action.

Performance Monitoring

Strategic placement of human resources plays a crucial role in the effective monitoring of performance and handling of events. This leads to the need to prioritize tasks. A service being used by many clients at the time when a problem occurs should have a higher priority than a service being used by few clients at the same time. By knowing the usage pattern of services, training programs on groups of services with similar usage patterns can be developed. This allows staff monitoring the services at certain times to have a more in-depth knowledge of particular services.

To identify services with similar usage patterns, similar time sequence analysis can be used (Peng, Wang, Zhang, & Patker, 2000). The input for such an operation is time-series data recording the number of clients using a particular service at any moment in time. Although such data is not normally collected explicitly, it is implicitly recorded in the Web server access logs. The steps in generating this time-series data from Web server logs are as follows:

1. Select from the Web server log all entries related to the offered Web services by extracting all entries containing the Web service's URL in the URL field.

2. Group the entries by Web services and client IP addresses, and then order the entries by time. This gives a set of a client's interaction with a Web service.

3.   Calculate the time between each interaction to determine separate client sessions with the Web service. A client session is one 'use' of the Web service. The duration of a client session for different services varies depending on the nature of the service. Setting the threshold of session boundaries thus requires the knowledge about the individual services.

4.   For each service, count the number of clients using it at specified time intervals. This can then be used to construct the time-series graph for each service.

Algorithms for approximate subsequence matching in time-series (Han & Kamber, 2001) now can be applied to find Web services that have similar usage patterns. These patterns can then be used to help in the design of roster schedules that optimize staffing levels and skill requirements while minimizing the number of employees that need to be present.

Service Innovation

It is important for service providers to establish themselves in the market by offering a range of quality services. The set of queries used by potential clients to find suitable Web services is a rich source for finding clues about what the clients want. If an unusual search term is used with other common search terms in the queries, and if the search terms are all related, then it is a good indication that there is a demand for a new service. The unusual search term may represent a new concept or a specialization of a general service currently being offered. As an example, short message service (SMS) sends text messages to mobile phones, while a more recent technology, multimedia message service (MMS), sends multimedia messages. SMS is a frequently used search term, but MMS is not. As the technology becomes more prevalent, demand for MMS Web services will emerge, and the appearance of MMS in query data will be evidence of this.

The simplest approach in discovering uncommon search terms is by deviation analysis (Devore, 1995). Having counted the frequencies of the search terms appearing, simple measures such as median, quartiles, and inter-quartile range (IQR) can be calculated. Then using the common heuristic that outliers fall at least 1.5^* IQR above the third quartile or below the first quartile, the unusual search terms can be identified. An alternative measure is the use of support to count the number of times the term appeared in total terms. If a search term has very low support, then it can be classified as an outlier.

Given that the demand for different services varies, applying these measures to the raw frequency count will produce biased results towards less popular services, producing many false positives. This is best illustrated using an example. A popular service is searched 1,000 times using a common search term Q_1 and 10 times using an uncommon search term Q_2. A very specific service aimed at a niche market is searched seven times using Q_3 and three times using Q_4, both of which are common for the service. When search terms for all the services are taken into account, and statistics is applied to the data, Q_2, Q_3, and Q_4 will be identified as uncommon search terms. However, Q_3 and Q_4 are false positives because they represent 70% and 30% of searches for the service. On the other hand, although Q_2 has 10 occurrences, it is only 1% of all searches for the popular service. Clearly, Q_2 is the only outlier that should be identified in this case. Extrapolating this to a real scenario, one can expect to find no true outliers for the popular services, which is far more important than outliers for less popular services. The solution to this is to group searches into search areas and then find the outliers for each search area. This can be done by:

1. Grouping the queries into search sessions
2. Joining all search sessions that are similar to form search areas
3. Form search term pools for each search area
4. Within each search term pool, apply statistics to find the uncommon search terms that suggest demands for a new Web service

Service Recommendation

The location of Web services using existing Web services search engines (keyword based) can be a lengthy endeavor. This method of service discovery suffers from low recall, where results containing synonym concepts at a higher or lower level of abstraction to describe the same service are not returned. Web service providers can recommend services to clients based on the services that other similar clients have used in the past with the use of DM, or by returning an expanded set of results to the user with the use of ontology (Beeferman & Berger, 2000; Bernstein & Klein, 2002; Wen, Nie, & Zhang; Yu, Liu, & Le, 2004). This is because similar clients are likely to have similar service needs. A single data mining operation or in combinations can be used to achieve this.

Based on Predictive Mining

Service providers have information such as the line of business, size of business, and what services their clients use. These can be used as inputs for predictive modeling operations and recommendations can be made to new clients. Inputs such as the interfaces, functionality, and security offered by the service, as well as the cost, and other resources required by the service can also be considered in analysis. Classification techniques such as decision trees can be used to build rules on service subscriptions. Since the only information service providers have about clients are those for billing purposes, the number of attributes available is small. Consequently, the structure of the resulting decision tree will be relatively simple and easily comprehensible to a human analyst. To further enhance the success rate of recommendations, service providers can find dissociations among the services they offer. Dissociations capture negative relationships between services with rules such as $X \Rightarrow Z; X \wedge Y \ni \neg Z$—that is, the use of services X and Y implies that it is unlikely service Z will also be used, even though X and Z are often used (Teng, 2002). By incorporating these dissociations in the recommendation process, more specific recommendations can be made.

Based on Association Mining

Web server access logs record all interactions between Web services and users. With the huge volume of Web service access, the amount of logs that can be collected makes a feasible source for identifying Web services with similar usage patterns. The tasks are: (1) selection from the Web server log all entries related to the offered Web services, (2) extraction of a set of a client's interaction with a Web service, (3) calculation of client sessions with the Web service, and (4) application of an association mining algorithm to find Web services with similar usage patterns.

Based on Clustering Mining

While previous approaches capture the intra-query relationships by clustering queries on a per query basis (Beeferman & Berger, 2000; Wen et al 2002), they omit the inter-query relationships that exist between queries submitted by a user in one search session. A better option is to group the similar search sessions and provide suggestions of search terms from search sessions that belong to the same cluster.

 The first task is to consolidate the data from the user query and Web server logs. This is done by matching the query recorded in the query log with the subsequent service descriptions viewed by the user recorded in the Web server log. The next task is to form search sessions to arrange a set of queries in sequence by a user to locate a particular service. Search session similarity now can be calculated based on the similarity of the set of search terms used and the set of service descriptions viewed between two search sessions. The Jaccard coefficient (Han & Kamber, 2001) can be used to calculate the similarity of the search terms and service descriptions sets.

Search sessions are assigned to the same cluster if they have many queries and service descriptions that are the same from the entire query and service description pool. The type of clusters desired is therefore globular in nature. Also the algorithm must be resistant to noise and outliers. The agglomerative hierarchical clustering

(Karypis, Han, & Kumar, 1999) is well suited to generate these types of clusters. After the clusters are formed, the support for each of the search terms in each cluster is counted and then assigned weights. The weights can be used to predict a user's service need by suggesting search terms from the cluster with the largest weight for the user's search term. Depending on the size and number of search terms that make up the clusters, the suggested terms can either be all search terms within the cluster, or be limited to those from a predefined number of most similar search sessions. A test was conducted for evaluating the effect of the measure combining both keyword and service description similarity. The results show that the search sessions clustered using the combined measure is more similar internally and thus the clusters are more compact. This is essential in the suggestion of search terms, as users would only be interested in suggestions that are highly similar to those submitted.

Existing Work

This section discusses the existing work that crosses paths between data mining and Web services.

Use of Data Mining in Improving Web Services Usage

The previous section discusses a number of possible applications of data mining to assist the Web services. In this section we outline some existing works. The majority of work is in the direction of addressing the shortcoming of UDDI by finding relationships between search terms and service descriptions in UDDI.

Sajjanhar, Jingyu, and Yanchun (2004) have applied the regression function called singular value decomposition (SVD) to discover semantic relationships on services for matching best services. Their preliminary results show a significant increase in correct matching between service descriptions and the search terms after application of their algorithm with IBM UDDI. The matched results are not merely based on the number of matched keywords within the service descriptions. The algorithm evaluates the keyword global weights within the SVD procedure and aggregates services containing the highest global weight words to find semantic matched services. Wang and Stroulia (2003) developed a method for assigning a value of similarity to WSDL documents. They use vector-space and WordNet to analyze the semantic of the identifiers of the WSDL documents in order to compare the structures of their operations, messages, and types, and to determine the similarity among two WSDL documents. This helps to support an automatic process to localize Web services by distinguishing among the services that can potentially be used and that are irrelevant to a given situation. Dong, Halevy, Madhavan, Nemes, and Zhang (2004) build a

Web service search engine to support the similarity search for Web services along with keyword searching with utilizing clustering and association mining. Starting with a keyword search, a user can drill down to a particular Web service operation. However, when unsatisfied, instead of modifying the keywords, the user can query for Web service operations according to the most similar and semantically associated keywords suggested by the engine using the data mining techniques.

Gombots et al. (2005) attempt to apply data mining to Web services and their interactions in order to analyze interactions between Web service consumers and providers. They toss a new term, "WSIM—Web services interaction mining," to analyze the log data to acquire additional knowledge about a system. They identify three levels of abstraction with respect to WSIM: the operation level, the interaction level, and the workflow level. On the *Web service operation level,* only one single Web service and its internal behavior is examined by analyzing a given log output of the Web service. On the *Web services interaction level,* one Web service and its "direct neighbors" Web services (that the examined WS interacts with) are examined. This analysis reveals interesting facts about a Web service's interaction partners, such as critical dependencies. On the highest level of abstraction—the *Web service workflow level*—the large-scale interactions and collaborations of Web services which together form an entire workflow are examined. This details the execution of the entire process: what is the general sequence of execution of various operations?

Malek et al. (2004) apply data mining in security intrusions detection while the Web services are in use. They show the impact of mining in detecting security attacks that could cripple Web services or compromise confidential information. They determine the relevance of different log records and define the attack signature with the use of sequential pattern mining with logs. Then they discover the highly compact decision rules from the intrusion patterns for pattern searching that help to describe some safeguard against the attacks.

Use of Web Services Technologies to Develop Data Mining Solutions

Web services techniques are increasingly gathering data from various sources that can be used for mining. Additionally, data mining tools are now required to access a variety of standards and platforms. The solutions for interoperability by using XML and SOAP as means of Web services communication can assist data mining by standardizing importing data and information to XML format. Web services can offer assistance to data mining in integration of data coming from various sources. The SOAP protocol enables data interaction on the Web and therefore makes the collection of data possible (Nayak & Seow, 2004). Some efforts have been made to implement these protocols, but in fact the full potential of these technologies has not yet been reached. An example is *Web services for DB2 Intelligent Miner* (http://www.alphaworks.ibm.com/tech/ws4im), "a collection of Web services that allow clients to describe and perform basic mining tasks using XML, XML Schema, and XPath on top of DB2 Intelligent Miner."

Another example of a SOAP-based data mining solution is *XML for Analysis* (http://www.xmla.org/tdwievent.asp), an open industry-standard Web service interface for online analytical processing and data mining functions. It provides "a set of XML Message Interfaces that use SOAP to define the data access interactions between a client application and an analytical data provider." The interfaces are aimed at keeping the client programming independent from the mechanics of data transport, but at the same time providing adequate information concerning the data and ensuring that it is properly handled. This data mining solution is platform, programming language, and data source independent.

There are many data mining applications that use Web services technologies to implement them efficiently. An example is online banking, which has recently grown substantially as a Web service. As the online transactions increase, so does the possibility of fraud, in particular credit card fraud. Chiu and Tsai (2004) proposed a Web services-based collaborative scheme for participating banks to share their knowledge about fraud patterns. The participating banks share their individual fraud transactions and new transactions via a central location. The data exchange in this heterogeneous and distributed environment is secured with WSDL, XML, and SOAP. The frequent pattern mining is then applied on this integrated data for extracting more valuable fraud patterns to improve the fraud detection.

Other research introduces a dynamic data mining process system based on Web services to provide a dynamical and satisfied analysis result to the enterprise (Chiu & Tsai, 2005). Each data mining process (data pre-processing, data mining algorithms, and visualization analysis) is viewed as a Web service operated on the Internet. The Web service for each activity provides its functionality. Depending on the user's requirement, the Web services are dynamically linked using the Business Process Execution Language for Web Service (BPEL4WS) to construct a desired data mining process. Finally, the result model described by the Predictive Model Markup Language (PMML) is returned for further analysis. PMML is an XML markup language defined for data mining functions and models (Wettschereck, & Muller, 2001) to make easy and efficient data models and result interpretation.

There are many application-oriented research studies as well. Zheng and Bouguettaya (2005) model the biological entities and the dynamic processes as Web services, and then propose a Web service mining approach to automatically discover the unexpected and potentially interesting pathways.

Future Directions:
Semantic Web and Ontologies

The Semantic Web (Berners-Lee, Hendler, & Lassila, 2001) is described as the next generation of Web architecture. It operates on new markup language standards such as Web Ontology Language for Services (OWL-S) (http://www.w3.org/Submission/OWL-S) and DARPA Agent Markup Language Semantic Markup extension for Web Services (*DAML-S*). OWL-S and DAML-S are high-level ontologies at the application level meant to answer the what and why questions about a Web service (Alesso & Smith 2004). An ontology defines the relations among terms (Maedche, 2003). The use of ontologies can relate the information on numbers of Web services to the associated knowledge structures and inference rules in a Semantic Web.

The Semantic Web with ontology is not merely an ordinary repository or normal online meta-data, but it becomes the intelligent Web having automated reasoning. An ontology-based Semantic Web describes its properties and capabilities so that: (1) software can automatically determine its purpose, thus automating service discovery; and (2) software can verify and monitor service properties, thus automating service monitoring. As the future of Web services greatly depends on their ability to automatically identify the Web resources and execute them for achieving the intended goals of the user as much as possible, OWL-S and DAML-S can achieve this, whereas UDDI cannot.

Recently, some preliminary works have been conducted to employ Web semantic techniques, showing its applicability in the concrete description of the Web resources. Bernardi et al. (2004) propose the process models to be described as first-order ontologies, and then habilitate the automatization of the searching and composition of Web services. Mandell and MacIlraith (2004) present an integrated technology for the customized and dynamic localization of Web services using the Business Process Language for Web Service (BPWS4J) with the semantic discovery service to provide semantic translation to match the user requirements. Soyaden and Singh (2004) developed a repository of Web services that extends the UDDI current search model. The repository in the form of ontology of attributes (based on DAML) provides a wide variety of operations such as the publication of services, costs of services, and service selection based on functionality. Similarly, Li, Yang, and Wu (2005) proposed an approach of ontology use in e-commerce service search based on generated query and decision-making process. The high-level ontology (based on DAML) positioning above WSDL relates service description of a WSDL document to descriptions of other WSDL documents. Benatallah et al. (2004) propose a matching algorithm that takes as input the requirements to be met by the Web services and an ontology of services based on logic descriptions, and recommends the services that best comply with the given requirements.

However, these approaches still require data mining to improve the user's search satisfaction. The semantic component must provide a mechanism for effectively classifying and selecting Web services based on their functionality and supporting the search of WSDL descriptions (in the form of tModel) of selected Web services in a non-sequential order within the directories or registries. So the requirements may be expressed by the user in terms of the functionality of the Web service needed instead of, for example, the name of the service, the name of the organization that provides the service, or the categories specified in an UDDI.

Data mining from the Semantic Web emphasizes the usage of Semantic Web technologies for mining purposes such as the usage of taxonomies in recommender systems, applying association rules with generalizations, or clustering with background knowledge in form of ontology. The applications may use association rules to discover relations on service descriptions in WSDL documents; for example, users who invoke a shopping service may possibly invoke another service in the area of banking. Furthermore, the structure of ontology can be implemented by a data mining application using trees. By defining each node in the tree as a service description of a WSDL document, each tree path can form an ontology that describes the similarity of a path with other paths.

Conclusion

In this chapter, we have discussed the domain of Web services and applications of data mining techniques in facilitating and improving the use of Web services. The data mining tasks that find applications in Web services mining include value prediction, similar time sequence analysis, deviation analysis, classification, clustering, and association mining. These applications range from delivering business value that can be used by management for strategic decision making, to providing technical benefits that target specialist end users. Further testing is required to identify the real value of the applications. Additionally, because some applications such as search term suggestion require real-time responses, techniques for providing results efficiently need to be developed. These may include new algorithms for scheduling the processing of requests and delivery of responses to multiple users so the information is returned as at close to real time as possible.

With some existing works, we show that the data mining techniques play an important role as the emerging technologies in Web service discovery and matching. On the other hand, as data mining applications built on Web services become more popular, there is growing need for further research to develop Web services-based data mining solutions which can scale the large, distributed data sets that are becoming more popular. Since HTTP, XML, and SOAP are platform independent, it is hoped that this will contribute to solving the blockage that has occurred among the competing proprietary protocols in the area of data mining. An example is a real-time Web services-based collaborative scheme involving data mining techniques to assist in detecting credit card fraud in online banking services.

The future holds for data mining techniques to apply with Semantic Web services and ontology to automate Web service discovery processes.

Acknowledgment

I would like to thank Cindy Tong and the ITB239, 2005 semester 1 students for assisting me in conducting the literature review on Web services and data mining usage.

References

Alesso, P., & Smith, C. (2004). *Developing the next generation Web services—Semantic Web services.* A.K. Peters Ltd.

Beeferman, D., & Berger, A. (2000). Agglomerative clustering of a search engine query log. In *Proceedings of the 6th ACM SIGKDD International Conference on Knowledge Discovery and Data Mining,* Boston.

Benatallah, B., Hacid, M., Leger, A., Rey, C., & Toumani, F. (2004). On automating Web service discovery. *VLDB Journal.* Berlin: Springer-Verlag.

Berardi, D., Grüninger, M., Hull, R., & McIlraith, S. (2004). Towards a first-order ontology for Semantic Web services. In *Proceedings of the W3C Workshop on Constraints and Capabilities for Web Services.*

Berners-Lee, T., Hendler, J., & Lassila, O. (2001, May). The Semantic Web. *Scientific American.*

Bernstein, A., & Klein, M. (2002). Discovering services: Towards high precision service retrieval. In *Proceedings of the CaiSE workshop on Web Services, E-Business, and the Semantic Web (WES): Foundations, Models, Architecture, Engineering and Applications,* Canada.

Booth, D. et al. (2004). *Web services architecture.* Retrieved December 11, 2005, from http://www.w3.org/TR/ws-arch/

Chen, M. (2003). Factors affecting the adoption and diffusion of XML and Web services standards for e-business systems. *International Journal of Human-Computer Studies, 58,* 259-279.

Chiu, C.-C., & Tsai, C.-Y. (2004). A Web services-based collaborative scheme for credit card fraud detection. In *Proceedings of the IEEE International Conference on E-Technology, E-Commerce, and E-Services (EEE 2004)* (pp. 177-181).

Chiu, C.-C., & Tsai, M.-H. (2005). A dynamic Web service-based data mining process system. In *Proceedings of the 5th International Conference on Computer and Information Technology (CIT'05)* (pp. 1033-1039).

Clark, D. (2002). Next-generation Web services. *IEEE Internet Computing, 6*(2), 12-14.

Cooley, R., Mobasher, B., & Srivastava, J. (1997). Web mining: Information and pattern discovery on the World Wide Web. In *Proceedings of the 9th IEEE International Conference on Tools with Artificial Intelligence (ICTAI'97),* Newport Beach, CA.

Curbera, F., Duftler, M., Khalaf, R., Nagy, W., Mukhi, N., & Weerawarana, S. (2002). Unraveling the Web services web: An introduction to SOAP, WSDL, and UDDI. *IEEE Internet Computing, 6*(2), 86-93.

Devore, J.L. (1995). *Probability and statistics for engineering and the sciences* (4th ed.). New York: Duxbury Press.

Dong, X., Halevy, J., Madhavan, E., Nemes, & Zhang. (2004). Similarity search for Web services. *VLDB.*

Fayyad, U.M., Piatesky-Shapiro, G., Smyth, P., & Uthurusamy, R. (1996). *Advances in knowledge discovery and data mining.* London: AAAI/MIT Press.

Gombotz, R., & Dustdar, S. (2005, September). On Web services workflow mining. In *Proceedings of the BPI Workshop* (LNCS), co-located at BPM, Nancy, France. Berlin: Springer-Verlag.

Han, J., & Kamber, M. (2001). *Data mining: Concepts and techniques.* San Francisco: Morgan Kaufmann.

Hoschek, W. (2002). Web service discovery processing steps. In *Proceedings of the IADIS International Conference WWW/Internet 2002,* Lisbon, Portugal.

Johnson, J.T. (2003). *State of the Web services world.* Retrieved April 17, 2003, from http://www.computerworld.com.au/index.php?secid=1398720840&id=622609517&eid=-180

Karypis, G., Han, E.H., & Kumar, V. (1999). Chameleon: A hierarchical clustering algorithm using dynamic modeling. *Computer, 32*(8), 68-75.

Kearney, A.T., & The Stencil Group. (2002). *The emerging Web services market.* Retrieved February 20, 2003, from http://www.stencilgroup.com/ideas_scope_200203atkws.pdf

Larsen, K.R.T., & Bloniarz, P.A. (2000). A cost and performance model for Web service investment. *Communications of the ACM, 43,* 109-116.

Li, L., Yang, Y., & Wu, B. (2005). Ontology-based matchmaking in e-marketplace with Web services. In *Proceedings of APWeb 2005* (pp. 620-631).

Maedche, A. (2003). Ontology learning for the Semantic Web. Kluwer Academic.

Malek, M., & Haramantzis, F. (2004). Security management of Web services. In *Proceedings of the IFIP/IEEE International Symposium on Integrated Network Management (NOMS 2004).*

Mandell, D., & McIlraith, S. (2004). A bottom-up approach to automating Web services discovery, customization, and semantic translation. In *Proceedings of the Workshop on E-Services and the Semantic Web.*

McIlraith, S.A., Son, T.C., & Zeng, H. (2001). Semantic Web services. *IEEE Intelligent Systems, 16*(2), 46-53.

Nayak, R. (2002). Data mining for Web-enabled electronic business applications. In S. Nanshi (Ed.), *Architectural issues of Web-enabled electronic business* (pp. 128-139). Hershey, PA: Idea Group Inc.

Nayak, R., & Seow, L. (2004). Knowledge discovery in mobile business data. In S. Nanshi (Ed.), *Wireless communication and mobile commerce* (pp. 117-139). Hershey, PA: Idea Group Inc.

Nayak, R., & Tong, C. (2004, November 22-24). Applications of data mining in Web services. In *Proceedings of the 5th International Conferences on Web Information Systems,* Brisbane, Australia (pp. 199-205).

Newcomer, E. (2002). *Understanding Web services: XML, WSDL, SOAP, and UDDI.* Boston: Addison-Wesley.

Paolucci, M., Kawamura, T., Payne, T.R., & Sycara, K. (2002). Semantic matching of Web services capabilities. In *Proceedings of the 1st International Semantic Web Conference,* Sardinia, Italy.

Peng, C.S., Wang, H., Zhang, S.R., & Patker, D.S. (2000). Landmarks: A new model for similarity-based patterns querying in time-series databases. In *Proceedings of the 2000 International Conference on Data Engineering* (pp. 33-42), San Diego, CA.

Sajjanhar, A., Jingyu, H., & Yanchun, Z. (2004). High availability with clusters of Web services. In J.X. Yu, X. Lin, H. Lu, & Y. Zhang (Eds.), *APWeb 2004* (LNCS 3007, pp. 644-653). Berlin: Springer-Verlag.

Soydan, A., & Singh, M. (2004). A DAML-based repository for QoS-aware Semantic Web service selection. In *Proceedings of the IEEE International Conference on Web Services.*

Srivastava, J., Cooley, R., Deshpande, M., & Tan, P.-N. (2000). Web usage mining: Discovery and applications of usage patterns from Web data. *SIGKDD Explorations, 1*(2), 12-23.

Systinet Corp. (2002). *Introduction to Web services architecture.* Retrieved January 6, 2003, from www.systinet.com/download/7la712f3fee0ed49a928bc6ed824/wp_systinet_SOA.pdf

Teng, C.M. (2002). Learning from dissociations. *Proceedings of the 4th International Conference on Data Warehousing and Knowledge Discovery (DaWaK 2002)*, Aix-en-Provence, France.

Vasudevan, V. (2001). *A Web services primer.* Retrieved December 11, 2002, from http://www.xml.com/pub/a/2001/04/04/Webservices/index.html

Yergeau, F., Bray, T., Paoli, *J.,* Sperberg-McQueen, C.M., & Maler, E. (2004, February). Extensible Markup Language (XML) 1.0 (3rd ed.) *W3C recommendation.* Retrieved from http://www.w3.org/TR/2004/REC-XML-20040204/

Yu, S., Liu, J., & Le, J. (2004). DHT-facilitated Web service discovery incorporating semantic annotation. In E Suzuki & A Arikawa (Eds.), *DS 2004* (LNAI 3245, pp. 363-370). Berlin: Springer-Verlag.

Wang, J., Huang, Y., Wu, G., & Zhang, F. (1999). Web mining: Knowledge discovery on the Web. In *Proceedings of the IEEE International Conference on Systems, Man, and Cybernetics 1999,* Tokyo, Japan.

Wang, Y., & Stroulia, E. (2003). Semantic structure matching for assessing Web service similarity. In *Proceedings of the 1st International Conference on Service-Oriented Computing.*

Wen, J.-R., Nie, J.-Y., & Zhang, H.-J. (2002). Query clustering using user logs. *ACM Transactions on Information Systems (TOIS), 20*(1), 59-81.

Wettschereck, D., & Muller, S. (2001). Exchanging data mining models with the predictive modeling markup language. In *Proceedings of Integration Aspects of Data Mining, Decision Support and Meta-Learning (IDDM-2001),* Freiburg, Germany.

Zheng, G., & Bouguettaya. (2005). A Web service mining for biological pathway discovery. In B. Ludäscher & L. Raschid (Eds.), *Data integration in the life sciences 2005* (LNBI 3615, pp. 292-295). Berlin: Springer-Verlag.

About the Authors

David Taniar holds a PhD degree in computer science, with a particular specialty in databases. His research areas have now expanded to data mining and warehousing. He has published more than 30 journal papers and numerous conference papers. He has published six books, including the recently released *Object-Oriented Oracle*. Dr. Taniar is now a senior lecturer at the School of Business Systems, Faculty of Information Technology, Monash University, Australia. He is on the editorial board of several international journals, and a fellow of the Institute for Management Information Systems (FIMIS).

* * *

Mafruz Zaman Ashrafi is a PhD student at Monash University, Australia. His research interests include data mining, distributed computing, e-commerce, and security. He received an MS in computer science from RMIT University.

Elizabeth Chang is a professor of IT and software engineering. She is a director for the Center Extended Enterprise and Business Intelligence (CEEBI) and Area Research Excellence for Frontier Technologies. She has published more than 200 scientific conference and journal papers in IT, and numerous invited keynote papers at international conferences. All her research and development work is in the area of frontier technologies and application to industrial informatics, business intelligence, and health informatics. Her key research areas include issues related to the process of producing an IT application, methodologies, Web services, trust management, XML, and ontology.

Zhengxin Chen received a PhD degree from the Computer Science Department, Louisiana State University, USA (1988). He is currently a professor at the University of Nebraska at Omaha (USA). His recent research interests include intelligent information systems, data mining, and text mining. Among his publications are *Computational Intelligence for Decision Support* (CRC Press, 1999), *Data Mining and Uncertain Reasoning: An Integrated Approach* (Wiley, 2001), *Intelligent Data Warehousing* (CRC Press, 2001), as well as research papers and co-edited books.

André C.P.L.F. de Carvalho received BSc and MSc degrees in computer science from the Federal University of Pernambuco, Brazil. He received his PhD in electronic engineering from the University of Kent, UK (1994). Dr. de Carvalho is an associate professor of computer science, University of São Paulo, Brazil. He has published two books and more than 200 papers in refereed conferences and journals. He is a founding co-editor of the *International Journal of Computational Intelligence and Applications,* published by Imperial College Press and World Scientific. His main interests are machine learning, neural networks, genetic algorithms, hybrid intelligent systems, data mining, and bioinformatics.

Tharam S. Dillon is the dean of the Faculty of Information Technology at the University of Technology, Sydney (UTS), Australia. His research interests include data mining, Internet computing, e-commerce, hybrid neuro-symbolic systems, neural nets, software engineering, database systems, and computer networks. He has also worked with industry and commerce in developing systems in telecommunications, health care systems, e-commerce, logistics, power systems, and banking and finance. He is editor-in-chief of the *International Journal of Computer Systems Science and Engineering* and the *International Journal of Engineering Intelligent Systems,* as well as co-editor of the *Journal of Electric Power and Energy Systems.* He is the advisory editor of the *IEEE Transactions on Industrial Informatics.* He is on the advisory editorial board of *Applied Intelligence,* published by Kluwer in the United States, and *Computer Communications,* published by Elsevier in the UK. He has published more than 400 papers in international and national journals and conferences, and has written four books and edited five other books. He is a fellow of the IEEE, the Institution of Engineers (Australia), and the Australian Computer Society.

Ling Feng is an associate professor at the University of Twente, The Netherlands. Previously, she was an assistant professor at Tilburg University, The Netherlands (1999-2002) and a lecturer at Department of Computing, Hong Kong Polytechnic University, China (1997-1999). Her research interests are distributed object-oriented database management system, knowledge-based information systems, data mining and its applications, data warehousing, data/knowledge management issues in the Internet era (including the integration of database and Web-based information technologies), XML databases, knowledge-based digital libraries, and mobile databases.

Alex A. Freitas received a BSc degree in computer science from FATEC-SP/UNESP and an MSc in computer science from the Federal University of Sao Carlos, both in Brazil. He received his PhD in computer science from the University of Essex, UK (1997). Dr. Freitas was a visiting lecturer at CEFET-PR, Brazil, in 1998, and an associate professor at PUC-PR, also in Brazil, from 1999 to June 2002. In July 2002 he moved to the University of Kent, UK, where he is currently a senior lecturer. His publications include two authored research-oriented books in data mining and more than 100 refereed papers published in journals, conferences, and book chapters. He is a member of the editorial board of two journals, namely the *Intelligent Data Analysis International Journal* and the *International Journal on Data Warehousing and Mining*. His main research interests are data mining, machine learning, biologically inspired algorithms, and bioinformatics.

Lixin Fu has been an assistant professor at The University of North Carolina at Greensboro, USA, since 2001. He has published more than a dozen papers in refereed journals and international conferences in the past five years. His main research areas include data warehousing, data mining, databases, and algorithms. Dr. Fu earned his PhD in computer and information sciences at the University of Florida (2001). He received his master's degree in electrical engineering from the Georgia Institute of Technology in 1997. He is a member of IEEE, ACM, and Upsilon Pi Epsilon Honor Society.

Xiuju Fu received a BS degree and an MS degree, both from Beijing Institute of Technology, China (1995 and 1999, respectively). She obtained her PhD from Nanyang Technological University in Singapore. She has co-authored one monograph, three book chapters, and more than 20 papers in conference proceedings and journals. Currently, she is working as a research engineer at the Institute of High Performance Computing. Her research areas include neural networks, support vector machine, genetic algorithms, data mining, classification, data dimensionality reduction, and linguistic rule extraction.

Li Ping Goh graduated in 1991 with a bachelor's degree (Hons) in statistics from Monash University, Australia, and obtained a master's degree from the National University of Singapore in 1994. She was involved in conducting social research on issues related to public housing in Singapore between 1992 and 1999. In 2000 she joined the Institute of High Performance Computing as a senior research engineer, focusing on applying data mining techniques to the industry.

Fedja Hadzic is a member of the eXel research group at the University of Technology Sydney. He obtained a Bachelor of Computer Science from the University of Newcastle, and completed a Bachelor of Science (Hons.) in IT from the University of Technology Sydney. His current research is mainly focused in the area of data mining and ontology learning. He was a part of the 'UTS Unleashed!' robot soccer team in 2004. His research work has been published in a number of international conferences. Further research interests include knowledge representation and reasoning, artificial life, lifelong learning, automated scientific discovery, robotics, and meta-physics.

Xiaohua Hu received a BS degree from Wuhan University, China (1985), an ME in computer engineering from Institute of Computing Technology, Chinese Academy of Science (1988), and an MS (1992) and PhD (1995) in computer science from Simon Fraser University, Canada. He is the founding editor-in-chief of the *International Journal of Data Mining and Bioinformatics* and currently is an assistant professor in the College of Information Science and Technology at Drexel University, USA. His current research interests are in biomedical literature data mining, bioinformatics, text mining, Semantic Web mining and reasoning, rough set theory and application, information extraction, and information retrieval. His research is funded by the National Science Foundation (NSF), the U.S. Department of Education, and the Pennsylvania Department of Health.

Gih Guang Hung is a senior program manager at the Institute of High Performance Computing, Singapore, for the Software and Computing Program. He leads various groups in research and development in the areas of grid computing, computational intelligence, and visualization. Dr. Hung graduated from the University of Illinois at Urbana-Champaign in 1993 with a PhD in electrical engineering. He currently holds an adjunct associate professor position with the School of Computer Engineering at the Nanyang Technological University of Singapore. His research interests include high-performance computing techniques, algorithm performance optimization, grid middleware, and remote collaboration technology.

Søren E. Jespersen is a consultant for Linkage Software. His research interests include Web usage mining and its applications in e-learning. He obtained his master's and bachelor's degrees in computer science from Aalborg University, Denmark (2002 and 2000, respectively).

Gang Kou is a PhD student in the School of Information Science & Technology, University of Nebraska at Omaha, USA. He earned his master's degree in computer science from the University of Nebraska at Omaha and his BS in physics from Tsinghua University, China. Mr. Kou's research interests cover knowledge discover in database and data mining, specifically concerned with theoretical concepts and algorithms for multi-criteria decision making and their practical application to real-world data analysis problems. He has published more than 20 papers in various peer-reviewed journals and conferences.

Wenyuan Li received BEng and MEng degrees, both in computer science and engineering, from Xi'an Jiaotong University, China (1999 and 2002, respectively). He earned a PhD in computer engineering from the Nanyang Technological University, Singapore (2005). He is currently holding a post-doctoral position in bioinformatics and text mining research at the Laboratory for Bioinformatics and Biomedical Informatics, University of Texas at Dallas, USA. Dr, Wenyuan's research interests include machine learning, data mining, and their application to data analysis. He also has interests in research on small-world and scale-free networks, and their relationships to information navigation and data analysis. To date, he has published more than 10 research papers in these areas.

Richi Nayak is a lecturer in the School of Information System, Queensland University of Technology, Australia. Her research interests are data mining, information retrieval, and Web intelligence. She has published over 40 papers in journals, conference proceedings, and books, and has developed various innovative mining techniques and applications related to XML, software engineering, e-commerce, m-commerce, Web services, and infrastructure. Dr. Nayak has been invited to serve as a program committee member in various conferences (KES06, PAKDD06, AMIT06, IRMA06/05, CITSA05, and UWSI06/05), and she is an editorial advisory reviewer board member of the *International Journal of Knowledge-Based & Intelligent Engineering Systems, International Journal of Cases on Electronic Commerce,* and *Information Resource Management Journal.*

Wee-Keong Ng is an associate professor at the School of Computer Engineering and director of the Center for Advanced Information Systems, Nanyang Technological University, Singapore. He received his PhD from the University of Michigan at Ann Arbor, USA. He has published more than 100 refereed journal and conference articles in the area of data mining, Web information systems, database and data warehousing, and software agents. He is currently a member of the editorial review board of the *Journal of Database Management* and the *International Journal of Intelligent Information Technologies*. He recently co-authored a book entitled *Web Data Management,* published by Springer-Verlag. He has served on the program committee of international conferences and has held tutorials, talks at conferences, and research seminars. He is a member of the IEEE Computer Society and of ACM.

Irene Ntoutsi received a BSc and an MSc from the Department of Computer Science and Informatics, University of Patras, Greece (2001 and 2003, respectively). Since 2003, she has been a PhD student with the Database Group of the Information Systems Laboratory, Department of Informatics, University of Piraeus. Her thesis concerns management of the data mining results in very large databases, with emphasis in similarity assessment between patterns, as well as in similarity reasoning with respect to the similarity of the underlying raw data. Her research interests include data mining, pattern management, similarity issues, and machine learning.

Kok-Leong Ong is a lecturer at the School of Engineering and Information Technology, Deakin University, Australia. He received a PhD from the Nanyang Technological University, Singapore (2004). He has published more than 20 papers in referred journals and conference articles primarily in the area of data mining. He serves on a number of program committees of international conferences, as well as being a reviewer for a number of international journals. He was also the session chair for "Knowledge Discovery in Data Streams" at the 9th International Conference on Knowledge-Based Intelligent Information & Engineering Systems 2005. His current research interests include data mining algorithms and application of data mining to discover business intelligence.

Torben Bach Pedersen is an associate professor of computer science at Aalborg University, Denmark. His research interests include multi-dimensional databases, data streams, OLAP, data warehousing, federated databases, Web usage mining, and location-based services. He received a PhD in computer science from Aalborg University in 2000, and a master's degree in computer science from the University of Aarhus, Denmark (1994). He is the (co-)author of more than 50 refereed publications in journals and conference proceedings. He is a member of IEEE, the IEEE Computer Society, and ACM.

Nikos Pelekis received a BSc from the Computer Science Department of the University of Crete, Greece (1998). He subsequently joined the Department of Computation at the University of Manchester Institute of Science and Technology (UMIST) to pursue an MSc in information systems engineering (1999) and a PhD in moving object databases (2002). Since March 2004, he has been a post-doctoral researcher with the Database Group of the Information Systems Laboratory, Department of Informatics, University of Piraeus, Greece. His research interests include temporal, spatial, and spatiotemporal databases; location-based services; geographical information systems; data mining; pattern management; and machine learning.

Yi Peng is a PhD student in the School of Information Science & Technology, University of Nebraska at Omaha, USA. She earned a master's degree in information science & quality assurance from same university, and a BS in MIS from Sichuan University, China. Ms. Peng's research interests cover knowledge discover in database and data mining, specifically concerned with systemic framework for the field of data mining. She published more than 20 papers in various peer-reviewed journals and conferences.

Karlton Sequeira is currently a research scientist at Amazon.com. He received a BE degree in electronic engineering in 1999 from the University of Mumbai, India. He obtained his MS and PhD degrees in computer science from Rensselaer Polytechnic Institute, USA (2002 and 2005, respectively). His research interests include algorithms for high-dimensional and heterogeneous datasets, computational biology, and manifold learning.

Yong Shi is the director of the Chinese Academy of Sciences Research Center on Data Technology & Knowledge Economy, and assistant president of the Graduate University of the Chinese Academy of Sciences. He has been the Charles W. and Margre H. Durham Distinguished Professor of Information Technology, College of Information Science and Technology, University of Nebraska at Omaha, USA, since 1999. Dr. Shi's research interests include multiple criteria decision making, data mining, information overload, and telecommunication management. He has published seven books, more than 60 papers in various journals, and numerous conferences/proceedings papers. He is the editor-in-chief of the *International Journal of Information Technology and Decision Making,* an area editor of the *International Journal of Operations and Quantitative Management,* and a member of the editorial board for a number of academic journals, including the *International Journal of Data Mining and Business Intelligence.* Dr. Shi has received many distinguished awards, including Outstanding Young Scientist Award, National Natural Science Foundation of China, 2001; Member of Overseas Assessor for the Chinese Academy of Sciences, 2000; and Speaker of Distinguished Visitors Program (DVP) for

1997-2000, IEEE Computer Society. He has consulted for a number of international companies in data mining and knowledge management projects.

Kate Smith is a full professor at the Faculty of Information Technology, Monash University, Australia. She holds a BSc (Hons.) in mathematics and a PhD in electrical engineering from the University of Melbourne. Dr. Smith has published more than 130 refereed journal and international conference papers in the areas of neural networks, combinatorial optimization, and data mining. She has received approximately $1.5 million in competitive research funding. She serves on several editorial boards and many program committees for international conferences. She regularly acts as a consultant to industry in the area of data mining.

Henry Tan is a PhD student working under the supervision of Professor Tharam S. Dillon. He graduated from La Trobe University in 2002 with a Bachelor of Computer System Engineering (Hons.) degree and was nominated as the most outstanding Honors Student in Computer Science. He is the holder of the 2003 ACS Student Award. His current research is mainly focused in the area of XML association mining. Other research interests include neural networks, AI, and game and software development. His research work has been published in a number of international conferences. He is currently on leave working for Microsoft as a software design engineer.

Yannis Theodoridis is an assistant professor of informatics, University of Piraeus, Greece. He received his Diploma (1990) and PhD (1996) in electrical and computer engineering, both from the National Technical University of Athens, Greece. His research interests include spatial and spatiotemporal databases, geographical information management, knowledge discovery, and data mining. Currently, he is the scientist in charge for the University of Piraeus for the IST/FET project, GeoPKDD (STREP project; 2005-2008), on geographic privacy-aware knowledge discovery and delivery, as well as several national-level projects. In the past he coordinated two IST/FET projects, PANDA (Working Group; 2001-2004) and CODMINE (Assessment Project; 2002-2003), on pattern-based management and privacy-preserving data mining, respectively. He has co-authored three monographs and more than 30 articles in scientific journals such as *Algorithmica, ACM Multimedia,* and *IEEE TKDE,* and in conferences such as ACM SIGMOD, PODS, ICDE, and VLDB. His work has over 350 citations in scientific journals and conference proceedings. He has served on the program committees for several conferences, including SIGMOD, ICDE, ICDM, and SSTD, and as general co-chair for SSTD'03, PaRMa'04, and PaRMa'06. He is member of ACM and IEEE.

Jesper Thorhauge is managing director of Conzentrate, a Denmark software company specializing in e-learning software. His research interests include Web usage mining and its applications in e-learning. He obtained his master's and bachelor's degrees in computer science from Aalborg University, Denmark (2002 and 2000, respectively).

Lipo Wang is (co-)author of more than 60 journal publications, 12 book chapters, and 90 conference presentations. He holds a U.S. patent in neural networks, and has authored two monographs and edited 16 books. He was keynote/panel speaker for several international conferences. He is associate editor for *IEEE Transactions on Neural Networks* (2002-), *IEEE Transactions on Evolutionary Computation* (2003-), and *IEEE Transactions on Knowledge and Data Engineering* (2005-). He is/was an editorial board member of six additional international journals. Dr. Wang is vice president of technical activities for the IEEE Computational Intelligence Society (2006-2007), and president of the Asia-Pacific Neural Network Assembly 2002/2003.

Daniel D. Wu received a BS degree in biochemistry from Xiamen University in China (1987), and an MS in physiology (1996) and MS in computer science (2001) from The Pennsylvania State University, USA. He is currently pursuing a PhD in the College of Information Science and Technology at Drexel University, USA. His research interests are in data mining, bioinformatics, and biomolecular network analysis.

Mohammed J. Zaki is an associate professor of computer science at Rensselaer Polytechnic Institute, USA. He received his PhD in computer science from the University of Rochester, USA (1998). His research interests focus on developing novel data mining techniques and their applications, especially for bioinformatics. He has published more than 150 papers on data mining and co-edited several books. He is currently an associate editor for *IEEE Transactions on Knowledge and Data Engineering,* action editor for *Data Mining and Knowledge Discovery,* and serves on the editorial boards of *Scientific Computing,* the *International Journal of Data Warehousing and Mining,* the *International Journal of Data Mining and Bioinformatics,* and the *ACM SIGMOD DiSC Digital Symposium Collection.* He is the recipient of the NSF CAREER Award (2001) and DOE ECPI Award (2002).

Index

A

aggregation logic 111
algorithm RulExSVM 278
apriori algorithm 135
artificial intelligence (AI) 297
artificial neural network (ANN) 199
association rules mining (ARM) 90
atomic change 113

B

base single tuple (BST) 33
bidirectional associative memory (BAM)
    298
big-bang 196
bipartite weighted matching 65
BOAT 101
bottom-up cubing (BUC) 32

brain-derived neurotrophic factor (BDNF)
    259
breadth first search (BFS) 18
business process execution language for
    Web service (BPEL4WS) 320

C

candidate rules 21
cellular automata (CA) 297
centroid 102
CFI 90
change detector mechanism 98
classification algorithm 198
classification error (CE) 106
CLIQUE algorithm 92
clustering 32, 61, 102, 107, 123, 213,
clustering genetic algorithm (CGA) 278
COBWEB algorithm 92

CommBuilder 219
common log format (CLF) 15
complete linkage 102
Complexpander 224
compression algorithm 145
condensed model 55
conditional market-basket probability
    (CMBP) 97
Connect-4 167
corridor-based heuristic 113
cost planning 311
coupling type 111
cover type 167
cube aggregation threshold 31
cube cardinality threshold 31
cube dimensionality threshold 31

D

DAG structure 185
DARPA agent markup language (DAML)
    312
DARPA agent markup language semantic
    markup extension for Web services
    (DAML-S) 321
database for interacting protein (DIP) 216
database management system (DBMS)
    2, 14
data cleaning 252
data mining (DM) 87, 176, 309
datasets selection 252
data warehouse (DW) 1, 15
decision tree (DT) 90, 99, 183, 201,
    261, 317
déclat algorithm 164
DEMON 112
density-based methods 92
depth-independent distance-based misclas-
    sification cost 189
depth first search (DFS) 18
Dif-Bits 157
direct acyclic graph (DAG) 176, 185
distance function 92
dominant eigenvalue 56
DOS group 266

E

éclat algorithm 151
enumerative 61
evaluation function 92
execution time 69
ExpandCore 219
expression component 89
extended common log format (ECLF) 15

F

false trail 11
fast update (FUP) algorithm 98
FindCore 219
FIs 90
FLP classification 258
FLP method 250
FOCUS measure 96
FP-tree 151
frequent itemset mining (FIM) 89
frequent pattern set (FREQ-PATTERN)
    129

G

G-Protein-Coupled-Receptor (GPCR) 201
GDS124 80
GDS38 80
GDS39 80
gene ontology (GO 81, 186, 199
general repository for interaction datasets
    (GRID) 216
generator 21
generic framework 186
generic rule model (GRM) 98
genetic algorithm (GA) 199, 277
GenMax algorithm 138
GN algorithm 214
Golomb encoding scheme 150
graphical user interface (GUI) 15
greatest common refinement (GCR)
    94, 110
grid-based methods 92
grid cell 56

H

hierarchical method 92
HIV-1 associated dementia (HAD)
        243, 271
horizontal compression 151
HPG model 12
hybrid 12
hybrid technique 3
hypertext probabilistic grammar (HPG) 8

I

IBL paradigm 183
in-community degree 217
instance-based learning (IBL) 182
inter-quartile range (IQR) 315
internal node 91
interval-based heuristic 113

J

Jaccard index 60

K

K-means algorithm 93
K-medoids algorithm 93
knowledge discovery in databases (KDD)
        86, 87

L

leaf node 91
learnability-based prediction 200
LINDO Systems Inc 252
low-dimensional 34

M

machine learning (ML) 176
mandatory leaf-node prediction 187
Markov random field (MRF) 297
maximal matching 67
MCP 244
mean field (MF) 297
measure component 89, 90
medoid 102

M

MFI 90
Microarray datasets 81
minSup 38
MMS 315
model-based method 92
model formulation and classification 252
molecular complex detection (MCODE)
        215
MonteCarlo sampling 69
multidimensional hierarchical clustering
        scheme (MHC) 32
multiple criteria linear programming
        (MCLP) 246, 259
multiple criteria programming (MCP)
        242, 243
multiple criteria quadratic programming
        (MCQP) 246

N

National Basketball Association (NBA) 53
nearest neighbor paradigm 182
neural network (NN) 298
Newton's method 285
NMDA 260
nominal attribute 91
non-empty cubes 35
numerical attribute 91

O

occurrence-based grouping heuristic 113
OLGA 71
optimization/ant colony optimization
        (PSO/ACO) algorithm 201
optimization based 61
optional leaf-node prediction 187, 193
ordinal attribute 91

P

pan-organism classification 186
PANDA 96, 109, 111
Parthasarathy-Ogihara 96
partitioning method 92
pattern comparison 86, 95
pattern monitor (PAM) 98, 112

permanent rules 113
post-checking 21
post check enhanced hybrid (PEHA) 20
ProductGraph 64
protein-protein interaction (PPI) 209
Protein Data Bank (PDB) 178
protein function 175, 179, 184
PSO/ACO algorithm 201

R

r-dimensional cuboids 34
Rand index 59
RBF kernel functions 286
referrer 13
restricted sparse statistics tree (RSST) 29
ResultSet 17
RLE (run length encoding) 169
RNA polymerase II 228
ROCK algorithm 101

S

scanner 143
selected values set (SVS) 44
self-organizing map (SOM) 121, 123
sequences 2
sequential pattern 3
service discovery 312
service innovation 315
session_dimension 19
similarity-based protein function predic-
      tion 181
simple object access protocol (SOAP) 310
simple quadratic programming (SQP) 269
single linkage 102
singular value decomposition (SVD) 318
SMS (short message service) 315
social network analysis (SNA) 298
SOM 126
specialized HPG 11
standard template library (STL) 46
star pointer 34
star value 34
STING 92
string tbp 19
structural component 89

subgraph 55
subsequence 6
subsession 6
subspace 57
support vector machine (SVM)
      244, 268, 276, 278

T

tidset/diffset datase 156
top-down 196
transaction ID (tid) 146, 168
transcription factor IID (TFIID) 225
tree-based data structure 151
true rule 20
true traversal 21

U

uniform misclassification cost 192
universal description, discovery, and inte-
      gration (UDDI) 310
unsupervised 91
update with early pruning (UWEP) algo-
      rithm 99
user session 2

V

validating 21
variation of information (VI) 104
vertical compression 150
VIPER 150

W

Web content mining 2
Web log 2
Web mining 2
Web ontology language for services
      (OWL-S) 321
Web services description language
      (WSDL) 310
Web structure mining 2
Web usage mining 2

X

XML (eXtensible Markup Language) 310

Z

Zscore 69

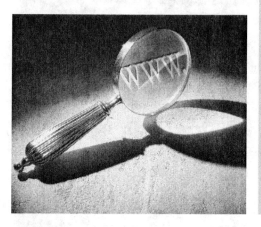